chy within the discipline that has defined what is and what is not legitimate for study within the discipline.

Philip Green received his B.A. from Swarthmore in 1954 and his Ph.D. from Princeton in 1965. He is currently an associate professor at Smith College, and has many magazine articles to his credit as well as two books, *Deadly Logic: The Theory of Nuclear Deterrence* and *The Political Imagination in Literature.*

Sanford Levinson received his B.A. from Duke University in 1962 and his Ph.D. from Harvard in 1969. Formerly an assistant professor at Ohio State University, he is now attending Stanford University Law School on a Russell Sage Fellowship. He is the author of articles which have appeared in *Dissent, Yale Law Journal, Harvard Review,* and *The New Republic.*

$10.00

For years political science has languished, caught in a web of categories both outmoded and irrelevant in a time of revolutionary change and reappraisal. Believing that political science ought to be a systematic effort to confront political reality, Philip Green and Sanford Levinson helped to found the Caucus for a New Political Science within the American Political Science Association. The Caucus has lobbied both for a democratization of the APSA and for a re-examination of the concerns of the discipline as a whole.

Power and Community, an anthology of original essays on the state of political science, as well as on the traditional concerns of the discipline attacked from radical perspectives, is the product of thinking by members of the Caucus on what political science ought to address itself to, in what way, and for whom. It is a discussion of the nature of teaching political science, as well as an examination of concepts such as community, authority, and legitimacy that political science has tended to exclude from its area of study.

It is an attack on the concepts of objectivity and science as political science has defined these; it is an assault on the oligar-

POWER AND COMMUNITY

Dissenting Essays in Political Science

Dissenting Essays

EDITED BY

Pantheon Books · A Division of Random House, New York

POWER AND COMMUNITY

in Political Science

PHILIP GREEN AND SANFORD LEVINSON

Three essays from this book have already appeared: "Legitimacy
in the Modern State" by John H. Schaar in the January 1970
issue of *New American Review* under the title "Reflections on
Authority," "Civil Disobedience and Corporate Authority" by
Michael Walzer in the September-October 1969 issue of *Dissent*,
and "Decentralization, Community Control, and Revolution:
Reflections on Ocean Hill-Brownsville" by Philip Green, in the
summer 1970 issue of *The Massachusetts Review*.

Library of Congress Catalog Card Number: 77–106360

ISBN: 0–394–44117–6

Manufactured in the United States of America
by H. Wolff, New York
2 3 4 5 6 7 8 9

First Printing

To Laura Morgan Green and

Robert Owen Green and

To Shirley Levinson and the memory of

Meyer Levinson

Preface

FOR SEVERAL YEARS now it has been clear that the consensus uneasily holding together the academic study of politics has been in the process of breaking down—a process highlighted in 1967 when a group of dissident political scientists joined together to form The Caucus for a New Political Science. This volume is one of several attempts now under way to hasten that breakdown and point our collective work in new directions.

As will be quickly apparent, not all the contributors are in complete agreement about matters of political philosophy or academic method; far from it. All, however, are united in sharing a dual critique of the dominant tendencies in our discipline. First, contemporary American political science has often been rendered irrelevant to vital political concerns by the pursuit of petty methodological purity. Second, this supposedly pure—i.e., value-free—work has always been strongly influenced by personal value-judgments, which with few exceptions have been supportive of the political status quo in the United States and have generally conveyed a false picture of political life in western democracies. Thus it is no coincidence that the two coeditors of and four additional contributors to this book have been on the executive committee of the Caucus, for the central purpose animating all our efforts is indeed to help create a "new political science" that will not be trivial and misleading.

It is not, of course, an easy task to indicate what a transformed political science might look like, and we make no claims that this volume will fulfill such a hope. Our historical era seems to be one in which everyone recognizes the necessity of new modes of thought, but no one has yet successfully put forth a convincing explication of that mode.

Transformative thought will never appear, though, if we merely sit around waiting for it; it cannot be willed into existence, but perhaps we can hasten its advent by attempting to sketch the paths such a transformation might take. Certain requirements do appear to be fairly obvious, given the nature of the critique we have stated above. A new political science must be able to focus its vision on important political issues and events, and it must be willing to confront rather than ignore the political ills of our own kind of social order. The essays which follow do at least that much, we hope, thus justifying both our criticisms of American political science and our claim to be pointing in a new direction.

The first three of these essays (those by J. Peter Euben, Sanford Levinson, and Kenneth Dolbeare), emphasize primarily the methodological and philosophical limitations of our colleagues' work, and thus lay the groundwork for the explorations of substantive political problems that follow. The remaining essays, with one exception, all attempt to illuminate aspects of the American polity inadequately analyzed by mainstream political science. Thus Michael Rogin shows how group theory has treated union members as mere subjects, pawns in a game of power played by their leaders, and calls our attention to working-class interests that are not so easily assimilable into that elitist model of democracy. Similarly Lewis Lipsitz reclaims the political voice of the poor from those social scientists who have viewed it chiefly as a symptom of pathology, and indicates what we might learn about our political system by listening to it seriously. Michael Parenti and Alan Wolfe demonstrate how problematic are some of our received notions about the nature of social integration and community; and Michael Walzer and Philip Green discuss the immense obstacles that the established legal order puts in the way of disadvantaged social groups that try to win a place in it. This section is concluded by John Schaar, who lays bare the "crisis of authority" that has transfigured American political life and that, in a small way, is manifested between these covers by our own unwillingness to accept any longer the myths by which social order has been maintained.

In the world of the academic social scientist, the chief of these myths has been that of the American polity as a working example of "democratic pluralism." The main substantive theme that unites all these essays is our rejection of that myth; our conviction that the concept of democratic pluralism has been ideological and obscurantist, in that our political order is neither genuinely pluralist nor always democratic.

Admittedly we have no agreed-on blueprint for the alteration of this condition, though several of our essays do attempt to explore new conceptions of democratic politics. We close with an essay by Tracy Strong that implicitly comments on this omission. Strong argues that in the long run the kind of new political philosophy that we are groping toward will require its own solid theoretical underpinning, such as mainstream political science has—falsely—claimed to be deriving from the behavioral approach. It is suggestive of the state of the discipline that he expects no help to be forthcoming from its conventional wisdom but rather directs our attention to such "outsiders" as Lévi-Strauss, Merleau-Ponty, and Nietzsche.

Finally, we have asked Wilson Carey McWilliams to read our essays and to present his thoughts on our efforts in an afterword.

Although we have had each contributor circulate his essay among his fellows for their comments and criticisms, the responsibility for the final products is strictly that of each individual; there has been no attempt made to impose an artificial unity on what is in fact a group of unlike minds.

Acknowledgments

WE WOULD LIKE to thank three members of Pantheon Books: André Schiffrin, who conceived the notion of a series of "anti-textbooks," of which this is one; and Tom Rivers and Jon Eisen, who served as the editors of this specific project.

Each of us would also like to take this occasion to express publicly his admiration for an ex-teacher whose conception of the proper study of politics served to goad him into disillusionment with the more mundane version of the discipline found in the graduate schools.

For Sanford Levinson it is particularly appropriate, because of his interest in the teaching of introductory courses in political science, to confess his debt to Hugh M. Hall of Duke University, his own first guide to the field. This is not to say that Professor Hall will necessarily be delighted with the outcome of his student's thoughts, but only that he will, perhaps, see some of his own willingness to confront head-on the problems of the American polity reflected in these essays.

Philip Green's similar debt is to H. H. Wilson of Princeton University, who has shown all his students what integrity in life and work really is.

Contents

Preface   vii

Political Science and Political Silence   J. PETER EUBEN   3

On "Teaching" Political "Science"   SANFORD LEVINSON   59

Public Policy Analysis and the Coming Struggle for the Soul of the Postbehavioral Revolution
KENNETH M. DOLBEARE   85

Nonpartisanship and the Group Interest
MICHAEL ROGIN   112

On Political Belief: The Grievances of the Poor
LEWIS LIPSITZ   142

Assimilation and Counter-Assimilation: From Civil Rights to Black Radicalism
MICHAEL PARENTI   173

Conditions of Community: The Case of Old Westbury College   ALAN WOLFE   195

Civil Disobedience and Corporate Authority
MICHAEL WALZER   223

Decentralization, Community Control, and Revolution: Reflections on Ocean Hill–Brownsville   PHILIP GREEN   247

Legitimacy in the Modern State   JOHN H. SCHAAR   276

"Hold On to Your Brains": An Essay in Meta-theory   TRACY B. STRONG   328

Political Arts and Political Sciences
WILSON CAREY MCWILLIAMS   357

Notes on Contributors   383

Index   387

POWER AND COMMUNITY

Dissenting Essays in Political Science

Political Science and Political Silence*

J. PETER EUBEN

Our collective and individual future, then, will inevitably be shaped by us, whether we choose inaction and passivity, regression and romanticism, or action, imagination, and resolve. Men cannot escape their historical role by merely denying its existence. The question is, therefore, not *whether* Americans will shape their future, but *how* they will shape it.　　　　　　　—Kenneth Keniston

IN ACT TWO of Rolf Hochhuth's impressive play *The Deputy,* a young priest, Riccardo, confronts a cardinal who is known to possess considerable influence over the Pope with his discoveries of Nazi "activities" against Jews. It is an enormously moving scene, made even more so by the flatness of Hochhuth's prose. For at this point Riccardo, alternatively pleading and demanding, must contend with a pedantic wisdom which oftentimes characterizes institutions—particularly those that emerge out of a revolutionary, heretical past. Though the play is relatively bare of symbolism, this particular confrontation takes place on several levels: the Church with its own past, man with himself, sympathy and indignation with calculation and *raison d'état.* Riccardo's fervid appeals and only partially repressed anger are greeted by what must surely be one of the commonest rallying cries

* I should like to thank my friends and colleagues who patiently read the manuscript and in their kindness criticized it: Terence Ball, John Schaar, Hanna Pitkin, Michael Rogin, Henry Kariel, and particularly Raymond L. Nichols. He, along with the other members of the Board of Studies in Politics, was particularly helpful when this essay was first read at a board colloquium.

3

of established men and institutions, a cry which, given the circumstances and development of the play, can hardly be unequivocal. Turning to Riccardo's father, who is also present at the encounter, the Cardinal admonishes him with sentiments that owe much to a former Inquisitor:

> Be careful, Count. Your Riccardo is an idealist, which is to say, a fanatic, you know. In the end the idealist always spills blood in the delusion that he is doing good—*more* blood than any realist.

Turning then to Riccardo the Cardinal continues in a tone which Hochhuth describes as "ironic hauteur, which is designed to make Riccardo seem a figure of fun":

> Riccardo—you idealists are *inhuman*. We realists are more humane, because we take men as they are. We laugh at their faults, for we know we share them.[1]

The insistence that "realism" is, in the long run, more humane than "idealism" is by now a cliché. The idealist has been, and is frequently still, the butt of jokes, the object of reprimands, warnings, and chastisement, subject to ridicule and scorn—in forms and tones as varied as those of Aristophanes, Machiavelli, and contemporary political science. The realist is "realistic," tough-minded, sensitive to what is "real" in and about men and history. He sees himself, as Norman Jacobson has noted, as a man of shrewd common sense, justly suspicious of ideologically oriented conduct, seeking the possible, possessing a firm grasp of the grand sweep of history.[2] He portrays his idealistic opponent as a victim of vain reveries, a chaser of shadows quixotically attempting to foist his visions and longings upon a recalcitrant mankind. The idealist, when not successfully ignored, is laughed at as an oddity or feared as a fanatic whose total commitment to his delusion or cause prevents his recognition of, and adjustment to, the imperatives and dictates of reality and the real world. By making do with given materials, by setting and accepting standards that are clearly attainable, the realist[3] becomes a kind of hero, restricting himself to what is available, shunning vain reveries, and thus reducing violence and bloodshed.

It is necessary, we are told, to insist on the hardness of our data and our world. Chasing shadows is not a pastime for serious men, and thus the decline of ideology, metaphysics, idealism, and "traditional" political theory is most fortunate. For some, "we have no political philosophy because politics has become too serious to be left to philosophers," [4] a welcome development, since "from a 'pragmatic' point of view, political philosophy is a monster, and wherever it has been taken seriously, the consequence, almost invariably, has been revolution, war, and the police state." [5] We do not need political philosophy, for from an equally "pragmatic" vantage point, our system "works." In the language of Bernard Berelson, and of Judge Learned Hand whom he quotes, "somehow the system not only works on the most difficult and complex questions, but often works with distinction. 'For abuse it as you will, it gives a bloodless measure of social forces—bloodless, have you thought of that?—a means of continuity, a principle of stability, a relief from the paralyzing terror of revolution.' " [6] Realistic analysis is necessary, we are told, in "times made dangerous by the operations of politics." [7]

We are continually counseled and encouraged to reevaluate our ideals, to assess their "realism." It is suggested, for instance, that we apply the term *democracy* to "existing realities," [8] that we forestall the possibility of a cynicism borne of disillusion by supplying "realistic" assessments of the way the system works.[9] We are even warned that as "political scientists learn more about the actual operations of political systems" we may have to reformulate democratic ideals "for fear that as unattainable and utopian goals, they serve merely to discredit democracy as an ideal." [10] It is more desirable to have political theory "written in reference to practice," for that kind of theory, as opposed to Locke's, Rousseau's, or Jefferson's, supposedly "has the advantage that its categories are the categories in which political life really occurs." [11] The work of many behavioralists may be understood as a response not so much to the critics of democracy as to democracy's overzealous defenders. In their intemperate enthusiasm, these apostles emerge as covert enemies of democracy, propagating impossible ideals and irrelevant standards, which become in turn the stimulus for disruptive ideologies and action. In their somewhat simplistic portraits of the moral and political corruptness of our society, of the discrepancy between moral rhetoric and political reality, in their unrealistic panaceas for reform, these defenders remain impervious to the complexities and realities of man and politics.

Realism is all the more attractive because the reality we confront is America, where, Seymour Lipset has asserted, in an oft quoted, frequently criticized, and since qualified statement, "democracy is not only or even primarily a means through which different groups can attain their ends or see the good society" but is really "the good society itself in operation." [12] We need not worry about what, on the first glance, seems worrying, for instance, the seeming indifference of many of our citizens toward politics, their seemingly disheartening "irrationality"; for "when one considers the data in a broader perspective," as Berelson writes, "how huge segments of the society adapt to political conditions over long periods of time—he cannot fail to be impressed with the total result." And, he concludes in a less secular vein, "Where the rational citizen seems to abdicate nevertheless angels seem to tread." [13] Louis Hartz provides the appropriate epigram when he writes that "the past had been good to Americans and they knew it. Instead of inspiring them to the fury of Bentham and Voltaire, it often produced a mystical sense of Providential guidance akin to that of Maistre." [14]

The presence of Providence can be more clearly and un-equivocally seen once we look not at what we might achieve but what we have avoided, not at Rousseau or Jefferson or Mill but at Auschwitz. As long as our gaze was upward, as long as a tradition of democratic thought provided, even partially, what was regarded as relevant and radical criticism, there was some hope that tasks undone and men forgotten would be faced up to and remembered. But once the American policy was contrasted, not with an image of its best self, but with "totalitarianism," it became all too easy to be seduced into a kind of relaxed complacency. Robert Dahl put the point and the mood well when he wrote:

> Nearly every group has enough potential influence to miti-gate harsh injustice to its members, though not necessarily enough to influence or attain a full measure of justice. The system thus tends to be self-correcting, at least in a limited fashion. If equality and justice are rarely attained harsh and persistent oppression is almost always avoided.[15]

And it is merely an extension of this position and attitude to conclude, as Dahl does in *Preface to Democratic Theory,* that "full assimilation of Negroes into the normal system already has occurred in many northern states and now seems to be slowly taking place even in the South," [16] and to omit discussion of what, in retrospect, seems so crucial—the role of racism in political involvement in the metal houses case presented in *Who Governs.* Though some regard "fear, pessimism, and silence" as dominating the community's social climate, "this is certainly not true," Dahl assures us, "of any community that I ever lived in." [17] Indeed, we are generally a peaceful people, for, again quoting from Dahl, "peaceful change is usually highly incremental." Partly for this reason, no doubt, "incremental change is the characteristic method of democracies; liquidation of the kulaks and the Great Leap Forward would not have been carried out by parliamentary governments." [18] Our political system is "durable" and we "seem to like it." With all its defects, "it does nonetheless provide a high probability that any active and legitimate group will make itself heard effectively at some stage in the process of decision." [19]

The relative political and social superiority of America is paralleled, if not enhanced, by a further judgment as to the merits of the behavioral approach, seen, interestingly enough, by many practitioners and critics as uniquely American. The scientific method and the possibility of a science of politics has been warmly embraced by most of those political scientists who insist on realism in politics and analysis. Behavioralism is advanced as a uniquely privileged perspective on political phenomena, one unencumbered by the metaphysics, ideology, and subjectivity that previously prevented a realistic description of action and facts. Heinz Eulau asserts that classical theories are, from the contemporary point of view, psychologically, sociologically, and anthropologically "primitive," "undeveloped," and "often mistaken." [20] Fortunately, both Eulau and Dahl find great promise in the new method for solving at least some of the problems previously regarded as insoluble.[21] Gabriel Almond, in what seems a self-serving misunderstanding of Thomas Kuhn's *The Structure of Scientific Revolutions*, insists that "in the last decade or two the elements of a new, *more surely scientific* paradigm seem to be manifesting themselves rapidly." [22]

This newest expression of optimism about achieving a science of politics and with it the ability to predict and control events stands in marked contrast to the diminished faith in man that was given a particularly modern impetus by the rise of Nazism. Under this impact, much older and deeper themes and fears received new articulation and definition. Altruism, the common interest, professions of sympathy, were determined to be epiphenomenal. Behind such protestations one could find, by the proper process of unmasking, "real" motives, drives, and goals. Unmasked man was truly intimidating in his potential for bestiality and his already realized depravity. A method that could promise prediction of human events and perhaps (benign) control of them seemed all the more imperative and welcome. For with the rise of Nazism it was clear that it no longer made sense (if it ever did) to regard human conduct as many men had come to regard science—as cumulative, progressive, and increasing human control over the environment. Faith in human capacity to contain human atrocity declined in the face of what was seen as Nazism's corroboration of profoundly liberal and American predispositions, and was replaced by a science which, though men could discover it, was itself suprahuman. Science could be used to control men, for the positivist notion of science was thought to have finally removed human elements from investigation and to have ensured that what would be discovered was reality, not some demented fool's conception of reality. Thus science came to be depicted as the progressive diminution of man's ignorance, while history was interpreted as revealing the impossibility of progress outside of scientific techniques and methods.[23] Science was and still is presented as the epitome of "rationality," at the same time that politics and political man are seen as basically vicious, if not "irrational." If men were capable of destruction and self-destruction, and if science seemed the only way men could control themselves, the task for political analysis and politics was set. Man had to be saved from himself, and this was the unique responsibility of American social science and politics. A science of politics could promise an end to Nazism and totalitarianism; at least promise it with more assurance than any rival approach to political phenomena. And America, as the most scientific country in the world, could best achieve, if not salvation, then the containment of evil; if we could not transcend original sin, we could, with Madison, at least control its effects.

I.

Certain aspects of Nazism, though not of course in historical isolation, graphically illuminated what came to be understood as a violation of expectations, an "anomaly" in terms
of previous paradigms of analysis and politics. Together
with Communism (which, once revelations concerning
Stalin became public knowledge, was seen in terms of
Nazism) and the general and bitter disillusionment with
political radicalism, Nazism was perceived as revelatory
about man, a reminder of what had always been a theme of
liberal thought: that naïve fantasies of inevitable progress
and of enlightenment were just that—naïve and fantastic—
and hence too dangerous to be countenanced. This was
given substance by the work of Freud—to whom Dahl attributes a "quantum jump" in our understanding of man
and to whose legacy he assigns the responsibility for having
"made us all acutely aware of man's capacity for irrational,
nonrational, impulsive, neurotic, and psychotic action in
politics, unfortunately, as much as elsewhere." [24]

Nazism came to play a role for many American political
scientist comparable to the place the state of nature played
in the thought of Thomas Hobbes. To a significant degree,
Hobbes's state of nature was a metaphor for the passionate,
prideful, unboundedly egotistical part of man—that portion
and those attributes which are destructive of authority and
ultimately of self. The state of nature, then, was a constant
possibility, since it was in fact part of man. One could not
still the destructive impulses in man, but one could subli-
mate and redirect such impulses and make them "functional." Hobbes was more or less convinced that his new
method would enable him to accomplish what others before
him had tried but failed to achieve—the quieting of destructive passions and thus the ceasing of present, and the precluding of future, civil disorder. From the fear of uncer-

tainty, from the terror of the unexpected, from the dread of the miraculous quality that Arendt finds in political action, Hobbes intended to rescue men by a sovereign, and by sovereignty. The state of nature as well as totalitarianism, and Nazism in particular, was partly an understanding of men and politics, a premise and a justification for political authority, and the basis for constricting the range of tolerable action.

In response to a critic, Dahl at once summarizes and expands this theme. He rejects the charge that he himself advocates a low level of participation and insists that on the contrary he should like to see much higher levels, particularly among some segments of the population whose participation has been lowest. He continues by questioning any automatic identification of high levels of participation with thriving democracy: "The rapid rise in electoral participation in the late years of the Weimar Republic did not make it a 'better' democracy, nor did it enable that Republic to solve its problems. Instead, it was associated with factors that transformed that experiment in democracy into a monstrous system, with very high rates of 'participation' of a kind, and where apathy was encouraged only in the concentration camps." Finally, in a footnote to the passage just quoted, Dahl writes:

Incidentally, while we may have recently emphasized the conditions of democratic "stability" too much, and the conditions of democratic change too little, I doubt whether anyone who remembers the failure of "stable" democracies to emerge in the USSR, Italy, Germany and Spain will ever find it in himself to scoff at writers who focus on the conditions of democratic stability. What such writers are likely to have in mind when they think of democratic "instability" is not cabinet changes nor even piddling differences in regime but the possibility of democratic failures eventuating in brutal dictatorships in comparison with which even the worst polyarchy will seem like the promised land.[25]

In these passages of great feeling we can see how, in the
face of Nazism and Communism, a new emphasis on stability
and authority became pronounced; an emphasis which characterized and sustained the values enshrined in the new paradigms of analysis and politics. David Truman, reflecting on
the history and state of the discipline in his presidential address to the American Political Science Association, notes
how disturbing were the "fascist coups in Italy and the later
Nazi take-over in Germany, with their open and effective
repudiation of the expectations and practices that underlay
the implicit agreements of the profession." [26] Almond suggests the new skepticism about progress, given a world "in
which fascism could capture strongholds in western culture." [27] And Daniel Bell, writing on contemporary discussions of "alienation," argues that "the sadism of the Nazis,
the ruthlessness of war, the existence of concentration
camps, the use of terror, had called into question the deepest
beliefs of the generation." [28]

In vivid contrast to ideological politics and the perceived
consequences of such politics—brutality, sadism, concentration camps, and widespread use of terror—was the New
Deal, which allowed none of these and during which a large
number of academics made their way to Washington and
government service. The moderate and celebrated pragmatic character of the New Deal presented such a benign
alternative to extremism, mass movements, and ideological
politics that drastic social change seemed both dangerous
and superfluous;[29] and thus it remained rather easy to overlook the way America treated her black, brown, yellow, and
red residents. Indeed, the contrast had lasting impact on
American political science. "The Second World War," Dahl
has noted, "stimulated the development of the behavioral
approach in the United States, for a great many American
political scientists temporarily vacated their ivory towers
and came to grips with day-to-day political and administrative realities in Washington and elsewhere: a whole genera-

tion of American political science later drew on these experiences." [30] The experience was of a nation united in war (with implications, perhaps, for the subsequent overemphasis of the presence of consensus in America), engaged in what appeared to be an unideological politics, hardheaded, pragmatic, and yet humane.[31] As we had fought our revolution, so we tended to fight our depression—with sobriety. It now became evident and imperative that men, if they were to avoid doing what they might, ought to embrace an ethic of timidity, celebrate compromise, applaud bargaining, and encourage moderation, negotiation, and incremental change. Such prudence, when joined with the insistence that democratic ideals are unrealistic and in need of revision, culminates in the belief that there is really no such thing as a good society—but that to the degree there is, we are it. What exists becomes, by default, what is ideal.

Thus the assimilation of a particular view of Nazism into the accepted political lore, as providing certain "lessons" about politics and man, made a definite conception of politics and political analysis appear self-evident, real, and necessary. This assimilation constituted both a break with the views of the immediate past and a resuscitation and reaffirmation of older themes definitive of the Western intellectual tradition,[32] more specifically, of Western liberalism,[33] and even more narrowly, of the American version and adaptation of that liberalism.[34] Indeed, the behavioral portrait of Nazism could be all the more convincing for its affinities with Madisonianism. Thus the behavioral understanding of Nazism did not so much create the recently dominant image of man and politics as give an older, thinly repressed understanding new elaboration, scope, and impetus.

As the predicament of man in Hobbes's state of nature made the authority of the sovereign more palatable and the arguments for his establishment more persuasive, so in like manner our willingness to emphasize stability, authority, and restraint (even though these have escaped accomplishment), our unabashed and only slightly camouflaged renunciation of democratic ideals, is more convincing given what we have avoided, what we might have but did not become, and what we did not do.

II.

Given what Nazism was understood to have once more revealed about men and the consequent dissipation of our historical exuberance, the problem for America—for both our politics and our political analysis—was obvious: how to ensure "democratic stability" and establish authority to guarantee the resilience of such stability. The political problem became, as it was for Hobbes, containment of violence, sublimation of pride, the elimination of brutality and destruction. Politics was assigned a central role in accomplishing these crucial purposes, with the paradoxical result that politics has by now become defined in terms most suspicious and repugnant to liberal men, without any compensating characteristics to assuage suspicion or mitigate repugnancy. As in much Christian theology, politics is a necessary evil, at best a limit on the consequences of human sinfulness, and is explicitly identified with force and violence. The traits men find most admirable—self-respect, common purpose—are discovered in private or perhaps social life, while those less admirable human traits and relationships—power, rule, authority, conflict, violence—are essentially, though not exclusively, identified with public life. Man is by nature a private rather than a public animal. Political life is not distinctively and pre-eminently the arena for human expression. It is in our private lives that we find what is distinctive about, and precious to, men. Given this understanding of the place of politics in human existence, it is not surprising that a re-examination of the place of political participation in human life should occasion tactical, but not moral, dilemmas. For once participation is no longer regarded as essential to a fully human life, it becomes possible to face apathy with moral equanimity. Fear of the obvious potential dangers of low participation, e.g., tyranny, mass disaffection, and potential repudiation of a government, are quieted by the belief both that our society has functioning self-corrective mechanisms and that nonparticipation indicates passive consent rather than latent hostility.

In strong words, Dahl insists:

> It would clear the air of a good deal of cant, if, instead of assuming that politics is a normal and natural concern of human beings, one were to make the contrary assumption that whatever lip service citizens may pay to conventional attitudes, politics is a remote, alien, and unrewarding activity. Instead of seeking to explain why citizens are not interested, concerned, and active, the task is to explain why a few citizens are.[35]

The politics that are remote, alien, and unrewarding are defined as "any persistent pattern of human relationships that involves to a significant extent power, rule, and authority." [36] "Wherever we find politics," Dahl writes, "we discover conflict and ways in which human beings cope with conflict." [37] "Conflict and politics," he says in another place, "are born inseparable twins." [38] Politics arise then "wherever there are people living together in associations, when they are involved in conflicts, and wherever they are subject to some kind of power, rulership or authority." [39] "The state is distinguishable from other political systems," we are informed, "only to the extent that it successfully upholds its claims to the exclusive right to determine the conditions under which certain kinds of severe penalties involving physical coercion may be legitimately employed." The state emerges as a "pawn of key importance in the struggle for power." Government steps into the picture "wherever conflict is thought to be beyond adjustment of nonpolitical means or by other governments than that of the state." Finally, consider the way the "political" sphere is distin-

guished from that area of existence which is warmly evocative, meaningful, and rewarding. "Probably no human
association is exclusively *political* in all its aspects. People
experience many *other* relationships than power and authority, experiences such as love, respect, purpose, dedication,
shared beliefs, and so on." [40]

Given a distinction posed in this manner, it is no wonder
that so few men participate, that politics is "remote, alien
and unrewarding." The question is open, however, as to
whether a different conception and kind of politics and political life—a political game with different stakes, rules, rewards, and rhythms—might be more rewarding, less alien,
and less remote. Perhaps for many of our citizens, or rather
residents, the political game as now defined and played does
not, but could, meet their deepest needs and desires. Apathy,
then, may be a product of American "politics" in the twentieth century and not part of political life.[41] Perhaps those
largely outside the system do not care for what those inside
the system are fighting about. "They want," John Schaar
suggests, "new issues and cleavages, new programs and goals,
new heroes and villains—in short a new agenda and a new
game." And Schaar goes on to ask whether it is possible, not
that men are apathetic because they have low socioeconomic
status, but that they have low socioeconomic status because
they are apathetic.[42]

I do not mean that Dahl's definitions or descriptions are
"wrong," but rather that they are so severely restrictive of
possibilities and yet presented with so little evidence or argument that attention ought to be focused on them. Why is
it that dedication, self-respect, common purposes, are found,
if at all, in private and not political life? What are the possibilities and potentialities of a politics revived and redefined
to engage these attitudes and commitments? What seems operative is a fear of too much politicization, a suspicion that
intense political commitment and passionate politics automatically eventuates in "total" politics—a "conception of

politics," Berelson reminds us, "advanced by such leading theorists of National Socialism and communism as Carl Schmitt and Lenin." [43] Nonliberal politics becomes guilty by association.

Now many behavioralists may well respond, as Dahl has recently responded to one of his critics,[44] that this line of argument confuses description and prescription, is and ought, facts and values. But again there is little systematic examination of these oppositions and the relationships between them. The response is virtually an incantation.[45] It ignores, for instance, the possibility that descriptions may, through political education, become a series of self-fulfilling prophecies; that "the social scientist actually helps make his objects of study what they are," so that his studies of his manufactured material redundantly confirm his science.[46] The failure to appreciate such possibilities and the dependence on the fact-value opposition is linked to the use of the phrase "in the real world." An appraisal of the uses and functions of that phrase in the behavioral literature will, it will be argued, reveal vacillation between modest attempts at description of American society at one point in time and the less humble objective of proposing a set of Neoplatonic categories which are seen as capturing and encompassing the essence of politics and man. This contention will, of course, be denied. Critics will insist that the findings in behavioral analysis are inductive rather than a priori. The unpersuasiveness of this response is indicated by Dahl's extrapolation from New Haven through America to politics in general in *Who Governs* and by the kinds of definitions presented in *Modern Political Analysis*.

III.

In *A Preface to Democratic Theory,* Dahl criticizes the theory of populist democracy as "no more than an exercise in axiomatics," because "it tells us nothing about the real

world." "However," he continues, "let us now pose the key
question in slightly different form: What are the necessary
and sufficient conditions for maximizing democracy in the
real world? I shall show that the words 'in the real world'
fundamentally alter the problem." [47] But there is no discussion of the real world, though there is an assumption that
there *is* a real world, one which can be grasped once and for
all. Yet without elaboration the "real world" seems merely
an attempt to force agreement on what the "facts" of political life are and thus on what values it is then "rational" and
intelligent to defend.

J. L. Austin has argued that though "real" is an "absolutely normal word," it is not normal in the way that "yellow" or "horse" or "walk" is normal, for it does not have one
single specifiable meaning. But neither, he insists, is it ambiguous. The word "real," Austin suggests, is a "trouser
word," in that "a definite sense attaches to the assertion that
something is real, a real such-and-such, only in light of a specific way in which it might be, or might have been *not* real."
He offers an example: " 'A real duck' differs from the simple
'a duck' only in that it is used to exclude various ways of
being not a real duck—but a dummy, a toy, a picture, a
decoy; and moreover I don't know *just* what, on that particular occasion, the speaker has in mind to exclude." [48] Now I
am not clear, and I am not sure Dahl is clear either, on what
is to be excluded from the "real" world. How and in what
ways does the phrase "exclude" whatever it is supposed to
exclude? Is what "exists" now, what "is" part of the American political scene at this moment, "real"?; i.e., part of an
unchanging and unchangeable reality? What are the spatial
and temporal dimensions of such exclusion?

Dahl's vagueness on these matters is significant, because it
permits him both to maintain the "fact-value" distinction
and, when useful, to ignore it. For "real" is a valuative, even
emotive, term—one which is implicitly meant to exclude
what is "false," "ideological," etc. But as such, the "real

world" becomes a metaphysics, perhaps *the* American metaphysics. For though the scientific method is understood as insisting that hypotheses be open and subject to falsification, yet the real world is unhypothetical. The phrase "real world" then seems to perform two different but complementary functions. Critically, it reaffirms the unreality of democratic theory (though it seems to confuse the nature of "traditional" theory in the process).[49] Positively, "real" is meant to give a preferred status to the world as portrayed by the behavioralist. "Once we get outside the models of the democratic theorists to the political life of the real world, we discover that politics which we in the West call democratic are in fact systems in which most policy is determined by a relatively small number of people."[50] The real world is the world unmasked by realistic political scientists, a world where choice, of necessity, is limited to marginal preferences; a world in which politics becomes, to use a phrase of Michael Oakeshott's, "the pursuit of intimations."[51] To be realistic, to take heed and account of the limiting imperatives of the real world, is to at once recognize the absurdity of "rationalism" (in Oakeshott's sense) or, what in many cases amounts to the same thing, "radicalism." Realism becomes an unargued and implicit conservatism—the best and perhaps the only kind. Incremental politics becomes, given this framework, both the only possible and the most desirable form of politics. Not only is it true that "the characteristics and effects of existing policies and institutions are more easily and more accurately and more confidently known than for hypothetical politics and institutions,"[52] but it is also the case that "to a great extent, everyone must take the boundaries of his political world as given by prior tradition and historical events. Such boundaries are not often open to rational change."[53] Such "givenness" demands appropriate forms of adaptation and adjustment. "Evidently," Dahl says, "we need to train people who can shift rapidly from a role in one kind of organization to a role in another without arous-

ing too great a burden of doubt and anxiety, and who therefore have the capacity partly to compartmentalize the values
required for each system. There is something a little terrifying about this picture of man compartmentalized. But we
cannot expect man to reject a development that society requires of him if he is to succeed and indeed to survive." [54]
Berelson shares this perspective when he marvels at how
"the political system adjusts itself to changing conditions
over long periods of time." The "system" appears as a dis-
embodied thing, unamenable to certain forms of human direction, though susceptible to marginal alterations. "Classic
theory" went wrong, we are told, by concentrating on the
individual citizen[55]—the language *we* need, it seems, is one
which deals with the "system of democracy," which takes
full cognizance of the incapacity of men to radically transform their world. Since we cannot do (and implicitly and
paradoxically ought not to do) too much (or can do only so
much), we are better off making peace with ourselves and
the real world by adapting and adjusting to that world. Failure to do so is to forget that politics is reflective of and par-
ticipates in all the limitations of man, that the only relevant
normative criticism is that which is incremental. To ignore
these injunctions is to be by definition utopian, irrational,
and ultimately destructive.

Furthermore, knowledge of the real world is "factual"
knowledge, for that world is an empirical world.[56] Scientific
theories, in politics or elsewhere, are in some simple way assumed to be symbolic reproductions of, or to correspond [57] to,
a reality that is, when all is said and done, "there." The object of analysis becomes, in turn, the purgation of distortions
that intervene between the investigator and the world which
stands ready to verify his hypotheses and propositions. And
because the real world is an empirical world, an empirical
method, such as behavioralism, is uniquely situated to provide privileged information about that world. But this
method is not, it is claimed, similar to that form of posi-

tivism which collected "brute facts." For behavioralists insist
on the fruitfulness of mutual interaction between facts and
theories—at least those "intellectually respectable" theories
which allow for "some more or less extensive validation" of
hypotheses.[58] Empirical propositions, i.e., those that propose
to say something about the real world we experience and observe,[59] must be differentiated from those normative propositions which insist on an "ought." "Whenever students of
politics scrupulously test their generalizations and theories
against the data of experience by means of meticulous observation, classification and measurement, then political analysis is scientific in approach." [60] Empirical theory is built up
by adding validated discrete propositions, analogous, it
would seem, to constructing a wall of bricks. Eulau proposes
that "a science of politics which deserves its name must
build from the bottom up by asking simple questions that
can, in principle, be answered. . . . An empirical discipline
is built up by the slow, modest and piecemeal cumulation of
relevant theories and data." [61] There is, then, a real world
which we can know and which seems to exist independently
of human will.

But Thomas Kuhn projects a quite different picture of
science and scientific research. For him, a "fact" and the
"fact-value" distinction is intelligible only within a previously defined context, what he calls "normal science," which
is in turn a function of a "paradigm." He insists, in what is,
at the very least, a significant qualification of Dahl, that if
"any and every failure to fit were ground for theory rejection, all theories ought to be rejected at all times." [62] Indeed,
Kuhn's analysis suggests that the real world of behavioralism
is a paradigm which like all paradigms is simultaneously
prescriptive and descriptive, normative and empirical, a partially (in two senses) articulated framework for analysis, a
set of mutually reinforcing images of man and politics
supported, as are scientific paradigms, by those authorities
who are given or assume responsibility for maintaining the

(politically) scientific community, and who thus are able to define in broad terms what constitutes appropriate and inappropriate behavior for "professionals" and to punish "deviancy." [63] Though the nature, "recognition," and impact of anomalies constitute a most perplexing problem in Kuhn's argument, still if we accept the notion that behavioralism is a paradigm of analysis and politics which largely replaced a previous mode of inquiry and conception of subject matter, we can better appreciate the way the events I have labeled "Nazism" were a violation of expectations, or an anomaly. It was the burden of the new paradigm to "resolve" in some acceptable way the newly emergent political "facts." This it did by a new "articulation" of a previous theory of politics and men, incorporated in the phrase "the real world." But the "real" world then is more a metaphysical mood than part of an articulated and defended argument. It is this vague awareness, this sense of resignation, which form the premise for the argument for realism and realistic analysis directed against previous modes of political analysis and political action. The response to Nazism as a liberal nightmare precluded detailed historical investigation of that atrocity at the same time that it generated a pervasive fear, useful in intimidating nonliberal politics. That crucial aspects of the behavorialists' position rest on unarticulated assumptions assists in explaining a recurrent lack of clarity as to the scope and durability of their findings, their belief that the categories of contemporary American political life capture political life generally—that the findings about the former are also valid for the latter.[64] It assists us, too, in comprehending the significance and implications of the argument that "traditional" political theorists were naïve in misperceiving the centrality of power and thus the nature of politics. For such a criticism is only plausible if one initially presumes that there *is* a political reality and nature of man against which theories of very different times and places can be referred. If there were no such "real world," the criticisms of political theory would have to be different indeed, and behavioralism would at best be seen as a method particularly appropriate for understanding American politics in mid-twentieth century, and its ideological character would be manifest.

IV.

The real world, because it is assumed to be an "empirical" world, is thought to be most fully revealed, comprehended, and presented by a method able to parenthesize and compensate for the various distortions that intervene between the observer and the world he observes. Indeed, an implicit argument for the new realism and an explicit one for the claimed superiority of behavioral analysis in laying bare the real world is that there exists a distinction variously formulated between the "is" and the "ought," "facts" and "values," "description" and "prescription," "empirical" and "normative." It is maintained that whether "empirical propositions are true or false is entirely independent of our values." [65] Political scientists are not alone, of course, in insisting on the logical separation of facts and values, or what is a corollary, on the necessity of keeping the role of scientist-scholar and concerned citizen distinct. These distinctions are at least as old as Hume, though the formulation of them owes more to the formulations of logical positivism than they do to the Scottish philosopher. The ideal of disinterested inquiry was stated most lucidly, as many things have been, by Bertrand Russell in the concluding lines of his *History of Western Philosophy*:

> In the welter of conflicting fanaticisms, one of the few unifying forces is scientific truthfulness, by which I mean the habit of basing our beliefs upon observations and inferences as impersonal and as much divested of local and temperamental bias, as is possible for human beings. To have insisted upon the introduction of this virtue into philosophy and to have invented a powerful method by which it can be rendered fruit-

ful are the chief merits of the philosophical school of which I
am a member.[66]

Objectivity has become for several behavioralists the sine
qua non of the scientific enterprise—of what it means to be a
political *scientist*. Thus Eulau suggests that only by maintaining the distinctions between facts and values, and what
is a corollary, the separation of roles in both theory and
practice, can a man aspire to the "values that scientists try
and live by . . . truth, objectivity, honesty and integrity." [67]
"Social research which requires direct observations and objective recording of reality," Daniel Lerner writes, is the
"natural enemy of *all* ideology." "Ideology," he goes on,
"*prescribes* a preferred future. . . . Research *describes* an
actual present—the way things in fact are." Ignoring the
way the research ideology rationalizes a threatened present,
Lerner goes on to say that "while the function of research is
to test social theory by observation of reality, the function of
agitprop [agitation and propaganda] is to make reality appear to conform to the ideology." [68] These distinctions
become the criteria for differentiating myths, ideologies, and
metaphysics from science, and so form a firm foundation of
arguments intended to demonstrate the superiority of scientific techniques, approaches, and methods. Furthermore,
they lend credence to the implicit claim that we can be precise about the political world in a way in which those who
are "subjective" cannot be.

The work of Kuhn, Feyerabend, and Hanson, as well as
that of contemporary philosophers whose primary interest
lies outside the area of science,[69] raises doubts about the
plausibility of these distinctions as formulated by political
scientists. Kuhn's discussion of paradigms, for instance, implies that the relation between facts, values, theories, rules,
observations, descriptions, myths, metaphysics, and science is
far more complicated than many behavioralists and scientists
acknowledge. He argues, "Scientific fact and theory are not

categorically separable, except perhaps within a single tradition of normal science." [70] It is misleading to say that the
world changes with a change in perspective, and yet it is
equally misleading to say that we see the same world after
what Kuhn describes as a scientific revolution and establishment of a new paradigm. In Kuhn's words, "though the
world does not change with a change in paradigm the scientist afterwards works in a different world." [71] Thus Eulau's
admonition that "it is the function of science to understand
and interpret the world, not to change it" [72] is only part of
the story.

There is, in addition, some reason for believing that any
description of reality makes certain courses of action and the
defense of certain values seem more "rational" and "realistic," at the same time that it facilitates or hinders the defense
of certain other values and modes of action. At one level,
perhaps the "final" one, disputes over values are importantly matters of persuasion, and the portrayed structure of
reality may well make such efforts more difficult or easy.
Thus, if one says of entities, institutions, etc., that they are
"real," or if one talks of "the real world" as containing a
limited range of objects or behavior patterns, then certain
things are seen as more possible than others, one alternative
deemed more or less realistic than another. If the real world
generates certain imperatives that are seen as conditions of
political action, these imperatives become the promise of
how one ought to act, or, more precisely, of how one can and
cannot act, of what is more or less feasible. Kuhn makes a
related point. Referring to the assumptions of physical scientists after 1630 and the appearance of Descartes' major scientific writings, he writes of "that nest of commitments"
which proved to be both metaphysical and methodological.
"As metaphysical, it told scientists what sorts of entities the
universe did and did not contain . . . as methodological it
told them what ultimate laws and fundamental explanations
must be like" [73] E. A. Burtt has put the argument forcefully:

If you cannot avoid metaphysics, what kind of metaphysics are you likely to cherish when you sturdily suppose yourself to be free from the abomination? Of course, it goes without saying that in this case your metaphysics will be held uncritically because it is unconscious; moreover, it will be passed on to others far more readily than your other notions inasmuch as it will be propagated by insinuations rather than by direct argument.

Now the history of mind reveals pretty clearly that the thinker who decries metaphysics will actually hold metaphysical notions of three main types. For one thing, he will share the ideas of his age on ultimate questions, so far as such ideas do not run counter to his interests or awaken his criticism . . . but the metaphysician will at least be superior to his opponent in this respect, in that he will be constantly on his guard against the surreptitious entrance and unquestioned influence of such notions. In the second place, if he be a man engaged in any important inquiry, he must have a method, and he will be under a strong and constant temptation to make a metaphysics out of his method, that is, to suppose the universe ultimately of such a sort that his method must be appropriate and successful. . . . Finally since human nature demands metaphysics for its full intellectual satisfaction, no great mind can wholly avoid playing with ultimate questions, especially where they are powerfully thrust upon it by considerations arising from its positivistic investigations, or by certain vigorous extra-scientific interests, such as religion. But inasmuch as the positivist mind has failed to school itself in careful metaphysical thinking, its ventures at such points will be apt to appear pitiful, inadequate, or even fantastic.[74]

Thus it is not at all self-evident that, as Charles Taylor rightly says, "the findings of political science leave us, as it were, as free as before." They "go some way to establishing particular sets of values and undermining others." [75] For in his implicit conception of political reality, of human needs, purposes, and values, a political scientist sets out and limits possible policies and actions, and it is because this is so that the phrase "the real world" and the injunction "be realistic" are intelligible.

In addition to this largely philosophical objection, there are various confusions which surround the claim for, and the insistence on, "objectivity." As Russell clearly says, the attempt to escape from bias is limited, not surprisingly, by what is "possible for human beings." But how much is possible? The behavioralists seem both to hold objectivity as an ideal and to believe that such an ideal is achieved in, and exemplified by, their work. Now insofar as objectivity is regarded as an ideal, one can demand, as Dahl does of previous democratic theory, that this ideal be "realistic," lest in establishing impossible goals it place present behavioral literature in disrepute. Indeed, this is partly what has occurred, as it has become obvious that the claim for, and insistence on, objectivity and neutrality have been employed in sustaining particular, principally "establishment," political views. This circumstance, together with a psychologically unsupported view of man as scholar and a failure to confront "Mannheim's paradox," also vitiates the less plausible, but more frequent, assumption that objectivity has been realized in behavioral studies.

Furthermore, it is never made clear or even discussed what kind of objectivity is possible or desirable in what sorts of political contexts and on what issues. How is objectivity, both idealized and actualized, related to political styles, to nonideological and "normal" politics on the one hand and to ideological or revolutionary politics on the other? What is the relation of liberal American politics to objectivity in particular and to a science of politics in general? Would objectivity be bearable in an intensely political society? What view of politics follows, and will be supported, if methodological certification demands political abstinence, and intellectual respectability is a function of scrupulous detachment from political involvement? What are the "objective"

political scientist's feelings about the phenomena he studies?
Does he too regard politics as unrewarding and alien and
thus something from which one is easily and eagerly detached?

The immediate response to such argument is a further insistence that men can and ought religiously to separate their
roles as scholar-scientists and citizens. The goal was put powerfully by Moritz Schlick:

> So long as the philosopher is concerned about his purely
> theoretical questions, he must forget that he has a human in-
> terest as well as a cognitive interest in the object of his in-
> vestigation. For him there is no greater danger than to change
> from a philosopher into a moralist, from an investigator into
> a preacher. Desire for truth is the only appropriate inspiration
> for the thinker when he philosophizes: otherwise his thought
> runs the danger of being led astray by his feelings. His wishes,
> hopes and fears, threaten to encroach upon that objectivity
> which is the necessary presupposition of all honest inquiry.
> Of course the prophet and the investigator can be one and the
> same person; but one cannot at the same moment serve both
> interests, for whoever mixes the two problems will solve
> neither.[76]

The same warning was offered in similar terms by William
F. Whyte when he insisted that preaching and "sermons"
ought not to find their way into classrooms. While he found
such sermonizing inefficacious, he was concerned with the
"neurotic compulsions" of the sermonizers.[77] Whyte, like
Schlick, takes it for granted that such role separation is possible.

With comparable sentiments, but in a different historical
and intellectual context, Eulau assures us that "I never concern myself with the problem of whether the result of research is critical or conformist; let us not confuse our role of
responsible citizen with our role of scientist." [78] In another
place he asserts that "political science, as all science, should
be put in the service of whatever goals men pursue in poli-

tics"; and Dahl, if I understand the purpose of *Modern Po-litical Analysis,* seems to agree.

Once again, such claims, insofar as they are presented as descriptions of the way men do or could act, are unsupported by evidence or argument. It is essential to ask whether the choice of research project and the willingness to make findings public would be unaffected if the political regime under which the social scientist lived were one which he regarded as engaged in inhuman practices? Are we to assume that a man is capable, while doing research on politics, of completely blocking out and ignoring the political context and ramifications of what he is doing? Or is it rather that a political scientist need not worry about the possible inhuman uses to which his research may be put, resting comfortably on his political commitment to the prevailing political values and rules? The distinction of roles, as Eulau states it, rests on an image of man and human behavior which is less than self-evident. This is not to deny that some men have greater self-consciousness than others or are more willing and able than others to maintain a certain degree of role separation. What we need is some subtle argument or evidence for such separation prior to accepting Eulau's argument and the more general view of science and objectivity which his argument is meant to buttress.[79]

Furthermore, such role separation is open to objections similar to the philosophical queries presented previously. For once again, it seems plausible to assume that the findings of the scholar-scientist become part of the "description" of political reality within which the concerned citizen makes his choices and assesses the possibilities of action. Either the findings of Eulau's research influence and create a framework for his notion of what is "realistic" and possible, or else those descriptions are oddly ignored when it comes time to act and decide. What forms of action are deemed possible and rational within the confines of the framework of reality that is disclosed by the method? What kind of knowledge is considered relevant and requisite for what sort of action? If we discovered certain ideological biases in research, certain implicit political commitments, then action on the basis of these biases would manifest the same ideology. Again, as Taylor suggests, a "framework," though it does not establish the validity of certain values, does support them, it distributes the onus of argument in a certain way.[80]

In *Modern Political Analysis,* Dahl states that "objectivity, neutrality, the capacity and opportunity for scientific detachment are impossible without certain social and political prerequisites." [81] Indeed, Daniel Lerner finds the identification between social science and America so close that the former is seen as a "tool and product" of the democratic West, while the "rule of social science" appears at times a new and more sophisticated form of imperialism.[82] Herbert Feigl also identifies "mature thinking," as found in science, with "mature social action as we find it in democracy." [83]

Thus all science, but particularly political science, and all scientists, but particularly political scientists, are seen as dependent on the presence of certain political and social prerequisites and conditions—those associated with open, Western, democratic societies. Now, given the division of roles enunciated by Eulau and this admission by Dahl, certain curious consequences seem to follow. For the scientist qua scientist has political commitments, insofar as he perceives a dependency between his ability to be scientific and certain political conditions, arrangements, institutions, and values. If the political scientist is more intensely concerned with science than with politics, his political views will be a function of his scientific commitment. He will then support any political regime which seems to him most committed to science. The division of roles will thus become merely a façade, for one role will be defined in terms of the other, more intensely felt role. Furthermore, the happy compatibility of science and democracy rests on the dubious assumption that the American community and the scientific one are, in fact, both open and democratic.[84]

But there may be a much more intimate relationship between the scientific community and political decisions than would appear from the positing of role divisions.

First of all, Kuhn suggests that we take the word "community" in the phrase "scientific community" far more seriously than we have done previously, and recognize that "normal science" is an orthodoxy supported by authorities who enforce distinctions between those who are and those who are not to be counted as part of the scientific community. Thus the image of an "open," internally "democratic" science may need revision. Furthermore, it is not even clear that science, at least in nonrevolutionary periods, is dependent upon an open society at all. For there is some evidence that those who are in positions of authority in the scientific community also have significant influence in the political community. It may even be the case that governments could be useful in assisting the scientific establishment in maintaining what would usually be portrayed as a scientific paradigm.[85] The Lysenko case may be merely a more extreme instance of what occurs in both Communist and non-Communist society.

V.

A frequent complaint of some behavioralists is that nonbehavioral analysis is not "precise" and "rigorous" enough to achieve accuracy of description. The achievement of the proper degree of precision would contribute, it is thought, to a realistic grasp of the real world by enabling us carefully to separate facts and values. In addition, adherence to certain canons of precision is sometimes used to distinguish those who are properly political scientists from those who are unwilling or unable to meet such standards ade-

quately.[86] While the methodological function of the insistence on precision may be clear, it is not equally apparent
that political purposes may be involved as well. Though
Hobbes was quite capable of using metaphor and image to
paint a somber, forbidding picture of masterless man, he
insisted that precision was an essential prerequisite for civil
order. Hobbes thought that a correctly applied method and
a language purged of passion-evoking words and images
might result in a nonideological politics and in public tranquillity.[87]

What is immediately confusing about an ideal of "precision" is that it is itself less than precise, i.e., it is not clear
what is counted as a precise (as opposed to an ambiguous)
statement about or description of a situation or experience.
Nor is it clear where one is to look for criteria that might
establish which description is more "precise" and in what
ways it meets such an ideal. Thus the insistence on being
precise in the abstract is too amorphous, for precision is a
significant demand within a particular context and in response to a definite question or problem.[88] To recognize a
description or explanation as lacking in precision is to assume sufficient familiarity with a problem and its context to
distinguish between precision and imprecision. Thus we
might be led to believe that an insistence on precision is
simply a demand for descriptions appropriate for coming to
terms with the phenomenon being described. But what then
becomes crucial is the way political phenomena are perceived, and the demand for precision may well presuppose,
or may have to presuppose, an ontology, a view of reality
and the nature of phenomena that inhabit that reality, and a
view of how such phenomena are to be described.

The demand for precision does, on occasion, appear to be
a rather straightforward request that descriptions should be
as unambiguous as possible. This weaker version of the demand might be construed as a warning—a warning which
would accept Feigl's admonition that "there is no point in

sharpening precision to a higher degree than the problem at hand requires." [89]

But if virtually every problem requires precision, this weaker demand becomes a stronger and more debatable claim—a claim that to be intelligible, ambiguity and poetic modes of expression ought to be purged from political analysis, for inherently they misrepresent and misdescribe political reality.[90] This version is stronger and more debatable because it assumes that there are descriptions of states of affairs which can be known to be ultimately correct and that for every state of affairs there corresponds a single correct description.[91] To be precise is to propound this description, and it is for this reason that precision is a precondition for accuracy. The process of seeking descriptions of increasing precision is the continual substitution of a clearer expression for what is deemed a misleading one, culminating in the ultimate clarity of a completely precise, ideally formal description in an equally precise and formal language. This ideal is perhaps suggestive of why Dahl seeks conclusive rather than exploratory or elucidative definitions (e.g., of the nature of politics) and why he is uneasy about ambiguity (e.g., on the notion of government).[92]

Now, a prime effort of recent British philosophy is to emphasize, in opposition to this process, that "language has many tasks and many levels," such that descriptions of the world cannot be reduced to one kind of description which is seen as the most proper or basic.[93] It is thus mistaken to believe that the physicist (or scientist or anyone else) "had got down to the level of what is really observed, such as logical atoms or sense data, and so has provided the basis for explaining events hitherto roughly accounted for by much less precise use of observation." For "what counts as the proper object of observation . . . does not constitute a particular class of things, meeting special criteria, but varies with the interest of the onlooker." [94] There is a danger of being gripped by what Waismann called a "clarity neurosis,"

where men are "haunted by fear, tongue-tied, asking themselves continually 'Oh dear, now does this make perfectly
good sense?' Imagine the pioneers of science—Kepler, Newton, the discoverers of non-Euclidean geometry, of field
physics, the unconscious, matter waves or heaven knows
what—imagine them asking themselves this question at
every step—this would have been the surest means of sap-
ping any creative power. No great discoverer has acted in
accordance with the motto 'Everything that can be said can
be said clearly.' " [95]

Furthermore, the emphasis on precision, even as pressed
in its milder form, ignores the role of symbols, poetry, and
ideology. It seems not to realize that certain kinds of descriptions of social phenomena cannot be made in the straightforward language used by scientists and emulated by social
scientists. "It may be," Michael Walzer reminds us, "that
certain sorts of statements about the state—vivid descriptions of, or bold assertions about, its essential qualities—
such as human beings are prone to make, simply cannot be
made, cannot even be thought, except metaphorically." [96]

Ultimately, the persuasiveness of an argument for precision rests on a specific view of reality and the acceptance of a
methodology deemed most useful in delineating and describing that reality. The demand for precision supports and
is in turn supported by the insistence on objectivity and the
unargued reliance on an implicit conception of the real
world.

The argument for precision has been linked at least once
in the history of political thought with arguments of an un-
deniably political nature. Hobbes's insistence on precision is
part of his argument for authority. In *Leviathan* he writes:

> [T]he light of human minds is perspicuous words, but by
> exact definitions first snuffed, and purged from ambiguity;
> REASON is the PACE; increase of SCIENCE, the WAY; and the bene-
> fit of mankind, the END. And, on the contrary, metaphors, and
> senseless and ambiguous words, are the *ignes fatui*; and rea-

soning upon them is wandering amongst innumerable absurd-
ities; and their end, contention and sedition, or contempt.[97]

Ambiguity and metaphor are not simply literary offenses
in this view; they are rather, and in an important way, politically dangerous. For Hobbes, these devices not only in-
truded into proper "ratiocination" but also could provoke
violent action and seditious thought. Part of Hobbes's objective was to establish a language that blunted those thoughts
and impulses which led to the kinds of actions depicted in
the state of nature. If one could eliminate those words and
phrases, those images and metaphors, that evoked, and pro-
voked, stability would be all the more secure. Precision and
method, in affording us certainty, would facilitate control
and remedy the frailty of human affairs.[98] Hobbes thought
(quite incorrectly, it turns out) that if the debate over politics could imitate the debate over geometry, we could have a
politics without passion and perhaps without action. The
advantage of a geometrylike politics was that, to use
Hobbes's words, "men care not, in that subject, what be
truth, as a thing that crosses no man's ambition, profit or
lust." [99] If we could only constrain, restrain, and parenthesize passion and spontaneity we could achieve, if not
community, then at least some peace. Words and reason and
a politically neutral vocabulary could, Hobbes suggested
and hoped, be used to stifle passions and redefine consciousness. One could end the state of war in the state of nature by
relying initially on man's fear and reason and ultimately on
science institutionalized in the person of the sovereign and
in the universities: by uniting political science and political
education. For Hobbes saw what Wolin finds the scientific
community to have seen: that the exercise of coercive authority can be made cheaper, more efficient, and less obtru-
sive if the modes of initiation and education of the members
predispose them toward the loyal behavior needed in para-
digm-workers,[100] or, we should say "good citizens."

For Hobbes, the Leviathan was both an answer to the English Civil Wars and a bulwark against the possibility of future sedition, disunion, and civil war. The state of nature epitomized and symbolized the unexceptionally egotistic, rapacious, and prideful nature of man. The desire to purge speech of objectionable forms of expression would be, Hobbes hoped, a supplement to, eventually even a replacement for, the legal force initially exercised by the sovereign.

Similarly, political objectives may be connected with the desirability of precision as expressed by various behavioralists. They too may find danger in metaphor and sedition lurking in the passionate prose of "fanatics" and "agitators," leading ultimately to ideological politics. Their state of nature—the nature of man as revealed by Nazism, explained by Freud, and "verified" by Communistm and McCarthyism —seems again answered by a politically useful methodology and precision. Most contemporary political scientists would agree with J. W. N. Watkins' summary of Hobbes's view: "A man's natural appetites are not sinful. What is objectionable is his moralized projection of them in the form of pseudocommandments to which other men are vainly expected to submit. This inflates conflicts of interest into ideological hostilities." [101]

Whatever the desirability of using a formal language for political analysis, the language so far used by most behavioralists is importantly "emotive." The choice of words belies a choice of sentiments, a "demonology," which functions as both premise and conclusion of the behavioral persuasion. The problem (from a different perspective, a benefit) is that our words have histories. Indeed, it may even be the case that an "evaluative" or "ideological" position is "so embedded within the framework of a language that it may perhaps resist even the most emphatic and explicit disavowals." [102] For a person who uses words is not, by his individual fiat, in control of their meanings. What they mean is determined for him by the "form of life" which he shares with other members of his society and in which the language he uses evolves.[103] The words *democracy, totalitarian, real, fanatic, realistic,* and many others as well, have such connotations and contextual variations of meaning that the kind of objectivity sought by various political scientists may be, given present linguistic forms, impossible to attain. If we should suggest what is perhaps a rather unsubtle criterion for assessing the objectivity of a work, that the readers be generally unaware of the author's political commitments, sentiments, and aspirations following close inspection of the work in question, then none of the works referred to so far has adequately managed to meet the test. (Perhaps it cannot be met outside of mathematics and other purely formal systems.) There is, in much behavioral literature, a series of oppositions between personal traits and political styles. These traits and styles emerge, despite qualifications, as separate and incompatible images of men, politics, and political science. There is little question as to which image is deemed more praiseworthy and admirable. On the one hand, there is the politics and analysis of the modest, tolerant, skeptical, sociable, civilized, humane, reasonable, marginalist, pluralist, compromising, moderate, methodical, incremental, realistic, scientific, bargaining, liberal, mature, reflective, adaptive, humble, professional man. On the other hand, there is the style of politics, action, character, and analysis of the arrogant, intolerant, dogmatic, antisocial, barbaric, inhuman, irrational, ideological, fanatical, radical, idealist, extremist, totalitarian, dictatorial, authoritarian, metaphysical, agitatorial, dilettantish, neurotic, and nonscientific man.[104] This latter coalescence of images, traits, characteristics, styles of action, behavior, and politics is seen as expressive of man's demonic potentialities, as evidenced by Nazism and totalitarianism, and perceived as a consequence of passionate, enthusiastic politics. We thus turn, for it seems that there is no choice, to mechanisms that can keep the latter image controlled, for men themselves seem unable to do so.

It would be possible to show how each characteristic or trait is seen as mutually reinforcing and sustaining—for instance, how the liberal is a pluralist-moderate with a willingness to bargain and compromise, a mature individual cognizant of the imperatives of life and thus more able to adjust peaceably to them. Or alternatively one could construct, in much greater detail, the full portrait of the agitator-fanatic who is suspicious of men's motives, "conjures away obstacles with ritualistic repetition of principles," [104a] sacrifices his family to the cause, prefers the liquidation of the kulaks to incremental politics, is intransigent, unrealistic, silly, and dangerous. The point is not, of course, that such characterizations and oppositions cannot be defended, for they can be. But the use of these words and classifications ought to be recognized for what they are: quite literally, a demonology, and not a simple, precise, unadorned description.

VI.

The preceding analysis has developed two separate but related arguments. I began with a rather broadly drawn portrait of the vision of America and politics held by a prominent section of American political science. In so doing I suggested that the assumptions of American political science have an important but until recently largely ignored political dimension which it is crucial to lay bare. This critique, centrally political in character, led me to focus on the phrase "the real world," which served as a transition from a political to an epistemological examination of behavioralism. More specifically, I chose to examine the claims for objectivity and for the goal of precision, which I see as really part of those claims. At each point I tried, sometimes rather cryptically, to suggest that the philosophical and political assumptions of behavioralism are mutually reinforcing, that the acceptance of one kind of assumption increases the plausibility of the other. I tried where possible to point out that at too many places and in too many ways behavioralism, particularly of the pluralist variety, presents us with unargued presuppositions and unhypothetical contexts. Drawing upon Thomas Kuhn's *The Structure of Scientific Revolutions,* by now a book with considerable currency in political science, I urged that the notion of science, including a "science" of politics, needs far more self-conscious and philosophically sophisticated discussion and defense than it now receives. For it is not sufficient for behavioralists to ignore or reject such discussion as obfuscating and interrupting what they are about and to rely instead on views safely ensconced in clichés and protected by a philosophical generation-gap. (Kuhn takes issue with their traditional view of scientific progress as a form of incremental advance based on scrupulous adherence to defined practices which govern theorizing. He rejects, too, the commonly held picture of cumulative knowledge and the firm belief that scientific theories are discarded on exclusively "scientific" grounds, i.e., when new "knowledge" has "disproved" or falsified them or when they fail to conform to accepted standards of scientific explanation and proof.[105]) I extended Kuhn's notion of paradigm ("universally recognized achievements that for a time provide model problems and solutions to a community of practitioners"[106]) and argued that there is now a dominant (though somewhat precarious) paradigm in political science —a paradigm which is both a product and a cause of an equally prevailing view of what constitutes "politics" and political "action." This paradigm, the "real world," is a partly conscious adherence to a theory, a way of doing things, and a picture of reality. The "acceptance" of this world was due to a series of specific yet generalized historical events (which I have lumped under Nazism) and issued in a new articulation of liberal politics and political analysis, a different principle of relevance, a redefinition of who and what was "scientific," and a reassessment of the place of "scientific" analysis in political study and political action.

Extending Kuhn's notions even further, I now want to suggest that in the same way that a paradigm and its "normal science" prescribe a certain range of questions and single out a limited part of nature for detailed and extensive investigation, thus making cumulative knowledge possible, so "cumulative" knowledge in politics is possible only during comparable periods of "normal politics." Furthermore, Kuhn's analysis of "scientific revolutions," a consequence of a puzzle (an unanswered problem that seems answerable in terms of the paradigm) becoming an anomaly (a difficulty which does not yield to intraparadigm resolution), has numerous parallels with the impact of Nazism on a certain understanding of politics and man.

Now Kuhn argues that a potential scientific paradigm must be able to cope with the anomalies which raised doubts about the adequacy of its predecessor, though he notes that the newer paradigm may be less adequate than the previous paradigm in other ways. The picture is not one of unambiguous progress but rather significantly one of replacement. It seems that to be accepted as a paradigm, a theory must seem better than its competitors, but it need not, never does, and perhaps cannot explain all the facts with which it can be confronted.[107] Again, this is the case with behavioralism.

The acceptance of a paradigm implies a new and (in terms of the older paradigm) a different but still rigid definition of the field. For a paradigm, and the normal science for which it is a necessary condition, are a proposed and enforced orthodoxy, a directive for, and restraint on, research, the boundaries of an inflexible box into which normal science attempts to "force nature." [108] It thus appears that a drastically reduced vision is a precondition for successful scientific research. Without a total concentration on one part of nature there would be a dissipation of energies, a babble rather than a conversation; a series of discrete, unrelatable experiments, vocabularies, and idioms eventuating in a form of "scientific" chaos. To have successful "mature" science is to avoid novelty steadfastly and explore minutely only that range of phenomena certified by the scientific community as worthy of consideration.

Now this does not seem too objectionable as long as the appearance of anomalies insures at least some openness and flexibility in science. But it is at just this point that Kuhn is unclear; a lack of clarity which makes the institutionalization of a paradigm seem a bit more sinister. The problem is as follows:

> Kuhn appears most uncertain in the matter of explaining why it is that a paradigm is ever successfully challenged. At one point he suggests that the arbitrary element inherent in the choice of any paradigm makes it likely that normal research will encounter anomalies which will eventually provoke a crisis. Elsewhere he simply notes that the rigidity of the scientific community may prevent insiders from challenging the paradigm but since its writ does not extend to "outside" fields, there is always the possibility of the scientific equivalent to *l'étranger* proposing a new paradigm, a possibility that has occurred frequently in the history of science. In the face of the resistance that any challenging paradigm is likely to encounter, Kuhn's uncertainty edges towards despair and his conclusion echoes the same doubts that haunted the medieval defenders of another kind of paradigm: "But so long as somebody appears with a new candidate for paradigm —usually a young man, one new to the field—the loss due to rigidity accrues only to the individual." [109]

If there is a paradigm in political science closely analogous to Kuhn's notion of a scientific paradigm, then some important but previously ignored consequences follow for both political analysis and politics. But here a note of caution is warranted, for the delineation of a paradigm is exceptionally difficult without some kind of historical perspective, and of course Kuhn's notion is historical. Furthermore, there are problems posed by the notion of "paradigm," such as the question of the proper level of generality and abstraction. E. A. Burtt for instance, because his concept of paradigm (he

does not use the word) is more general, finds greater continuities in the development of science than does Kuhn.
Nevertheless, both Almond and Truman suggest, in their
assessments and appraisals of the discipline, that a new "paradigm" is emerging in political science. Almond sees the development "in the last decade or two, the elements of a new,
more surely scientific paradigm," [110] and Truman evidently
looks forward to a "redefinition and redirection" [111] of the
discipline toward a new, broadly based consensus.

But I wish to demur on the desirability of the new consensus and paradigm. Though it looks as if we cannot do without paradigms (whether behavioral or otherwise) if we desire a science of politics, yet any scientific understanding of
politics (and perhaps any systematic understanding whatever) "far from arising out of the concerted quest for endless
theoretical novelties seems to require the suppression of
competing viewpoints." [112] If Kuhn and Wolin are correct,
the success of science (and I am suggesting, by extension, all
forms of analysis) depends on a reduction of the field of experience and imagination, thus contributing to a diminished source of inspiration and a routinization and circum-
scription of the mind and action.[113] The most recent diminution is, I have argued, a consequence of a series of historical
events clustered around and interpreted in terms of Nazism.
The result seems to have been an insensitivity to novelties,
an insensitivity to the condition of our excluded minorities,
to their growing frustration and rage, an attitude that some
men are "inorganic background," in Fanon's terrifying
phrase. Imagination and passion have been banished from
political analysis and political life, thus precluding a politics
that might engage men's attention as it becomes significant
for their lives. Thus while a paradigm in science excludes
novelties in the form of natural phenomena, the political
scientist excludes novelties that are movements, groups, and
people. These outsiders become all the harder to see as we
give up the distinction between a polity where men adapt

and survive and one where they flourish and thrive. Reluctant or fearful in the face of recent history, we seem to have been passive in the face of fact, of current idols and assumptions. Questions of means have become, by default, questions of ends.[114] In the process, we have ignored those who have been outside, those men whose needs have been ignored by our politics. It is, of course, possible to argue that because men speak and act they cannot remain disregarded novelties for long. But how long is long? The inarticulate seldom have historians to tell of their acts or listen to their speech.

A paradigm must be "enforced." To achieve a science of politics, we need enforcers, we need those whose authority in a community of political scientists would function in ways comparable to that in the community of science. Tolerance for diversity within such a community, as within the "normal political science" it would be there to defend, would necessarily be limited in order to guarantee cumulative knowledge.

Not only does a paradigm function as a set of necessary blinders but it also tends to "insulate the [scientific community] from those socially important problems that are not reducible to the puzzle form, because they cannot be stated in terms of the conceptual and instrumental tools the paradigm supplies." [115] If this were, and it seems it would have to be, the case in the community of political scientists, then we might see a community of such scientists isolated from those they study, researching only those aspects of politics that receive methodological certification as defined by the paradigm. Indeed, if we push the point further and assume that the "community" of political science will be fairly small, embrace the concept of professionalism maintained by the one or two core journals and the key textbooks, provide opportunities for closeness, common purposes, etc., then political scientists may come to identify not with the larger political community but with their own ever growing and yet exclusive community. As attention and concern focus inward into the community instead of outward toward the larger political society, we may find ourselves moving once again toward the kind of ivory tower from which behavioralism sought initially to escape. It is a mistake to believe that an ivory tower is a place rather than a frame of mind or a perspective, that it accompanies us in the library but not in the field or research center.

My objection to the newly developing ivory tower is related to the protest of Baratz and Bachrach that pluralists have overlooked the crucial significance of "nondecision making," i.e., "the practice of limiting the scope of actual decision-making to 'safe' issues by manipulating the dominant community values, myths and political institutions and procedures." [116] Dahl similarly recognizes, but does not follow up, the point when he writes in *Preface to Democratic Theory:* "What we balk at in accepting the vote of the Soviet citizen as an expression of preference is that he is not permitted to choose among all the alternatives that we, as outside observers, regard as in some sense potentially available to him." [117] The argument I am making was eloquently put by Henry Kariel when he wrote that by "postulating functions which have the effect of shifting our perspectives, we expose previously unseen institutional forms. We perceive a new reality—lives *not* lived (or not lived decently) because of decisions *not* made. When the empty space in which potentialities might have been realized is bared, we become aware of our losses." [118] Because we account ourselves pragmatic, realistic, and scientific, it seems as though we have no myths or metaphysics but just the real world. But "the myth of an age can be found in the issues it takes for granted—in the questions it never asks, in the assumptions so universally shared they remain tacit." [119] We need a constant source of new pictures, images, and visions of reality—whether they are supplied by an uncondescending comparative politics, a newly dynamic empiricism, or the power and exciting possibilities supplied by "traditional" political theory.[120] Thus we may overcome the complacency of confusing our theory with reality,[121] of insisting that political theorists use the "categories in which political life actually occurs," of pejoratively labeling radical criticism and action by identifying it with Nazism and totalitarianism.

Again let me emphasize that my concern with methodology is not primarily a methodological concern, but rather a political one. What is worrisome is that the social scientist, in the interests of his science, will help make his objects of study what they are and assist in establishing a political world in which, to use Arendt's terms, action is transformed into "behavior." Though I have argued that part of behavioralism is "wrong," the greater danger is that it may come to be true, that our interest in becoming a science, in "achieving" and maintaining a behavioral paradigm, may blunt our sensibilities to any politics except the kind particularly suited for behavioral analysis. The repeated emphasis on predictability is perhaps indicative of a desire to make politics predictable, for the more we can predict, and thus assuage our fear of uncertainty, the more fearful do uncertainty and unpredictability become.

The insistence on realism, the demand for objectivity, precision, and science, and the philosophical and political refuge provided by the "real world" are too confining and limiting in terms of both political analysis and political life. A paradigm of analysis which sustains, and in turn is sustained by, a form of political life too often makes questions about the quality of such life or the adequacy of such analysis seem unaskable, or if formulated, silly or superfluous. Believing that our propositions capture reality, we sometimes forget that any theory of politics and mode of political organization favors certain values, life styles, and people at the expense of others. Material abundance does not alter this situation. The promise of such abundance is not itself material. To be rich and yet desperate seems somehow absurd. That it is not absurd remains an unanswered and at least potentially a political challenge. The recognition that many are poor and despairing, without dignity, commitments, or self-respect, is a prerequisite for escaping from the intimidation of liberal politics and scholarship without ignoring their significance.

Too often we take the path of least resistance, and agree with Riccardo's father in *The Deputy* that "There isn't anything one of us can do." His son, a priest who dies in a concentration camp, addressing no one and everyone, asks, "How shall we ever find apologies for our silence?"—or indeed for our inaction.

NOTES

1. Rolf Hochhuth, *The Deputy* (New York, Grove Press, 1964), p. 115.
2. Norman Jacobson, "Political Realism and the Age of Reason: The Anti-Rationalist Heritage in America," *Review of Politics,* October 1953, p. 448.
3. I am aware that here I gloss over a number of distinctions which it might, in a different context, be necessary to emphasize and elaborate. There are many ways one might be called, or term oneself or an opponent, an "idealist" or "realist." Furthermore, it is true that "realism" is often confined to political scientists writing in the area of international relations. For relationships between domestic and international liberalism, behavioralism, and various forms of realism, see Kenneth Waltz, *Man, the State and War* (New York, Columbia University Press, 1959). My concern in this essay is with the work of "domestic realists," many but not all of whom are behavioralists.
4. The words, but not the sentiments, are from Peter Laslett's Introduction to *Philosophy, Politics and Society,* 1st Series (New York, The Macmillan Company, 1956), p. vii.
5. As in the previous footnote, the words, not the sentiments, are from Henry David Aiken "The Revolt Against Ideology," *Commentary,* April 1964, p. 29. The "end of ideology" debate is closely

related to the argument about the "decline of political theory" and the "status" of metaphysics.

6. Bernard Berelson, Paul F. Lazarsfeld, and William N. McPhee, *Voting* (Chicago, University of Chicago Press, 1954), p. 312.

7. Nelson W. Polsby, Robert A. Dentler, and Paul A. Smith, *Politics and Social Life: An Introduction to Political Behavior* (Boston, Houghton Mifflin Company, 1963), p. 1.

8. Robert A. Dahl, *Who Governs* (New Haven, Yale University Press, 1961), p. 311.

9. Robert A. Dahl, "The Analysis of Influence in Local Communities" in Charles A. Adrian, ed., *Social Science and Comunity Action,* (East Lansing, Michigan State University Press, 1960), p. 25. I am focusing my critical remarks on the work of Robert Dahl for two reasons. First, he is in my opinion perhaps the most subtle and well read of the behavioralists, and secondly, what seems to me partial confirmation of the first statement, he no longer holds many of the views I criticize here, at least in the way he did previously. See his *Political Oppositions in Western Democracies* (New Haven, Yale University Press, 1966), Preface and Chs. 2 and 11–13; "Evaluation of Political Systems" in Ithiel de Sola Pool, ed., *Contemporary Political Science: Toward Empirical Theory* (New York, McGraw-Hill Book Company, 1967); *Pluralist Democracy in the United States: Conflict and Consent* (Chicago, Rand McNally & Co., 1967); and particularly "The City in the Future of Democracy," *American Political Science Review* (APSR), December 1967, pp. 953–70.

10. Robert A. Dahl, "What Is Political Science?" in Stephen K. Bailey, ed., *American Politics and Government* (New York, Basic Books, 1965), p. 16. For a critical discussion of these points see Peter Bachrach, *The Theory of Democratic Elitism* (Boston, Little, Brown and Company, 1967).

11. Berelson *et al., Voting*, p. 306.

12. Seymour M. Lipset, *Political Man* (New York, Harcourt, Brace & World, 1960), p. 403. A persuasive criticism can be found in James Farganis and S. W. Rousseas, "American Politics and the End of Ideology," *British Journal of Sociology*, December 1963, pp. 347–62. The qualification can be found in "My View from Our Left," *Columbia University Forum;* Fall 1962, pp. 31–37. See also Lipset's "Equal or Better in America," *Columbia University Forum*, Spring 1961, pp. 17–21. Criticisms of behavioralism are being discussed with increasing frequency. See, for instance, the collection of articles in Charles A. McCoy and John Playford, eds., *Apolitical Politics* (New York, Thomas Y. Crowell Company,

1967), and Henry S. Kariel, ed., *Frontiers of Democratic Theory,* (New York, Random House, 1969). See also Robert A. Dahl, "Further Reflections on the 'Elitist Theory of Democracy,'" *APSR,* June 1966, pp. 296–305.

13. Berelson *et al., Voting,* p. 311.

14. Louis Hartz, *The Liberal Tradition in America* (New York, Harcourt, Brace & World, 1955), p. 47.

15. Robert A. Dahl, "Equality and Power in American Society," in William V. D'Antonio and Howard J. Erlich, eds., *Power and Democracy in America* (Notre Dame, Ind., University of Notre Dame Press, 1961), p. 89. See also Dahl, "Analysis of Influence in Local Communities," p. 35.

16. Robert A. Dahl, *Preface to Democratic Theory* (Chicago, Phoenix Books, 1963), pp. 138–39.

17. Dahl, "Equality and Power in American Society," p. 75.

18. Robert A. Dahl, "Reflections on Oppositions in Western Democracies," *Government and Opposition,* I, No. 1 (November 1965), 12. (Yet liquidation of Indians was carried out by a parliamentary government.) There is a complex and subtle problem here, and I want at least to indicate my awareness of it. The identification of incrementalism and conservatism is explicitly denied by Dahl and Charles Lindblom in *Politics, Economics and Welfare* (New York, Harper Torchbooks, 1963), esp. pp. 82–88, and in Lindblom and David Braybrooke, *A Strategy of Decision,* (New York, The Free Press, 1963), esp. pp. 106–10. The question as to whether their position is fully persuasive cannot be assessed in a short space, for the arguments themselves are extremely subtle and rest on certain conceptions of "conservatism" and "incrementalism" which would require close and extensive analysis. Whatever the conclusion of such analyses might be, Dahl's sentiments as expressed in this quote do not seem fully consistent with the argument he and Lindblom make in the pages cited above.

19. Dahl, *Preface to Democratic Theory,* pp. 4, 150.

20. Heinz Eulau, *The Behavioral Persuasion in Politics* (New York, Random House, 1964), p. 7 and *passim.* For an anthropological critique of the belief in the superiority of modernity and the facile opposition between "primitive" and modern, see Claude Lévi-Strauss, *The Savage Mind* (Chicago, University of Chicago Press, 1966). For congruent through different criticisms of the same point, consult Thomas I. Kuhn, *The Structure of Scientific Revolutions* (Chicago, Phoenix Books, 1964), and E. A. Burtt, *The Metaphysical Foundations of Modern Science* (Garden City, N.Y., Doubleday Anchor Books, 1954).

21. Robert A. Dahl, *Modern Political Analysis* (Englewood Cliffs, N.J., Prentice-Hall, 1963), Preface.

22. Gabriel Almond, "Political Theory and Political Science," *APSR*, December 1966, p. 869 (emphasis supplied).

23. See Lee S. Halprin, "American Liberalism, Literature, and World War II," *Minnesota Review*, Winter 1963, p. 181.

24. Dahl, "What Is Political Science," p. 13. See also Dahl, *Modern Political Analysis*," pp. 60–61; "Hierarchy, Democracy and Bargaining in Politics and Economics," in Heinz Eulau, Samuel J. Eldersveld, and Morris Janowitz, eds., *Political Behavior* (New York, The Free Press, 1956), pp. 88, 89.

25. All quotations are from Dahl's "Further Reflections," p. 301.

26. David Truman, "Disillusion and Regeneration: The Quest for a Discipline," *APSR*, December 1965, p. 868.

27. Almond, "Political Theory and Political Science," p. 875. Almond lists a number of other reasons for the change in paradigms: the rise of communism, the inadequacies of "separation of powers" as an explanatory concept, and the rise of new nations.

28. Daniel Bell, "The 'Rediscovery' of Alienation," *Journal of Philosophy*, LVI, No. 24 (November 1959), 949.

29. Michael Paul Rogin, *The Intellectuals and McCarthy: The Radical Specter* (Cambridge, Mass., The M.I.T. Press, 1967), p. 9.

30. Robert A. Dahl, "The Behavioral Approach in Political Science: Epitaph to a Successful Protest," *APSR*, December 1961. Citations are to the reprint of the article in Polsby, Dentler, and Smith, *Politics and Social Life*. The quote is on p. 16.

31. The "end of ideology" literature is enormous and varied. See Lipset's *Political Man;* Daniel Bell, *The End of Ideology*, rev. ed. (New York, The Free Press, 1965); Albert Camus *Resistance, Rebellion, and Death* (New York, Modern Library, 1960), pp. 185 ff.; Karl Mannheim, *Ideology and Utopia* (New York, Harvest Books, 1966); Farganis and Rousseas, "American Politics and the End of Ideology"; Aiken, "The Revolt Against Ideology." Clifford Geertz, "Ideology as a Cultural System," in D. E. Apter, ed., *Ideology and Discontent* (New York, The Free Press, 1964), p. 51, writes: "invoking the extreme pathologies of ideological thought—Nazism, Bolshevism, or whatever—as· its paradigmatic forms is reminiscent of the tradition in which the Inquisition, the personal depravity of Renaissance popes, the savagery of the Reformation wars, or the primitiveness of Bible-belt fundamentalism is offered as an archetype of religious belief and behavior." There is, of course, a very intimate relationship between the literature on the end of ideology and those arguments which discuss the nature

of mass society and mass participation. A fine summary of this material can be found in Joseph Gusfield, "Mass Society and Extremist Politics," *American Sociological Review*, XXIX (Fall 1962), 19–30.

32. See, for instance, Kenneth Keniston, *The Uncommitted* (New York, Delta Books, 1965), Ch. 11, "The Decline of Utopia"; and Judith Shklar, *After Utopia: The Decline of Political Faith* (Princeton, N.J., Princeton University Press, 1958).

33. See Sheldon Wolin, *Politics and Vision* (Boston, Little, Brown & Co., 1960), Chs. 9 and 10, and George H. Sabine, "Two Democratic Traditions," *Philosophical Review*, October 1952.

34. See Hartz, *Liberal Tradition*. But see also John Higham, "Beyond Consensus: The Historian as Moral Critic," *American Historical Review*, LXVII (1961–62), 609–25.

35. Dahl, *Who Governs*, p. 279.

36. Dahl, *Modern Political Analysis*, p. 6.

37. Dahl, "What Is Political Science?" p. 6.

38. Dahl, *Modern Political Analysis*, p. 73.

39. Dahl, "What Is Political Science," p. 6.

40. Dahl, *Modern Political Analysis*, pp. 50–51, 51, 18, 7 (emphasis supplied).

41. Walter Dean Burnham, "The Changing Shape of American Political Universe," *APSR*, March 1965, pp. 7–29.

42. John H. Schaar, "Insiders and Outsiders," *Steps*, I, No. 2 (November 1967), 2–14.

43. Berelson *et al.*, *Voting*, p. 319.

44. See Dahl, "Further Reflections."

45. There is some analysis by Dahl in response to Strauss and to "transempiricists" in *Modern Political Analysis*, pp. 100 ff.

46. Schaar, "Insiders and Outsiders," p. 5. *Cf.* Norman Jacobson, "Political Science and Political Education," *APSR*, September 1963, pp. 561–69.

47. Dahl, *Preface to Democratic Theory*, p. 64.

48. J. L. Austin, *Sense and Sensibilia*, reconstructed from the manuscript notes by G. J. Warnock (New York, Oxford University Press, 1964), pp. 62, 70. See also Austin's essay "Other Minds" in Antony Flew, ed., *Logic and Language* (Garden City, N.Y., Doubleday Anchor Books, 1965), pp. 353 *et passim*.

49. The charge against the theory of populism is similar to Dahl's arguments on the nature of traditional political theory. See, for instance, "Political Theory: Truth and Consequences," *World Politics*, October 1958, pp. 89–102, and "The Science of Politics:

New and Old," *World Politics,* April 1955, pp. 479–89. Political theories frequently reject the existing limits of action and fact and seek, in their theoretical visions, to redefine that reality which constitutes the very boundaries of action and fact. Facts are taken seriously by political theorists, some of course more than others; indeed it is their extreme sensitivity to "fact" that inspires the image of different facts. The object, particularly for philosophical political theory, is alteration of political universe and the establishment of new and different boundaries for action and factuality.

50. Robert A. Dahl, "Atomic Energy and the Democratic Process," *The Annals of the American Academy of Political and Social Science,* CCXC (November 1953), 1.

51. See Michael Oakeshott's "Political Education" in his book of essays, *Rationalism in Politics* (New York, Basic Books, 1962), pp. 111–36, for similarities between his explicitly conservative views and Dahl's arguments.

52. Dahl, "Reflections on Oppositions," p. 12.

53. Dahl, *Preface to Democratic Theory,* p. 53. It must be made clear that the first line of the paragraph from which this quote is excerpted concerns "geographical governmental units" and thus my point might seem out of place. But the entire paragraph and the one immediately following sustain my interpretation. Again, see the work of Oakeshott for similar views, for instance, his "Contemporary British Politics," *The Cambridge Journal,* I, 1947–48.

54. See Dahl, "Hierarchy, Democracy, and Bargaining," p. 90, and *Who Governs,* p. 223.

55. Berelson *et al., Voting,* p. 312.

56. Dahl, *Preface to Democratic Theory,* p. 59.

57. Dahl, *Modern Political Analysis,* p. 8. See also Eulau, Eldersveld, and Janowitz, *Political Behavior,* p. 4. Eulau seems to espouse a "coherence" theory of truth in *Behavioral Persuasion,* pp. 20 and 134, as opposed to Dahl's "correspondence" theories of truth. See John Passmore, *A Hundred Years of Philosophy* (London, Gerald Duckworth & Co., 1966), pp. 378 ff.

58. Dahl, "Hierarchy," p. 84. *Cf.* A. J. Ayer's remarks in a debate with Father Copleston reprinted in Paul Edwards and Arthur Pap, eds., *A Modern Introduction to Philosophy* (New York, The Free Press, 1957), pp. 586–618.

59. *Cf.* Dahl's "The Science of Politics: New and Old," pp. 481–82, where he writes, "an empirical theory can be produced only by constructing and testing propositions about the real world, not by defining political science." And this test, we know from *Modern Political Analysis,* is a matter of correspondence. If the proposi-

52 J. PETER EUBEN

tion corresponds to the real world, then it is, by Dahl's account, both empirical and true. It is not clear that we could ever, on this account, have a false empirical proposition. The problems with "observe" are legion. Compare Norwood Russell Hanson, *Patterns of Discovery* (London, Cambridge University Press, 1958) with Dahl, *Modern Political Analysis,* p. 51; *Preface to Democratic Theory,* pp. 91, 99, 118; "What Is Political Science?" p. 19.

60. *Modern Political Analysis,* p. 2.

61. Eulau, *Behavioral Persuasion,* p. 9.

62. Kuhn, *Structure of Scientific Revolutions,* p. 145; also Hanson, *Patterns of Discovery.*

63. See Alfred DeGrazia, ed., *The Velikovsky Affair: The Warfare of Science and Scientism* (New Hyde Park, N.Y., University Books, 1966).

64. Norman Jacobson, "Political Science and Political Education," and Henry Kariel, *Open Systems: Arenas for Political Action* (Itasca, Ill., F. E. Peacock Publishers, 1969).

65. Dahl, *Modern Political Analysis,* p. 103. What we need from behavioral (and other) analysts is a closer investigation of the degree to which it is necessary to specify conditions and contexts in which something is more or less true (or false) and in what sense such terms are properly applied or misapplied. Terrence Ball has suggested to me that many behavioralists seem to confuse the analytic and the synthetic and that the polar antithesis true/false is applicable only in deductive postulational systems, where x is defined as not-y, and where true is characterized as not-false. See Paul Feyerabend, "Explanation, Reduction, and Empiricism," in Herbert Feigl and G. E. Maxwell, eds., *Scientific Explanation, Space, and Time* (in Minnesota Studies in the Philosophy of Science; Minneapolis, University of Minnesota Press, 1962).

66. (London, George Allen & Unwin, 1946), p. 864. See also Russell's essay, "Scientific Method in Philosophy," in *Mysticism and Logic* (Garden City, N.Y., Doubleday Anchor Books, 1957), pp. 93–119. The relevant philosophical issues are discussed in the following works. On logical positivism see the historical discussions in G. J. Warnock, *English Philosophy Since 1900* (London, Oxford University Press, 1958); J. O. Urmson, *Philosophical Analysis: Its Development Between the Two World Wars* (London, Oxford University Press, 1965); John Passmore, *A Hundred Years of Philosophy,* esp. Chs. 15 and 16. For various statements and restatements of logical positivism see A. J. Ayer, ed., *Logical Positivism* (New York, The Free Press, 1959), and his *Language, Truth and Logic,* 2nd ed. (London, Victor Gollancz, 1964). I have tried to re-

late logical positivism to behavioralism in *The Destructive Understanding of Politics,* unpublished doctoral dissertation, University of California, Berkeley, 1968, Ch. 4.

67. Eulau, *Behavioral Persuasion,* p. 11.

68. Daniel Lerner, ed., *The Human Meaning of the Social Sciences* (New York, Meridian Books, 1959), pp. 24–25. In his *Promise of Politics* (Englewood Cliffs, N.J., Prentice-Hall, 1966) Henry Kariel quotes the citation given by the Woodrow Wilson Foundation to Dahl for *Who Governs* (p. 109, footnote):

> "In a time when democracy is being seriously questioned by its empirical friends and while it is being attacked by its ideological enemies, this work, affirmative in tone, but neither complacent nor conservative, serves a public as well as scholarly purpose. It demonstrates that pluralistic democracy is at present a viable system in our own country: and, although its institutions and processes are more difficult to understand than we may have thought, they do work and are worth defending.

69. For examples of the latter see the enormously influential works of Ludwig Wittgenstein, e.g., *The Blue and Brown Books* (New York, Harper Torchbooks, 1965), and his *Philosophical Investigations* (New York, The MacMillan Company, 1959). See also J. L. Austin, *Philosophical Papers* (Oxford, Clarendon Press, 1961) and John Wisdom, *Paradox and Discovery* (Oxford, Basil Blackwell & Mott, 1965). A recent collection of essays in a similar genre is the one edited by Bernard Williams and Alan Montifiore, *British Analytical Philosophy* (London, Routledge & Kegan Paul, 1966). For a sharply critical assessment of all these trends, see Ernest Gellner, *Words and Things* (London, Victor Gollancz, 1959).

70. Kuhn, *Structure of Scientific Revolutions,* p. 7.

71. *Ibid.,* p. 120.

72. Eulau, *Behavioral Persuasion,* p. 9; that this is how he would like his science to operate is itself revealing.

73. Kuhn, *Structure,* p. 41.

74. Burtt, *Metaphysical Foundations of Modern Science,* p. 229. John Gunnell, in "Social Science and Political Reality: The Problem of Explanation," *Social Research,* XXXV (Spring 1968), 160–61, makes a similar argument.

    On the meaning and nature of metaphysics see P. F. Strawson, *Individuals: An Essay in Descriptive Metaphysics* (Garden City, N.Y., Doubleday Anchor Books, 1959); W. H. Walsh, *Metaphysics* (London, Hutchinson University Library, 1963); D. F. Pears, ed., *The Nature of Metaphysics* (New York, St. Martin's Press, 1965).

54   J. PETER EUBEN

75. Charles Taylor, "Neutrality in Political Science" in Peter Laslett and W. G. Runciman, eds., *Philosophy, Politics and Society*, 3rd Series (New York, Barnes & Noble, 1967), p. 27.

76. Morris Schlick, "What is the Aim of Ethics," in Ayer, ed., *Logical Positivism*, pp. 247–48.

77. William F. Whyte, "Politics and Ethics: A Reply to John Hallowell," *APSR*, April 1946, pp. 306–71.

78. In James C. Charlesworth, ed., *A Design for Political Science: Scope, Objectives and Methods*, Monograph, American Academy of Political and Social Science (Philadelphia, 1956), p. 115. The argument generally assumes a particular and often undefended notion of "science," "responsibility," and "citizenship."

79. Eulau, *Behavioral Persuasion*, p. 137. See a criticism on this point by Christian Bay, "Politics and Pseudo-Politics," in McCoy and Playford, eds., *Apolitical Politics*.

80. Taylor, "Neutrality in Political Science," p. 57.

81. Dahl, *Modern Political Analysis*, p. 102.

82. Lerner, ed., *Human Meaning of the Social Sciences*, Preface and Ch. 1.

83. Herbert Feigl, "The Scientific Outlook: Neutralism and Humanism," in Herbert Feigl and May Brodbeck, eds., *Readings in the Philosophy of Science* (New York, Appleton-Century-Crofts, 1953), p. 10. What Feigl no doubt means is "ideal" democracy. Here as elsewhere, e.g., in the phrase "the real world," there is a "useful" confusion between the is and the ought.

84. Kuhn, *Structure of Scientific Revolutions, passim,* and Sheldon Wolin's extension and elaboration of several of Kuhn's points in his "Paradigms and Political Theories" in Preston King and B. C. Parekh, eds., *Politics and Experience* (Cambridge, Cambridge University Press, 1968). The euphoria and idealization of scientists and the scientific community as found in J. Bronowski's *Science and Human Values* or, in a more sophisticated way, in Robert Merton's *Social Theory and Social Structure* (New York, The Free Press, 1957), Part IV, is under increasing criticism. See, for instance, the startling response of the scientific community to the works of Immanuel Velikovsky in Alfred DeGrazia, *The Velikovsky Affair.* See also H. L. Nieburg, *In the Name of Science* (Chicago, Quadrangle Books, 1966) and Daniel S. Greenberg, *The Politics of Pure Science* (New York, The New American Library, 1967) for arguments which challenge the conception of the scientific community as democratic and open.

85. On this point the Greenberg and Nieburg books cited in the preceding footnote are particularly instructive. There are many ques-

tions on the role of foundations both as extensions of government agencies and as stimulators of certain kinds of research. Thus Dahl in "The Behavioral Approach" regards the role of foundations as essential in the development of behavioralism but does not discuss some serious implications of the importance of foundations. Marian D. Irish accounts "foundation grants" as one of the two "hallmarks of modern political science." See p. 16 of the book she edited, *Political Science: Advance of a Discipline* (Englewood Cliffs, N.J., Prentice-Hall, 1968).

86. See Dahl, "Political Theory: Truth and Consequences," p. 97; *Preface to Democratic Theory*, p. 64 and *passim*.

87. My general and only partially elaborated argument on Hobbes is from a more complete and subtle analysis by Norman Jacobson. To my knowledge he has not published his views in detail, though hints of them are in his "Political Science and Political Education.

88. See Kuhn's *Structure of Scientific Revolutions*, p. 31, and also p. 65, where he suggests that a precisely demarcated paradigm facilitates the recognition of anomalies. But Kuhn is not fully persuasive on this for reasons discussed below.

89. Feigl, "Scientific Outlook," p. 12.

90. What Dahl calls in *Modern Political Analysis* (p. 24) "Plato's brilliant fancy."

91. Dahl is fully aware that the interests and values of the investigator play a role in the kind of research topic he chooses. But this admission may be a very serious one indeed, depending on what those values are and the kind of role they play. Dahl would also agree, I believe, that one of the major issues of the is–ought distinction is psychological in character. On both points see *Modern Political Analysis*, Ch. 8.

92. See Gunnell, "Social Science and Political Reality," p. 162, and Dahl, *Modern Political Analysis*, pp. 6 and 12.

93. Urmson, *Philosophical Analysis*, p. 180.

94. A. R. Louch, *Explanation and Human Action* (Oxford, Basil Blackwell & Mott, 1966), p. 44.

95. F. Waismann, "How I See Philosophy," in Ayer, ed., *Logical Positivism*, pp. 359–60. F. P. Ramsey put a similar point differently: "The chief danger of our philosophy," he writes, "apart from laziness or wooliness, is scholasticism, the essence of which is treating what is vague as if it were precise and trying to fit it into an exact category." "Philosophy" in *ibid.*, p. 325.

96. See Michael Walzer, "On the Role of Symbolism in Political Theory," *Political Science Quarterly*, No. 2 (June 1967), p. 195 n. On

precision language and politics see also Geertz, "Ideology as a Cultural System"; Abraham Kaplan, *The New World of Philosophy* (New York, Vintage Books, 1961), pp. 56–57; Gunnell, "Social Science and Political Reality," pp. 179 ff; Dahl, "Political Science: Old and New," p. 483, and particularly Dahl's sensitivity to the problem as revealed in his "Evaluation of Political Systems" in Pool, ed., *Contemporary Political Science*, p. 174.

97. Hobbes, *Leviathan*, ed. with intro. by Michael Oakeshott (Oxford, Basil Blackwell & Mott, 1957), pp. 29–30. Rolf Dahrendorf has written: "Politics is one of the most exciting subjects of study for the social scientist. It would be a great shame indeed if by an undue concern with methods of limited applicability, we managed to dampen this excitement for our students, our public, and for ourselves." "Three Symposia on Political Behavior," *American Sociological Review*, XXIX (1964), 736.

98. Hannah Arendt, *The Human Condition* (Garden City, N.Y., Doubleday Anchor Books, 1958), p. 174.

99. Hobbes, *Leviathan*, p. 68.

100. Wolin, "Paradigms and Political Theory," p. 134.

101. J. W. N. Watkins, Hobbes's *System of Ideas* (London, Hutchinson University Library, 1965), p. 151. See also p. 14 and p. 165. I would agree that the insistence on precision and clarity need not always be conservative. See for instance Lenin's insistence on the proletariat's need for clarity quoted in Michael Walzer, *The Revolution of the Saints* (Cambridge, Harvard University Press, 1965), p. 314.

102. Alan Montifiore, "Fact, Value and Ideology," in Williams and Montifiore, eds., *British Analytical Philosophy*, p. 190.

103. E. A. Burtt, *In Search of Philosophical Understanding* (New York, New American Library, 1965), pp. 25 ff.

104. Various aspects of the demonology are discussed in, or derived from, Joseph Tussman, *Obligation and the Body Politic* (New York, Oxford University Press, 1960), p. 115; Lerner, *Human Meaning of the Social Sciences*, Preface and Ch. 1; Lester Milbrath, *Political Participation* (Chicago, Rand McNally & Co., 1965), p. 89; Berelson *et al.*, *Voting*, p. 315; Geertz, "Ideology as a Cultural System," pp. 49 ff; Dahl, *Modern Political Analysis*, pp. 88–89, "Hierarchy, Democracy and Bargaining," "Reflections on Opposition," p. 12, *Preface to Democratic Theory*, pp. 31, 50–51 and *passim*, and "Analysis of Influence in Local Communities"; Jacobson, "Political Education" and "Political Realism"; Rogin, *The Intellectuals and McCarthy*, p. 44 ff. and 272 ff.; Eulau, "A Design for Political Science," p. 119; Robert Mer-

ton, "The Mosaic of the Behavioral Sciences," in Bernard Berelson, ed., *The Behavioral Sciences Today* (New York, Harper Torchbooks, 1963), pp. 267–68; and Daniel Lerner and Harold D. Lasswell, eds., *The Policy Sciences* (Stanford, Cal., Stanford University Press, 1965), Foreword and Ch. 1.

104a. Harold Lasswell, *Psychopathology and Politics* (Chicago, University of Chicago Press, 1930), pp. 77f.

105. Wolin, "Paradigms and Political Theories," p. 131. Kuhn himself elaborates these views in regard to a specific scientific revolution in his *The Copernican Revolution* (New York, Vintage Books, 1959), esp. pp. 25–44.

106. Kuhn, *Structure of Scientific Revolutions*, p. x.

107. *Ibid.*, pp. 17–18.

108. *Ibid.*, pp. 19, 23.

109. Wolin, "Paradigms and Political Theories," p. 137.

110. Almond, "Political Theory and Political Science," p. 869.

111. Truman, "Disillusion and Regeneration," p. 873.

112. Wolin, "Paradigms and Political Theories," p. 133.

113. See Robert A. Nisbet, "Sociology as Art Form," in Maurice Stein and Arthur Vidich, *Sociology on Trial* (Englewood Cliffs, N.J., Prentice-Hall, 1963), p. 155.

114. Several of these arguments are from Keniston, *The Uncommitted*.

115. Kuhn, *Structure*, p. 37.

116. "Decisions and Non-Decisions," *APSR*, September 1963, pp. 632–42, and "The Two Faces of Power" in *APSR*, December 1962, pp. 947–52. The quote is from the former article at p. 632.

117. Dahl, *Preface to Democratic Theory*, p. 69. See also K. W. Kim, "The Limits of Behavioral Explanation in Politics," in McCoy and Playford, eds., *Apolitical Politics*, pp. 48 f., and Schaar, "Insiders and Outsiders," p. 6.

118. Kariel, *Open Systems*, p. 130.

119. Keniston, *The Uncommitted*, p. 316.

120. "Traditional" is a significant misnomer. The difference between political theorists and behavioralists is partly a political one. For if behavioralism is the "normal science" of political science and if it is only with the breakdown of normalcy that alternative theories are deemed relevant, then political theorists, insofar as they not only are historians of political thought but want their theories regarded with seriousness, are radical rather than "traditional."

121. For similar arguments see H. R. G. Greaves, "Political Theory Today," *Political Science Quarterly*, March 1960; and Paul Feyerabend, "Explanation, Reduction and Empiricism," pp. 28–97,

"How to be a Good Empiricist" in William L. Reese, ed., *Philosophy of Science: The Delaware Seminar* (New York, John Wiley & Sons, 1963), pp. 3–40, and "Realism and Instrumentalism: Comments on the Logic and Factual Support," in Mario Bunge, ed., *The Critical Approach to Science and Philosophy* (New York, The Free Press, 1964), pp. 280–308.

On "Teaching" Political "Science" *

SANFORD LEVINSON

Thus, if we are competent in our pursuit (which must be presupposed here) we can force the individual, or at least we can help him, to give himself an *account of the ultimate meaning of his own conduct*. This appears to me as not so trifling a thing to do, even for one's own personal life. Again, I am tempted to say of a teacher who succeeds in this: he stands in the service of 'moral' forces; he fulfils the duty of bringing about self-clarification and a sense of responsibility. And I believe he will be the more able to accomplish this, the more conscientiously he avoids the desire personally to impose upon or suggest to his audience his own stand.

—Max Weber, *Science as a Vocation* (Italics in original.)

I.

ONE OF THE cardinal debates of political science, and indeed of all the academic disciplines, concerns the notion of "objectivity" in the classroom. The teacher "buys" academic freedom, with its independence from overt regulation by the state, by agreeing to a ruthless and self-imposed segregation of "teaching" from "preaching." Just as the liberal state rests on a separation of church and polity, so does the modern secular liberal university rest on a separation of "fact" and

* I wish to thank Dennis F. Thompson of Princeton University and John Champlin, William Harrison, and David Kettler, my colleagues at Ohio State, for the invaluable help they provided me in criticizing earlier drafts of this article. In addition, previous versions were read at the faculty colloquium of Ohio State and at the Center for the Study of Democratic Institutions in Santa Barbara, California, at a meeting arranged by the Caucus for a New Political Science, on May 2, 1969. I am grateful for criticisms received on both occasions.

59

"value." A teacher of political science gains his authority
from mastering "data," whether it be the nature of the
American party system or the internal problems within
Thomas Hobbes's body of thought. In either case, he quietly
and dispassionately dispenses his information, and the student is free "to make up his own mind" about any of the
moral implications of the allegedly neutral "facts."

The fact-value distinction is based on at least two assumptions: (1) the basis of value judgments is ultimately arbitrary, there being no cognitive means of confirming or falsi-
fying the validity of moral statements; and (2) an external
world of objects exists and is knowable in terms of empirical relationships. One cannot, therefore, be "objective"
about a value statement because there is no source external
to the speaker to validate that statement, whereas "objectivity" can be demanded in reference to empirical relationships
because such external controls are perceived to exist. (If
they share no other views, both Marxists and their liberal
critics agree that such "objectivity" of social analysis is possible, and both are quick to denounce scholars with unacceptable views for being "ideologues," even though each
would give a different definition of the term "ideology.")

Peter Euben's essay in this volume, however, exemplifies
the attack leveled by contemporary philosophers of science
upon any easy acceptance of the notion of such "objective"
knowledge about the external world. Yet a possible danger
of Euben's argument is that it may prove too much, for it
seems to lead to a complete relativism regarding the possibility of social knowledge.[1]

What I would like to do in this essay is to explore some of
the implications of the comments above insofar as they affect
us in our role as "teachers" of political "science." I put both
words in quotation marks because I regard both as problem-
atical. To be a teacher implies having something to teach,
and this something is what constitutes a discipline. Whether
one is a rabbi, a professor of physics, or a teacher of astrol-

ogy, the authority involved in the role comes from the perception by students and colleagues that the claimant has mastered the knowledge of his discipline. The rabbi conveys the Word of God, while the physicist transmits the laws of physics, and the astrologer the techniques of casting horoscopes and thus foretelling the future. All link an alleged transpersonal reality with the novices seeking to know more about that reality.

What differentiates the physicist, however, from his two counterparts is his commitment not only to a discipline but also to a methodology which would exclude revealed religion and astrology as claimants to verifiable knowledge. The political scientist, too, claims a privileged status for his "knowledge," even when he rightly rejects as the only model of rigor the natural scientist.

As John Schaar notes, however, corroborating Euben from a different perspective, the crisis of our age is a crisis of authority, and evidence of the extent of this crisis can be found in the increased questioning of the legitimacy of established institutions even by participants within them. All of us in this book have committed ourselves to the discipline of political science. As teachers, we necessarily pledge ourselves to transmitting the insights and methods of the discipline. Yet the very disaffection with our discipline symbolized by this volume calls into question any naïve hope that we can confine our worries only to our research while continuing to "teach" as usual.

One of the most influential statements ever made about the task of the teacher of social science was Max Weber's. Weber is not only one of the chief architects of the accepted notion of the vocation of the teacher but also the major proponent of the "fact-value" dichotomy and its concomitant emphasis on "objectivity" within the "factual" realm. Within Weber's own argument, however, are contained profound dilemmas, and these problems reveal themselves most vividly when we consider the main focus of interaction be-

tween the discipline and the student—the classroom. These
problems are most clearly illuminated, moreover, when we
focus on the task of teaching an "introductory" course,
where the role of the teacher in initiating a novice into the
discipline is most unambiguous.

Radical political scientists have performed very well in
the past several years in terms of offering a critique of some
of the assumptions of the mainstream of the profession.
What has not been done adequately is to relate the concerns we all feel about the deficiencies of our discipline to
the teaching tasks we are engaged in.

II.

The very title of the series within which this volume appears—the Pantheon Anti-textbooks—points to a critical
problem involved in the notion of a discipline. As Thomas
S. Kuhn has noted in *The Structure of Scientific Revolutions,* the presence of an agreed-upon textbook is a key factor denoting the existence of a mature "science." Though a
given natural science may have textbooks that compete in
terms of writing style, price, etc., what distinguishes what
Kuhn calls a "normal science" is general agreement on the
guiding paradigms of a discipline and thus the potential at
least of a single "textbook." And the purpose of such textbooks is to socialize the scientific novice into his discipline.
"Why, after all, should the student of physics, for example,
read the works of Newton, Faraday, Einstein, or Schrödin-
ger, when *everything he needs to know* about these works is
recapitulated in a far briefer, more precise, and more systematic form in a number of up-to-date textbooks?" [2] The
"everything" needed by the student is the conceptual models employed by the field at that particular point in time—
those models which define the very notion of an empirical
world and consequently the notion of "factuality" within
that world. A natural scientist is defined by his ability to

work from these models in an approved manner, and not at all by his knowledge, say, of their history. In addition, a key function of textbooks is to rebut or more commonly to ignore competing general theories which have been rejected by the mainstream of the discipline. No textbook in chemistry, for example, would spend much time, if any, "refuting" phlogistic chemistry. The "objectivity" of the natural scientist in no way entails his inability to choose very sharply between "valid" and "invalid" answers to problems; we do not usually consider an astronomer "intolerant" for rejecting with scorn a pre-Copernican notion of the universe.

Similarly, in the teaching of introductory courses in the natural sciences, a "discussion leader" has the purpose mainly of clarifying the "truths" of his discipline. He does not engage in "debate" with students about the validity of the fundamental theories, except in a relatively trivial way exemplified by "labs" whose purpose is to prove that, yes indeed, beams will balance on a lever if equal weights are placed equal distances from the center. If a student, however, declares that the time span assumed by geology or evolutionary biology is "wrong" because it is "disproved" by the Holy Bible, he is not argued with, beyond a certain point, but either ignored or advised to drop the course on pain of failure. As Kuhn notes, many of the natural sciences use textbooks well into the graduate phase of their respective programs; only Ph.D. candidates will be presented with problems about whose answers there is meaningful dispute, and even they will be expected to resolve the dispute by using conventional methodology.[3]

It is a truism, on the other hand, that the situation is extremely different in political science. Even though many texts present themselves for consideration, most of us rightly reject them as inadequate for a student seeking to know about his world. This volume itself is an illustration of the extent to which political science is caught within what Kuhn terms a "scientific revolution," when paradigms compete

with one another and there is no agreed-upon method for
distinguishing their validity or invalidity. Concomitantly, in
this situation it is questionable whether or not one can speak
of any given political scientists as "authorities," for that
raises the begged question of the transpersonal standards
upon which the designation must be based if it is to have any
real meaning. Not only the definition of what it means to be
a political scientist but also the criteria by which we distinguish a superior from a poor political scientist raise basic
philosophical questions. (I am assuming here that we are
talking of more complex matters than whether or not a
scholar fabricates evidence, blatantly ignores negative evidence, or even passes the test of logical consistency.)

As Weber said in one of his major essays on the methodology of social science, "The relationship between concept and
reality in the cultural sciences involves the transitoriness of
all such syntheses. The great attempts at theory-construction
in our science were always useful for revealing the limits of
the significance of those points of view which provided their
foundations. The greatest advances in the sphere of the social sciences are substantively tied up with the shift in practical cultural problems and take the guise of a critique of
concept-construction." [4] This aptly summarizes the development in political science following the collapse of the illusions of post-World War II American liberalism in the
flames of Saigon, Ben Tre (the city the United States "had
to destroy in order to save"), Watts, and Detroit. The
"practical cultural problem," in brief, has shifted from trying to maintain a political order assumed to maximize democracy, as much as reasonably possible, to attempting to
rid that order of the newly rediscovered cancers of poverty,
racism, and political imperialism. And, as Weber predicted,
political concepts which blinded us to these ills are indeed
being met with the critiques they richly deserve.

If many of the core approaches of contemporary political
science, such as "pluralism," have turned out upon closer

examination to be ideologies both justifying existing structures and distorting proper understanding of their bases, it still cannot be said that successful alternative paradigms have presented themselves. As we pointed out in the introduction, what motivates the contributors to this volume is discontent with the principal existing schemes rather than agreement on a single system of replacement. (This was also true, I might point out, of the contributors to the previous volume in this series, *Towards a New Past, Dissenting Essays in American History*. Whatever may be the political sympathies which join together at times Eugene Genovese and Staughton Lynd, they fundamentally disagree, as will be seen later, about the task of the historian and about what constitutes evidence for explanatory schemes.)

What, then, should students be taught about political science in an introductory course? What criteria can be used for decision about materials? Is there any meaning to the notion that a teacher should present "all sides" of an issue? I am made uncomfortable by my own question, but *not* because it involves restricting the number of "sides" or points of view presented. I trust there are few of us who offer astrological explanations of political events as acceptable alternatives to more secular interpretations, even though there are literally millions of people who believe in astrology and even though there is a large body of "textual" astrological theory that asserts itself paradigmatically. Nor would most of us accept a paper from a student, however original, that used astrology as the explanatory system.

As Professor Julian Markel of Ohio State noted when reporting to the local chapter of the AAUP regarding the injunction calling for "objectivity" on the part of the teacher, in all disciplines, even those lacking general paradigms, "The normal state of controversy is one in which at any given time certain alternatives appear more plausible than others, and in which still others seem irrelevant or even frivolous." Few graduate seminars, even on a narrow topic, con-

sider "all" points of view; it is simply misleading, at the very
least, to regard the presentation of a wide multiplicity of
alternatives as possible for an introductory course. The
question remains, though, if there is any basis of choice regarding what *will* be pursued in the classroom, and here it
becomes germane to return to Weber.

Weber's own injunction heading this essay contains some
very real problems, if not contradictions. There is a powerful resonance of Socrates within Weber. "The shallowness of
our routinized daily existence," he exclaims, "in the most
significant sense of the word consists indeed in the fact that
the persons who are caught up in it do not become aware,
and above all do not wish to become aware, of this partly
psychologically, part pragmatically conditioned motley of
irreconcilably antagonistic values." [5] There are few thinkers
who could as honestly have had as their motto "Know Thy-
self" as could Weber. And, as with Socrates, this self-
knowledge is bound up with a moral purpose—the clarification of the "ultimate meaning of [one's] own conduct."

Unlike Socrates, Weber did not believe in any kind of
ethical transcendentalism which could overcome the conflict
among values. The only real answer for Weber to a moral
dilemma was that provided by one's conscience; indeed,
Weber's hostility to a teacher's attempting to influence a
student's values flowed from his belief that the student
should not be "prevented from solving his problems on the
basis of his own conscience." [6] Conscience should not be entirely arbitrary in its choice, however, and here Weber
called for a vital set of tasks to be undertaken by the teacher,
tasks which made him a servant of "moral forces." The tasks
are twofold: the selection of questions to be examined and
then the statements that can be made concerning these questions.

"An attitude of moral indifference," Weber stressed, "has
no connection with scientific 'objectivity.'" Moreover, "in
social sciences the stimulus to the posing of problems is in

actuality always given by *practical* 'questions.' Hence the
very recognition of the existence of a scientific problem co-
incides, personally with the possession of specifically oriented motives and values." [7] In fact, this is a principal
theme of his essay: "objectivity" applies only to the criteria
for analyzing social problems; the choice of problems is satu-
rated with value commitments. "To be sure, without the investigator's evaluative ideas, there would be no principle of
selection of subject-matter and no meaningful knowledge of
the concrete reality." [8]

The first choice facing the teacher is the selection of problems to be presented in his course, and as we have seen, his
selection will be intimately bound up with his evaluation of
what constitute "practical" issues. In this sense, the problem
of choice is perhaps not overly difficult for those of us whose
perceptions of America demand confrontation with the implications of the war in Vietnam and the meaning of our
various domestic crises. In my introductory course in political science at Ohio State, I raise questions about the existence of poverty, hunger, etc., in the United States and imply
thereby that any acceptable "political science" must relate
political structures to these problems.

This problem of choice, however, is not the most significant issue. Merely to raise popular issues like hunger, etc., is
a cheap form of whetting the student's appetite for "relevance." The crucial question remains, Having recognized
the "practical" (moral) import of a question like hunger,
do we have any tools for helping the student to come to grips
with the problem?

I spoke above of Weber's emphasis on the "moral" role of
the teacher. This role, however, was strongly connected with
his own stress on the importance of the "ethics of responsibility" for the social actor. By this concept he meant a teleological ethics, one which took into account the consequences
of one's actions. He contrasted this to a Kantian "ethics of
perfection," in which consequences had nothing to do with

the "goodness" or "badness" of an action. Though he professed his own neutrality as to the ultimate validity of either scheme, there is no doubt that he was scared of those who acted "regardless of consequences." Indeed, it was because of his own recognition of the ubiquitous role of violence in politics that he condemned those who would hastily use force in the pursuit of "perfection" in politics.[9]

The function of the social scientist, therefore, was to make teleological calculation possible, and this entailed the possibility of intelligible prediction:

> . . . when the possibility of attaining a proposed end appears to exist, we can determine (naturally within the limits of our existing knowledge) the consequences which the application of the means to be used will produce in addition to the eventual attainment of the proposed end, as a result of the interdependence of all events. We can then provide the acting person with the ability to weigh and compare the undesirable . . . action. Thus, we can answer the question: what will the attainment of a desired end "cost" in terms of the predictable loss of other values?[10]

If it is Weber's anguish about the derivation of moral values which has made him so attractive to contemporary intellectuals, it is still this vestigial positivism which denotes his birth in the nineteenth century. It is, I believe, not disputes about values, at least in the ordinarily understood sense, which are tearing the discipline of political science apart (though, of course, value conflict is present), but rather the demise of positivism and the consequently irresolvable disagreement about what in fact are the effects of certain kinds of social action. Far too much attention has been paid to the alleged consequences of attempting a "value-free" social science and much too little to the disputes about the validity of the "facts" themselves which are at the core of much political controversy. In the language of Kuhn, what political science as a discipline obviously lacks are epistemological paradigms within which the kind of work postulated by Weber could in fact be done. Moreover, as Ken Dolbeare points out elsewhere in this volume, the emphasis of contemporary political science on studying only the political process, and even then often using only static models rather than the consequences of political outcomes, makes even more difficult the realization of a truly Weberian social science.

As Weber stressed, a linkage between ends and means is vital to any responsible political action. The phrase "the end justifies the means," for all of its emotional resonance, is surely only a truism, at least when one adds the all-important caveat that the means must be causally related to the attainment of the end at an acceptable cost; this truism is at the heart of Weber's own stress on the importance of calculation. It follows for Weber that the task of the teacher is to help the student understand these ends-means relations; otherwise, the moral questions raised by the teacher would be, in a sense, merely abstract and "perfectionist." That is, they would be divorced from their necessary context of social interrelations. To discuss, for example, whether political violence—or even assassination—is always "bad" demands, if the discussion is to be anything more than simplemindedly moralistic, an acute perception of the actual historical consequences of such acts. The problem is that the kind of social theory demanded by this side of Weber does not exist.

The great hope of nineteenth-century social thinkers, the primary exemplar obviously being Marx, was to construct a "science" of society. The consequences of the rejection of Marxism—the last great edifice in the tradition of comprehensive theory extending back to Plato—has been the involuntary embrace of chaos, and most definitely *not* the creation of a more satisfying theory of social processes. This is not to say that political science has faced up to its condition of intellectual chaos, for as Theodore Lowi has recently argued, the "pluralism" so favored by the discipline is in real-

ity a warmed-over version of nineteenth-century economic
liberalism, with its benign faith in a self-regulating unseen
hand preventing any untoward breakdown of the political
and social system.[11] The political history of the 60s has made
us all too aware of the delusion of such faith, and we realize
once more the need we have for comprehensive theory. We
hope, as did Weber, for its emergence.

The great—and almost tragic—achievement of Weber
was to destroy the confidence behind this hope. If Weber did
not believe that social events occurred randomly, he did
help to remove the epistemological foundation on which a
predictive social science might be based. "The number and
type of causes which have influenced any given event are always infinite and there is nothing in the things themselves to
set some of them apart as alone meriting attention. . . .
Order is brought into this chaos only on the condition that
in every case only a *part* of concrete reality is interesting and
significant to us, because only it is related to the *cultural
values* with which we approach reality." [12] Later sociologists
of knowledge, moreover, have been unable to find a resting
point at which "true" social analysis can take place. To
study an aspect of social reality because of its value implications is an existential necessity of being a social scientist, but
this says little about the problem of validation of the insights
one comes up with.

What I am suggesting is that the traditional debate about
the "objectivity" of the teacher, defined as it is in terms of
the linked distinction between "facts" and "values," may
simply no longer make much sense, if indeed it ever did.
The notion depends for its effectiveness upon the acceptance
of a stable external world of cause and effect, and Weber
served as his own most effective critic in terms of destroying
such a perceptual basis.

My argument at this point is, in a sense, a twist on the
"end of ideology" assertion, for I would agree that we may
be bereft of any ideology in the sense of explanations of the

world which serve to bring order out of chaos. The optimism of the "end of ideology" ideologues like Daniel Bell and Zbigniew Brzezinski comes only from their naïve belief that in fact professional social scientists have developed paradigms to explain (and direct) social change and that such social scientists will be the "technotricians" of the coming postindustrial age. Alas, such faith appears without merit, and brute nominalism makes more sense.

Insofar, therefore, as the role of the teacher is to make the student morally aware of the consequences of his acts, it is enormously more difficult than Weber recognized. The teacher must choose not only the problem he wishes to study; much more importantly, he must choose, among competing empirical theories, those one or two which he will impress upon a student. And two things are clear about our own choices: first, that they are exceedingly complex; secondly, that they may carry with them profoundly different import in terms of the means-ends relations postulated by competing theories.

Political discourse is full of such words as "reasonable," "responsible," etc. Most American political scientists, for example, seem to view the risk-taking of the Kennedy response at the time of the so-called missile crisis as, in some sense, "reasonable." Similarly, the policy of a dominant elite, such as the policy of the war in Vietnam with its maiming and destruction, is viewed as "reasonable" by most political scientists, at least in the sense implied by the statement "reasonable men can disagree." What would it mean, though, to call it "unreasonable," that is, to indicate one's belief that the paradigm on which it is based is substantially without foundation in the empirical world? Few of us would hesitate, in the classroom, to view the Nazi image of the world as "unreasonable"; is it anything more than parochial attachment to the United States which prevents a similar recognition in the case of Vietnam?

Do we, as political scientists, really have the tools by

which to indicate meaningful means-ends relations, or are
words like "reasonable," etc., doomed to continue merely
for ideological cant? This is simply another way of asking
whether or not we have any real insights to contribute to
students interested in "responsible" action, within Weber's
meaning, concerning society. And this is itself only another
way of asking about the status (and possibility) of social
theory.

The tragic ethos of Barrington Moore's *Social Origins of
Dictatorship and Democracy*, for example, comes from his
reluctant conclusion that great violence and suffering may
be causally linked to the solution of problems of agricultural
production and thus the alleviation of misery in modernizing societies. Moore, I would argue, is very "Weberian" in
suggesting that enormous "costs" might be attached to the
nonrevolutionary development of India, just as there have
been real "benefits" in the Chinese pattern of development.[13] In addition, one of Moore's implicit criticisms is that
the American cultural predilection for emphasizing the absence or presence of formal governmental institutions kept
us from asking other questions that would more truly have
awakened us to the implications of our own conduct as a
nation.

Similarly, the basis of Eugene Genovese's remarkable critique of Staughton Lynd's writings on American history and
thought is Lynd's use of universal values wrenched from any
meaningful historical context. "Lynd must necessarily de-
clare slavery and servitude evil and immoral for every time
and place; I would argue that at certain times through history they contributed to social development and that the
moral case against modern slavery must rest on its being a
historical anachronism."[14] Genovese, as a Marxist, goes
beyond Weber by assuming that history carries within it its
own moral justification, but he joins Weber in pointing to
the importance of teleological, rather than simply moral,
reasoning. The task of the social scientist is indeed to try to

clarify empirical relationships between means and ends
rather than merely to denounce abstractly the evils of the
day or praise the vague desirability of reform (or revolution). Genovese also belies those who would use Marx's
Eleventh Thesis on Feuerbach—"The philosophers have
only *interpreted* the world, in various ways; the point, however, is to *change* it"—as an excuse for avoiding the hard
tasks of seeking accurate descriptions of the social world. We
must indeed reject static conceptions of the world which
deny the possibility of change, but change can only come in
the wake of an accurate understanding of the world.[15]

This is obviously where the rub comes in. The teacher of
political science cannot perform his Weberian (or Marxist)
task with confidence precisely because he generally does not
share Genovese's conviction that sufficiently exact tools of
analysis exist by which to judge the "necessity" or "superflu-
ousness" of historical events or programs. To revert to
Kuhn's terminology once more, we lack the paradigms
which could make such analysis feasible. Let me give an example from my own classroom: After we had discussed the
book *The Politics of Poverty*, by John Donovan, and I had
pointed out my own qualms about Charles Lindblom's ignoring, in "The Science of Muddling Through," the role of
violence in social change, a student asked me whether or not
the black riots-rebellions-revolts (the language is, to put it
mildly, ideologically bound) had been "effective" in helping the cause of racial justice. My answer was that maybe we
would know in twenty or fifty years, but that attempts to
answer the question now seemed fruitless. I added that perhaps I was being too optimistic even then, for we do not
know three hundred years after the Puritan Revolution
whether its violence was "necessary" either to the development of capitalism or to the growth of parliamentary democracy. The answer to such questions as that asked by the
student depends on the possession of a theory of social
change.

Still, the necessity of presenting more than nominalistic statements of fact manifests itself to the teacher, and the problem cannot be sidestepped merely by throwing up one's hands. Richard Hofstadter, in a splendid passage in his study of the Progressive historians Turner, Beard, and Parrington, captures the "fact-value" linkage that is a part of all serious social analysis and of all "teaching" in the social sciences:

[The historian] need not be, indeed ought not to be, merely a dispenser of "moralistic epithets" or a public prosecutor, nor need he necessarily presume to settle the moral questions at issue, but he will do well at least to remember that in his choice and arrangement of facts he is establishing the estimations of reality upon which well-considered moral judgments are based. For example, Beard in an astonishingly casual footnote, states: "The ethics of redeeming the debt at face value is not here considered although the present writer believes that the success of the national government could not have been secured under any other policy than that pursued by Hamilton." Now an interpretative judgment like this is not exactly a moral judgment, but it plainly provides a necessary part of the structural frame within which moral judgments are set. If one makes the premise that, from the standpoint of the common well-being, a firmer national government was necessary and also that Hamilton's way of funding its debt was essential to its success, then one's view of any moral deficiencies that attached to the funding process will be of a wholly different order than if one starts with the opposite premise. Thus, while the historian does not have to set himself up as a moralizer, he is constantly dealing with the substantive setting within which moral judgments are made, constantly trying to provide a sense of the requirements and limitations of social situations, of the effects that actions and decisions have had upon large numbers of people. And while questions about men's intentions and motives have a certain interest in their own right, they are less important than questions about the range of possibilities actually open to historical agents and about the effects of their behavior.[16]

III.

Thus we come to what is perhaps another way of stating the central question of this essay: What is the role of the political scientist in the "political education" of his students? As Michael Oakeshott noted, the very term "political education" for the contemporary mind often carries with it "a sinister meaning." [17] It is viewed as the entering wedge of totalitarian doctrines, by which autonomy is to be denied in favor of manipulation and "brainwashing."

Several things need to be said immediately. First, the very notion of autonomy presumed by many educators working out of the liberal tradition needs to be reexamined. The process of education is at the very least a process of overcoming the fantasied omnipotence (i.e., the ultimate "autonomy") of childhood by being made aware of the limits of the external world. Moreover, an infinite number of potential possibilities of life are quickly reduced to those few generated by one's particular cultural and sociopolitical milieu, quite without the child's engaging in "choice" in any serious sense of that word. For once, political science is right on the mark when it calls that branch of the discipline which studies this process "socialization." One can certainly object to what children are socialized into, but it is the worst kind of obfuscation to continue to parade the notion of autonomy without coming to grips with the questions generated by the reality of education.

This obviously is most relevant to primary and secondary education. One may feel that by the time a young man or woman gets to college his "political education" is over and that the college educator has no role in this process. However, if my remarks above about Weber say anything, it is that the social scientist plays a crucial role in that "political education," for it is his responsibility, it is in his way of standing "in the service of 'moral' forces," to make the stu-

dent aware of those ways in which reality *can* be changed and
with what consequences. It is the teacher's responsibility to
focus on aspects of the world which the student would prefer
not to examine; the teacher should, that is, make his students uncomfortable with their own ideas by making them
cognizant of the costs of action or inaction.

Perhaps I can illustrate the direction of my concerns best
by discussing briefly one aspect of my own graduate school
experience, for it encapsulates what I reject most fully in the
present mode of political science. I want to analyze a course
taken in my first year at Harvard, a seminar on national security policy led by Professor Henry Kissinger.

Having become interested as an undergraduate in the
problems of nuclear weapons strategy, I had come to Harvard in part in order to study with Kissinger. What was
striking about the seminar, however, was that at no time
during the year were the basic parameters of American foreign policy ever seriously questioned. That is not to say that
all American policy was accepted without reservation; Kissinger certainly had doubts about the ill-fated multilateral
nuclear force and similar particulars of security policy. But
the broad goals of American foreign policy were unchal-
lenged; the assumption that American "security" could be
discussed in isolation from the impact of our policies on the
rest of the world was left unexamined. No critique of deterrence theory was ever made from the perspective that it is
insane to consider blowing up most of the world in order to
protect "vital American interests" as they are conceived by a
particular regime in power. We were being "politically educated" in the most fundamental sense as Harvard-trained
technicians for the American government.

During that year, moreover, the Cuban missile crisis occurred, with its threat of a thermonuclear holocaust. There
was discussion only of the Soviet "provocation"; there was
none about the fact that John Kennedy and his staff, including the ex-Dean of the Harvard Faculty and member of the

government department McGeorge Bundy, were risking our lives so that they could maintain their "credibility." The notion of alienation has become a cliché, but it is surely one of the most awful proofs of the pervasiveness of alienation that to this day most Americans (and certainly almost all political scientists) continue to accept blithely the possibility of worldwide catastrophe as an adjunct of protecting the "security" of the United States. Their own lives are separated from themselves and made the "property" of a reified state.

To put it mildly, such a theme was never discussed in Kissinger's course, perhaps because to do so would have violated the postulates of "realism" as portrayed by Peter Euben in the first part of his essay. Political science as it is now constituted seems to regard it as "unrealistic," "unprofessional," and "ideological" to wonder whether any "national security policy" which risks thermonuclear war might be quite irrational. Surely a Weberian teacher who took his responsibilities seriously might, at least, have raised the fact that the consequences of failure of the Kennedy policy might well have been millions of deaths. Surely the political scientists who have been quick to condemn almost in toto the New Left for their alleged unwillingness to take into account the consequences of their actions might spare some of their outrage for an existing political elite which seems as "extreme" in its own peculiar mode of calculation. Insofar as academic political science refuses to take seriously the discussion of alternatives to a "security" policy which threatens our obliteration, it serves the function of educating its students into the continued acceptance of that policy. As a fillip, it then designates this self-alienation with the term "realism."

However, a sympathetic reader might interject here that it is an open question whether alternatives do in fact exist. This is precisely the point, and it is to these kinds of questions that we should direct our students' and our own concern. The most subtle form of "political education" is the

treating of events and conditions which are in fact amenable
to change as though they were natural events. This is not a
question of treating what is as what ought to be but rather as
what *has* to be.

Do we, for example, teach our students that there is nothing "natural" about the persistence of hunger in the United
States, that it persists because of the operation of certain aspects of our social and political structures, aspects which in
turn could be changed? Moreover, do we argue that change
could occur by a device so simple as passage of legislation or
so fundamental as violent revolution? If the former, do we
teach them that the method of bringing about such
legislation is to write to their congressman or to demonstrate
in the streets? Or do we simply adopt Oakeshott's thunder-
ing conclusion to his article and inform our students that
"The world is the best of all possible worlds, and *everything*
in it is a necessary evil." [18] To adopt this view of the empirical world is to extend a blanket exculpation to political
leadership or a political system for its deficiencies and to
suppress the very raising of certain "value" questions.

Why would we consider it irrational to blame (or to
praise) Lyndon Johnson for the eclipses of the moon which
occurred during his administration? Is it not because our
image of the natural world does not allow for causal connections between the activities of the American President and
natural events like eclipses? A basic tenet of ethical theory is
that a man can be blamed only for doing those things over
which he had some control; the formula, thus, is that "ought
implies can." But what, however, if we would wish to blame
Johnson, or the political system that he represents, for the
persistence of hunger in the United States? Would this be
any "fairer" than blaming him for the eclipse? To raise the
question of hunger in a classroom, even though it may
represent a response to the "practical" question, the "value
judgment" that hunger is "bad," also implies a particular
view of the empirical world, one in which hunger is no

longer to be treated as a natural event similar to eclipses, but rather as an aspect of a political and socioeconomic system which could be eliminated by sufficient exertion of will.

Our most fundamental task of "political education" is thus to try to make students aware not only of the implications of their own conceptions and conduct but also of the existence of alternative possibilities. Moreover, we might try to make the student aware of how the political world looks from the perspective of those worst off within it, instead of continuing basically to offer apologias for the leadership which now exists. It *is* valuable for a student to realize that the President is under an enormous amount of conflicting pressures, and that consequently presidential leadership is extremely difficult; it is also valuable for a student to learn that the poor white or black ghetto resident is faced with *his* own pressures, and that the quality of a political system may be measured more by how those at the lowest spectrum are treated than by the affluence of the top.[19] If we are successful, we may help create in our students (as well as sharpen for ourselves) conceptions of politics in which the existing deficiencies can be overcome. We must, that is, not only encourage the student's development of his own "values" but also make him aware of alternative conceptions of the empirical world which might, in fact, transform those values.

The teacher must recognize the enormous responsibilities of his role. In addition, like the psychotherapist, he must recognize the possible existence of resistance to his arguments. Especially if their purpose is to discomfort the student in his acceptance of certain points of view. This is not to argue that any disagreement with a teacher's argument is to be explained away as a "resistance"; surely this is not the case. But I do repeat that even the most minimal commitment to the notion of "teaching" a discipline implies that we are doing more than simply spewing forth idiosyncratic thoughts, with nothing more than our own charisma to back them up, and it is sheer pretense to collapse entirely the distinction between teacher and student as an over-compensation for what is too often too great a separation.

Perhaps the most complex personal dilemma of the teacher, as with the therapist, is finding the mean which preserves the student's own autonomy while at the same time subjecting him to the necessary work of developing self-consciousness. The principal difficulty in this whole discussion, however, is suggested by the last word in the previous sentence, for the question of consciousness, with its corollary of "true" or "false" consciousness, raises once again the question of trans-personal standards against which to measure a momentary self-understanding.

IV.

A complete discussion of the problems involved in teaching would take far more space than is now available and would consider issues ranging from whether or not political science should continue to be treated as a separate discipline (and I trust it is clear that I have reservations on this point) to the extent to which our nation's universities must be radically transformed if they are ever to engage seriously in the function of "education" rather than serving as mere selection agencies for the corporate order. All of these questions merit the widest possible discussion. What I am arguing, though, is that even in the most radically restructured university genuine intellectual problems would remain regarding the notion of "teaching" political "science" (or any other rubric denoting the systematic study of society), and I hope that they do not get lost in our eagerness to reduce the crisis of the contemporary university simply to matters of politics.

NOTES

1. This seems to be the conclusion, for example, of Peter Winch's vigorous essay *The Idea of a Social Science* (New York, Humanities Press, 1963). However sympathetic one may be to his attack on the rigid scientism exemplified by a book like Richard S. Rudner's *Philosophy of Social Science* (Englewood Cliffs, N.J., Prentice-Hall, 1966), it is still somewhat maddening to be left with the impression that it is all a matter of taste whether one accepts "magical" or "scientific" explanations of events. For an attempt at treating this dilemma, see Israel Scheffler, *Science and Subjectivity* (Indianapolis, The Bobbs-Merrill Co., 1967).
2. Thomas S. Kuhn, *The Structure of Scientific Revolutions* (Chicago Phoenix Books, 1962), p. 164. Italics added.
3. See Christopher D. Stone, "Towards a Theory of Constitutional Law Casebooks," 41 *University of Southern California Law Review* 1 (1968) for a very interesting discussion of the implications for the legal profession of its widespread use of "texts" in the form of "casebooks." It is not at all coincidental that the developing critique of the social inadequacies of the legal profession also takes the form of casting a dubious eye at the underlying assumptions transmitted in the process of legal education through the texts.
4. Max Weber, " 'Objectivity' in Social Science and Social Policy," in Edward A. Shils and Henry A. Finch, eds., *The Methodology of the Social Sciences* (Glencoe, Ill., The Free Press, 1949), pp. 105–6. Hereafter cited as " 'Objectivity' . . ."
5. Max Weber, "The Meaning of 'Ethical Neutrality' in Sociology and Economics," in *ibid.*, p. 18.
6. *Ibid.*, p. 3.
7. " 'Objectivity'. . . ," pp. 60, 61. Italics in original.
8. *Ibid.*, p. 82. See pp. 72–82 generally for Weber's very important statements regarding the implications of presuppositions.
9. See pp. 120 ff. of "Politics as a Vocation," in Hans Gerth and C. Wright Mills, eds., *From Max Weber: Essays in Sociology* (New York, Oxford University Press, 1946). See also Harry Eckstein's brilliant essay on Weber, "Political Science and Public Policy," in Ithiel de Sola Pool, ed., *Contemporary Political Science* (New York, McGraw-Hill Book Company, 1966), pp. 122–65. Julian Freund discusses these aspects of Weber in the opening chapters

of *The Sociology of Max Weber* (New York, Pantheon Books, 1968).

10. " 'Objectivity'. . . ," p. 53.

11. There is Ralf Dahrendorf's concise comment that for Marx, "social conflicts were not random occurrences which forbid explanation and therefore prediction." *Class and Class Conflict in Industrial Society,* (Stanford, Cal., Stanford University Press, 1959), p. 125. For Lowi's argument see *The End of Liberalism* (New York, W. W. Norton & Co., 1969).

12. " 'Objectivity'. . . ," p. 78. Italics in original. Mention should be made of George Lichtheim's invaluable essay "The Concept of Ideology," reprinted in his collection of that name (New York, Vintage Books, 1967), which both traces the development of the notion of ideology and discusses the consequences of the breakdown of the Hegelian-Marxist synthesis.

13. See also Moore's essay, "Tolerance and the Scientific Outlook," in Robert Paul Wolff, Barrington Moore, and Herbert Marcuse, *A Critique of Pure Tolerance* (Boston, Beacon Press, 1965), pp. 53–73.

14. The exchange between Lynd and Genovese occurred in *The New York Review of Books,* December 19, 1968, pp. 35–36.

15. David Kettler develops this argument at length in his forthcoming article, tentatively entitled "The Vocation of Radical Intellectuals," in Kettler and Gottfried van den Bergh, eds., *Truth Against Power* (Amsterdam, Van Gennep, 1970).

16. Richard Hofstadter, *The Progressive Historians* (New York, Alfred A. Knopf, 1968), pp. 229–30. The quotation is from Charles A. Beard, *An Economic Interpretation of the Constitution of the United States* (New York, The Macmillan Company, 1913), p. 35n. See also Charles Taylor's essay "Neutrality in Political Science," in Peter Laslett and W. G. Runciman, eds., *Philosophy, Politics and Society, Third Series* (New York, Oxford University Press, 1967), pp. 25–57. "In setting out a given framework, a theorist is also setting out the gamut of possible polities and policies" (p. 55).

A striking complement to the views of Hofstadter and Taylor is provided by the following quotation of R. D. Laing, the English existential psychotherapist:

"A woman grinds stuff down a goose's neck through a funnel. Is this a description of cruelty to an animal? She disclaims any motivation or intention of cruelty. If we were to describe this scene 'objectively,' we would only be denuding it of what is 'objectively,' or better, ontologically present in the situation. Every description presupposes our ontological premises as to the nature (being) of man, of animals, and of the relationship between them.

"If an animal is debased to a manufactured piece of produce, a sort of biochemical complex—so that its flesh and organs are simply material with a certain texture in the mouth (soft, tender, tough), a taste, perhaps a smell—then to describe the animal *positively* in those terms is to debase oneself by debasing being itself. A *positive* description is not 'neutral' or 'objective.' In the case of geese-as-raw-material-for-*pâté,* one can only give a negative description if the description is to remain underpinned by a valid ontology. That is to say, the description moves in the light of what this activity is a brutalization of, a debasement of, a desecration of: namely the true nature of human beings and of animals." R. D. Laing, *The Politics of Experience* (New York, Pantheon Books, 1967), pp. 37–38.

17. Michael Oakeshott, "Political Education," in Peter Laslett, ed., *Philosophy, Politics and Society* (New York, The Macmillan Company, 1956), p. 1.

18. *Ibid.,* p. 21.

19. This old notion of looking at society "from the bottom up" has recently received renewed support from such different scholars as Jesse Lemisch and John Rawls. Lemisch, a young American historian, outlined his argument in "Towards a Democratic History," an occasional paper published by the Radical Education Project in Ann Arbor, Michigan. Rawls, professor of philosophy at Harvard, is working on what promises to be a major reinterpretation of democratic political theory in which one of the key moral criteria will be distributive justice relative to the people worst off in any given polity.

The present tendency of political science to look at politics "from the top down" is confirmed by the eagerness with which several major universities were quick to offer Lyndon Johnson and Hubert Humphrey academic positions after their respective withdrawals from the American government. None of the political science departments so eager to take advantage of the "special knowledge" provided by these men have been willing to offer similar appointments to, say, Eldridge Cleaver or George Wiley, the head of the National Welfare Rights Organization, who might also be felt to have "special qualifications" to interpret the operations of the American political system. This is not to argue, incidentally, that it would necessarily be desirable to start appointing a wide range of political activists to academic positions, but only that the appointment mechanisms of the profession now are biased in favor of one kind of political activist—those who have succeeded within conventional American politics.

Public Policy Analysis and the Coming

Struggle for the Soul

of the Postbehavioral Revolution *

KENNETH M. DOLBEARE

FOR PURPOSES of professional put-down, few epithets in political science have ranked with the phrase "policy-oriented." And yet the substance of public policy is, if anything, enjoying a modest renascence among political scientists, albeit with a variety of definitions, purposes, and perspectives. The recent Social Science Research Council-sponsored volume *Political Science and Public Policy*[1] certifies some of these research interests. "Policy Institutes" and similarly oriented "Schools of Public Affairs" have sprung up on at least ten major campuses. Various recent meetings of political scientists have heard in plenary sessions and elsewhere that the study of domestic-policy consequences will be a central factor in a "postbehavioral revolution" in political science—a move toward the social use of the skills developed by the behavioral movement. These are exciting deeds and words —at least potentially—for all those who hope to see political science dealing critically and evidentially with the crucial

* I am grateful to several colleagues at the University of Wisconsin for the inspiration and provocation that led to this paper. It is an extension of thoughts developing over a period of time and expressed in fragments elsewhere, but now seen as more pressing and therefore stated more bluntly.

85

problems of our times. Along with many others, I welcome this growing concern for the difference government policies actually make for people and problems within the society.

But an enthusiastic welcome and a quick engagement in policy research should not be allowed to obscure some very real problems—even dangers—in this new research focus. Most of the empirical research done by political scientists in the last decades is irrelevant to the great policy problems of the late twentieth century; a good proportion of it merely endorses the status quo and/or promulgates benevolent images of "American democracy." [2] Policy research, however, poses the threat of relevance. Policy makers and public alike may be guided in part by what some political scientists offer them in the way of data, interpretations, and (perhaps) recommendations. Thus our research premises, standards, and performance may take on importance outside our discipline, and we risk fates worse than irrelevance. Inadequately done policy analyses may lead to the wrong actions by governments, they may touch off intradisciplinary disputes of various kinds, or they may make us mere technocratic instruments of the status quo.

My concern here is with the latter prospect. Uncritical extension of some current research premises and approaches seems to me likely to further rigidify perceptions of available policy alternatives and institutionalize the very value premises and assumptions which have led to or now sustain existing problems. In short, they may inhibit rather than speed up the fundamental changes that are our alternative to either breakdown and chaos or an internal garrison state. We can avoid such results only by frank and early consideration of the implications of reviving policy research. The essence of the problem is the frame of reference employed— the unstated (and perhaps unrecognized) premises and assumptions involved in the design of research, interpretation of data, and articulation of conclusions. We are all, particularly *because* we are students of politics, more or less acculturated to liberal ideology, democratic mythology, and the "value-free" aspirations of social science methodology. For these reasons, the study of public-policy consequences runs the risk of assuming the perpetuity of existing values and power distribution, thereby focusing efforts toward change on minor aspects of the means to be employed in government programs and assisting policy makers to more finely gauge the level and character of actions necessary to manage deprived populations.

The conduct of empirical research requires the making of *some* assumptions and the acceptance of *some* givens, of course, but an excessively narrow range of inquiry is no real service to either the society or the needs and demands of scholarship. Herein lies a crucial distinction: (*a*) policy research undertaken explicitly (or *implicitly*) under assignment, for purposes of better achieving policy makers' established goals, and (*b*) policy research as an independent scholarly enterprise culminating in increased understanding of the performance and prospects of this political system. Policy makers require research which will render them more effective in attaining their goals, of course, and skilled technicians are vital agents for that purpose. But scholarship demands a much wider-ranging, value-probing critical and judgmental perspective. If policy research is to become part of the scholarly discipline of political science, it should be only on these terms. A focus on the consequences of present policies provides an initial empirical base, thereby avoiding many speculative or normative pitfalls. If resourcefully and imaginatively undertaken, however, such research can lead to significant evaluative opportunities. I shall try to highlight the promise of a scholarly approach to policy analysis, identify and isolate some of the probable dangers, and then suggest some ways in which the former may survive uncorrupted by the latter. In short, I shall ask, What is involved in a policy-consequences focus? What does it offer? What dangers are posed by some contemporary empirical approaches?

I. THE "POSTBEHAVIORAL REVOLUTION"

At least since the end of the decade of the thirties, empirically oriented political scientists have concentrated almost exclusively upon aspects of the political *processes* through which policies are made. Voting behavior, political parties, interest-group activities, decision making in institutions, etc., have all been prominent fields of concentration for those who specialize in American politics. Analysis starts with a claim made for government action of a particular kind and ends when a statute is passed, a decision rendered, or a regulation issued in that subject area. Relatively little attention has been paid to the *content* of the policies produced through these processes or to the *effects* which they may have on the people and problems which are their objects.

The return to a substantive policy focus on the part of some political scientists now is apparently due to the convergence of several disparate factors. Not least among these causes are pressures from our students for us to deal intellectually with the realities that confront them personally. We should frankly acknowledge the substantial debt that we owe them for forcing us to reexamine the nature and purposes of our discipline. Clearly, the pressing nature and unavoidable salience of domestic-policy problems in the United States have also been a major factor. The "social indicators" movement, the concept of a presidential "social report" to accompany the Economic Report, and the various study commissions of the late 1960s have all risen on this tide of social concern. More narrowly professional reasons are also involved: students of developing areas have been obliged to relate government actions to the nature of problems and to the attainment of target goals, and they have developed both some expertise and considerable equanimity about the task in the process. Further, it is sometimes embarrassing to find other social scientists such as economists or sociologists apparently confidently filling the role of policy adviser while political scientists have nothing to offer. But the great majority of the studies of public policies which are visible in political science today have developed from a very limited extension of the long-established process focus within the discipline. Two very broad characterizations encompass practically all of this recent body of work.[3]

One usage employs policy characteristics (frequently expenditures) as the dependent variable for analysis and seeks to add new dimensions of understanding about the policy-making process by relating such characteristics to process or environmental features such as the competitiveness of the party system or the per capita income of the community. Some recent theoretical extensions of these interests have begun to conceptualize policies in terms of their substance or to create categories based on observers' impressions of the "impact" of policies, but none of these have detached themselves from a primary focus on characteristics of the policy-making process. This primary interest in explanation of the political process, as well as an affinity for quantitative methods, links this category of approaches closely with the mainstream of process-oriented empirical political science and insulates it against contact with the value components of current policy problems.

A second and even looser category of approaches includes research which takes a policy problem (welfare, urban renewal, the space program, economic growth, medicare) as its focus and analyzes the processes surrounding its making or implementation. Such studies include both national and local (particularly urban) policy problems, and their goals usually are to understand why particular policies were produced at specific times or how implementation has been shaped by political actors and forces. Although the problem area has been selected because of its special importance, analysis is directed primarily at the policy-making processes in which it is embedded rather than at the substance of the policies or their consequences for the problems which inspired them.

Patently, these approaches neither have taken nor will take us very far into the substance of public policy: they ask *why policies have their present form,* and they look for answers exclusively within certain narrow subareas of the visible political process. At no time do they ask *what difference it made* to people or problems that such policies were enacted. Only in the area of judicial-impact studies do political scientists ask such questions, and then only with regard to whether or not compliance with a Supreme Court decision was forthcoming.[4] In short, what government does is studied chiefly in terms of how it came to be that way, not in terms of whether it was effective or ineffective, better or worse than some other way of solving a problem, or good or bad in the absolute or overall sense.

Thus we come to what has been termed by some a major theme in the "postbehavioral revolution." Nascent within the current movement into the study of public policy is a concern for the substance of policies which takes the form of systematic empirical tracing of the tangible consequences of a policy within the society. Dropping (for the purposes of this research) all concern for why the policy has its present form, such an approach undertakes to spell out precisely what the allocations of burden and benefit actually are—in short, who wins and who loses, and what, by virtue of the policy in question. Components of policies are linked empirically to specific consequences wherever possible, and an effort is made to trace direct and secondary effects on the society and economy as far as they can be identified. People's reactions are assessed, together with the manner in which their attitudes toward the policy and the government itself are affected. Finally, attention is paid to the way in which one set of policies may affect popular desires for more or less or different policies in the same field and to the way in which unanticipated effects of a policy create new circumstances affecting government action.[5]

Regardless of its sharp contrast to process-focused analysis, this shift involves no dramatic conceptual breakthrough. Such an output-focused approach has long been explicit in the works of major general theorists. More than three decades ago, Harold Lasswell suggested that politics be understood as who gets what, when, and how.[6] More recently, David Easton has stressed output, outcome, feedback, and support as crucial stages of political activity.[7] But the fact is that such areas remain empirically unexplored: we cannot really know *who* gets *what,* or what outputs produce which outcomes or generate what types of feedback, until such questions are studied systematically and empirically. We have left half of the entirety of politics unexamined because of an apparent fascination with the dynamics of the other half, and we have not even explored that side fully. We cannot know what aspects of the policy-making process are really important, for example, until we know what effects specific provisions of a statute or a regulation have actually had. Quite often, the actual consequences of policies may be different from either the hopes or the fears of policy makers, interest-group leaders, newspaper editors, or the general public at the time of enactment. (No study yet shows, for example, that the Supreme Court's much-criticized defendants'-rights decisions have resulted in a lower conviction rate among complying police departments.) Nor can we know to what extent government policies are achieving designed objectives, or what unexpected results they are producing, until such studies are made. Thus, although this movement is no conceptual innovation, it surely implies a major shift in the focus of empirical investigation.

Opening this vast new terrain for careful empirical inquiry may indeed have a profound effect on the scientific understanding of politics. It may render political science considerably more useful in regard to immediate social

needs—and it may even justify the label of the "postbehavioral revolution." Clearly, this type of policy analysis is not
merely a return to the nonempirical, policy-prescribing
days of the prebehavioral or traditional era in the study of
politics. It is a synthesis of the newest and best empirical
techniques with the worthy substantive concerns of the past.
It might well mark a new stage for the discipline—provided,
of course, that we avoid the dangers inherent in uncritically
extending some of our present approaches. Let us look in
depth at the promise and the dangers.

II. OPPORTUNITIES IN THE ANALYSIS OF
POLICY CONSEQUENCES

The essential impact of a focus on the consequences of
public policies lies in its inescapable reintroduction of the
substantive dimension to the concepts and definitions which
are central to our understanding of the nature of politics.
Americans generally, and American political thinkers (including political scientists) particularly, have always placed
heavy emphasis on the procedures by which governmental
decisions are made and relatively little emphasis on the concrete substance or results of government actions. Definitions
of politics, and the choices of researchers as to what is most
important to study, suggest implicitly that the crucial questions are the rules for taking part in politics, the procedures
under which elections are held, the fairness and openness of
decisional processes, the nature of representative-constituent
relationships, the extent of participation by nonelites, and
other questions of law and practice relating to how a political system reaches a decision to act on a particular subject.
Judgments about the quality of that system or about the
propriety of any decision made through it are often made
solely on the basis of whether established procedures have
been followed. If all the rules and familiar practices are observed to have been carried out, in other words, then *by*

definition the policy produced is appropriate, inevitable, or at least the best possible.

But if we begin to view politics through the eyes of the consumer, to consider the substance and consequences of policies for people and problems within the society, we are in effect greatly expanding the horizons of the political. Procedures and processes are indeed important, we say in effect, but they are not the only things that are meaningful; it is also vital to see what happens and to whom through these processes. A few examples may be in order. Judgments about a policy or a program will take into consideration not just how it happened to be produced, but whether it produces results in keeping with the expressed intentions of policy makers, with the preferences of particular groups or of the people generally, and whether it is rationally responsive to the character of problems. Democracy, for example, becomes not just civil rights and participation, but the consistency of results with the desires of masses of people. The symbolic aspects of politics, patently a factor in the behavior of both elites and masses, may be more readily identified by contrasting tangible consequences with expectations and assumptions. The unperceived dysfunctions of various policies may be highlighted for ameliorative action. These implications are random illustrations, and many more undoubtedly will suggest themselves to the reader; the point is that the number and range of such effects for our understanding and approach to politics are very large. I shall discuss in detail only two major opportunities which seem to me to be particularly promising: (1) establishing an empirical basis for evaluation of the performance of both particular policies and of the American political system itself; and (2) being able to grapple empirically with the process (and problem) of political change in the United States.

Policy Consequences and the Evaluation of Performance

Descriptions of the actual consequences of public policies will provide multiple opportunities for evaluation. The *objects* of evaluation may range beyond specific policies or programs to the political system as a unit or to the value premises and ideology which give rise to and support both system and program. Precise specification of the consequences of several policies in a variety of subject areas will provide an empirical base for assessing such aspects of the system as its responsiveness and problem-solving capabilities. Ultimately, such data will permit inferences as to the operative values which animate decision makers. Recurring patterns of policy consequences, for example, might provide an empirical base for measuring the relative significance of the contending values of property rights and equality in the United States. Evaluative efforts need not (*should* not) be limited to individual programs in isolation, lest such opportunities for understanding be lost.

Murray Edelman's hypotheses about the many possible ways in which symbolic issues and satisfactions may structure our politics[8] offer another illustration of possible objects and purposes of evaluation. A focus on the tangible consequences of public policies will shed light on the extent to which reality differs from rhetoric—on the gap between substance and symbol—in American politics. To what degree are Americans deflected from attention to the real actions of their government by the manipulation of symbols? Are policy makers and masses equally attracted to the symbolic rather than the real? On occasion, of course, symbolic goals are the primary stakes and rewards of political activity, and tangible consequences relatively less significant. It is often the case also that what actors and public believe to be true is more significant to the character of their political activity than the actual conditions which exist. But these are hardly reasons for a detached observer to eschew reality when he can find it. Analysis of tangible consequences not only would show clearly the occasions and extent of symbolic deflection but also provide a basis for assessing the relative significance of various actions within the policy-making process.

The *standards* for evaluation may range from the orthodox liberal values perhaps unconsciously preferred by most political scientists to frankly normative, value-justifying standards more characteristic of some activists. Researchers with a concern for scientific evaluation will seek some relatively objective standards, while others may be content to apply standards of their own contrivance to the same findings. *The particular standard employed is less important than that (1) the data and findings be set out comprehensively, and (2) the standards be specified precisely and defended independently of the judgment to which they lead the evaluator.* The inevitable lack of unanimity on judgmental criteria should not deter development of descriptions of policy consequences. Once the descriptive base has been established, debate over criteria and conclusions can be rendered more rational at least, and perhaps the general problem of scholarly evaluation will become more tractable.

Some of the dangers encountered in policy analysis become visible at this point. An initial objection to the act of evaluation itself may be anticipated from those whose commitment is to "scientific" inquiry and therefore to "value-free" research and presentation of data—and the avoidance of evaluative judgments. It is at least debatable whether the strictest self-discipline could render researchers, unavoidably children of our culture, truly value-free. It seems clear that the choices of what is important enough to research and the interpretation of the meaning of data involve definitions, assumptions, and choices of what is relatively more plausible and logical. Inevitably, these are affected by the heritage and life experience of the researcher. Further, any research findings which are meaningful must support some value-based arguments or assumptions within the polity and refute others.

Thus, we are involved in value realms today, and we have no choice in the matter. Not expressing value judgments does not mean, therefore, that we are not affecting value-laden outcomes or actions. It means only that for the most part our findings are (or may be rendered) supportive of the status quo because we do not say they are at odds with it. Or our findings may be given totally contradictory or erroneous interpretations by contending parties, again, because we have failed to *say* what these findings mean. The only way that research can avoid these prospects is to confine itself to essentially trivial questions or methodological minutiae. This is apparently the route preferred by some political scientists, but they by such self-limitation remove themselves as sources of danger to the useful study of policy consequences. The danger here flows from the pretensions, on the part of those who do relevant research, to value-free scientific standards: not only are these political scientists self-limiting in what they study, but through a misplaced "professionalism" (and perhaps concern for preservation of access and expert status), their contribution becomes either uncritical endorsement of the status quo or just another bit of ammunition for use by various partisan contenders.

But even greater danger may be anticipated from the well-intentioned but uncritical empiricist who offers his services (including his judgmental capacities) in the cause of social improvement. The evaluative standards he is prone to use may serve as an illustration of three interrelated components of what I have previously referred to as the central problem of reviving policy research as a scholarly enterprise: the frame of reference within which research is conducted. The three leading prospects I see for faulty evaluative standards, all reflecting limitations in the contemporary frame of reference of much empirical research, are as follows:

(1) Extra-empirical convictions stemming from liberal

ideology or democratic mythology will structure judgments. Because we (as Americans and as political scientists) know from extra-empirical conviction that our political system is just, that it balances the interests of all, and that the United States is a democracy, we lose judgmental perspective on the facts that we find from our research. As a result, we may innocently redefine justice or participation or equality or democracy to fit what we find. What is, is right. Or at least (in the United States), it is the best that is practical under the circumstances. The same phenomenon may develop in regard to stability and change. Stability is necessary because we have had it in the United States in recent decades, and it is definable as what we have experienced. Change should be at the pace that we have experienced it—to proceed faster would be dangerous, impossible, and (no doubt) undesirable.

(2) The only questions asked will be essentially procedural, rather than substantive, despite an ostensible focus on policy substance. Did the officials have authorization to take a particular action? Were established procedures followed, rules of the game observed, familiar forms used? The unstated assumption is, as we have noted earlier, that any policy produced without violation of established procedures would be "good" and any requiring new or different procedures would be "bad." This avoids the very strong probability that the procedures themselves are value-laden and favor one set of people or values over others. Nothing in politics— Constitution, laws, rules, and hallowed traditions particularly included—is either neutral or value-free: structures and procedures alike militate toward some ends and to the exclusion of others. Thus, to say that whatever emerges from established procedures is "right" is to beg the important question. Who wins (and who loses) under such conditions is not just a coincidence.

(3) The values and priorities of policy makers will be accepted without question as "givens" within the context of

which analysis must be conducted. If we apply no evaluative
standards except those which accept these parameters, we
can be no more than skilled propagators of whatever those
preferences happen to be. To preserve our position as detached, independent observers and evaluators, we must examine those very premises and priorities, pointing out, if
necessary, occasions where they themselves are the prime
sources of problems or the inability to solve problems. To do
less is to be controlled by the values and assumptions of the
policy makers. Thus circumscribed, we may not only obscure the basic causes of problems, but also endorse illusory,
minimal, or chiefly rhetorical "solutions," and thus in effect
perpetuate the very problems we seek to solve.

A related faulty standard emerges from taking the stated
intentions or expressed purposes of policy makers at face
value and making assumptions to the effect that policies actually achieve such goals *and were really intended to.* In
either case, research and evaluation will be controlled by
whatever the policy makers accepted or articulated. Alternative policies, or different value premises or priorities which
would lead to alternative policies, may be excluded as part of
the evaluative criteria. To evaluate comprehensively what
was done, of course, we must consider what other options
were available under exactly the same conditions, what
could have been done (given existing resources and *other*
priorities), and what the nature of the *problem* suggests is
requisite to solution.

Explicit definition of policy consequences and the incorporation of a substantive dimension into concepts of politics
raise the possibility of employing much more revealing and
useful standards of evaluation, reflecting a broader and more
critical frame of reference. Relatively objective standards
might include (*a*) the stated intentions of a statute or regulation, or of its supporters and promoters—or a carefully
framed synthesis of the purposes behind such action; (*b*)
various possible alternative policies which might have been

undertaken under the same perceived circumstances and somewhat variant value premises and priorities; (c) the nature of popular preferences where and as determined by survey evidence; and (d) widely accepted values generally thought to be applicable within the system, such as equality. Somewhat more speculative and value-justifying standards for evaluation might also be developed, such as (e) assessment of the resources and capabilities of the society, and (f) definition of the depth and scope of public problems facing the polity, such as racial discrimination and poverty. Any or all of these might in particular circumstances be used as measuring standards against which the tangible consequences of government policies could be evaluated. From such comparisons, we might reasonably expect to build a comprehensive assessment of the desirability of some of our procedures, of whether the needs of citizens are being adequately fulfilled, of whether the government and the economy are performing at the level of their capabilities—in short, whether the American political system is working well or not. (Again, I do not mean that the procedures by which it works are irrelevant, but only that the results of its workings are a necessary and fundamental component of any overall evaluation.) Similarly, the extent and rate of "improvement" in each of these categories would be ascertainable. Various other more prescriptive standards will no doubt suggest themselves to observers, but again, judgment and inevitable controversy may at least proceed from an established set of findings.

In more general terms, several studies of policy consequences might make it possible to begin to define the major values of the political system in operational form. That is, the values and priorities which actually (rather than merely rhetorically) animate the major actors in politics might be inferrable from recurring patterns of policy consequences. These patterns, as well as the priorities implicit in their origins, might then be contrasted with the describable prob-

lems of the society, the needs and aspirations of various
groups within it, and some of the widely celebrated values of
the culture, such as equality. It seems clear that there are
many ways available to build an empirical base for scholarly
judgment about the performance of the American political
system.

Policy Consequences and Political Change

All political systems undergo change through time, including well-developed industrial systems such as the United
States. But political scientists have not addressed themselves
to the study of change processes in this country. This may be
due in part to assumptions that all was now in good order or
would inevitably work out for the best, or that the really
crucial questions were not change but the reverse: how to
maintain the stability of governments in a world overly bur-
dened with the threat of change. Some part of this omission,
however, may be attributable to the difficulty of coming to
grips empirically with such an elusive objective of inquiry as
political change.

The identification of the tangible consequences of public
policies offers an empirical entry point from which to begin
the study of political change and could both justify and encourage much greater investment of research energies in this
direction. If we understand politics at least partly in terms of
substantive effects, of who gets what and when, then changes
in the patterns of allocation of burdens and benefits are occasions of political change. Further, they may identify occasions when associated changes in other areas of politics also
occur—such as changes in the character of decision-making
rules and procedures, in the composition of elites, in the
context of environmental forces and the distribution of political power, and in the underlying value premises which
sustain the political system in its present form. From identification of such changes, we may proceed to the specification
of the conditions which permit and promote change, and by

indirection, the conditions which impede or prevent change. Dangers are encountered in this area at the earliest conceptual stages. Again, the dangers stem from a too narrow frame of reference, from the inclusion of limiting and structuring assumptions and value premises. What *is* change, and what are the various possible reasons why it does or does not occur? Economic and technological changes (inflation, automation, consumption and employment patterns, mergers, etc.) are constantly occurring, with little direction, regulation, or coherent planning. In time, they may be highly visible, and they may have sharp social consequences. But such changes must be distinguished from changes in political values, ideology, power distribution and usage, and allocations of burdens and benefits through public policies—from political change as such. Even where economic or technological changes work severe social dislocations, there may be little or no political change following; the two are not necessarily linked, although of course we might expect special pressure on established political ideas and institutions to arise from sweeping economic and social changes. The point is that political change is a separate phenomenon which may or may not follow from economic change, may or may not take place in the absence of social or economic change, and in any event ought not to be confused with other forms of change.

But even when we distinguish political change as a distinctive process which is not to be taken for granted or assumed, we have not opened our frame of reference far enough. At least two further steps remain before all possibilities have been comprehended. First, we must not only examine occasions and processes of political change when we can identify them, but we must also explore the instances where political change did *not* occur despite efforts to secure change or during periods of severe economic or social dislocations. Second, we must seek reasons for both results along the widest spectrum of possibility. Change might be responsive to felt needs on the part of masses; or it might be

responsive to special interest groups or elites and be subse-
quently ratified by masses; or it might be generated exclusively by elites, or some of them, and accomplished through
manipulation of mass consent or in defiance of mass preferences. Stasis might be due to a general consensus on the un-
desirability of change or to elite repression of needs felt by
masses or some of them. These are not comprehensive illustrations, but they show several possibilites not built into
contemporary research designs. Stability and status quo
we have, but we cannot provide a definitive empirically
grounded explanation and we cannot say therefore whether
it is good or bad. One way to start is to acknowledge the
range of possible explanations and to do our research accord-
ingly.

Illustrations of how tracing consequences may yield
findings relevant to the process of political change (or
stasis) are available from the one subfield of political science
which has undertaken such inquiry. This is the area of judicial-impact studies, in which efforts are made to understand
when and to what extent compliance with Supreme Court
decisions has occurred on the part of local officials, police,
and the general public. One study, for example, found that
initial public opposition to elimination of school prayers
was easily overcome and change, consistent with the Court's
ruling, instituted by decisive action and continued follow-
through on the part of the key official in the process—the
school superientendent.[9] Another study of responses to the
prayer decision over a five-year term found that significant
issues of this kind had two distinct dimensions in the minds
of people.[10] For the most part, they were national issues with
deep emotional overtones, which in this case led to a viru-
lent campaign in which many people signed petitions and
otherwise campaigned for a constitutional amendment to
permit prayers in the schools. To a much lesser extent, they
were local questions about actual practices in the schools of
local communities. In this instance, there was great agitation

and controversy directed at the national level and in criticism of the Court, but no manifestation, from either pro or con side, of concern over the extent of religious activity in the schools in any local district in the state, and of course, therefore, no controversy whatsoever on the local level. Perhaps this suggests an important reason why images of change abound in the United States, but the status quo of local practice—which is all that tangibly affects most people—endures with apparent perpetuity.

Another illustration of the utility of tracing policy consequences for understanding of change or the lack of it may be drawn from studies of the operations and impact of the Selective Service System.[11] In this policy area, data demonstrate that having nearly 4,100 local draft boards results in extreme variability in inducting men, arbitrary procedures and decision making, and exacerbation of the economic discrimination inherent in current deferment policies. Further, majorities in the population (and large majorities of the affected registrant groups), would prefer a centralized and nondiscretionary mechanism. But the normally more influential professionals, managers, and other upper-middle-class strata of the population strongly support the local board system, perhaps because the members of such boards are men like themselves. Thus, despite a detailed proposal by a presidential study commission, it was easy for strategically located congressional supporters of Selective Service to extend the agency and its policies unchanged for another four years.

But the larger requirements for understanding political change—such as specification of the conditions under which change does and may come about in the American political system—go beyond the contrasting of reality with rhetoric or intentions or the generation of incidental insights into aspects of the change process. Studies of changes in patterns of allocation of burdens and benefits through time may make possible measurement of "improvement" in the direction of various established goals and also provide the opportunity to search for associated changes in the distribution of power within the political system. Must new elites rise to power before there are substantial changes in government allocations, for example? Or are meaningful tangible changes possible with no change in elite composition, and if so, under what circumstances of perceived threats or advantages to such elites? Political science has not sought to answer such questions on the basis of contemporary empirical evidence, but surely these are pressing questions—for which tracing of policy consequences offers a beginning.

I do not mean that the only way to study political change in the United States is through a focus on changing patterns of public policies or their consequences. This is only one approach, albeit one which satisfies the need for hard data and uncontestable evidential weight. Once the underlying consensus explanation for the static nature of the American political system is undermined by the combination of a more searching conceptual approach to change/nonchange *and* the demonstration of our professional capacity to deal with such problems empirically, we may move to a generally more dynamic view of politics and how to study it. One approach, for example, would be to draw upon analysis of present power distribution and usage in the United States in order to set up a series of critical juncture points, at some or all of which, change of some kind would have to occur before there could be significant changes in the political system or its policy products. One such crucial point might be the nature of electoral coalitions, another the composition of elites surrounding the executive branch, another the level of perceptions of crisis within the society, another the concentration of wealth and apparent threats to it. Depth analysis could then be directed at each of these critical junctures in search of any evidence of change or pressures toward change, and an overall estimate of the prospects of change developed for various hypothesized alternative conditions and circumstances.

Another approach would be the even simpler one of focusing on change-seeking movements of past and present and building a comparative analysis relating the conditions which made for success and failure in the past to the present context of American politics. From such an approach, we might anticipate a heightened appreciation of the obstacles to change, the sources of flexibility in the present system, and the realistic prospects for success of any particular movements today. We might find that there are some directions or some styles in which change is more readily accomplished than in others, or that elite flexibility exists within parameters which could be defined empirically, and so forth. Many valuable insights into the most pressing social needs might be generated in these and other ways once the subject area was opened for investigation and the conceptual horizons of political science expanded to include the consumer's perspective on the results of government actions.

III. APPLYING A NEW FRAME OF REFERENCE

Perhaps the next stage is to illustrate how the problem of a too narrow frame of reference evidences itself in some major recent work in the policy field. It may then be possible to establish some bench marks which will help indicate the way toward a more comprehensive, and therefore more productive, approach to policy research.

I have chosen for this purpose perhaps the best—and certainly the best known—recent critique of the community action program, Moynihan's *Maximum Feasible Misunderstanding*.[12] Moynihan is much criticized from the Left, perhaps to his enhanced usefulness in government; but none can successfully deny his sophistication as a social scientist nor the sincerity of his efforts toward social improvement. He deserves better from his academic critics. But, these deserved acknowledgments tendered with genuine respect, it becomes even more important to see how a sensitive policy-oriented social scientist may exemplify most of the characteristics of tunnel vision which I have attributed to the frame of reference of contemporary empirical political science. (The poverty program in general is a useful area for illustration of the importance of one's frame of reference: in this case, what seems clearly to be in the long run a conservative program, in the sense of drawing deprived groups into having a stake in the established system, becomes in the short-run eyes of some observers a radical program.)

No analysis of approaches to policy research should minimize the acute problem the reformer encounters in seeking to bridge the gap between research and action. Is it possible to design and accomplish change that is meaningful in terms of redistribution of power or the tangible benefits of government action, yet that will still stand a chance of acceptance by existing policy makers and other established groups? The dilemma is surely a cruel óne, and its resolution may be impossible. The reformer may have to opt for one or the other side, either minimizing the reallocations so as to make his program acceptable to established forces or insisting upon more far-reaching changes which are anathema to them. In the former ("pragmatic," easier, job- and status-preserving) situation, he runs the risk of becoming a mere technician for power holders' purposes—and perhaps effectively makes himself part of the status-quo-preserving (rather than reform-achieving) forces of the society. In the latter situation, of course, he risks being branded a radical, or at least a maverick, who is so lacking in "responsibility," "political realism," or "good judgment" as to be closed out of future opportunities to affect government policy making.

But both the policy technician and the policy-oriented political scientist should at least recognize the dilemma and face squarely the constraints it poses. No effort to cross the bridge should fail to take into account the differences in the range and character of the value premises, assumptions, and commitments to established power and practices which distinguish the two sides. Moynihan cannot be unaware of these distinctions. Indeed, he is highly sensitive to the professional role of the social scientist. And yet he drifts back and forth rather casually en route to his conclusion that the community action programs were ill-advised efforts to apply controverted social science "theories" and consequently ended in predictable chaos and resentment on all sides. (The other possible conclusion, of course, is that he has simply opted for the status quo and opposes meaningful change on value preference grounds.) Let us see how his analyses and conclusions find their origins in his frame of reference.

Moynihan's approach to the problem of improving the economic and social status of poor people is based on two crucial (but unarticulated) assumptions. First, the basic political structure, including not only the institutions and practices of governments but the particular incumbents of public office and the patterns of power distribution, values, and interests which they represent, are fixed parameters within which reform must be accomplished.[13] Second, conflict within the society, particularly between "have-nots" and "haves," is undesirable and should be avoided at almost any cost.[14] These are neither remarkable nor inappropriate structuring assumptions for the policy technician who has adopted (for these purposes, at least) the values and priorities of incumbent policy makers and other power holders. But they are unacceptable and wholly inappropriate self-limitations for one who would critically evaluate policies from an independent scholarly perspective. Moynihan's frame of reference illustrates how *not* to approach policy research and analysis for scholarly purposes, and to the extent that he purports to speak as other than a policy technician he exemplifies the dangers described earlier in this paper.

From the above preliminary assumptions, Moynihan proceeds to find the CAP a faultily designed application of uncertain social science "theories." One of his major points is that participation by the poor created substantial conflict with established local power structures; this should have been foreseen, he argues, and the fact that the prospect was not made clear becomes an indictment of the services rendered to policy makers by the social scientists involved.[15] Patently, even modest changes in the status quo of political power and prerogatives are likely to create conflict. But to term such conflict an unmitigated evil, and to use it as evidence of the failure of social science, is tantamount to saying that the federal government should not be an agent of significant change. Satisfactory to the policy technician of the moment, perhaps, but the independent scholar can hardly be bound by such limits. Did the CAPs fall short of expectations (what *were* those expectations?) because of flaws of design? Or because the Vietnam war poisoned the political environment and ended all hope of adequate funding? Or because of the propensity of local power holders to resist any diminution of their prerogatives? Perhaps if one (with a broader frame of reference) saw participation by the poor as a necessary preliminary stage in generating motivation and mobilizing resources so that the poor could secure a larger share in the rewards of this system, in a relatively peaceful manner, before lines become so rigidified that the chance was lost, one might have a kinder judgment of the CAPs. At least, Moynihan should make clear that any "failure" of these social scientists was a failure *as policy technicians:* in effect, a failure to accept the ground rules—fixed political structures and no conflict—which Moynihan saw fit to adopt.

In a provocative and important final chapter, Moynihan offers suggestions about the proper role which social scientists might play in the policy field. Again, he may mean no more than how they should structure their work to be better policy technicians—in which case I would enter no reservations. If his suggestions are taken as directed at the scholarly approach to policy analysis, however, as some might understand them, the context in which they are made means that they can serve only as illustrations of some of the dangers we have discussed.

It should be clear that this is no more than a beginning at the kind of critique that careful empiricists themselves would make if they turned their attention to the problems of ideology, assumptions, and unrecognized value parameters likely to be encountered in policy research. Nor is there any reason why scientific standards and objectivity need exclude social relevance and utility: the problem is only that we need to ask the further question, Utility and relevance from what perspective? Any approach to the study of policy consequences which does not first confront the question of the nature of the frame of reference to be applied is likely to wind up as a disservice to the uses of critical intelligence. All research must adopt some assumptions and begin with some givens, of course; but the act of taking on such a frame of reference is probably the most crucial determinant of conclusions. Only by acknowledging the full range of possible value priorities which might obtain (present *and* future) and the widest possible range of alternatives to any present policy, shall we gain the necessary perspective on the policy consequences which we document, and be of true service to our society.

Policy analysis of the kind here proposed is at best only a minor element in developing an overall understanding of the strengths and weaknesses of the American political system and the ways in which it can, should, and may be improved. The discipline of political science itself is of marginal relevance to the problems and prospects of America's future. But it is where we work, and we must make our efforts where we work, or we shall make no efforts at all. Policy analysis as it is how developing within the discipline is at least unencumbered by the encrustations of the past. It synthesizes a healthy concern for the substance of what government action means to people and to problems with the newer empirical techniques for evidence-gathering about what actually occurs in politics. And it offers opportunities to move toward analysis of political change and empirically grounded evaluation of the performance of the political system, promising developments both for the discipline and for the goal of socially fruitful use of our intellectual resources. Most needed now are several studies of the consequences of various public policies, in which responsibly executed empirical research is set in wide-ranging value frameworks and employed openly for evaluative purposes: if we do our work promptly and well, it may be that the field of policy analysis can be developed into a model of the critical use of politically sophisticated intelligence. Evaluative conclusions will probably not be unaminous, of course, but at least we shall disagree over relatively well-focused value questions. Perhaps this is the ultimate promise: political science could be well satisfied if it provided the evidence about operations of the political order and focused the value questions for decision by the citizenry.

NOTES

1. Austin Ranney, ed., *Political Science and Public Policy* (Chicago, Markham Publishing Company, 1968).

2. This is a vast oversimplification, made necessary by space, time, and relevant considerations. But I cannot leave it unexplained. Those who wish to rebut my characterization may find it presented more fully in my *Power and Change in the United States: Empirical Findings and Their Implications* (New York, John Wiley & Sons, 1969).·

3. Summaries of the literature included in this category may be found in Ranney, *Political Science,* and Herbert Jacob and Michael Lipsky, "Outputs, Structure, and Power: An Assessment of Changes in the Study of State and Local Politics" in Marian Irish, ed. *Political Science: Advance of the Discipline* (Englewood Cliffs, N.J., Prentice-Hall, 1968).

4. A collection of such studies which offers useful perspectives in introductory essays is Theodore L. Becker, *The Impact of Supreme Court Decisions* (New York, Oxford University Press, 1969).

5. See James W. Davis, Jr. and Kenneth M. Dolbeare, *Little Groups of Neighbors: The Selective Service System* (Chicago, Markham Publishing Company, 1968) for further explanation and an attempt to apply these goals in research. In some ways, however, this book is subject to the very criticisms made in this essay.

6. Harold Lasswell, *Politics: Who Gets What, When, How* (New York, McGraw-Hill Book Company, 1936).

7. David Easton, *A Systems Analysis of Political Life* (New York, John Wiley & Sons, 1965).

8. Murray Edelman, *The Symbolic Uses of Politics* (Urbana, The University of Illinois Press, 1964).

9. Richard M. Johnson, *Compliance : Supreme Court Decision-Making From a New Perspective* (Evanston, Ill., Northwestern University Press, 1967).

10. These illustrations are drawn from a forthcoming monograph by the author and Philip E. Hammond of the University of Wisconsin.

11. The principal studies relied upon for the findings described in this paragraph are Davis and Dolbeare, *Little Groups of Neighbors,* and Gary Wamsley, "Decision-Making in Local Boards: A Case Study" in Roger Little, ed., *Selective Service and American Society* (New York, Russell Sage Foundation, 1969).

12. Daniel P. Moynihan, *Maximum Feasible Misunderstanding* (New York, The Free Press, 1969).

13. *Ibid.,* pp. 156, 164, 182 and *passim.*

14. *Ibid.,* pp. 142–143 and *passim.*

15. *Ibid.,* p. 187.

Nonpartisanship and the Group Interest

MICHAEL ROGIN

I. NONPARTISANSHIP AND THE GROUP INTEREST

"NAME THE POLITICAL SCIENTIST who has made the most important contributions to the discipline since World War II," members of the American Political Science Association were asked in 1962. David Truman was among the six men most often mentioned.[1] Truman's classic work of "group theory," *The Governmental Process*,[2] had legitimized both a politics of group conflict and a process-oriented approach to the political world. Obscured by the frenetic activity Truman presented, however, were the mass of largely inactive group constituents. How were these masses connected to the political process? How could one assert that the active minority represented the inactive majority? Truman's great achievement, without which his theory of democratic politics could hardly have had its impact, was to provide reassurance on those questions.

The original focus on organized groups had not been reassuring at all. Robert Michels, the first modern writer seriously to consider the internal life of private associations, concluded that leaders failed to represent members. Large formal organizations, wrote Michels, were inevitably run by leaders insulated from rank-and-file control. Oligarchs not only ruled the organizations, they also developed interests of their own which they sought to realize at the expense of membership interests. Leaders desired to maintain themselves in office. They formed friendships with other group leaders and with prestigious individuals in the wider society. Their desire to protect the organization led to activities divorced from membership goals. In short, for Michels leadership positions carried with them perceptions and interests opposed to those of the rank and file.

After Michels discovered his "iron law of oligarchy," writers attempted to disprove it. But their efforts largely missed the point. For Michels' assertion that group leaders monopolized power was not his most significant contribution. Here he was impressionistic, inconsistent, and often unpersuasive. Michels' major insight was not empirical but theoretical. He focused attention on possible conflicts of interest among leaders and members. His work ought to have made it difficult to assume that leaders' actions automatically represented members' interests. It ought to have led to studies of the role leadership interests play in the genesis and content of voluntary association policies.

But this was not the direction taken in *The Governmental Process*. Michels' insight opened a Pandora's box for democratic philosophy that Truman had no desire to face. He did not ask whether group leaders "represented" their constituencies. Perhaps the question seemed too theoretical and normative for empirical political science. Perhaps it would have provided a standard to judge the actual operations of the group process. Instead, Truman buried the problem of representation within a reified group, in which leader and member interests were made identical by definition. Truman located the interests of each group in its ruling elite.

Truman, I will argue, turned interest groups into what his theoretical forebear Bentley called "spooks." He created "soul stuff" that distorted the real interest group and its operations. This accusation may seem perverse, since Truman, after all, is pre-eminently concerned with power and interests. A self-proclaimed realist, he is impatient with abstractions which disguise the presence of conflict. Consider, for example, his analysis of the public-interest spook. Many people, he writes,

> assume explicitly or implicitly that there is an interest of the nation as a whole, universally and invariably held and standing apart from and superior to those of the various groups included within it . . . such an assertion flies in the face of all that we know of the behavior of men in a complex society. . . . The differing experiences and perceptions of men not only encourage individuality but also, as the previous chapter has shown, inevitably result in differing attitudes and conflicting group affiliations. "There are," says Bentley in his discussion of this error of the social whole, "always some parts of the nation to be found arrayed against other parts.[3]

But Truman himself falls victim to the error of the group whole. For the abstraction of the public he substitutes the abstraction of the interest group. Having refused to speak of a public interest, he speaks continuously of group interests. In the real world, however, groups do not "claim," "wish," or have "interests," as Truman's language suggests; only individuals do.[4] To paraphrase Bentley, the group itself is nothing other than the complex of individuals that compose it.[5] "When we personify the choosing capacity of a society [read group], we are putting a spook behind the scenes." [6] Truman understands that persons have interests and abstractions do not, but he treats groups as persons rather than as abstractions. He is thus a group fetishist; he treats the group spook as if it had real and concrete existence. This is less the epistemology of a realist than of a Realist.[7]

According to one definition of interest, however, which Truman ignores, it might be legitimate to speak of group interests. For political thinkers of an earlier day, to say that the interest of x was y meant that y was good for x. By this token, an individual's interest was what benefitted the individual, a group interest was what benefitted the group—and the public interest was what benefitted the nation. In rejecting a public interest, however, Truman joins other social scientists in discarding this definition of interest. What benefits an actor is, after all, inevitably subjective and value-laden; it may permit us to understand what an interest is in theory but leaves us with the enormous problem of determining what does in fact benefit the individual, group, or nation. Therefore, Truman defines interest as what someone wants, not what is to his benefit; interest becomes synonymous with desire. Thus the interests of a group are the attitudes "shared" among its members "toward what is needed or wanted in a given situation." [8] But if there is no public interest, because all citizens never want the same thing, surely all members of a group are equally unlikely to share a desire unanimously.

Indeed, Truman knows that group members have conflicting points of view. Leaders of voluntary associations often present a picture of unanimously supported group decisions arrived at through mass participation.[9] But groups, as Truman sees them, are no freer from conflict than is the nation as a whole, and group decisions are not the outcome of mass democratic discussion. Truman does not assume internal group unity, as many group leaders do. The primary task of the group is to *achieve* unity. If a group is not cohesive, argues Truman, it cannot be effective.[10] But how can Truman speak so repeatedly of group cohesion and effectiveness without raising the very questions he himself would ask about concerted public action, namely, cohesion on whose terms and effectiveness for whose interests?

Here group leaders enter the picture, not to undermine the concept of group interest, as with Michels, but to rescue it. The social affiliations of ordinary people, Truman asserts, provide them with special interests. But leaders develop from their leadership positions no social affiliations or special interests, only an interest in achieving "group" goals. In a complex modern society, Truman explains, "no individual is wholly absorbed in any group to which he belongs." Each individual is a member of many groups and has many interests. These overlapping group memberships constantly threaten the cohesiveness of a group, and therefore its effectiveness. Having discussed various intraorganizational conflicts stemming from these overlapping memberships, Truman continues:

> It is at this point that the skills and strengths of the group leadership, to which we shall turn later, become relevant and crucial. Leaders can scarcely control the multiple group memberships of the rank and file, but within limits they can isolate or minimize the effects. The maximization of cohesion in such circumstances, whether to perpetuate the tenure of leaders or to achieve group goals, is the continuing and primary task of leadership in the internal politics of interest groups.[11]

For Truman, group members bring different and conflicting interests to the group; conflicting interests do not arise out of organizational positions within the group. The organized group is subject to conflicting interests, but it does not create them. Like a billiard ball, Truman's reified group is hit from the outside but does not generate its own activity from the inside. There is no room for conflict generated from intragroup roles. Conflicts of interests occur only among members, as in a union whose members are Catholic and Protestant, Democratic and Republican. Leaders as leaders (and members as members) do not have interests.

True, leaders may desire to maintain themselves in office. But this, Truman informs us, will help promote group cohesion, "the continuing and primary task of the leadership." Threats to the group come from internal conflicts of interest, not from the self-perpetuation of leaders. Conflicts of interest are dangerous because in threatening group cohesion they threaten group effectiveness. Leaders desire cohesion; they therefore have the function of reconciling various interests.[12] Thus, since leaders will normally want increased cohesion, Truman can in effect identify their goals with the goals of the group as a whole. In the real world, however, leader-created cohesiveness will not necessarily increase group effectiveness in achieving *members'* goals. Since Truman equates cohesiveness with effectiveness, he cannot consider this problem.[13]

"The problem of internal politics," concludes Truman, is to achieve "maximum cohesion." A "secondary" and "incidental" problem is the "matter of continuing the existing leadership of the group in the privileges that its status provides." This problem is secondary, we are assured, "not for moral reasons, but because the make-up of a particular leadership element depends primarily upon the group's situation and only secondarily upon the leaders' skills."[14]

The meaning of Truman's sentences is not immediately clear. One should not be misled into thinking that he presents the "matter of continuing the existing leadership of the group in the privileges that its status provides" as a threat to the membership. From the phrase quoted one might have expected a discussion of the stake existing leaders have in their privileges, and the consequences for membership interests. Instead, we are told that in the achievement of group goals the perpetuation of the existing leadership is of secondary importance. Not only can the existing leaders achieve group goals, but other individuals in leadership statuses probably could as well. Far from worrying about existing leaders, Truman is reassuring us about potential ones.

Again the problem is "instability" and the solution is cohesion. "Leadership skills" can help promote cohesion, but in providing these skills no particular individuals are indispensable. If this is the only significance of leaders in organizations, no wonder that maintaining existing leaders in their positions is a secondary problem. For the conflict of leadership and membership statuses has been made into no problem at all.

By identifying leader with member interests, Truman has avoided inquiring into whether or not, under what circumstances, and by what standards group leaders "represent" their members. Without such an inquiry, empirical information about how much power leaders and members actually have is beside the point. The problem with the Truman volume is not that it attributes too much power to members, just as Michels' significance did not lie in attributing so little.

Truman has sidestepped the difficult problem of representation by allegedly restricting the use of the term "interest" to cases where all group members agree. The absence of unanimity is sufficient to refute the idea of a public interest, and its presence (under the heading of "shared attitudes") defines the group interest. But the goal of unanimity is a utopian one; more than that, Truman recognizes that there will indeed be conflicts of interest among group members. He is thus driven to the expedient of other theorists of unanimity. He must take refuge in a leader assumed by definition to represent the group. The leader's interests (defined as desires) implicitly stand for what is in the interest of the members (interests now equated with benefits). By sleight of hand, Truman has located the interests of the group in its ruling elite.[15]

The major work of group theory ironically avoids the major problems organized groups present—conflicts of interest between leaders and members, the extent of democracy in a group-dominated society, and the possible genesis of group goals in special leadership preoccupations. Such monumental blindness suggests a hidden purpose. Again Truman's own discussion of the public interest points the way. How does Truman explain the use of "public interest" terminology, given its scientific absurdity? He writes:

> There is a political significance in assertions of a totally inclusive interest within a nation. . . . Such claims are a tremendously useful promotional device by means of which a particularly extensive group or league of groups tries to reduce or eliminate opposing interests.[16]

Alleging a totally inclusive group interest clearly serves political functions for group leaders. It permits them to claim to represent members when in fact they may not.[17] The group-interest spook also performs an important function for Truman. In spite of his protestations, Truman does believe in a public interest—the survival of the American political system. He has come to believe that one must rely on leaders to protect that system and favors more centralized elite control to meet recurrent crises. Thus Truman's confidence in leaders is more than a matter of definition; it reflects personal normative political choices.[18] These, however, are hidden in an allegedly scientific analysis. Burying the question of representation, Truman need not defend his preference for leaders against charges of elitism. Instead, he can assume that group conflict achieves the goals of the constituents of a constitutional society.

Reifying the group permits Truman implicitly to transpose the classical model of individual competition among equals to the organizational-political sphere. Many writers have noted that concerted group activity is the only way in which individuals can achieve their political goals in a large and complex society. But it is also possible that groups, although necessary to achieve representation of individual interests, also frustrate that representation. Whether they do so, and to what extent, are empirical questions. They are among the most important empirical questions raised by the existence of groups. But to raise those questions is to permit doubts about the extent to which modern constitutional societies like the United States have solved the classical democratic problems of representation and power. One who can assume that groups represent their members is an essential step closer to asserting that the conflict between organized groups realizes the popular will.

II.

Truman's normative evasion has, like all others, serious empirical consequences. Clearly, it is difficult to understand the internal processes of voluntary associations if one ignores leader-member conflicts of interest. More important for our purposes, the group-interest spook distorts understanding of interest-group demands and tactics. Having identified leaders' interests with group interests, one accepts as accurate leaders' statements about their goals and behavior. A theory of groups ought to examine the impact of organizational structures and leadership behavior on the constituency allegedly represented. Truman's group theory was an elaborate effort to avoid such questions. I want now, analyzing the political approach of the American Federation of Labor, to address them.

Large, craft-based international unions dominated the American Federation of Labor in the years before the New Deal. Within these internationals craft-union officialdom was preeminent.[19] Yet no study of AFL political tactics has taken off from these facts. Instead, AFL tactics[20] have been presumed to flow directly from the position of American workers,[21] an assumption which has distorted the substance of the strategies, the reasons for them, and the consequences for the working class.

Long before group theory became prominent, Federation leaders and labor historians had described labor's political approach as "nonpartisan." That their description remains widely accepted, however, owes much to group theory.[22] Samuel Gompers' admonition that the AFL would "reward its friends and punish its enemies" has become the classic epigram of nonpartisan politics. Scholars view the approach of the pre-New Deal AFL as a prototype for the political methodology of interest groups in general. In the words of one historian, AFL leaders "proposed to attempt to keep labor's vote 'independent,' and thus induce the two parties and their candidates to vie with each other for 'labor's vote.' " [23] Another explains the general tactic at greater length:

> . . . Nonpartisan political action turns largely on the use of pressure techniques and the lobby, and it rests on the possibility of exchanging labor votes for governmental behavior favorable to labor. . . .
>
> . . . To the extent that it aims to win support on issues significant to labor from all political parties—in practice from the two major parties—and not at causing the parties to divide over these issues, it may be accurately described as bipartisan. Up to the present, this has been the dominant pattern in organized Labor's political behavior. . . .
>
> . . . [Nonpartisanship] is, of course, also the characteristic mode of behavior of employer, business, farmer, and other more specialized interest groups.[24]

This picture of AFL political tactics bears little relation to reality. The description is probably no closer to the activities of other groups. Nonpartisanship served to disguise political strategies, not to describe them. Let us examine the nonpartisan ideology, the actual political approach it rationalized, and the interests it served.

THE SHIFTS IN LABOR TACTICS

National leaders of the American Federation of Labor never expressed enthusiasm for politics. As they saw it, previous attempts to organize workers had foundered on the rocks of political controversy. Politics diverted attention from and created disagreement about the immediate economic issues which most concerned workers. "When it is so difficult," said Henry White at the 1903 AFL convention, "to get the working men to agree upon the simple everyday issues, how can you expect to get them to agree upon the complex propositions that political action implies." [25]

But labor's stated coolness toward politics manifested itself in very different ways. In the forty years following its birth in 1886, the AFL adopted three distinct political strategies, all covered by the nonpartisan label. For the first twenty years of its existence, the Federation combined an antagonism for party politics with a long and socialist-sounding set of political demands (including compulsory education, an ˙eight-hour day for government employees, municipal ownership of streetcars, waterworks, and gas and electric plants, and nationalization of the telegraph, telephone, railroads, and mines).[26] Federation spokesmen emphasized the corruption of bourgeois politics and stressed the antagonism of the bourgeois state to the interests of workers. This attitude, although suspicious of bourgeois party politics, was not inherently antipolitical. In its earliest years the Federation had greeted independent political action on a local level "with pleasure." [27] But as these local attempts met with universal failure, the Federation became discouraged. AFL leaders still held out union political power as an ultimate goal but did not want to jeopardize the young and growing unions by premature political experiments. Gompers explained, "Before we can hope as a general organization to take the field by nominating candidates for office, the workers must be more thoroughly organized and better results achieved by experiments locally." [28]

For the present, however, the Federation would not involve itself in reform politics, which had decimated unions in the past. In practice, the AFL ignored its political demands. Gompers refused to endorse Bryan in 1896, explaining that there was a difference between political action in the interests of labor (which he was for) and party political action.[29] In 1900 Gompers asked AFL Treasurer Lennon not to stump for Bryan; again the Federation based its refusal to endorse a presidential candidate on nonpartisan principles.[30]

By 1906, however, it was clear that this antipolitical stance was hampering union growth and activity. Employer hostility to unions had increased, and cooperative judges were

using the labor injunction promiscuously. Judge-made law
challenged labor's traditional economic weapons—the
strike, the boycott, and the picket line. For violating injunctions union officials were fined and imprisoned. Moreover,
with the formation of the IWW in 1905, there was increased
competition from left-wing groups. Politics could no longer
be relegated to the future, attacked, or ignored. If political
activity introduced divisions into trade unions, these would
have to be faced.[31]

In the period before 1906 AFL leaders had accepted the
party preferences of workers as givens and therefore sought
to steer clear of issues which would divide workers along
partisan lines. Now the goals must be to emancipate workers
from political party allegiances, so that they could exert
their united strength at the polls.

> The American Federation of Labor has often declared and
> often emphasized that, as our efforts are centered against all
> forms of industrial slavery and economic wrong, we must also
> direct our utmost energies to remove all forms of political
> servitude and party slavery, to the end that the working peo-
> ple may act as a unit at the polls of every election.[32]

The meaning of nonpartisanship changed drastically. Before 1906 no one spoke of rewarding friends and punishing
enemies. The only political activity countenanced by nonpartisanship was an occasional "local experiment" in
independent political action. According to Gompers, support for partisan political candidates violated nonpartisan
principles. Now nonpartisanship was revised to include,
even to insist upon, rewarding friends and punishing enemies within the major parties. As Gompers explained:

> If an endorsement of our contention by a political party is to
> compel us to abandon these contentions, then it needs but
> such endorsement of our very existence to compel us to dis-
> band. . . . Partisanship is exhibited by adherence to a party
> which refuses its endorsement, and nonpartisanship consists in

continued work for our principles regardless of what any political party may do.[33]

One should not conclude, however, that the AFL's nonpartisan principles required it to shuttle between the major parties. From our knowledge of the strength of traditional party loyalties, the low issue-consciousness of American voters, and the relatively minimal electoral impact of pressure groups, we should be suspicious of any organization which claims to propel voters between the major parties on the basis of the issues. Moreover, the Federation and its affiliates engaged in virtually no grass-roots political activity. Between 1906 and 1922 the AFL simply allied itself with the national Democratic Party. The *Federationist* and most leaders of the AFL endorsed the Democratic presidential candidate every four years and supported most northern Democratic congressional candidates.[34]

After 1914, although the AFL-Democratic Party alliance continued, the AFL attitude toward politics shifted once again. The organization had entered politics, not in the service of broad social reforms, but to emancipate itself from the labor injunctions and the antitrust laws; with the passage of the Clayton Act, labor leaders mistakenly believed this had been accomplished. Progressives in the unions had seized on increased labor political interest to push for unemployment insurance, wage and hour laws, and other social legislation. But Gompers and other Federation leaders, wanting unions to be the only source of welfare benefits, opposed such laws.[35]

Federation leaders therefore returned to the antipolitical attitudes of the turn of the century. There was a significant difference between the two periods, however. Union antipathy for politics was no longer characterized in radical, syndicalist terms. Politics was a corrupt and coercive arena, not because it was controlled by business but because of its inherent nature. For many years Federation leaders, parroting

Social Darwinist doctrine, argued that all politics was coercive. The economic sphere, dominated by voluntary associations, permitted free, uncoerced activity. By the 1920s labor-management cooperation became the alternative to working-class political action. In his autobiography Gompers wrote:

> I have often allowed myself to dream of the possibilities of production if all were to work unretarded by the existing restraints. . . .
> . . . Foremost in my mind is to tell the politicians to keep their hands off and thus to preserve voluntary institutions and opportunity . . . to deal with problems as the experience and facts of industry shall indicate.[36]

World War I hastened the incorporation of the AFL into business-dominated America. The war inspired Federation leaders to heights of patriotic nationalism. In addition, it brought them into friendly contact with businessmen serving in Washington. As a result many trade-union officials overcame their suspicions of business and saw little need for politically engendered conflict. They looked forward to a postwar period in which all problems would be worked out in a spirit of patriotic cooperation, as they had been during the war.

Nevertheless, Federation leaders were temporarily and reluctantly drawn into reform politics after World War I. Hundreds of thousands of workers, organized because of government muscle behind war-born "cooperation" (and soon to become unorganized when that muscle was taken away) were receptive to political action. The flurry of postwar radicalism, and the open-shop campaign that followed, further pressured AFL officials. In 1920 the convention adopted a resolution favoring government ownership of the railroads, over the opposition of Gompers and the old guard. Four years later progressive pressure and major party rebuffs forced the AFL to endorse La Follette for president.[37] But as we shall indicate later in another connection, the Federation

did little for La Follette beyond the formal endorsement.
After the 1924 presidential campaign, national political
activity played an insignificant role in AFL operations. Although the AFL lost members and strength during the
1920s, its antipolitical attitude lasted well into the Great
Depression.

CRAFT UNIONS AND URBAN MACHINES

Throughout the history of the American Federation of
Labor, its leaders justified almost every conceivable political
tactic with the nonpartisan label. Nonpartisanship justified
refusal to endorse major-party candidates but also required
their endorsement. It was an alternative to third-party political action but permitted the endorsement of a third-party
candidate. It justified labor's flight from politics but held
out the hope of ultimate labor political power. It required
the AFL to shuttle between the major parties but obscured a
national alliance with one of those parties. But one consistency does appear to underlie this welter of inconsistencies.
Nonpartisanship permitted a great variety of political tactics; that was perhaps a virtue. It always explicitly excluded
any permeation of union affairs by politics, and any close
and continuing tie to a single political party machine. But
for the first forty years of its existence, local union alliances
with political machines dominated the affairs of the urban
craft unions.

Labor historians and group theorists alike are fond of
pointing out the disadvantages which attach to labor's exclusive dependence on a single political party. The AFL sur-
vived, it is often said, because it knew how to resist the lure
of politics.[38] However, in local politics, the most important
political arena for the craft unions which dominated the
AFL, nothing could be further from the truth.

Whatever the abstract virtues of labor, coolness toward
politics, there were concrete reasons which thrust local craft

unions into political alliances. First, these unions needed favorable legislation—safety and sanitation laws, licensing and
apprenticeship statutes, building and other codes. Proper
enforcement of these laws was essential to protect union interests; labor must have friendly appointments to building
inspectors' jobs, for example. City contracts—an immense
source of jobs—must be awarded to union labor; the police
must be friendly or at least neutral during strikes; and the
local administration could perform a variety of other political favors for the unions. There were also the leaders to consider; business agents and local officers wanted patronage
plums and often their share of political graft.[39]

The common theme was jobs—for members and leaders.
National and reform politics did not help craft unions supply and protect jobs. Local politics did.[40]

Given labor's need for local political involvement, AFL
unions could not be nonpartisan. Most large cities were
under the control of the political machine of a single party.
In city after city, unions obtained political access through a
close and continuing friendship with the political machine
of the dominant party. Despite nonpartisan principles, local
Gompers supporters made no attempt to "remove all forms
of political servitude and party slavery," to steer clear of partisan entanglements, or to choose between the parties on
specific issues.

In New York, for example, craft-union officialdom maintained a continuing alliance with Tammany Hall. Every
power in the New York building trades in the first three
decades of the twentieth century had Tammany backing;
many held Tammany offices.[41] Tammany provided many
services for craft-union officials. While Hylan was mayor, political influence was exerted so that public works would be
built of natural stone instead of terra-cotta.[42] This move protected the Stone-Cutters, whose international president,
James Duncan, was one of the staunchest verbal opponents
of labor political involvement.[43]

Tammany also aided New York officials in crushing rank-and-file revolts. These sometimes occurred, in New York and other cities, because machine unionists had sacrificed bread-and-butter union goals for their personal aggrandizement. Some revolts also had a political thrust. Machine-union ties thwarted worker involvement in national and local political reform movements.

In the folklore of labor history, unions opposed labor parties in order to steer clear of political involvements. Often the close ties between local leaders and political bosses provided more persuasive reasons. The central labor bodies of Brooklyn and Manhattan, under the influence of Jewish socialist and other progressive trade unionists, endorsed a local labor party following World War I; Gompers and Tammany Hall quickly intervened. State AFL leaders with Tammany connections packed one meeting of the Manhattan body with ostentatiously armed "delegates." These men physically prevented a walkout by the regular representatives and voted to support Gompers' "nonpartisan" policies. After the central bodies were reorganized, Gompers personally taking a hand, many anti-labor-party union officials received Tammany appointments.[44]

Four years later Tammany became anxious to promote the Al Smith presidential boom. A New York city statute, long ignored, required that day laborers for the city be paid the prevailing wage. Now the law was generally enforced. "The only exceptions were in those trades whose loyalty to Tammany had not been the order of the day." [45] After the Democratic Party refused to nominate Smith, powerful craft unions like the carpenters, with local political ties, bitterly fought the AFL endorsement of La Follette. Although the Federation did endorse the Wisconsin senator, the national office of the AFL immediately began hearing from local officials, who saw their carefully constructed arrangements with urban machines endangered. As a result of this local pressure, the AFL gave little to La Follette beyond the formal endorsement. In New York the Central Trades and Labor Council urged the election of Davis.[46]

Gompers' nonpartisan policies received their most important New York support from local craft-union officials integrated into the political machine. Craft-union connections with the dominant Republican machines in Wayne County (Detroit) and Philadelphia paralleled the ties with Tammany in New York. In Chicago and San Francisco, labor-machine connections were also intimate.[47]

Union alliances with political machines violated nonpartisan principles, and their existence was not publicized. Instead, nonpartisanship disguised and protected the alliances. First, the main enemies of the machine unionists were Socialists and progressives friendly to independent labor political action. Support for labor parties could always be attacked on nonpartisan grounds. Second, nonpartisan principles prevented an explicit national alliance with one of the major parties; such an alliance might harm local political arrangements. Nonpartisanship permitted local unions to be Democratic in Democratic cities and Republican in Republican cities. Third, nonpartisanship promoted emphasis on narrow issues of immediate significance to union organizations; it allowed labor endorsement of machine politicians indifferent or opposed to broader working-class demands.[48] Most of the unionists opposed to a labor alliance with machine politicans were not supporters of Gompers' nonpartisan policies. Unlike Gompers, they supported progressive social legislation and were sympathetic to various local labor-party ventures.[49] In theory the nonpartisan attack on general programs of political reform permitted unions to steer clear of politics; in practice it protected their local political ties.

Others besides machine-oriented trade unionists supported nonpartisanship for antiradical rather than antipolitical reasons. Urban craft-union officials were largely Irish Catholics. During the first decades of the twentieth century the Church took an increasing interest in labor affairs.

Though many priests favored social legislation, all were anxious to halt the spread of socialism among organized workers. Catholics utilized non-partisan rhetoric, not because they were antipolitical, but rather because they sought to undermine the political emphasis of the Socialists.[50] Like the craft-union politicians, Catholics found nonpartisanship a convenient ideological mask for their activities.

Finally, nonpartisanship de-emphasized national politics and political reforms. It thus protected the trade union against such potential competitors for working-class loyalty as the state, the labor political-action committee, and the political party. Opposing unemployment insurance, one powerful craft-union official explained,

> If you feed lions cooked meat, they are not going to roar. . . .
> The only way to get wage-earners interested in the trade union
> movement and make it a driving force is to convince them
> that . . . it is only through the strength, the fighting strength
> of that economic organization that you are going to get higher
> wages and shorter hours.[51]

III.

Nonpartisanship did not describe the actual political tactics of the American Federation of Labor. It obscured some and contradicted others; that was its function. Nonpartisanship provided an unanalyzed abstraction around which a number of union factions with their own political interests could unite. It promoted the cohesion of the AFL.

Cohesion is a word we have encountered before; it is the centerpiece of Truman's analysis of the internal process in groups. Moreover, in stressing the lack of concrete content in nonpartisanship, we have argued that the ideology restricted the AFL to no specific political strategy. Truman also stresses the need for flexibility in the choice of effective political tactics. Nonpartisanship was meant to be a pragmatic weapon, not a consistent theory; perhaps the variety of tactics it could sanction simply indicated its viability.

To function as a unifying ideology, however, nonpartisanship had to disguise actual Federation policies, deny that these were generated by special leadership interests, and insist that they benefitted all members equally. Truman, anxious to bolster the myth of neutral leaders, has treated nonpartisanship at face value,[52] as if no organization intervened between working-class experience and nonpartisan politics. There is limited validity to this. Nonpartisanship did grow out of the experience of craft workers as well as union officials. It reflected the failure of the broadly based, reform-oriented Knights of Labor, and the craft-worker concern for immediate wages, hours, and working conditions. Certainly, the broad attitudes of American workers and the structures of a business-dominated society limited the alternatives open to the AFL. The development of a powerful, independent labor party was extremely unlikely.[53] But to argue that the multitude of specific decisions made in the name of nonpartisanship in the first forty years of the Federation's existence were equally inevitable—that the leaders had no choices if they were to preserve their unions—is to subscribe to a remarkable degree of historical determinism. Certainly there were limits beyond which union leaders could not consistently go without provoking serious rank-and-file dissension. But from what we know of the internal structure of the international unions and the political awareness and sophistication of the mass of the population, the bounds within which leaders could act freely were very wide.[54] Moreover, except perhaps for the time of original organization, unions lacked utilized participatory structures which could form and activate mass consciousness of interests.[55]

Leadership independence, then, was a fact in the AFL. What did it mean for the representation of members' interests? Most social scientists argue that legitimate functions attach to leadership. Leaders are better informed than members. They can better see long-term consequences; they are more skilled in organizational tacties. Leaders are better able to achieve members' demands, it is argued, than members themselves.

This justification of leadership may be a good starting point, but its implications are not always understood. If leaders are permitted to act independently of the specific desires of members, then how is one to judge leadership actions? No longer are the members' desires alone sufficient. The ultimate or long-range desires of the members remain crucial. But in the vast intermediate range in which most political decisions are made, the members are not the best judges of their own interests. The interests of the members are implicitly no longer equated with their desires, but rather with what is to their benefit.

Given their special interests and the extent of their power, however, group leaders are not the only legitimate judges of what policies will benefit the membership. Truman equates leadership desires with membership benefits, having denied the appropriateness of an inquiry into benefits in the first place. This approach is both internally inconsistent and unreasonable. If the actions of group leaders are to be judged by whether they benefit the group constituency, then the outside observer as well as the group leader must investigate that question.[56]

This conclusion could lead to a thicket of normative disagreements about what was best for American workers in the pre-New Deal period. But the question of representation, while it forces us to acknowledge value disagreements, also requires examination of the organizational sources and constituency consequences of group policies. These matters are at least in principle empirical, and my interpretation of nonpartisanship focuses around them.[57]

Nonpartisanship met many leadership interests—desire to maintain friendly relations with local political machines, fear of competitors for working-class loyalty, anxiety to discredit Socialist unionists, among others. These interests derived from intraorganizational and wider social concerns. First, union leaders became committed to their organizations and to their own tenure in office, often divorcing these commitments from the original, substantive union goals. Since their prestige, power, and personal identities depended on the stability of their organizations, craft-union officials exaggerated the dangers from dual unionism, internal factionalism, and other competitors for working-class loyalty. They tended to be cautious in adopting new tactics, preferring to safeguard gains rather than to risk them.

Second, the more established their organizations and the longer they remained in office, the friendlier the AFL officials became toward business leaders and others powerful in the outer world. They developed continuing relations with these men, which often turned to admiration. They often used their organizational positions to obtain wealth and status outside the labor movement. Many writers now praise this process of embourgeoisement, arguing that it creates moderate leaders more willing to compromise.[58] Yet the embourgeoised AFL leadership of the 1920s was more extreme in its antipathy to politics, its suppression of internal disagreement, and its superpatriotic rhetoric, than at any other time in its history. Surely much depends on what leaders become embourgeoised into. AFL leaders in the 1920s resembled the nationalistic, Social Darwinist businessmen against whom their unions had originally been organized.[59]

The security sought by union leaders colored Federation political action. AFL unions had organized around narrow constituencies, as homogenous as possible. To use Gompers' words, nonpartisanship also followed the line of least resistance, both vis-à-vis the external environment and in relation to different factions within the AFL. It sought to find a least common denominator around which different factions with different interests could unite. It sought to protect union organizations in a hostile environment and promote their cohesion. In the process, the AFL helped defuse potential working-class opposition to capitalist America.

Nonpartisanship helped incorporate the organized working class into the dominant values and institutions of American society. Locally, unions reinforced the power of political machines. Nationally, the Federation avoided large-scale reform political action that would have challenged the centers of power and used politics to restructure society. Instead of a divisive, conflict-oriented politics, the AFL offered a two-pronged consensus approach. Narrow demands for political favors benefitted job-hungry leaders and entrenched craft unions, without challenging upper-class holders of wealth and power. Nonpartisanship also expressed broad Americanist rhetoric which could unify workers because it was shared throughout the society. At best such rhetoric was so vague it required no action; at worst it was racist and superpatriotic.[60] In either form it sought, like the nonpartisanship offered by conservative municipal reformers in the same period, to obscure and avoid conflict. Nonpartisanship was a means of adapting, more and more as the AFL matured, to the dominant values and powers of America.

There are analogies here to the ethnic assimilation Michael Parenti discusses in this volume. AFL politics helped promote cultural assimilation far more than structual assimilation. Culturally, it reinforced the emphasis on narrow, business values, as the Federation even adopted business opposition to social legislation. Nonpartisanship also supported working-class superpatriotism analogous to the ethnic superpatriotism Parenti describes. Instead of trying to organize the unskilled, AFL leaders supported, with racist arguments, immigration restriction and Oriental exclusion. During the war and the 1920s superpatriotism and antiradical hysteria dominated the rhetoric of the organization.

Nonpartisanship opposed, on the other hand, structural assimilation, or at least an effort to redistribute power and wealth through political action. Such politics would have benefitted unskilled workers, weaker unions, and the unorganized.

Perhaps AFL leaders did reflect the normal preferences of the bulk of craft-union members. But two points are crucial here. First, the leaders and the organizational structures helped form and reinforce the attitudes of trade-union activists surely and probably of workers as well. A labor party, unlikely as it was to be formed, would have promoted a different set of values. Second, no theory of social change posits a permanent crisis mentality among the potential radical agents. In normal times the organizational bureaucracy may well reflect the attitudes of its constituency. When objective conditions radicalize sections of the masses, however, the bureaucratic leadership becomes a brake both on the development of radical consciousness and on the creation of new organizational structures. As we have seen in the case of the labor-machine alliance, the intervention against radical action was often open and brutal. If other obstacles to radicalization are strong, the role of the conservative bureaucracy may be crucial.[61] Socialists remained strong in the labor movement until the 1920s; orthodox AFL leaders, both through their ideological impact on the rank and file and through their coercive intrusions in times of crisis, helped keep them from triumphing. The failure of American radicalism was surely overdetermined. Nonpartisanship, as practiced and defended by leaders of the AFL, played its own humble part.

Group conflict over narrow goals is the politics of *The Governmental Process* and the AFL alike. For Truman, in theory, as in the practice of the AFL, this politics is conservative, accepting and working within the dominant social structures. But Truman, in making such a politics natural, has obscured its enforcement by group leaders and its consequences for the mass of the population. Obliterating any critical consciousness outside the process, the American science of politics fails to comprehend the society it mirrors.

NOTES

1. Albert Somit and Joseph Tanenhaus, "Trends in American Political Science," *American Political Science Review*, LXVII (September 1963), 944.
2. New York, Alfred A. Knopf, 1951.
3. Truman, *Governmental Process*, p. 50.
4. *Ibid.*, pp. 31, 35, 37, 213, 227, *passim*. It is one thing to speak of acting groups as analytic categories, as Bentley did. It is quite another to refer to the actions of concrete collectivities like real interest groups. One may create an abstract model which contains "group" actors. In the real world only individuals act.
5. Bentley's real words were, "Society itself is nothing other than the complex of groups that compose it." *Cf.* Arthur F. Bentley, *The Process of Government* (Evanston, Ill., The Principia Press, 1935), p. 222.
6. *Ibid.*, p. 154.
7. Truman's group fetishism is analogous to the fetishism of commodities described by Marx. In both cases, "the productions of the human brain appear as independent beings endowed with life, and entering into relations both with one another and the human race." *Cf.* Karl Marx, *Capital* (New York, Modern Library, 1906), I, 83. The reification of "realism" in contemporary political science is the theme of Peter Euben's essay in this volume.
8. Truman, *Governmental Process*, pp. 33–34.
9. *Cf.* Grant McConnell, *Private Power and American Democracy* (New York, Alfred A. Knopf, 1966), pp. 51–154; Michael Rogin, "Voluntarism: The Political Functions of an Anti-Political Doctrine," *Industrial and Labor Relations Review*, XV (July 1962), pp. 525–30; Oliver Garceau, *The Political Life of the AMA* (Hamden, Conn., Archon Books, 1961), pp. 83–103.
10. Truman, *Governmental Process*, p. 112.
11. *Ibid.*, pp. 156–59, 164.
12. *Ibid.*, p. 193.
13. Only once does Truman recognize that "the well-situated minority [may] take action that does not conform to the decisions or prefer-

ences expressed by the rank and file or by their elected representatives" (*ibid.*, p. 141). But this does not lead to any discussion of bases for leadership-membership conflict of interest. Instead, when Truman returns to this problem (p. 194), he asks why followers sometimes tolerate "mediocre" leaders. The members' problem, as Truman writes of it, is never what leaders want, but leaders' incompetence in getting what members want.

14. *Ibid.*, p. 210.

15. Some comments by Bentley are apropos. "Now this social will appears in many forms," he writes. "As a curious development of it we have a Novicow, who, needing an 'organ' to carry the will— for how absurd to have a function without an organ—places it in the élite. . . ." Then, addressing himself to proponents of a social will, he challenges "anybody who believes in its substantial participation in social life to locate it somewhere—not humourously, as in the élite, but seriously." *Cf.* Bentley, *Process of Government*, pp. 155, 158.

16. Truman, *Governmental Process*, p. 50.

17. *Cf.* McConnell, *Private Power*, pp. 51–154; Rogin, "Voluntarism."

18. *Cf.* David B. Truman, "The Politics of New Collectivism," unpublished manuscript, Columbia University Library, pp. 10–11, 13, 19, 21, as quoted by Shin'ya Ono, "The Limits of Bourgeois Pluralism," *Studies on the Left*, V (Summer 1965), 64–66. *Cf.* also Peter Bachrach, "Elite Consensus and Democracy," *Journal of Politics* XXIX (1962), 439–52; Jack L. Walker, "A Critique of the Elitist Theory of Democracy," *American Political Science Review*, LX (June 1966), 286–87.

19. *Cf.*, among other works, James O. Morris, *Conflict Within the AFL* (Ithaca, N.Y., Cornell University, 1958), pp. 10–13, *passim;* Lewis Lorwin, *The American Federation of Labor* (Washington, D.C., The Brookings Institution, 1933), pp. 301–5, 447–52, *passim;* Philip Taft, *The A.F. of L. in the Time of Gompers* (New York, Harper & Brothers, 1958); Robert Franklin Hoxie, *Trade Unionism in the United States* (New York, D. Appleton & Co., 1919), pp. 177–87, 350–75; Sylvia Kopald, *Rebellion in Labor Unions* (New York, Boni and Liveright, 1923), Rogin, "Voluntarism."

20. When I speak of the Federation's political "tactics" or its demands, operations, etc., I do not mean to reify the group and ignore membership-leadership conflicts. The Federation is personified solely in the interests of stylistic convenience.

21. *Cf.* Truman, *Governmental Process*, pp. 299–304; Avery Leiserson, "Organized Labor as a Pressure Group," *Annals of the American Academy of Political and Social Science*, CCLXXIV (March 1951),

108–10, 114–16; Selig Perlman, *A Theory of the Labor Movement* (New York, Augustus M. Kelley, 1949; first published 1928).

22. *Cf.* Truman, *Governmental Process,* pp. 299–300; Leiserson, "Organized Labor as a Pressure Group."

23. Marc Karson, *American Labor Unions and Politics 1900–1918* Carbondale, Southern Illinois University Press, 1958), p. 48. Karson argues, as I will, that this statement does not describe actual union political behavior.

24. Henry David, "One Hundred Years of Labor in Politics," in J. B. S. Hardman and Maurice F. Neufeld, eds., *The House of Labor* (New York, Prentice-Hall, 1951), pp. 91, 92.

25. AFL, *Proceedings,* 1903, p. 194.

26. AFL, *Proceedings,* 1894, pp. 36–40.

27. AFL, *Proceedings,* 1886, p. 8.

28. AFL, *Proceedings,* 1894, p. 14.

29. AFL, *Proceedings,* 1896, pp. 21–22.

30. Philip Taft, *A.F. of L. in the Time of Gompers,* p. 292.

31. *Cf.* Karson, *American Labor Unions,* pp. 29–41.

32. AFL, *Proceedings,* 1906, p. 32.

33. AFL, *Proceedings,* 1908, p. 223.

34. Karson, *American Labor Unions,* pp. 54–62, 71–73, 81–89, 285.

35. For the AFL's opposition to social legislation, *cf.* Rogin, "Voluntarism," pp. 530–34. The AFL had supported hours legislation in 1894 and 1899 before opposing it in 1914. This is a measure of the difference between the antipolitical stances of the two periods.

36. Samuel Gompers, *Seventy Years of Life and Labor,* 2 vols. (New York, E. P. Dutton & Co., 1925), II, 26.

37. Since 1906 nonpartisanship had been presented in practice as the alternative to support for third-party candidates. But Gompers explained that the AFL, in punishing the old parties and rewarding its friend La Follette, was not departing from nonpartisan tradition. *Cf.* Samuel Gompers, "We Are In To Win," *Federationist,* XXXI (September 1924).

38. *Cf.* Leiserson, "Organized Labor as a Pressure Group"; Truman, *Governmental Process,* pp. 302–4; Perlman, *Theory of the Labor Movement,* p. 219.

39. In 1902, while Gompers was denying politics had any relevance to union goals, the AFL convention defeated a Socialist resolution forbidding union organizers from holding political jobs. *Cf.* AFL *Proceedings,* 1902, p. 154.

40. *Cf.* Philip Taft, "Labor's Changing Political Line," *Journal of Political Economy,* VL (October 1937), 635. At the 1895 AFL convention Jacob Weissman of the Bakers, a staunch Gompers supporter, opposed sending a delegate to the International Conference of Social Work. "It embodied political action," he explained, "to which we were opposed." At the same convention Weissman introduced a resolution favoring municipal regulation of bakeshops. Two years earlier he had favored laws requiring a day of rest for California bakers and preventing the construction of bakehouses in basements. *Cf.* AFL, *Proceedings,* 1893, p. 73; 1895, pp. 53, 64.

41. *Cf.* Harold Seidman, *Labor Czars* (New York, Liveright Publishing Co., 1938), pp. 11–17, 51, 81–85, 222–27.

42. *Cf.* Louis Stanley, "Prosperity, Politics, and Policy," in J. B. S. Hardman, ed., *American Labor Dynamics* (New York, Harcourt, Brace & Co., 1928), pp. 197–99.

43. Duncan was known throughout the Federation as a philosophical anarchist, business-union variety. "Why wait for the slow process of law," he had once asked, "when we can exert a sure and certain economic power?" *Cf.* AFL, *Proceedings,* 1902, p. 182.

44. This story is recounted in Lawrence Rogin, "Central Labor Bodies and Independent Political Action in New York City: 1918–1922," unpublished master's dissertation, Department of Political Science, Columbia University, 1931, pp. 16–34.

   In Chicago labor-political ties also thwarted reform politics. There was a fight over municipal ownership of Chicago's street railways in the early 1900s. Fearing aggressive labor support of municipal ownership, Mayor Harrison appointed many union officials to jobs on the city payroll, as building inspectors, bridge inspectors, and members of various bureaus. When, in 1903, the formation of the Union Labor Party threatened Harrison's reelection, these men threw their weight against the new venture. *Cf.* Ray Ginger, *Altgeld's America* (New York, Funk and Wagnall's, 1958), p. 281.

45. Stanley, "Prosperity, Politics, and Policy," p. 199.

46. *Cf.* E. E. Cummins, "Political and Social Philosophy of the Carpenters Union," *Political Science Quarterly,* XLII (September 1927), 410; Eric F. Goldman, *Rendezvous with Destiny* (New York, Alfred A. Knopf, 1952), p. 228; L. Rogin, "Central Labor Bodies," p. 29.

47. *Cf.* William Lederle, "Political Party Organization in Detroit: 1920–1934" unpublished master's dissertation, University of Michi-

gan, 1934, p. 63; Stephen V. and Vera H. Sarasohn, *Political Party Patterns in Michigan* (Detroit, Wayne State University Press, 1957), pp. 28, 31, 48; Robert Hunter, *Labor in Politics* (Chicago, Socialist Party, 1915), pp. 47–64; Henry John Gibbons, "The Labor Vote in Philadelphia's Political Upheaval," *Charities and the Commons*, XV (February 3, 1906), 588–90; George P. West, "American Labor's Political Strategy—A Failure," *Nation*, CXIV (March 29, 1922), 367. Seidman, *Labor Czars*, pp. 30, 57–61; Ginger, *Altgeld's America*, p. 281, *passim;* Alvah Eugene Staley, "The History of the Illinois State Federation of Labor," unpublished Ph.D. dissertation, Department of Economics, University of Chicago, 1928, pp. 224–28, 282–92; Walton Bean, *Boss Ruef's San Francisco* (Berkeley, University of California Press, 1952; Alexander Saxton, "San Francisco Labor and the Populist and Progressive Insurgencies," in *Pacific Historical Review*, XXXIV (November 1965).

48. For example, of the five Chicago congressmen mentioned as prolabor by Gompers in 1920, four had voted for the hated Esch-Cummins railroad labor act and the fifth was a tool of the anti-union Chicago meat-packers. *Cf. Federationist*, "No Time for Experimenting with Labor Party Theories," XXVIII (May 1920), 439; Harry Bird Sell, "The AFL and the Labor Party Movement of 1918–1920," unpublished master's dissertation, Department of Sociology, University of Chicago, 1922, pp. 79–80, 121–22.

49. In St. Louis the city-central emancipated itself from machine politics only thanks to the influence of the powerful Socialist Brewery Workers. *Cf.* Edwin James Forsythe, "The St. Louis Central Trades and Labor Union: 1887–1945," unpublished Ph.D. dissertation, Department of Political Science, University of Missouri, 1956, pp. 41–47, 55–58.

50. *Cf.* Karson, *American Labor Unions,* pp. 212–84; David J. Saposs, "The Catholic Church and the Labor Movement," *Modern Monthly,* VII (May 1933), 225–30; (June 1933), 294–98.

51. AFL, *Proceedings, 1932,* p. 342.

52. *Cf.* Truman, *Governmental Process,* pp. 65–74, 300–304.

53. Hindsight, however, minimizes Socialist strength during the progressive period. The Socialist candidate against Gompers obtained one-third of the vote in the 1912 AFL convention.

54. *Cf.* Angus Campbell *et al., The American Voter* (New York, John Wiley & Sons, 1960), pp. 165–215; V. O. Key, Jr., *Public Opinion and American Democracy* (New York, Alfred A. Knopf, 1961), pp. 153–201; and note on p. 13, *supra.*

55. *Cf.* Michael Walzer's comments in this volume.

56. This is also Hanna Fenichel Pitkin's conclusion in her authoritative *The Concept of Representation* (Berkeley, University of California Press, 1967).

57. Sanford Levinson's essay raises legitimate objections to the tack I have taken here. Levinson reminds us that the basic conflicts in contemporary political science go beyond values to conflicting interpretations of the facts. The standard American retreat from value conflict to agreement on the facts no longer seems to work.

58. *Cf.* Seymour Martin Lipset, "The Political Process in Trade Unions: A Theoretical Statement," in Walter Galenson and Seymour Martin Lipset, eds., *Labor and Trade Unionism* (New York, John Wiley & Sons, 1960), pp. 238–39.

59. Support for the war in Vietnam by contemporary labor leaders is also best explained by leadership organizational rather than working-class experience. Crucial were the internal fight with Communist and other left-wing unionists in the 1930s and 1940s and the incorporation of trade-union leadership into the Democratic Party.

60. *Cf.* Alfred S. Cleveland, "NAM: Spokesman for Industry?" *Harvard Business Review*, XXVI (May 1948), 359–62; Karson, *American Labor Unions*, pp. 136–41; Alexander Saxton, "The Indispensable Enemy: A Study of the Anti-Chinese Movement in California," unpublished Ph.D. dissertation, Department of History, University of California at Berkeley, 1967.

61. *Cf.* Carl Schorske, *German Social Democracy 1905–1917* (Cambridge, Mass., Harvard University Press, 1955).

On Political Belief:

The Grievances of the Poor *

LEWIS LIPSITZ

WHEN MEN are politically silent, what should we make of it? Perhaps it indicates a sort of satisfaction: the gourmet's quiet, his mouth full of life's peach flambée. Or perhaps the silence of some men tempts us to consider them politically irrelevant: misplaced IBM cards that don't show up in any of the totals. Or perhaps we should conclude that those who are silent are too transfixed, confused, ignorant, busy, tormented, or afraid, to know what to say or how to say it—stutterers who cannot get the first word out; people ducking into an alley away from the police; moviegoers who have lost their breath.

Whether we intend to or not, we have to deal with those who are politically silent, even if we do so only through our failure to consider them. When we confine a study of foreign-policy making to a discussion of elite decisions, we have probably made the implicit judgment that on these matters the mass of men are usually silent followers. But we have also learned that silence is not necessarily a lifetime occupa-

* I am especially indebted to David Tabb who helped to design the study, carry out the interviews and interpret the findings. I also wish to thank the Social Science Research Council for the initial grant that made this work possible; the Political Science Department of the University of North Carolina for its assistance along the way, Richard Hamilton of the University of Wisconsin for his helpful criticism, and Skip McGaughey who put in the time.

142

tion. We have learned that when a society evidences a "domestic tranquillity," the "domestics" may not really be tranquil.[1] Protest may suddenly emerge where before there was only acquiescence, fear, and inner conflict. Then rage, envy, and repression may flourish where before there was only deference and orderliness. We have learned that there are dangers and possibilities in mass politics, as in all politics.

Some writers have become preoccupied with the fear of mass politics—the vision of previously silent people barging into the political arena, threatening civil liberties, supporting demagogues, and scapegoating. Such anxieties have commonly inhibited the perspectives of political scientists when they come to grips with the significance of political silence. But other writers have argued that mass movements hold out a democratic promise: changing society's agenda; creating new leaders; shaping articulate voices from the explosive and hesitant cries of the powerless. In any particular situation, writers disagree about the degree of danger and promise involved when people once silent begin to take on the burden of speech.

For those interested in the meaning and functioning of "democracy," political silence has to be an important concern. Democracy ought to have some connection with men's needs and desires—and that includes all men, whether they are politically articulate or not. We have seen theories elaborated which praise mass apathy or indifference, but even such defenses of democracy have to be understood with reference to a political system meeting the needs of the many and hopefully of all. The hidden assumption in many of these "theories" is that the kind of political arrangements we now have actually *do* meet the needs of the many—though the nature of these needs and their satisfaction is rarely brought up.

We have to decide about political silence. If we can understand it, we can gain a perspective on our society. It is

important to know if the quiet we often hear is the sound of
the gourmet or the stutterer, the hum of other enterprises,
the muteness of the inchoate, or some combination of these.
We have to grasp the nature of the political ideologies of
ordinary people, or the nature of the absence of such ideologies. We have to see how people focus or fail to focus
on "politics" in the usual sense, and how this is related to
the rest of their life situation. A man may, for example, feel
deep grievances about his position in life and yet be unable
to connect such grievances with any social criticism, even of
the most conventional sort. Perhaps this makes sense; perhaps his grievances are purely personal; perhaps not. A man
may not be able to speak about politics in the ideological
terms usual in his day, but the political significance of his
grievances or opinions may be considerable, at least from the
point of view of democratic theory. A man may be able to
tell you that the shoe pinches but may have a difficult time
figuring out exactly where and why, how things got that
way, how the pinching is related to the structure of the shoe,
and what he can do about it.

MARX, BURKE, AND MASS IDEOLOGY

The very events and vicissitudes of the struggle against capital, the
defeats even more than the victories, could not help bringing home
to men's mind the insufficiency of their favorite nostrums and preparing the way for a more complete insight into the true conditions
of working-class emancipation.   —Friedrich Engels, 1888

The occupation of a hairdresser, or of a working tallow-chandler,
cannot be a matter of honour to any person. . . . Such descriptions
of men ought not to suffer oppression from the state; but the state
suffers oppression, if such as they, either individually or collectively,
are permitted to rule.   —Edmund Burke, 1790

Marx and Burke present us with radically conflicting
views about the nature of mass belief systems. If we have a

look at these opposed analyses, it will help us understand more recent conclusions about mass publics and also help us to gain some perspective on the general question of the connection between ideology and grievances. We might characterize Burke's analysis as emphasizing the statics of "prejudice," while Marx is concerned with the dynamics of grievance. Burke is obsessed with authority structures and historical continuities. C. Wright Mills said about himself that he worried "with" the Cuban Revolution, not "about" it; so, fundamentally, Burke worried "with" the established institutions of his time, not "about" them. For Marx, the legitimacy of existing institutions is a temporary phenomenon, and revolutionary discontinuity is characteristic of Western historical development.

Marx and Burke agree, however, on the enormous role of the past in shaping men's perception of the present and future. When Marx says in the *Eighteenth Brumaire,* "The tradition of all the dead generations weighs like a nightmare on the brain of the living," he is referring to a process that Burke recognized and elaborated upon. But Burke saw not the past's nightmarish "weight," but rather the "weightness" of inheritance. Reflecting on the French Revolution, Burke asserts triumphantly of the English: "We fear God; we look up with awe to kings; with affection to parliaments; with duty to magistrates; with reverence to priests; and with respect to nobility." [2] Burke goes on to explain that the mass of the British are what he calls "men of untaught feeling." They are the sort who "instead of casting away all . . . old prejudices, . . . cherish them to a very considerable degree, and, to take more shame . . . cherish them because they are prejudices." Burke argues repeatedly for the importance of such "prejudices," including as they do the ordinary man's relationships to those in authority. For Burke, as for many conservatives, man is a religious animal, needing such prejudices, habits, unconscious affiliations, to help him deal with his own feelings and to orient himself in an otherwise

confusing and embittering world. Speaking of the philosophers of reason who would destroy the French monarchy,
Burke talks of the need for illusion: "But now all is to be
changed. All the pleasing illusions, which made power
gentle, and obedience liberal, which harmonized the different shades of life, and which, by a bland assimilation, incorporated into politics the sentiments which beautify and
soften private society, are to be dissolved by this new con-
quering empire of light and reason. All the decent drapery
of life is to be rudely torn off. . . . On this scheme of
things, a king is but a man. . . ."

What then is the nature of mass belief systems, according
to Burke? Under a settled constitution, the mass of men will
tend to private affairs, deferring to their betters in political
matters. They will exhibit a tenacious attachment to established procedures, rituals, and authorities—and never raise
fundamental questions about the legitimacy of a regime.
Government does not derive from the consent of the governed, in any conscious, articulated sense, but maintains its
solidity through behavioral inertia and successful socialization plus that modicum of ameliorative governmental remedies clearly required by considerations of prudence. Ideology, from Burke's point of view, is alien to the normal
condition of most men. It is true that partisan questions
must come up in political life, but the mass public will
rarely have a part or want to have a part in such quarrels.
The mass of men, then, accept their place in the scheme of
things, and together with this fundamental acquiescence accept the places assigned to others. The emphasis in Burkean
politics must fall upon ritual and proper procedure, rather
than upon mass organization and struggle.

Reading such a discussion of mass beliefs, Marx might say
to us: "The demand to give up the illusions about its condition is the demand to give up a condition which needs illusions." He is speaking here of religion and the social conditions which he believes give rise to it and which it helps to

perpetuate. The Marxist critique of religion would apply equally to the other "decent drapery of life" so significant for Burke. All of these "illusions" share religion's "ideological" quality, serving to mask from men the real nature of their condition as historical actors. Marx's expectation is that systemic contradictions within the capitalistic political economy will slowly awaken the working class from the "nightmare" of the past. Workers will begin by experiencing their grievances separately, each worker within the chamber of his individual life. But the factory system will provide a communal context for these grievances. Slowly the workers will become enlightened, connecting personal grievances with group grievances, group grievances with social concerns, and social concerns with a scientific knowledge of social change. At each step, the workers will gain subtlety in their appreciation of the connection between their personal conditions, the condition of their fellows, and the nature of the system in which they play a part. Their grievances then acquire a dynamic quality, leading them on in a problem-solving manner into social struggle and organization building. The worker class becomes the agency of its own liberation because ordinary men and women have acquired a nose for reality, a clear-sighted and determined appreciation of the "true conditions for working-class emancipation." Marx's discussion of the Paris Commune shows his expectation that once in power, the workers would continue to exhibit the problem-solving scientific orientation they developed in the struggle. The workers are men who can dispense with illusions because they are dealing with the real problems of life from a historical perspective they have successfully internalized.

It is possible to overdo Marx's ideas about the democratization of history making. I am not asserting that Marx regarded leadership as unnecessary or dangerous, though he certainly seemed to credit leaders with a somewhat different significance in different writings. He clearly thought that

some form of ideological and organizational leadership was
essential to building a mass movement. Leaders help to define issues, structure priorities, and plan strategy. What
Marx does emphasize, however, is that history making involves mass action and mass enlightenment. It involves
struggles which grow more or less naturally out of the grievances of the mass of men. To paraphrase Burke, for Marx "a
leader is but a man," yet one who can articulate mass grievances.

A Marxist explanation of political silence then would coincide in large part with Burke's ideas of "prejudice" but
would see this inertia as a victimization of men. In the
Marxist vision, ordinary people are capable not only of
understanding social conditions, but, at the appropriate
time, of participating in altering them decisively. If, for a
time, most men are silent, this is because they have grown
numb to the pinching of their shoes and cannot imagine any
better fit. For Marx, man is a religious animal only for the
time being; as a species he remains capable of becoming
critic, organizational activist, and social theorist.

For Marx, once men see that no divine sanction infuses
the social order, they begin to free themselves from idolatry.
Social life then is essentially a world of practical questions.
For Burke, however, the issue of rebellion is an unnatural
one, since where institutions are held to be sacred, all the
answers have already been provided. Burke's analysis would
lead us to believe that most men will lack broad political
ideas except customary "prejudices" and those notions supporting the legitimacy of the regime. They will not bring an
independent, critical perspective to bear on the existing
order. Their knowledge will be limited to matters immediately connected with their own little "platoon," and their
interests will be similarly limited. Marx, on the other hand,
foresees the development of a coherent political perspective
that connects those grievances close to home with a system-
level analysis. In the Marxist world, the leaders and the

masses will increasingly share a common perspective; in the Burkean world, many of the concerns of the political elite will be remote from the day-to-day ideas of the mass of men.

SOME CONTEMPORARY POLITICAL SCIENCE IDEAS ABOUT MASS BELIEFS

Robert Lane told us that the "common men" of Eastport lacked a utopian vision, a well-defined sense of justice that would provide them with a conscious and powerful instrument for scrutiny of their social order.[3] Jack Walker then argued that these men "share this disability with much of the American academic elite."[4] But perhaps Walker accepted Lane's testimony about the common man too readily; after all, the terms of the argument are rather vague—can't a man have a sense of grievance, if not a conception of justice? a few hopes, if not a utopian vision? When do we pass from one into the other? Walker's own critique of what he named "the elitist theory of democracy" called attention to mass-based movements of social protest. The very existence of such movements must testify to the presence of some grievances and some hopes, however ill-defined. Clearly, not all of the common men are deeply satisfied with the existing order, though they may have considerable difficulty articulating their criticisms.

Yet Lane's picture of the "ideology" of America's common men has much that is persuasive about it. It helps to explain what seems to be the relative "conservatism" of most working-class Americans. Discussing the fear of equality Lane tells us, "Lower-status people generally find it less punishing to think of themselves as correctly placed by a just society than to think of themselves as exploited or victimized by an unjust society." Such a generalization explains a great deal: a lack of interest in ideology; hostility toward the "left"; sensitivity to status concerns; a lack of political activism. This helps us understand why the American working

class has been called the "least revolutionary proletariat in
the world." But perhaps such a generalization, vague as it is,
tells us too much—like a TAT picture into which we project our own inner lives. Perhaps it was not only that Lane's
analysis was persuasive, but that it seemed to suit the temper
of the times, that it was a convenient sort of analysis to believe. It implied that the world was probably about as acceptable as it could be and that ordinary men, sensibly
enough, accepted it.

Stretching things a bit, we can see in Lane's analysis a sort
of liberal Burkeanism. His study of the ideology of the common man, broad-gauge and deep as it was, failed to focus on
the grievances these men felt. It emphasized instead how
fully they had accepted both their own place in the social
system and the workings of that system itself. It showed how
nonideological they were (in the normal, more specialized
sense of "ideological"). They, like Burke's common men,
were guided by "prejudice," not grievance.

Lane interviewed fifteen men, and these were all white,
New Haven residents—the time was the late 1950s. Accepting what Lane describes, we can still see his conclusions as
valid only for white Connecticut residents who are upper
working class. Yet, the nonideological quality Lane found is
to be found again in the American electorate as a whole. It is
the conclusion of Philip Converse that the vast majority of
American voters do not have any cohesive "ideology" that
guides their views on the controversial social issues of the
day.[5] Converse finds that only a small fraction of Americans
can speak substantively about the meaning of a "liberal-
conservative" dimension in relation to political parties. The
best most voters can do is to discuss parties in terms of the
social groups these parties supposedly favor. Converse also
finds that individual views on specific issues appear to vary
widely over time, indicating the lack of personally coherent
political perspectives. The picture Converse conveys of the
nature of mass belief systems is this: a sharp divorce between

the ideological conflicts among elites and the vague, nonspe-
cific, contradictory views of the mass public. Between these
two, Converse suggests the presence of issue publics, attuned
to questions in some specific area.

Converse draws sensible and sobering conclusions from
the American survey data of the 1950s, on which his analysis
is based. Yet the article has a startlingly unreal quality about
it. He seems to be describing to us a mass public that has few
issue-related views except perhaps on matters concerning
race. We get the image of people with certain traditional
"prejudices" (such as an inherited party affiliation), but
with little evidence of political grievances, opinions, or perspectives. This public orients itself in terms of its "prejudices" and for the rest appears to change its mind from time
to time about "controversial" questions. No doubt, there is
much truth in this image, perhaps particularly as drawn
from the America of the 1950s. Yet it leaves us with too va-
cant a picture of the nonviews of the mass public. Most
Americans may not evidence ideological "constraint" of the
sort Converse is looking for; yet at the same time, they may
harbor serious grievances and hopes which they may or may
not be able to relate to politics. The lack of constraint in the
beliefs of the mass public requires some explanation: is it
that most people know very little; that they care very little;
that they care, but don't understand; that they hold a good
many views but don't make them cohesive; that there are
underlying perspectives that individuals have trouble relating to the political system—exactly what? Are most people
really "silent"—that is, without serious political grievances?
Lane tacitly maintains that this is so, and it appears that
Converse has only documented it more broadly, if in less
depth.

LOOKING AT SOME OF THE POLITICAL
GRIEVANCES OF THE POOR

If we turn to the American poor, then, what would we expect to find? We encounter here the least educated, least knowledgeable, and probably the most politically apathetic segment of the population. We would expect, then, to find an absence of ideological constraint, a vagueness about politics, a failure to see that politics are personally relevant, a skepticism, and a feeling of futility. Other studies have given us strong indications of these things. Yet, in the general silence of the American poor, a few voices have made themselves heard. We have seen some of the poor mobilized for political goals. We have see some poor people gaining a bit of political sophistication. And we have, if we are honest, been educated by them. Political silence, then, is sometimes a relative matter, sometimes a temporary matter—related to the circumstances in which people find themselves and the way in which they comprehend those circumstances.

But how ideological or nonideological are the poor? Would Converse's generalization hold with them, or must we make some revisions? Let me examine these questions in the context of a study of poor whites and poor Negroes in a southern city; a survey made in the mid-1960s. This survey attempted to combine some of the features of Lane's depth-interviewing with more typical survey styles. Each of the eighty-two men (fifty-three white, twenty-nine black) who were selected by street address, randomly, from a low-income census tract, completed a three- to four-hour interview, much of which was open-ended. This kind of interview cannot make any pretense of obtaining real "depth"—it is mostly "breadth," rather, that is achieved.

To begin with, we find among these men the same absence of meaning in the liberal-conservative dimension that

Converse shows in the American population as a whole. Eighty-six percent of the men could say nothing about this dimension at all in relation to the political parties; and of the other 14 percent, a good many had only a vague notion. One of the most articulate men saw the liberal-conservative dimension in primarily racial terms. "Conservative is to me just another word for not liking somebody. Talking about clinging to the old ways. That's what makes me mad. They cling to the old ways. The race thing is the only thing they want to cling to the old ways on. They're modernizing everything else. So if you're conservative, to me you're prejudiced." We have to be a bit cautious here, since at the same time that we find this absence of an ideological perception of the parties, we also find that 35 percent of the men would like to see a new political party get started, and of this 35 percent, most favor a party oriented toward labor and the poor.[6] On the question of a socialist or labor party, most of the men feel such a party would be more in touch with the need for better jobs and wages. One man brings a comparative perspective to bear: "It would be interesting to see a Labor Party like in England. They have a Labor Party over there and they seem to be doing fairly well. I always wondered how it would work here in America." Not all the men who are interested in a "labor" party emphasize economics, however. Consider the following exchange between interviewer and respondent:

—Well, socialists wouldn't be too bad if they would get the right man in head there.
—Why?
—Well, they'd be more equal about some of the things they do there. Any damn thing would be a change to beat what's there.
—What would a socialist President do that Johnson wouldn't?
—Well, if he was gonna fight a country he'd fight it and if he wasn't gonna fight it he wouldn't. He'd more equalize each one than Johnson.

Some of the men explicitly rejected the idea of another
party, and a common reason for doing so was that we had
enough trouble as it was—another party would just make a
bad situation worse.

Yet when we turn to other questions, we find that these
men do have political opinions, in many cases fairly specific
ones, and are often critical of government action and inaction. Taken as a whole, their views lend support to the idea
that poor people do find ways to orient themselves to the
political arena and develop points of view which we would
expect to be fairly consistent over time. The views outlined
below show that many of the American poor are anxious for
the government to help them with their own problems and
that their concern with their own economic well-being plays
a significant role in orienting the poor politically. It may be
true to argue, as Converse does, that Americans lack ideological clarity; but where the poor are concerned, we should
not mistake this absence of clarity for a total absence of
views. Many views are deeply felt; many grievances grow
out of personal life and affect men's politics. Lacking a way
of talking about the liberalism and conservatism of the
political parties, a man may still think he smells something
rotten in the state and (rightly or wrongly) be able angrily
to point his finger at what he means.

To begin with, we find that these men show a hostility
toward spending money on space exploration and foreign
aid.

TABLE 1

Opinions Concerning Space Programs & Foreign Aid

	SPACE		FOREIGN AID	
	%	N	%	N
Favor & In-Between	15	(12)	45	(37)
Oppose	75	(62)	50	(41)
Don't know	10	(8)	5	(4)

In both cases, a majority of the critics felt that there were better uses for this money here in the United States, and many cited the need to aid the poor. Several men mentioned specific "earthly" uses for these funds: "They should cut down on this mess about trying to beat the Russians to the moon. That is the main thing. It is the most senseless and the most useless thing I've ever heard tell of. That money they spend for that could be putting up a lot more hospitals and housing projects and schooling facilities."

"I think you better take care of your problems right here on earth. Everybody talking about a poverty program, making everybody equal and giving a poor family a fair share and making it better for the children to go to school; better homes for everybody to live in. Where are you going to get all this money from if you keep putting it into rockets and ships and things trying to get to the moon?"

The specificity of these statements is, however, unusual. It was common for opinions to be somewhat vaguer and frequently to emphasize a religious prohibition. For example: "The Lord wanted you up there, he'd have put one up there. I don't see no point in shooting to the moon. The Lord put that moon up there to stay. I don't think man should play with the moon and the sun. The Lord put that there to give us a little light at night."

The tendency to emphasize welfare issues is shown again in the responses to the question, Do you think the government in Washington spends too much money or not enough money? A majority of the men say "too much." But what is perhaps more important is that almost 80 percent of those who say "too much" specify that it is space expenditures, foreign aid, and Vietnam and military spending that should be cut. Of those who say the government does not spend enough, over 90 percent call for more government spending in nondefense areas, such as aid to the poor, housing, food, and education.[7]

TABLE 2
*Does Government Spend Too Much, Not Enough,
Or About Right?*

	%	N
Too much	52	(43)
Too much on some, too little on others	12	(10)
Not enough	12	(10)
About right	6	(5)
Don't know	17	(14)

TABLE 3
*What Does Government Spend Too Much
Or Not Enough On?*

On What?	TOO MUCH* %	N	NOT ENOUGH* %	N
Space, Foreign Aid, Military	79	(41)	5	(1)
Domestic welfare state programs	0	0	95	(18)
Miscellaneous (e.g., highways)	21	(11)	0	

* The numbers in each column include responses from people who offered various responses as categorized in Table 2. For example, the TOO MUCH column in Table 3 includes people from TOO MUCH ON SOME, etc.

These sorts of inclinations find expression in another way. The men were asked which of three items was most important for good government:

TABLE 4
Most Important for Good Government

	% Saying	N
Enough jobs to go around	48	39
Freedom of speech	36	30
A powerful army, navy, and air force	12	10
Don't know	4	3

On another set of three alternatives, there was a similar pattern of choices:

TABLE 5
Most Important for Good Government

	% Saying	N
Equal treatment for all	60	49
Fighting communism	17	14
Lots of aid to the poor	15	12
Don't know	8	7

Questions of equality and employment are foremost, with military and anticommunist options chosen by relatively few. This appears in accord with the previous findings which show the "domestic" politics, bread-and-butter orientation of the poor.[10]

Many of the men brought the Vietnam war up spontaneously during their interviews, emphasizing that they felt the cost of the war was hurting the chances for aid to those who need it at home. One man makes this point very emphatically:

The only way to help the poor man is to get out of that war in Vietnam. They're spending so much money the poor man— I mean—like social security—that goes up all the time. I don't mind paying social security if the old people going to get it. 'Cause some day I might be old. These taxes—high taxes—it's going over yonder to kill people with and I don't see no cause in it.

Another man can't understand why America can't end the war after having invested so much in powerful armaments.

. . . And another thing I can't understand is this war in Vietnam. They send billions and billions of dollars for missiles and atomic warfare and stuff like that and now this war's going on there for a right good while and I read in the paper how many Americans have been killed. I can't see no use in

that if they're going to have this war and spend money for
these things and have that kinda power if they're not gonna
use it. . . .

Here we see an implicit connection established between a
concern with the government's wasting money and a desire
for an escalation of the war.

But we can approach the question of grievance in another
fashion: by asking people about the problems of daily life
and finding out how they think government might relate to
these problems. We went about this in two ways. First, we
asked a set of questions about matters such as rent, prices,
and interest rates that we thought might concern poor
people. Second, we asked people what they found to be their
biggest personal problem. In both cases, we then followed
up by trying to find out if the person saw any role for the
government in helping him to deal with what he perceived
as a problem.

It turns out that most of the people we spoke to felt, first,
that there were things they needed day-to-day but couldn't
afford; second, that things cost too much these days; and
third (for that half of the sample which had borrowed
money), that interest rates were too high. Asked about
their biggest personal problem, approximately 75 percent
spoke of troubles that would come under the heading of
health, money, education, and housing. Twenty percent said
they had no big problems, and a few simply didn't know.

While 96 percent of the sample say that things cost too
much these days, 77 percent say they favor governmental
price controls (20 percent don't know). When asked whether
the government should help them with things they can't
afford, 75 percent (of those who say they need things they
can't afford) say yes. On the question of interest rates, 94
percent of those who have had to make a loan feel that the
government should help people like themselves borrow
money. (And 76 percent of these people feel that interest
rates are not fair.)

On the question of personal problems, 32 percent feel they are already receiving some assistance from the government, and all are able to specify what that assistance is.[11] Less than half, however, feel that the government is helping them enough, and most of those who complain can particularize their demand for additional aid. When we turn to those individuals who say that the government is not helping them with their biggest personal problem, 61 percent feel that it ought to be helping, and many of these people can spell out what sort of help they mean.

Speaking about their personal problems and the government's relationship to those problems, these men show four tendencies. First, many call openly and explicitly for government assistance and, in addition, make specific recommendations. One man, who states that he needs milk and meat and other proper food for his family (instead of dry beans), responds in the following way to a question about whether the government is helping him now:

—I don't see where it helps—they taking money away from us.
—Why don't they help?
—They just ain't worried about the man. I mean the average man. The men up in Congress and all, they got money. They know their family going to eat. . . .
—Should the government help?
—I think they ought to . . . they ought to have a store, some kind of store where clothes is not as high as they are in other places . . . I think they ought to have stores set aside for a man with a certain income . . . when you file your income tax, if your income is so low, they send you like an ID card and you go in that store, that grocery store, and buy foods. . . . Have stores in each town set up and let you buy your food, clothes, maybe a man could make it.

Other men have other remedies to suggest, which focus on increasing present benefits and services and instituting controls on costly items. A second tendency is ambivalence in regard to government assistance: some men seem to want ad-

ditional help but cannot bring themselves actually to ask for
it or demand it. Complaining that he has trouble buying
medicine and food, one man says the government ought to
let him draw more money.

> —Does the government help in this way now?
> —Yes, they help some
> —What do they do?
> —Well, they give me $71 and something or other, or some-
> body's giving it to me. Anyway, it comes.
> —Do you think anything else should be done?
> —I wouldn't say that, because the government is spending a
> lot of money now, and I tell you I can make out with what
> I'm getting but I would *love* to have more. But if it's going
> to end with the war, or end with—I wouldn't want to—in
> fact, the more you give people, the more they want. But I'm
> talking about people who need it and just aren't able to
> work. . . .

A third pattern might best be called bewildered resignation. For example:

> —Does the government help with your personal problems?
> —No
> —Why not?
> —I don't know. I guess they go down the line, and I'm at the
> bottom of the line.

The expression of ignorance about why the government fails
to provide help or to take proper action is extremely common. When pressed on the question of why the government
does not do what they would like it to do, very few of the
men can even begin to provide an answer. One man, who
begins by endorsing what the goverment is doing, concludes
with an unusually open expression of personal bewilder-
ment:

> Oh, they going to provide better jobs. There ain't no use to
> even get in an argument in politics about that. 'Cause the gov-
> ernment is doing a good job as it is. I don't see a thing wrong
> with the way government is doing things. The government is
> set up all right. They're doing a good job and everything.

But there could be a lot of changes made which there should be changes made. The onliest way they'll get this world out is to change things. But I don't know what to tell 'em to change 'cause I don't know. I don't know what the trouble is and I don't know what the set-up is.

A few men argue against government assistance with their personal problems or feel that the government is already providing enough help. Drawing on a metaphor of moccasined individualism, one man maintains:

I believe in each man carrying his own canoe.

We approached the question of grievance in another fashion—this time more abstractly, by asking questions about America and the American government. We wanted to see if poor people saw the government as benevolent or malevolent; if they saw the society as free or oppressive. Beyond these questions of mood, we wanted to see if people could speak in specifics, to what degree they could particularize their grievances. The results are set out in the tables below.

Sometimes people say this is a "free country." Does that mean anything to you?

	%	
Yes, free country	45	(The major meaning assigned to freedom was in personal terms—"doing what you want to do." A very few people mentioned religious freedom and equal rights.)
No, not free	44	(The answers here included nine different meanings. The major ones were: discrimination against Negroes; the cost of things and taxes; government regulation; the powerlessness of the poor; foreign involvements, and forcing integration. A plurality of responses focused on racial questions.)
Don't Know	11	

The question about "freedom" often evoked easily understandable responses, such as the one from a man who argued
this way:

> There's not but two free people in this country, and that's a
> Negro woman and a white man . . . because a Negro woman
> can go anywhere she pleases and so can a white man. A white
> woman cannot go in the colored neighborhood . . . and a
> Negro man better not be caught in a white neighborhood.

But in many cases, responses seemed to refer to deeply felt
but unfocused feelings—whether of anger or relief.

> If this is my home, I can go in and out. There are some places
> where you don't have the privilege of going out at night. If
> they tell you to go in you have to.

> It's free to a certain extent and then it's not. . . . There's a
> lot of ways it's not free. You about pay your way for every-
> thing you do. . . . You gotta right to go when you want to
> and do what you want to as long as you don't break the law.
> But there are a lot of laws. You can't hardly go down the
> street that you don't break a law.

Such statements are hard to interpret. Behind them, perhaps, stands a fear of powerlessness, a sense that the world is
beyond one's control. The privilege of going in and out of
one's house can mean a great deal to someone who feels
excluded from most aspects of a society's life. It is also probably worth noting the association of "freedom" with the idea
of paying-your-way. This severe limitation on "freedom," as
the poor experience it, finds more complete expression in
another man's response to this question:

> . . . you can't ever go out here and work and make a living.
> You got to pay taxes on what salary you make. That's buying
> your job. . . . Your food's taxed. You got to pay the grocery
> man's price and a tax on top of that . . . the water that God
> made for everybody—you got to pay for that. You can't even
> go fishing or hunting—you got to have a license. . . .

Now some people say that the government in Washington mostly takes away people's freedom, but others say that the government helps to make people free. How do you feel about it? (People were allowed to choose both responses if they wanted to.)

	%	
Takes away freedom	45	(Most responses focus on government regulation and forcing racial contact. But others include the draft, laws favoring the rich, and the role of police.)
Helps freedom	58	(Again a plurality of the responses assign meaning in terms of race—in this case, the government promoting integration and upholding rights; other responses cite help for the poor, the need for laws and regulations, and protection provided by the military.)

Do you feel the government ever really hurts (helps) the ordinary person these days?

	%	
Hurts, Yes	64	There are three main specifics here: the government's failure to do enough for the ordinary man, high prices, and taxes—the last being most common.
Helps, Yes	72	Nine different specific areas are mentioned: social security, welfare, housing, poverty programs, highways, mental-health programs, civil-rights laws, education, government jobs. A majority mention as "help" something in the social security-welfare-housing category.[12]

Many of those who agree that the government does supply some help to the ordinary man maintain there is more it could be doing. The following quotes are from men all of whom thought that the government did help already:

. . . I drawed $54 social security and I drawed $27 welfare and health.
—Are there other ways the government could help?
—Well, I look at it this way—if every man in America I'd say 73 years old or the ones at the proper age—I think if he drawed $100 a month I don't think it would be too much.

. . . the country's in such a shape. The only way to help the poor man is to get out of that war in Vietnam. They're spending so much money, the poor man—I mean like social security, that goes up all the time. . . .

. . . they're too busy spending money on roads and abroad.
. . . The government is looking out for, shall I say . . . they're taking money building up the rich areas, people that have the money. And the other, they're sending it to people in Europe when they should be keeping some money over here to help their own people.

But when we move from a discussion that can focus on grievances to questions related to particular programs and to linkages between grievances and public action, we see that a considerable number of these people have not formulated opinions. For example, we saw earlier that more than 90 percent of these men feel day-to-day items cost too much, and more than 75 percent of them favor price controls. We then asked them why price controls were not in effect right now. Our expectation here was that in attempting to explain the absence of a government action they felt was important, these men would spell out the dynamics of the political system as they saw it. We might even encounter a certain degree of "ideological" analysis here. It didn't turn out that way. On the question of why there weren't price controls, 73 percent couldn't respond at all. A few (7 percent) argued that price controls *were* in effect; another 21 percent offered the sort of answer we expected would be more common—an answer, vague though it was, that placed blame for unresolved grievance. They said, The leaders don't try. The same pattern prevailed on other questions about the "why" of political events. And few of the men could name groups that believed as they did or opposed their beliefs.[13]

CONCLUSIONS

A recent survey finds that poorer Americans (under $5,000) are far less likely to favor a race to the moon than are wealthier Americans (over $10,000). The figures are 22 percent compared with 56 percent.[14] This is in accord with what we saw of poor people's attitudes in Durham. Richard Hamilton, in a recent discussion of mass support for "tough" military initiatives, found that poorer people were less likely to favor American involvements in Korea and Vietnam and were more likely to support negotiations and de-escalation.[15] This also finds some support in the Durham interviews.[16] The content of those interviews gives us some idea of why poorer people should react in this fashion. The dominant theme is the sense of being cheated: one's government is not concerned enough with one's well-being; one's government is willing to spend money on what appear to many of these men as frivolous or illegitimate enterprises while it fails to meet their own deeply felt day-to-day needs.

In keeping with this sense of deprivation, we also found a desire among the poor for some sort of assistance from the government, and a series of dissatisfactions with the kind of work the government was engaged in. It is interesting to reflect that Herbert McClosky, in his article "Consensus and Ideology in American Politics," [17] found that mass attitudes were far more favorable to economic equality than were the attitudes of political elites. Oddly, McClosky took some pains to show the greater agreement on democratic "essentials" that existed among political activists as compared with

the mass public: essentials such as censorship, procedural
due process, academic freedom. McClosky, curiously, chose
to ignore in his analysis his own data on economic equality.
He refused to allow this set of findings to disturb his conclusions and brushed it off by arguing that economic welfare
was not so clearly a component of what democracy meant.
But to whom? It was, he argued, a matter of opinion. Yet he
failed to acknowledge that censorship, due process, and Fifth
Amendment rights were also controversial matters—this was
precisely why he had investigated opinion about them.[18]
More recently, Form and Rytina[19] have found that poorer
people are more likely to support an image of politics in
which no one group has predominant power, while wealth-
ier people are more likely to support business dominance.
They also find, in keeping with the Durham interviews and
many other attitude surveys, that poorer Americans are
more likely to favor government involvement in helping
the disadvantaged in our society.

Discussions of ideology have frequently overlooked or
slighted the obvious preference of poorer Americans for an
increased degree of economic well-being. In particular, if we
reflect now on the analyses of "ideology" offered by Converse and Lane, we can draw the following conclusions:

1. The particular questions asked and the manner in
which they are asked will probably have decisive effects on
the findings, particularly among the poorer, less educated
respondents. Converse bases his discussion of the lack of
ideological "constraint" in the American public on responses to questions administered in survey style and based
upon political issues, such as public ownership of utilities,
that were of concern to elites at the time. He is probably
right when he questions the reliability of such questions and
methods in getting at the concerns of much of the American
population.[20] A failure to respond to such questions in a consistent way does not imply, as Converse concludes, that large
portions of the electorate do not have meaningful beliefs

about politics. We have seen, for example, that within certain limits people can reflect meaningfully on what they expect of government within the context of their own personal problems. One would expect such responses to show considerable consistency over time—depending both on life circumstances and on the strategies of various political groupings.

More specifically, we should acknowledge that poor people have many grievances concerning both what the government does and what it does not do, ranging from taxation to racial integration to space programs and foreign wars. In addition, we should expect that poor people, again within certain limits, will be able to speak meaningfully about what they want to see government do or stop doing.

2. Ideology must be thought of in a manner more subtle than either Lane or Converse allowed for. First, grievances and issues must be distinguished. Significant portions of a population may have grievances without those grievances being shaped into issues by political activists. The reverse is also true: issues which many portions of the population neither understand, nor care much about may be debated among elites. Beyond this, latent grievances may exist which people are themselves unaware of and which can only be grasped or defined through unusually sensitive interviewing. These latent grievances are important if we are to understand the potentialities of a situation and some of the deeper emotions people feel. Neither Lane nor Converse makes these sorts of distinctions.

Second, politically relevant views have to be distinguished from concepts of how political systems work. A man may have grievances without knowing exactly who his friends and enemies are. The global concept of ideology as a utopian vision or a well-developed sense of justice encompassing a thorough world view should not obscure more common, mundane concerns. Lane's failure to deal with latent grievances, in the absence of what he regarded as a radical ideology, led him to conclude too quickly that because there were no revolutionaries there was also no bitterness.

One way to restructure the concept of ideology is to see it as an expression of concern about the distribution of resources—as the individual sees that distribution.

We would expect constraint among those issues an individual perceives as immediately relevant to himself. Among poor whites, for example, the race issue will be important because these people feel what they experience as the "bite" of equality.

3. The most vaguely developed aspect of poor people's (and most people's) political views is likely to be the area of explanation—why things happen and don't happen; who opposes what and why; how things can be changed. It is in this area that the linkage is made between personal grievances and political action. Without such a link, the grievances may remain inchoate or feebly articulated. This is where mass movements function: setting agendas, ordering priorities, communicating what is possible. Such movements have the most meaning for the creation of democracy where established institutions and parties have not been in touch with the latent sentiments of portions of the population. Such movements also serve as a focus for rage and resentment—such as the civil-rights movement does for many whites.[21]

I have not attempted here a thorough elaboration of the ideology of the poor, either black or white. I have tried to suggest, instead, that the poor have politically meaningful ideas and that it would be easy to miss this when reading some contemporary political science.[22] I have tried, implicitly, to argue for a focus on "grievance" when investigating the political ideas of poor people, rather than accepting the Burkean focus on legitimacy. Such an approach has importance for democratic theory, for it helps us to distinguish among the various "silences"—to differentiate between the bitter and the complacent. It will help us identify more clearly which people feel their needs are not being met and to identify grievances which have not been formulated as issues by political activists. If the political scientist is to be the physician of the body politic, he will first have to remove his own cataracts.

NOTES

1. This insightful pun is Howard Zinn's.
2. All quotes are from Burke's *Reflections on the Revolution in France.*
3. Robert E. Lane, *Political Ideology* (New York, The Free Press, 1962), esp. Ch. 21.
4. Jack L. Walker, "A Critique of the Elitist Theory of Democracy," *American Political Science Review,* LX (June 1966), 285–95.
5. Philip E. Converse, "The Nature of Belief Systems in Mass Publics," in David E. Apter, ed., *Ideology and Discontent* (New York, The Free Press, 1964), pp. 206–61.
6. Here racial differences seem significant. Among whites, of the 47 who responded, about a third (16) favored a new party. Of these 16, eight spoke of a socialist or labor party, and six of the Dixiecrat-type party. Among the Negroes, 25 of 29 respondents commented on the new party issue, and of these 25, twelve favored a new party. Of these 12, nine looked toward a party oriented toward labor, the poor, or the Negro. From this point on, a footnote will elaborate on those findings on which racial differences are significant. If no such footnote is found, this indicates that racial differences were relatively trivial.
7. There are sharp racial differences here. Three whites out of four say the government spends too much, whereas less than a third of the Negroes argue this way. The responses here show clearly the general tendency among whites to see government aid as going to other groups, particularly Negroes. Taking such a view, the best they can hope for is lower taxes, rather than imagining an improvement in the way government assistance is distributed.

8. Racial differences here are fascinating:

% SAYING

	WHITES	NEGROES
Enough Jobs	51	38
Freedom of Speech	26	55
Powerful army, etc.	17	3
Don't Know	6	3

The Negro emphasis on free speech probably reflects the problem of demonstrations and voting rights, which were important at the time.

9. Both whites and Negroes choose "equal treatment" about 60 percent of the time. But whites are more likely to choose Fighting Communism, and Negroes, Aid to the Poor.

% SAYING

	WHITES	NEGROES
Equal Treatment	59	59
Fight Communism	21	10
Aid to poor	11	21
Don't Know	10	10

This emphasis on equal treatment has different meanings to different men. For Negroes its meanings are obvious; for whites it represents a preference for what they regard as a fair shake from the government, as well as the notion that poorer people ought to receive more attention. The Aid to the Poor alternative may have been chosen by relatively few because of the widespread sense among these men that poor people ought to receive only the aid they really need to get started: the word "lots" therefore could be interpreted as meaning excessive aid. Equal, not preferential, treatment is what most of these men favor, at least verbally.

10. Overall, the picture on domestic vs. military priorities is a confusing one. The two previous tables have indicated a strong emphasis on welfare-state priorities, but other evidence is not as clear-cut. For example, asked if America should build additional military power, 46 percent were in favor, 27 percent against, and 27 percent didn't know. Sixty-six percent favor the Test Ban treaty, with 15 percent opposed. Twenty-nine percent favor the Bay of Pigs, with 24 percent opposed. On questions concerning the Vietnam War, the picture is also mixed, but on the whole, the Durham sample is more dovish than the national sample reported in S. Verba, et al., "Public Opinion and the War in Vietnam," American Political Science Review, June 1967. The Durham sample is

less likely to favor escalation and less likely to favor additional expenditures involving tax increases or cutting welfare state payments. On the other hand, this sample is less likely than the national sample to favor a coalition government and slightly more likely to favor atomic war with China. These issues will be explored more fully in a future article.

11. Of those who say they have serious problems, a somewhat larger percentage of Negroes is receiving government assistance.

12. On these questions, racial issues become prominent, and the differences between Negro and white responses are marked. On the question of a "free country," Negroes are less likely to respond negatively than are whites, 31 percent to 57 percent. On the question of taking away or helping freedom, whites are more than twice as likely (53 percent to 24 percent) to see the government taking away freedom, but only a little less likely to see it helping freedom (38 percent to 45 percent). When it comes to specifics, the racial issue is clearly dominant on this question—a plurality of the answers in terms of taking away freedom cite forced racial integration; a plurality of those in terms of helping freedom concern racial integration. On the question of the government helping or hurting the ordinary man, the pattern is somewhat similar. Four whites say the government hurts for every three who say it helps, where two Negroes say it helps for every one who says it hurts. Yet the racial issue itself does not loom large in the substantive responses to this question.

13. Of the twenty-two whites (42 percent) who named a group they felt was against the things they favored, seven spoke of business and the "rich," while ten named civil-rights groups. Among the Negroes, nine of the ten (34 percent) who named a group named business and the "rich."

14. Harris survey, *Washington Post,* July 31, 1967.

15. Richard F. Hamilton, "A Research Note on the Mass Support for 'Tough' Military Initiatives," *American Sociological Review,* XXXIII (June 1968), 439–45.

16. Harris has also reported on the greater reluctance of poorer Americans to support the sending of U.S. troops to aid Israel. Those in favor were: Under $5000, 17 percent; $5–10,000, 23 percent; $10,000 and up, 32 percent. *Washington Post,* June 10, 1967.

17. Herbert McClosky, "Consensus and Ideology in American Politics," *American Political Science Review,* June 1964.

18. There are other serious problems with McClosky's interpretations of his findings. See my "Communication," *American Political Sci-*

ence Review, December 1966, pp. 1000–1. Unfortunately, McClosky's data have not thus far been analyzed further in class or other terms.

19. William H. Form and Joan Rytina, "Ideological Beliefs on the Distribution of Power in the United States," *American Sociological Review*, XXXIV, (February 1969), 19–31.

20. The full passage in which Converse expresses his doubts goes this way: ". . . the discouragingly large turnover of opinion on these issues in the total mass public might be taken as evidence that the questions were poorly written and thus extremely unreliable and that the main lesson is that they should be rewritten. Yet the issues posed are those posed by political controversy, and citizens' difficulties in responding to them in meaningful fashion seem to proffer important insights into their understanding of the same political debates in real life. More crucial, still, what does it mean to say that an instrument is perfectly reliable vis-à-vis one class of people and totally unreliable vis-à-vis another. . . ." Converse, "Nature of Belief Systems," p. 244.

21. Goldwater was a popular candidate among whites. Forty-seven percent reported voting for him, 28 percent for Johnson, and 25 percent didn't vote. Johnson received the votes of 83 percent of the Negroes, 17 percent not voting. The conflicts within whites about race versus class orientation will be explored more fully in a future article.

22. See, for example, the discussion in Walter Dean Burnham, "The Changing Shape of the American Political Universe," *American Political Science Review*, March 1965, and A. Campbell and H. Valen, "Party Identification in Norway and the United States," *Public Opinion Quarterly*, Winter 1961.

Assimilation and Counter-Assimilation:

From Civil Rights to Black Radicalism

MICHAEL PARENTI

HISTORY, the anthropologist Irving Goldman once said, moves forward and it moves backward, and just when we think it is going one way we discover much to our grief, though sometimes to our gratitude, that it has turned in the other direction. It should come as no surprise that history is unpredictable and even perverse, yet to admit as much is somewhat un-American, for we Americans are dedicated to the proposition that events travel along a clearly defined, albeit occasionally bumpy, trajectory of progress; progress for our country in particular, and—to the exent that the experience of others is assumed to represent a linear extension of the American experience—progress for all mankind: from the howling wilderness to the machine-fed garden, from hardship to well-being, from bigotry to brotherhood.

The same holds true concerning our perceptions about ethnic life in America: there has been the long-standing belief held by public official and lonely scholar alike that the poor, downtrodden, and alien would become the prosperous, equal, and assimilated, and that the marginal group members would eventually immerse themselves indistinguishably in American life. A subvariant of this theory assumed that during the course of assimilation the different groups would contribute portions of their own culture to the dominant white Anglo-American culture, so that American society would emerge as a unique and exotic blend, an image immediately recognizable as the "melting pot"—undoubtedly the most popular and the least substantiated of all theories about ethnic life.[1]

For a student of ethnicity it has often been difficult to distinguish ideology from science. With a few notable exceptions, such as Horace Kallen, who valiantly advocated the preservation of subgroup cultural autonomy, most students have worked within an assimilationist ideological paradigm. Deeply committed to the belief that assimilation was ultimately the most desirable social solution, they have found it easy to conclude that assimilation was actually happening. History was thought to be moving along its trajectory, from divisiveness to unity, from alien pluralities to brotherly blends.

More recently a number of social scientists have begun to find the assimilationist paradigm unsatisfactory as an explanation. While others make conjectures about rates of assimilation, these social scientists are questioning whether assimilation actually has been taking place.[2] Perhaps the ethnics have not been assimilating, at least nowhere to the extent we have assumed. At first glance this seems a rather startling assertion. Have not old-world immigrant cultures all but disappeared? Are not the ethnics scattering into Americanized suburbs? Are they not enjoying better educational and income levels and wider occupational distributions?

As I have tried to indicate elsewhere[3] the analytic distinction between a *cultural* system, i.e., the system of beliefs, norms, symbols, and ideas, and a *social* system, i.e., the system of structured relations among individuals, institutions, classes, and groups, becomes a useful model for understanding the ethnic experience in America. Most studies show that by the second generation the ethnics make dramatic cultural transitions in the direction of the mainstream culture, i.e., they accomplish a more or less successful acculturation, but it is not at all clear that they incorporate themselves into the structural-group relations of the dominant social system. The group may become "Americanized" to a great extent in its cultural practices, but this says little about its social relations with the host society. In the face of widespread acculturation, the minority still maintains a social substructure encompassing primary and secondary group relations composed essentially of fellow ethnics of the same class status. This has been shown to be true in numerous community studies of Polish, Irish, Italian, Jewish, Scandinavian, and certainly black groups. Indeed, it is the absence of wide-scale assimilation that allows us to talk about such communities as identifiable ethnic entities.

Other studies indicate: (*a*) Ingroup social links persist even when the geographical continuity of the first settlement area is broken up. That is to say, there is frequently a regrouping in second settlement areas, with suburban ethnic-class stratification and residential patterns bearing a rough resemblance to urban patterns. (*b*) There still exists a vast proliferation of ethnic formal associations, be they professional, business, labor, veteran, educational, church, charitable, recreational, fraternal, political, or informal ingroup associations as found in neighborhood, work, personal friendship, and extended kinship relations. (*c*) The upward occupational mobility of ethnics has been generally overrated. While individual ethnics have won access to professional roles previously beyond their reach, there is no evidence of any substantial convergence of intergroup status levels. If today's ethnics enjoy a better living standard than did their parents, it is due to the across-the-board rise throughout America. Fewer pick-and-shovel jobs and more white-collar positions for minority members are less the result of upward mobility than of an overall structural transition in the composition of our labor force.[4]

The structural changes in the economy have not worked to much advantage for the black man. Recent years have brought a massive obliteration of the unskilled jobs which were the mainstay of the earlier immigrant work force (down from ten million to four million in the last decade), with the poor black being the hardest hit.

Any discussion of assimilation should take account of economic and class realities. To expect total ethnic assimilation is to expect a kind of social mobility and absorption which is not commonly found in a society characterized by highly advanced class divisions. While we have not been taught to think of America as a class-divided society—indeed, we have been quite consistently taught to think just the contrary— the fact is that relative income and occupational distributions among various ethnic groups in urban and suburban areas have remained in a more or less stable relationship to each other over the last two generations, with the WASPs and Northern Europeans on top, the relatively latecoming Eastern and Southern Europeans further below, and the blacks, Indians, Mexicans, and Puerto Ricans on the very bottom. Social stratification among ethnic groups, then, is at least partly a function of class stratification; ethnic cohesiveness is not merely the result of personal preference, but also the outcome of sharing more or less similar, and somewhat limited and particularized, accesses to the social structure. Minority cohesion is a phenomenon highly influenced by material and class considerations, and what we so often describe as "ethnic pluralism" might better be seen as inequalities in the class structure.

Besides the distinctions made between the cultural and social systems, one must take into account the personality system when discussing ethnic identity.[5] Even among those upwardly mobile individuals who achieve a pattern of social relations extending almost exclusively beyond their original ethnic and class group, that is, those who are both acculturated and assimilated, we find quite visible ethnic identifications. Insofar as the individual internalizes formative experiences from earlier social positions and subcultural matrices, he is never merely responding to his present sociocultural world; his character structure and his earlier identifications operate to some limited extent as independent mediators. It is a rare person, no matter how well assimilated, who reaches adulthood without some internalized feeling about his ethnic identifications, especially since such identifications are rarely neutral but are usually associated with affects and images relating to social status, marginality, and personal worth. Just as social assimilation moves along a slower path than that of acculturation, so does identity assimilation, or rather nonassimilation, enjoy a pertinacity not wholly dependent upon the other two processes. This is worth keeping in mind when we discuss black identity.

AMERICAN CULTURAL IMPERIALISM

Historically, the theoretical choice posed for the ethnic has been either isolated existence in quasi-autonomous cultural enclaves or total identificational immersion into American society. A few groups such as the Hasidic Jews, the Hutterites, and the Amish have sought the cultural-enclave solution, but the great bulk of ethnics have chosen neither of these "either-or" conditions. In 1915 Woodrow Wilson observed: "America does not consist of groups. A man who thinks of himself as belonging to a particular national group in America has not yet become an American." [6] Wilson's remark demonstrates that behind every questionable ideology there is bound to be some bad sociology. For example, note the following mistaken assumptions:

(1) There is an assumption that the behavior patterns and norms of two different cultural matrices are in all major respects mutually exclusive, and therefore, that communal unity necessitates the eradication of the weaker matrix. In fact, the marginal and dominant cultures *are* mutually exclusive in some ways; hence there is always a need for some acculturation in the direction of the cultural group which owns and controls the dominant social, economic, and polit-

ical institutions. The ethnic who wants entrance into the mainstream in order to make a living finds that he must master some of the linguistic and social skills of the dominant society and learn to behave like something close to the Anglo-American prototype. But acculturation is a multifaceted process covering everything from religious beliefs to gesticulation styles, and even among those who have acculturated to certain American life patterns, residual subcultural practices and values may be retained. Some of these may be marginal to important social action, e.g., certain food preferences, while others, e.g., religious value orientations, may affect social and political predispositions in vital ways.[7] In short, cultures are not completely mutually exclusive; there is room for transmutation, synthesis, overlap, and ambidexterity. Unable to recognize this, the nativists embarked upon a protracted Americanization program, conducted by public officials, local communities, patriotic societies, the mass media, and by that most effectively chauvinistic of all American social institutions, the public schools; it was a campaign predicated on the belief that a thorough eradication of alien cultural traits, no matter how innocent, beautiful, and lively these traits might have been, was a precondition for producing Americans. No consideration was given to the cost paid by the ethnic in self-respect and cultural growth.[8]

(2) The nativist-assimilationist view that an individual cannot be both American and something else fails to recognize that a person's position in the social system is not exclusively determined by one particular group but that all individuals enjoy multiple group membership. It follows that a person's identity is not, as Woodrow Wilson and other nativists assumed, an indivisible quality. In reality, a person experiences cumulative identities which are sometimes incongruous but usually complementary. For the ethnic, a minority-group identity is not necessarily incompatible with an American loyalty any more than is a regional, class, or

other particular group attachment. Indeed, *the ethnic identity is usually asserted in a context of American chauvinism.* Thus, parading on Columbus Day and taking pride that an Italian discovered America and that Italians "helped build this country" is as much an affirmation of one's Americanism as of one's ingroup pride. The affirmation of the group's worth and status is measured by the standards of nationalism and patriotism set down by the dominant belief system.

(3) Finally, the nativist assertion that one is either 100 percent American or else un-American does not coincide with actual nativist practice. Since the beginning of our nation, the native population has wanted minority groups to acculturate or "Americanize," a process entailing the destruction of alien customs and appearances offensive to American sensibilities. But this was not to be taken as an invitation into Anglo-American primary-group relations. It seems the nativists well understood the distinction between acculturation and assimilation: in a word, die for Old Glory but stay out of my country club. They wanted the ethnic to feel undivided loyalty to America without his demanding an undivided social acceptance into Anglo-American society, and more specifically, without his demanding a greater return for his labor and a fairer allocation of the system's material wealth. Demands which were intended to ease the hardships of his lower-class existence were taken as signs of "alien subversion." [9] Loyalty to Americanism became loyalty to the system as it was, an acceptance of the dominant credo of a capitalist culture, a credo which assured the populace that men got pretty much what they deserved and that ours was the "most perfect system." While strenuously propagating an ideological acculturation, dominant white Protestant America discouraged any tampering with the ongoing arrangements of class privilege and power which was the material base of structural nonassimilation.

BLACK IDENTITY AND COUNTERASSIMILATION

Turning specifically to the blacks and to the question of
an emerging black identity, I think one can get the sense of
my opening statement about history moving in a direction
contrary to our anticipations. The agitations and demonstrations of the late 1950s and early 1960s, which we saw as
the great leap forward in race relations, "the Negro Revolution," some called it in 1963, now seem to have changed direction and taken a counterassimilationist course.

Some obvious things must be said about black people in
America, to wit: of all the marginal groups they have
experienced the cruelest material and psychic deprivations,
the most thorough destruction of their self-respect and manhood, the most frequent and ruthless violence against their
persons. The occasions on which they could forget their
marginal identity are more limited than for other groups.
Few things so perpetuate ingroup awareness as outgroup oppression; generally, the greater the animosity, exclusion,
abuse, and disadvantage caused by class and race oppression,
the more will ethnic self-awareness permeate the individual's feelings.

The same may not be true of *class* awareness. To be sure,
poor blacks know they are poor, but the diagnosis of cause
and the idiom of protest are most readily couched in racial
rather than class terms by both blacks and white liberals. By
ascribing the black man's plight to a universal white racism,
undifferentiated in its motives and effects, liberals do not
have to look into the system of economic exploitation, price
gouging, and profit seeking which has victimized the black
man from his earlier days as a seasonal hand on the corporate-
owned farm to his present life in the northern ghetto.

Those who anticipated that blacks would "work their way
up the ladder" quietly and gradually as other minority
groups had done entertained an imperfect notion of both

the future and the past. The white minority groups have not moved *up* but have moved *in* at certain modest levels of the social structure. While unskilled jobs have been disappearing over the last two decades, semiskilled and moderately skilled and just plain stable ones are not opening up fast enough. The bulk of the Poles, Italians, Irish, Jews, etc., who took over the building and garment trades, the sanitation, fire and police departments, school teaching, welfare, and other such municipal services, and the small businesses and marginal services, including the rackets, did not move on to greater heights—as the American Dream would have it; they were still there and very much in control when the blacks began to demand entry. *Rather than following in the immigrant experience, the black man has been a victim of it,* held back and even displaced from trades and jobs in order to make way for the immigrant white newcomers.

Until recently, with notable exceptions, blacks remained, like other Americans, firm suporters of the assimilationist tradition, it being assumed that with time and fortitude the battle for easier access into mainstream society would eventually be won. It was further assumed by many that if the Negro, as he was then called, was to win a fairer share of the available life chances, he would need integration, first and foremost. It was the deeply internalized credo of the black bourgeois moderate and of the white liberal (and often still is) that America was to move away from color distinctions and color awareness. There was an assumption that integration was not only the ultimate goal, it was the necessary first condition for race betterment. Just as A. J. Muste used to say, Don't ask what is the way to peace, peace is the way, so it was believed that integration was not only the goal, it was the way, the means to effect all sorts of psychic and substantive benefits for blacks and whites.

By the mid-1960s blacks began to say publicly what they had known all along, that a deprived group's advancement in the face of majority hostility depends in part on its ability to develop countervailing power. Stripped of its rhetoric, this is what black power is about. One of the first explanations of black power was presented by a Negro leader several years before the term actually came into vogue: "History is the long and tragic story of the fact that privileged groups seldom give up their privileges voluntarily. . . . We know through painful experience that freedom is never voluntarily given by the oppressor; it must be demanded by the oppressed." So wrote Martin Luther King from Birmingham City Jail in 1963. However, to achieve such power the black man would have to develop his own organizational structure and leadership, and this essentially is black separatism. Stated in those terms, why did such a conventional idea cause such anguish? Considering that most ethnic groups have advanced their positions in part by developing their own labor, business, political, legal, educational, and communal institutions, "it is," as Piven and Cloward note, "puzzling to hear that Negroes must restrain themselves from following the same course." [10] Actually, it is less puzzling when we recall that those who insist that blacks must achieve total social assimilation into American life remain either ignorant of, or indifferent to the fact that no prominent ethnic group has achieved such assimilation. Once we realize this we might pause and ask, What exactly do we mean by "total integration" for blacks? The negative reaction against black power also arises in part from the failure to appreciate that power is not colorless. As James Boggs observed, power in America is white, and Americans "accept white power as so natural that they do not even see its color." [11]

Finally, the opposition to black nationalism is less puzzling if we keep in mind that people do not easily surrender their ideologies and that no one is more committed to the ideology of limitless assimilation, and hence more resistant to the ideas of black power and black separatism, than the integrationists—specifically, the black moderates and white liberals. For the black militant leaders, however, the goal is not integration but self-realization, and this means the propagation of cultural, social, and identificational forces that are counterassimilationist. Assimilation into white society is rejected as unattainable in its idealized version (i.e., the total social integration of black and white in loving brotherhood and the eradication of all antagonistic racial distinctions), unattainable in the foreseeable future, and therefore a cruel chimerical goal to hold before the black man.

Assimilation, the militants believe, is also self-defeating in its present piecemeal tokenism, insofar as it dissipates black militancy, absorbs black talent, and obfuscates black consciousness, while bringing very little substantive return to the black masses. "Those institutions in the black community which are 'integrated,' whether political organizations, the rackets, or social welfare agencies—actually contribute to black impotence," suggest Piven and Cloward, "for they are integrated only in the sense that they are dominated by whites and serve white interests." [12] "Integration," Nathan Wright, Jr., argues, ". . . has clearly failed. There can be no meaningful integration between unequals. . . ." So that we do not conclude that the antiassimilationists are really segregationists, we might quote Wright further: "No rising ethnic group in this nation has, on its own, asked for integration. All have asked simply for desegregation. Desegregation involves some integration as a means to an end but not as an end in itself. Desegregation involves the clearing of the decks of all barriers to free choice relationships which do not interfere with the rights of others." [13] Black nationalists support the removal of legal and de facto barriers that loom as instruments of racial insult and oppression. What they deny is that the black man's salvation can come only through piecemeal absorption into white institutions. They contend that integration is predicated on the presumption that only the white man's presence can make the black man feel whole. "Integration," Stokely Carmichael believes, ". . .

speaks to the problem of blackness in a despicable way. As a goal, it has been based on complete acceptance of the fact that *in order to have* a decent house or education, blacks must move into a white neighborhood or send their children to a white school. This reinforces, among both black and white, the idea that 'white' is automatically better and 'black' is by definition inferior. This is why integration is a subterfuge for the maintenance of white supremacy." [14] The Negro who cries "Love me so I can love myself; accept me so I can accept myself" is still waiting for the white man to set him free.

"Assimilation," Alvin Poussaint, a psychiatrist, said, "by definition always takes place according to the larger societal (white) model of culture and behavior, and thus the Negro must give up much of his black identity and subculture to be comfortably integrated." [15] Here Poussaint is using assimilation to include acculturation as I have defined it, and this might lead us to a second point concerning the emerging black nationalism: it is not only counterassimilationist, it is to a large extent counteracculturationist. It calls not only for new black social organizations but for a new cultural metaphysics, a new valuational system, and a new self-identity. Until recently, as just noted, assertions of Negro identity were integrationist, a commitment described by Harold Isaacs, after extended interviews with numerous Negro leaders and Negro professional men, as "the most vehement insistence on being *American,* a refusal to entertain any notion of a hyphenated identity like Afro-American." One of his respondents is quoted as saying, "I'm an American first and a Negro second." [16] Included in such an identification was an internalized conviction concerning one's inferiority, a sense of shame and even loathing about one's African origins and black heritage,[17] an evasion of black identifications and a desire for association with traits deemed desirable by the dominant culture, described in brief as "the longing for whiteness and the flight from blackness." This "escapist" phenomenon, as it affected the Negro middle class, has been described by E. Franklin Frazier and by Nathan Hare.[18]

What we have now is a "revolution" in cultural and personal identification—a change in historical direction which might be summarized as the unwillingness to strive for or accept the value definitions of the white world. The group no longer measures its own worth by the standards set down by the dominant culture; instead it seeks to construct distinctly black moral, social, and aesthetic values. This reconstruction entails an emphasis rather than a de-emphasis on color awareness. It is no longer contended that blacks are really just like whites, only a little darker, but that they are something distinct unto themselves, something quite different. Blackness is celebrated as virtuous, meaningful, and beautiful. There is a new commitment to a distinct cultural heritage, an open association with African history, language, music, art and aesthetics, and the neglected subject of black history in America, a new assertion of black manhood, and an assertion of the right to armed self-defense against white violence. Here one cannot overestimate the influence of the Black Muslims. Propelled from the status of obscure cult to national limelight in 1962–1963 by white mass media that were shocked by Elijah Muhammad's "black racism," the Muslims have offered a model of moral regeneration, racial aesthetics, and psychocollective identification which other black nationalists have wholeheartedly adopted, minus the more exotic Islamic paraphernalia, cultist theology, and authoritarianism that one associates with the Black Muslim sect.[19]

This new cultural and identificational assertion is qualitatively different from the kind of ingroup self-glorification common among the other ethnic groups which always emphasized the group's devotion and contribution to America and the legitimacy of its status in America, a kind of celebration which the black bourgeoisie often indulged in on behalf of the Negro.[20] The new black identification has little room in it for the liturgy of American patriotism. The assertion "I am an American who happens to be a Negro" is replaced by the declaration "I am a black man who happens to be living—and not very freely or happily—in white America." The standard pluralist rhetoric about how one individual is many things, an American, a teacher, a veteran, a family man, a citizen of Philadelphia, and a Negro, is replaced by the all-abiding "I am a black man." There is a shift away from multiple role identifications and toward a more compelling monochromatic role definition (quite literally monochromatic—one color) which operates as a determining and pre-emptive factor in the individual's other role performances; hence one thinks of oneself as a black teacher, a black veteran, a black father, a black citizen; ideally the ordinary life roles are now endowed with a special expectation and commitment.

Most black nationalists seemed to agree that blacks should not be dedicated to advancing themselves within the white system but to creating that which is distinctly black, the assumption being that black cultural and social arrangements will be purer, finer, and more "soulful" than those devised by the joyless, grasping white man. At this point, the students of European, Slavic, Asian, and American nationalisms should be impressed by the accuracy of the designation "black *nationalism*." There is the same call for a people to find themselves, return to their sacred heritage, cast off the oppressor, and *not change places with him but become something better than he*. It is the familiar theme that the oppressed shall regenerate and lead, a theme as old as the Old Testament reiterated by Treitschke, Mazzini, Gandhi, and by almost every nationalist and nativist movement.[21] Blacks must develop what is most revolutionary, revitalizing, and regenerating, and this, it is contended, can only come from a deep attachment and experience with black culture and black institutions.

As a first step toward achieving this revitalization, black

separatists have advocated community control of local schools, and separate black studies programs in colleges, to counteract what is felt to be the suffocating and oppressive influence of white cultural imperialism and white American superpatriotism. Black control of local schools would probably bring an immediate improvement in *élan* and a more realistic and relevant curriculum—as was the case in the Ocean Hill-Brownsville district in New York in the autumn of 1968. Though a community-controlled education would be far from perfect, it could never be as demeaning, punitive, mindless, and bureaucratic as that usually found in the ghetto school system. Black community control of such things as schools, housing, businesses, police, and welfare services will not be easy (if at all possible) to achieve. As the United Federation of Teachers demonstrated in New York, there are many entrenched interests which do not care to see control of material resources pass into other hands; this resistance has led growing numbers of black militants to conclude that the challenge must be directed against the entire sociopolitical system itself.

BLACK RADICALISM

It is a measure of the times that those "gains" which would have seemed so heartening in 1960, viz., a Negro on the Supreme Court, a Negro in the President's Cabinet, a Negro in the Senate (all accomplished during the Johnson administration), seem so much less impressive in 1970. Rather than taken as a sign of inevitable progress, such advances are usually discounted by black militants as tokenism. The accession of a select few to new positions in the old system represents no gain for the masses. That Ralph Bunche had brunch at the White House brings neither peace to the urban ghettos nor food to the Mississippi Delta. To some black militants, the black sheriff or black senator or landlord or bureaucrat who replaces his white opposite number but propagates the same values and gives the same performance as his predecessor is merely an extension of the same white power structure in dark face.

To be sure, most black leaders still think in a racial rather than a class idiom and their major concern is not for the dispossessed of all colors but for the special plight of the black man. To the extent that attention is accorded to the exploitative features of the system, the victims are seen as blacks and the exploiters as whites. Some militant blacks have even denounced white radicals—as when LeRoi Jones spoke of the "subversives" in Newark in 1968. But militants such as H. Rap Brown and Eldridge Cleaver have moved beyond the simple "white is oppressing black" theme and toward a critique of American society as a system maintained by oppressive economic and political institutions which must be overturned root and branch. According to this view, the abolition of white racism within the present social structure will not cure the black man's ills, since both black and white will still be living under the same oppressive economic system. Thre is even some question as to whether the white man could *ever* discard his racism in a system which measures the value of his life and soul by his capacity for competitive acquisitiveness. Only the end of class privilege, profit, and exploitation along with all the coercive abuses, anxieties, and warped values which are needed to maintain and protect such a system, the radicals contend, will bring justice for the black poor and other dispossessed groups.

The emphasis on *class* consciousness rather than *race* consciousness is especially pronounced among the Black Panthers. The party's chairman, Bobby Seale, stated:

> The Black Panther Party is not a black racist organization . . . because Huey P. Newton and Eldridge Cleaver understood and taught us that it was not a race struggle but a class struggle—A CLASS struggle. . . .
> Every human being must understand—every . . . brother and sister must realize we will not fight racism with racism

but that we will fight racism with *solidarity*. We will not fight capitalism with capitalism (black capitalism) but we must fight capitalism with socialism. We can never—nor can they (other nations)—even try to fight U.S. imperialism, with more imperialism, but we will fight it with proletarian internationalism.[22]

The move toward a reassertion of black culture is dismissed by the Panthers in the harshest terms. "Cultural nationalism" is treated as a foolish charade propagated, as one Panther irreverently puts it, by "the cultural nigger nationalist draped in a dashiki, sandals, and other cultural paraphernalia, and speaking ooga booga," [23] the effect of which is to distract the black man from the real revolutionary class struggle and divide the poor and the oppressed along color lines. In a similar vein, H. Rap Brown writes: "To be Black is necessary, but not sufficient . . . when you begin to stress culture without politics, people can become so hooked up in the beauty of themselves that they have no desire to fight." [24] Better to read Mao than Jones; better to learn revolutionary discipline than Swahili. Black culture, the radicals in SNCC and in the Panther Party are reminding the Afro-nationalists, is not black power, and black power itself is a meaningless concept unless a proper diagnosis is made of the causes of powerlessness. These causes are to be found in the system of ruling-class profit and control which victimizes both black and white at home and throughout the world.

Whatever the merits of the Panther attack on cultural nationalism, it does raise a question which the black separatists have not confronted: By what process does the propagation of African dress, art, language, and other such cultural accouterments bring about the structural changes needed to better the lot of the black masses? If, as I noted earlier, social, cultural, and personality systems often respond to imperatives that operate independently of each other, then we might well witness a black identificational-aesthetic-cultural revolution without ever seeing a social revolution, that is, without the kind of fundamental reallocations of goods, services, property controls, and operational values which the more radical blacks claim are needed in order to bring justice and freedom to the dispossessed. (Parenthetically, I might observe that it is not a settled point that black cultural awareness is, as the Panthers say, a distraction from effective radical protest. It may well be that many blacks cannot embrace the kind of commitment to revolutionary challenge which the Panthers advocate without first asserting a separatist racial identity of the kind that leaves them less inclined to follow the path of Thurgood Marshall and Ralph Bunche and more inclined to experience and express the full extent of their alienation from, and disgust with, the present white social system. Cultural awareness may nurture a sense of self and group and a criticism of the oppressive system, thereby moving the ex-Negro first toward black nationalist militancy and then toward a more ideological class position.)

The issue of "black community control" also poses some unresolved questions. A tenuous control over municipal services and eventually over the municipal government itself and other such gains may not bring the kinds of beneficial transformations which the separatists desire. As various municipal officials have noted, the problems which the cities face are greater than their ability to deal with them. Municipal governments are highly dependent and vulnerable creatures whose options are limited and preempted by socioeconomic forces which command markets, resources, and political power extending far beyond the city limits. Black control of local governments may bring certain ameliorations (which are not to be lightly dismissed), but such control is not likely to effect any fundamental changes in the national economic order and in those priorities which are determined by the dominant political and economic powers of America.

In sum, there seems no easy solution for blacks in America. The view that with more time and more education, blacks will assimilate into an Anglo-American culture and social structure, as have the immigrant groups, proffers an outdated and incorrect assimilationist ideology based on a misapprehension of what actually did happen to the other minority groups. The "immigrant analogy" of inevitable ethnic upward mobility breaks down in other respects also: while opportunities in colleges, firms, and professions seem to be opening up faster than the few mobile blacks can fill them, the pre-emption by other ethnic groups of what otherwise might be considered natural employment areas for working-class blacks, and the technological changes in the urban and rural labor markets, are militating against the black masses.[25] Nor does the counterassimilation of cultural-identificational nationalism seem to promise solutions for the problems of racial and class oppression. Even the search for community control and the cry for "black power" seem but demands for some rather limited and insufficient resources within an essentially unsympathetic social structure.

The one challenge which seems commensurate with the enormous systemic inequities confronted by blacks is that which is posed by black radicals and revolutionaries. For that very reason, it is also the one which appears most improbable of realization, given the power realities of the present system. There seem few immediate prospects for successful revolutionary change in America. The combination of neglect, dole, co-optation, tokenism, economic exploitation, legal oppression and harassment, police violence, and selective assassination utilized by ruling whites to keep blacks in a deprived condition for the last three hundred years may keep them there for the foreseeable future. As of now (June 1969), almost every black radical leader, especially those in the Black Panther Party, is either under indictment or on appeal, in hiding or in jail (many have been incarcerated without trial because of an inability to raise astronomical bail sums). Numerous black radicals have been subjected to

interminable harassments, arrests, beatings, and stake-outs
and raids by police in states throughout the nation.[26]

Unless black consciousness becomes radical consciousness,
blacks will have to be content with the cultural trappings of
a new identity rather than with the substance of a new life
complete with equality and justice. But once black militancy assumes a genuine radical dimension, it becomes the
object of systematic police and court oppression.

It is not too much to say that only a transformation in the
political consciousness of black and *white* Americans can
bring about fundamental social change. To say that the
white majority must learn racial "tolerance" is to fall back
on the rhetoric of the 1950s. What whites need to develop is
a growing *intolerance* of the socioeconomic and political
values that have ruled and regulated the lives of all Americans in what William Sloane Coffin, Jr., describes as "the
established disorder." The irony of black militancy is that it
cannot achieve its fullest realization without a regeneration
of white sociopolitical values, especially if the goal is not
merely a decentralization of certain municipal services but
the reallocation of all political, social, and economic powers.

At present, widespread revolutionary commitments in the
white community do not seem imminent. But history, as we
noted, moves forward and it moves backward; yet if it
teaches us anything, it is that we must not close our eyes to
unexpected developments.

NOTES

1. For a critical discussion of the melting-pot and assimilation theories see Milton M. Gordon, *Assimilation in American Life* (New
   York, Oxford University Press, 1964).
2. See Erich Rosenthal, "Acculturation without Assimilation?" *American Journal of Sociology,* LXVI (November 1960), 275–88; Amitai
   Etzioni, "The Ghetto—a Re-evaluation," *Social Forces,* March

1959, pp. 255–62; J. Milton Yinger, "Social Forces Involved in Group Identification or Withdrawal," *Daedalus*, XC (Spring 1961), 247–62; Gordon, *Assimilation in American Life.*

3. Michael Parenti, "Ethnic Politics and the Persistence of Ethnic Identification," *American Political Science Review*, LXI (September 1967), 717–26; see also A. L. Kroeber and Talcott Parsons, "The Concepts of Culture and of Social System," *American Sociological Review*, XXIII (October 1958), 582–83.

4. References to the empirical evidence supporting these propositions can be found in Parenti, "Ethnic Politics."

5. See Talcott Parsons, "Malinowski and the Theory of Social System," in R. W. Firth, ed., *Man and Culture* (New York, Humanities Press, 1957).

6. Quoted in Oscar Handlin, *The American People in the Twentieth Century*, rev. ed. (Boston, Beacon Press, 1963), p. 121.

7. For examples of the latter see Michael Parenti, "Political Values and Religious Cultures: Jews, Catholics and Protestants," *Journal for the Scientific Study of Religion*, LX, No. 12 (1967), 259–69.

8. Oscar Handlin's poignant treatment of the immigrant child's experience in the public school is still worth reading; see his *The Uprooted* (Boston, Little, Brown and Co., 1951), Ch. 9.

9. See William Preston, Jr., *Aliens and Dissenters* (Cambridge, Mass., Harvard University Press, 1963).

10. Frances Fox Piven and Richard A. Cloward, "What Chance for Black Power?" *The New Republic*, March 30, 1968, pp. 19–23, one of the most penetrating analyses of the systemic, structural, and power realities which blacks face in America.

11. Boggs is quoted in Nathan Hare's "How White Power Whitewashes Black Power," in Floyd D. Barbour, ed., *The Black Power Revolt* (Boston, Sargent, Porter, 1968), p. 182.

12. Piven and Cloward, "What Chance for Black Power?"

13. Nathan Wright, Jr. "The Crises Which Bred Black Power," in Barbour, *Black Power Revolt*, p. 117.

14. Stokely Carmichael, "Power and Racism," *New York Review of Books*, September 22, 1966.

15. Dr. Alvin Poussaint "The Negro American: His Self-Image and Integration," *Journal of the American Medical Association*, LVIII (1966), 419–23; reprinted in Barbour, *Black Power Revolt*.

16. Harold R. Isaacs, *The New World of Negro Americans* (New York, John Day Co., 1963), p. 178.

17. *Ibid.*, pp. 105–324.

194   MICHAEL PARENTI

18. E. Franklin Frazier, *Black Bourgeoisie* (New York, Collier Books, 1962); Nathan Hare, *The Black Anglo-Saxons* (New York, Marzani & Munsell, Publishers, 1965).
19. E. U. Essien-Udom's *Black Nationalism: A Search for an Identity in America* (Chicago, University of Chicago Press, 1962), is the best treatment of the Muslims.
20. See Hare, *Black Anglo-Saxons,* especially Ch. 10, "The Supercitizens."
21. Cf. Hans Kohn, *Prophets and Peoples* (New York, The Macmillan Company, 1946); also Vittorio Lanternari, *The Religions of the Oppressed* (New York, Alfred A. Knopf, 1963).
22. *The Black Panther* (newspaper of the Black Panther Party), April 20, 1969, p. 13.
23. *Ibid.,* statement by Brother Jymbo, p. 8. See also the statement by George Mason Murray, Panther Minister of Education, quoted in *The Guardian,* April 19, 1969, p. 8.
24. H. Rap Brown, *Die, nigger, Die!* (New York, Dial Press, 1969).
25. For a critique of the immigrant analogy see *Report of the National Advisory Commission on Civil Disorders* ("Kerner Report"), ed. The New York Times (New York, E. P. Dutton & Co., 1968), Ch. 9.
26. To cite one fairly common action: Thirty-five FBI agents carrying machine guns, tear gas, and sledge hammers attacked and vandalized the Black Panther headquarters in Chicago on June 4, 1969. Smashing down doors, tearing posters, trampling loaves of bread intended for the children's breakfast program, smashing the mimeograph machine and desks, the agents then stole some $3,000 in cash intended for the free medical clinic, several typewriters, and firearms, and arrested the eight Panthers in the office on charges of harboring a federal fugitive, although no fugitive was found among them. Damage was estimated at $20,000. *The Guardian,* June 14, 1969, p. 3. In April and May of 1969 at least sixty-eight Panther leaders were arrested in five different states on various criminal charges.

Conditions of Community:

The Case of Old Westbury College

ALAN WOLFE

THERE IS little community present in the study of community. Various writers put forth their definitions and concepts and argue for them vehemently in the face of competing sets of concepts and definitions.[1] Meanwhile, back in the
real world, things called communities are being established
by diverse groups which see themselves as powerless; community control has become a major symbol of internal warfare in New York; the lack of some sort of international
community is continually deplored; and within certain experiments in higher education much talk is heard of community government. Somewhat dismayed by the irrelevance
of political theory and sociological conceptualization to
these new experiments in and uses of community, I propose
in this essay to attempt to develop a meaningful concept of
community and then use it to explore some of the political
dilemmas of creating community by describing my experiences in a new experimental college which had the building
of community as one of its professed aims.

I think we can expect to see more and more political con-
troversies based on communitarian concepts, coming especially from the ends of the ideological spectrum. The foremost example of this pattern is in New York City, where the
Ford Foundation, the Republican administration, and local
black organizations formed a loose alliance around the term

"community control of public schools." [2] In doing so, they demonstrated that almost nobody knew what the term "community" meant. The three areas selected as demonstration districts included a school complex bordering on Harlem and East Harlem, a section of the Lower East Side known primarily for its access to Brooklyn, and Ocean Hill-Brownsville, an area with no geographic *raison d'être* except its poverty. One thing leads to another, however. The school strike went a long way toward creating community solidarity, and whatever Ocean Hill-Brownsville was before the strike, it is becoming a community now.

White radical organizations are also promoting the concept of community. The Newark Community Union Project tried to develop a sense of identity and solidarity in that city's central ward. In attacking trustees with heavy outside interests, student radicals have been trying, so far without notable success, to make legitimate the question of who rules the university, thus asking for the parameters of particular educational communities. Part of the concern of the antiwar movement is that basic decisions over people's lives have been removed from their control. In each area, a partiality for face-to-face contact and a distrust of distance and hugeness, elements in a concept of community, are heavily present.

By far some of the most fascinating experiments with community are the least publicized. Consider the following intentional communities, all established in recent years, all with diverse purposes, and all heard about through the grapevine:

NAME	LOCATION	PURPOSES
Washington Free Community	Washington, D.C.	Communal life; publishing; barter
Centers for Change	New York City	Educational methods

Esalen Institute	Big Sur, Cal.	Sensitivity training; communal life
Drop City	Trinidad, Colo.	Arts and crafts; psychedelic commune
Synanon	various	Drug rehabilitation; communal life
Morningstar	West Coast	Communal life
Hog Farm	nomadic	Communal life; barter
USCO	Santa Fe, N.M.; rural New York	Arts and crafts commune
New Buffalo Commune	New Mexico	Religious and spiritual exchange
Living Theatre	various	Political and artistic expression and involvement
Koinona	Georgia	Farming; communal life

It is clear that in spite of the widespread feeling that utopian, communal living has been proved impossible, there are a variety of intentional communities existing, some of which are even flourishing.

A similar reexamination of community is beginning to take place among academics. Community has been a long-ignored term among political scientists. The index of the *American Political Science Review* from 1905 to 1963, which was compiled on the basis of key words in the titles of articles, lists nine articles with the word *community* in the title, compared with ten for *bureaucracy*, twenty-two for *group(s)*, forty-six for *committee(s)*, and fifty-seven for *system(s)*. Of the first nine, we find that one deals with *Othello*, two with the British Community of Parliaments, two with the state of Ohio, one with international politics, and three with local politics. It is my guess that this avoidance and confusion of meaning will soon be corrected. Sociologists have long been concerned with the term, a sure sign

that political science will follow. And a major critique of
political liberalism begins its last chapter with this:

> . . . I wish to take one step forward by analyzing the concept
> which, I am convinced, must serve as the key to a new social
> philosophy, namely the concept of community.[3]

If I am right and community is considered more and more
a major alternative, politically and theoretically, to what we
have now, then a discussion of the practical difficulties which
community presents is clearly in order. What interests me in
this discussion is not that a group of people failed to build
community, but how they went about failing. In that process, there is much about community to be learned.

THE CASE OF OLD WESTBURY COLLEGE

Old Westbury College of the State University of New
York was established by the legislature and the state Department of Education as an innovative laboratory for higher
education. Excerpts from SUNY's 1966 master plan give an
indication of the school's mandate:

> The State University will establish in Nassau County a col-
> lege that pays heed to the individual student and his concern
> with the modern world. Specifically this college will
> 1. End the lock-step march in which one semester follows
>   another until four years of youth's most energetic years
>   have been consumed; to this purpose qualified students
>   will be admitted to college without high school gradua-
>   tion, and those who attain competency will be granted
>   degrees without regard to length of collegiate study.
> 2. Admit students to full partnership in the academic
>   world and grant them the right to determine, in large
>   measure, their own areas of study and research. . . .
> Since the campus is to be built literally from the ground up,
> the President and the faculty members the President recruits
> will have an almost unrestricted opportunity for innovation
> and creativity.[4]

Various educational concepts have been combined in an attempt to provide that experimentation. To put it complexly, an attempt has been made to combine the basic principles of St. Johns College and the Hutchins-era University of Chicago with an Antioch-type field studies program related to the problems of race, poverty, and urbanism, with an overlay of Goddard-type independent study. The first-year program gives an idea of how this was to be done. Running through both semsters of the first year is a Common Humanities Seminar which deals generally, although not exclusively, with the so-called Great Books. Participation in the seminar constitutes one-third of the student's program. The other two-thirds of the first semester consists of participation in one or more social science seminars (every member of the first-year faculty of nine teaches one social science and one humanities seminar) and a faculty-sponsored independent study project. In the second semester the student engages in a field program somewhere in the world, probably in New York City, continuing with his seminars. This is obviously a hodgepodge, but at this writing it is too early in the college's first year to evaluate its success or failure.

Experimentation is not limited to the academic side alone. The internal governing of the college is considered by many of its participants to be also open to experimentation. Every member of the college community—faculty, students, administration, staff—is expected to play a role in the college's affairs, although the exact nature of that role is open to dispute. In rhetorical form, the role was expressed in the words "full partnership" in the mandate and in these words from the catalogue, which is also a statement of the first program:

> In creating this new college the State University sees the restlessness, curiosity and questioning of youth not as a specter, but an opportunity. The turbulent, critical mood of today's students is a great occasion for education. . . . For both stu-

dents and faculty the curriculum and the community of learning will be demanding. Taking responsibility for one's own education and accepting partnership in a common venture will put pressure on each participants.[5]

This statement, emphasizing so much the word "common," led some students and faculty who were attracted to the place to conclude that here a real community could form and a political experience occur which in the long run might prove more valuable than the educational one. With these hopes in mind, I would like to discuss some of the problems and dilemmas which arose as some of us made the attempt to translate those words into a communal experience.

Power and Community

Power was the first issue to be confronted. A major aspect of the communal experience described above was a relative equality of power among the participants. While the words "full partnership," used so often in the college's catalogue, seemed to guarantee that equality, such was not the case. The problem of power had to be fought out in, of all things, a power struggle.

Basically, the problem was that full partnership meant one thing to the president and another to the more radical faculty and students. Old Westbury, it seems, was both blessed and cursed with a president who believes in personal leadership. His name is Harris Wofford, former Associate Director of the Peace Corps, and the idea of full partnership originated with him. This was the result of his working for Sargent Shriver, an administrator who appeals to Wofford as the ideal of what an enlightened leader could do. Wofford's concept of full partnership, like Shriver's, does *not* include the idea that all members of the community would collectively make all decisions. That idea conflicts very strongly with his own concept, that leadership must be dynamically provided and that he has been called upon, in his appointment as president, to provide it. This conflict between full partnership and executive leadership is thus built into the structure of the college as it now exists. What this means has been described by one of the college's student planners in these terms:

> Staunch in his opposition to government by committee, Wofford led when leadership was called for, and when decisions were made, it was normally he who made them (this not always being apparent at the time). "Full partnership" essentially meant all had equal status in attempting to influence the leader. The seminar-style planning process, indeed, was sometimes referred to as "educating the President." [6]

That description of the decision-making process before the arrival of faculty and students was not how things had to be, some of us felt. A review of some of the most significant power struggles is helpful in discovering that, given the people there, that is how it did have to be.

The first confrontation in the college's decision-making structure occurred over the issue of faculty recruitment, appropriately enough, since the current (1968–1969) faculty of nine is to be increased to twenty-five in one year. Wofford's concept was that since he had been given a mandate to lead, these appointments should be his to make, after full consultation with all members of the community. To the faculty, all of whom came to the college to plan it according to their quite diverse educational theories, this concept was anathema. Some did not trust Wofford's judgment, some smelled political patronage, others appealed to the historical role of faculties in defining themselves. The faculty presented a plan in which a joint faculty-student selection committee would in effect do the hiring, although the appointment letter would go out under the president's name, as is required by state regulations.

Power plays take on strange forms in nascent communal organizations. At one meeting, the faculty literally lit into Wofford, tearing him apart across a table while he remained

unmovable and unmoved. Two weeks later, after a trip to
South America, Wofford presented a plan similar to that of
the faculty except that it came from him. Two committees,
one dealing with the urban studies aspects of the college
and one with the humanities, would search for candidates
and propose names to a selection committee composed of
seven students, seven faculty, and the academic vice-president.
The selection committee would make recommendations to
the president, who would then make the appointment. So
the decision was reached, and the faculty selection process
was instituted and completed its operations. But on the
theoretical level, what happened to the problem of power?
The faculty got its plan, but by the good graces of the president, although his plan was approved in a faculty meeting.
In other words, Wofford solidified his power by giving some
of it up, and the faculty gained power by approving someone else's plan. Although the faculty and students became
the initiators of new faculty appointments, Wofford chose to
veto an abnormally high 20 percent of the names proposed
to him. It is difficult to say who "won" that particular confrontation, except to point out that an equality of power had
not been approximated—the president could, and did, sub-
stitute his personal whims for the whims of a representative
body.

The inequality of power on the campus is more vividly
demonstrated by another clash. A suggestion by the Black
Caucus in the college that 50 percent of the incoming class
for 1969–1970 be nonwhite was taken up by many students
as a desirable goal. In meeting after meeting, the merits and
demerits of the plan were debated until it was generally
agreed that a vote should be taken. But a vote for what? The
students, like the faculty, never had any power status given
to them, except to advise the president. (Indeed, Old Westbury was the only campus I have ever seen where the formal
powers of the students and faculty approached equality;
both had none.) Would a vote of the students in favor of the

plan, combined with a faculty vote in its favor, make the policy operative? Or would it just be a suggestion to the president? One way to find out was to go ahead and vote.

The students first asked the faculty to join them in a "one-man, one-vote" community gesture. If the constantly used term community were to have any meaning, the students said, then on an issue as overwhelmingly important as this, all members of the community should vote together. The faculty laughed, knowing that community was something you say, not something you act on. They rejected the student proposal in favor of having their own vote. The students then held a meeting and voted overwhelmingly in favor of the 50/50 proposal. At this point, President Wofford made it emphatically clear that he considered the proposal repulsive and that he would ignore any advice on it. There we were again—advising the president. At the next faculty meeting, a vote was not taken on the issue. Wofford was so adamant and unmovable that it seemed silly to go ahead. The proponents of the 50/50 issue among the faculty, including myself, agreed to a meaningless compromise in order to end the meeting; something to the effect that the admissions committee would use all available resources to encourage nonwhites to come to the school, and so forth. In other words, in spite of the support for the idea on the part of a majority of the students and a near majority of the faculty, the president decided the issue again. It was now clear what the power relationships on the campus were, and talk of full partnership and community began to fall off.

The lesson I read from these confrontations is that the search for community is a search for a new theory of democracy, one based upon a rough equality of access to decision-making power. Communal decision making stands in direct contrast to two other modes of making decisions: the bureaucratic and the autocratic. In neither of these is there any attempt to provide access to power for all participants in the organization. To talk of community with respect to either of

these two forms would be nonsense, because individuals
would not have in common what is most fundamental:
power.

The situation at Old Westbury was not as clear-cut. The
decision-making structure was neither bureaucratic nor
autocratic, but a third form, lying closer to the latter than
the former. What made it distinctive was that the autocrat
had adopted the rhetoric of community, and the result was
confusion. If there is a hierarchy of power, and if community is a term constantly used, the result will be that those at
the top will, in the classic manner of elites everywhere,
translate their own personal will into the communal will.
And because something has the ring of community to it,
people not at the top will tend to give a decision more legitimacy than it perhaps deserves. The result is that the term
community, which implies a democratization of decision
making, is used to perpetuate nondemocratization. For this
reason, the context of community is crucial. Community can
never be discussed apart from power, and when power is discussed, advocates of community may find that they wish the
term not be used if power is being exercised in certain ways.
For obvious reasons, I never use the term any more at the
college but refer instead to that new social entity, "so-called
community."

Space and Community

A second problem of community concerns space. Put in
question form, it is this: Does community exist within a certain physical location, or is it a state of mind which people
can share though they are in different places? Nearly all of
the examples of community given earlier in this essay are
based upon a common living principle within a specific area.
Old Westbury College was similarly organized. All students
are expected to live on the college grounds or near them.
Commuting from home is frowned upon and in the first year
does not exist at all. All but three of the faculty live on or

near the campus. In such fashion, the college was conceived of as an isolated island surrounded by the luxurious splendor of the North Shore country of Long Island.

It didn't work, at least in my opinion. Eighty-three students living in an isolated area with few cars, to put it bluntly, got on each other's nerves. In a community that tight, as one faculty member put it, a tremendous capacity for forgiveness becomes a necessity. One knows so much about everyone else that if one holds grudges, he might find himself talking to nobody within a month. Although things never went that far, tensions did begin to arise over seemingly trivial issues. It became apparent to many that so small a student body in that location was a mistake, that instead of breeding community, it bred antagonism and distrust. Something had to be done, and something eventually was, although to most people it had nothing to do with community at all.

That something was the teachers' strike in New York City. One of our faculty members who had previously been involved in community organizing in Bedford-Stuyvesant proposed a plan in which students at the college would teach in elementary schools during the remainder of the strike, which at that time was of indeterminable length. He asked the faculty to reschedule their classes at night and on the weekends to accommodate this activity. The response was soul-searching. The best—best in the sense that people confronted one another honestly with their feelings—"community" meetings were held in which the strike and the effects of student participation in breaking it were discussed. One of the questions raised there is also being raised here: would the physical removal of over half the students destroy the community or give it a chance to flourish? Although this was not foremost in the minds of those who went to teach, many speculated about the effects of such an action on the "community."

My impression is that the three-week absence (it turned

out) of large numbers of people from the college during the
day was a stimulus in the direction of genuine community.
The earlier commingling had been without purpose, a
group of people brought together by an admissions office
around some vague words the meaning of which was unclear
to all, presumably even to those who wrote them. After the
strike, many participants realized a new purpose, some type
of college, perhaps with an urban studies focus, which would
enable them to both understand and change their society.
Many who did not go to Brooklyn discovered that they were
after an intensive liberal arts education which would help
them achieve self-understanding. College planning, lacka-
daisical before this interruption, started in earnest. Curriculum planning began. Faculty recruiting finally started. Con-
troversies still existed, but they tended to be about much less
trivial, even about important, items. To be sure, there was
tension between those who taught and those who did not.
But within each group, community as a state of mind rather
than as a spatial entity began to become a reality.

The question of whether community needs a spatial dimension has been discussed by sociologists with typically inconclusive results. Leo Schnore, for one, argues that the
term community must refer to people within a given area.[7]
My experience at Old Westbury would lead me to disagree
with Schnore and agree instead with a former colleague of
mine at the college—the one with the greatest interest in
community and the first to resign—who has argued as follows:

> As conceptually difficult as it may be, it is undoubtedly use-
> ful to consider limited interest groups organized apart from
> space as communities in the usual sense of that term. I say this
> because in essence the notion of community refers to an
> ordered set of social relationships. The fact that such sets of
> social relationships are bounded in space is, from a sociologi-
> cal point of view, incidental and relatively unimportant.
> What is important is that these relationships themselves

promulgate interpersonal processes necessary to the development, the elaboration, and the persistence of organized social life.[8]

The question of space is not trivial. If community can only exist within certain locations, and if locations are indeed declining in importance with urbanization, industrialization, and bureaucratization, then we had better forget community. If we choose to remember it, conceiving of community as nonspatially defined enables the concept to become applicable to large institutions while permitting individuals within these institutions a personal life of their own.

Diversity and Community

Easily the most intellectually complicated problem facing the emergence of community at Old Westbury was diversity. Reference was made before to the tensions which existed at the college between students who broke the teachers' strike and those who did not. This is reflective of an admissions policy which consciously went after as many different types of students as possible. Each of the following categories includes at least one of the eighty-three students at Old Westbury: transfer students from inferior colleges and universities; high school graduates with excellent board scores and grades; transfer students from superior colleges and universities; high school graduates with poor records; high school dropouts of middle- and upper-middle-class backgrounds who just grew bored with high school; high school dropouts from lower-class areas; upper-class blacks; middle-class blacks and Puerto Ricans; lower-class nonwhites; lower-class whites; upwardly mobile Jews; very young foreign students; older foreign students; army veterans; draft resisters; community organizers; people with no formal schooling at all; graduates of "street academies"; prep-school graduates; and none of the above.

The notion of bringing together as diverse a group as pos-

sible and having them confront one another is part of Harris
Wofford's vision shared by nearly everyone on the campus,
including one part of me. Another part of me just wonders.
There simply does not seem to be much that emerges when a
community organizer from El Barrio disagrees over the use
of drugs on campus with a suburban middle-class white
transfer student from an Ivy League school. An elaboration
of this example of drug policy should indicate some of the
dilemmas of diversity.

Old Westbury has perhaps the most unique approach to
drugs of any campus in the country. Wofford, a lawyer, believes strongly in civil obedience unless one is willing to pay
the consequences of civil disobedience. He therefore drafted
a letter during the summer to all incoming students indicating what the law was and how he expected everyone to obey
it. "Naïve and ineffective," everyone thought. But it
worked; there is, after a brief flurry, almost no drug activity
on campus at all, except for some use by nonstudents. It
worked, but for reasons which few could have predicted; it
worked because the drug issue became intertwined with the
race issue in a way that I hinted at in the previous paragraph. Many of the nonwhite students had been addicts or
friends of addicts. They were investing a good deal in the
college, having left a familiar way of life for an unfamiliar
and quite innovative one. The use of drugs by white students was seen as both dangerous and a middle-class luxury
which could destroy the college and hence the investment
the black students had made. The result: an informal policy
of enforcement in which the nonwhites announced that they
would simply bash in the heads of drug users. This was remarkably effective, much more so than the various inconclusive community meetings periodically held on the subject. I
find myself totally ambivalent about this situation. The violence and lack of free choice and privacy are almost as disturbing as the effectiveness of the policy is pleasing. But the

point to be emphasized here is not my view, but the effects on community. The diversity was so pervasive that a decision was not made by communal methods but by the imposition of one group's values upon the other.

It may be the case, then, that community in a situation of enormous diversity is impossible. That hypothesis need not be as illiberal as it at first sounds. One should at all costs avoid absolutes (a statement containing an obvious absolute), and that includes the absolute that diversity is inherently good. Rather, one should ask this question: do the advantages that accrue from diversity outweigh the disadvantages? And the answer to that question always depends upon the context, specifically, the purposes for which the people were brought together. Thus I would argue that from an educational point of view, the diversity at Old Westbury is healthy; one Jewish student from Long Island told me in effect that he has learned more from his Puerto Rican roommate than he has from his seminars. But from the standpoint of community, the same diversity is pernicious. It has created subcommunities, like that of the strike-breaking students, but it has inhibited formation of a community which includes everyone at the college. One simply has to choose whether the communal or the educational experience is more important. I haven't made that choice yet.

I am not totally endorsing the view of Herbert Marcuse in his famous essay, "Repressive Tolerance." [9] But I am suggesting that there is something there which should not be dismissed as simply totalitarian raving. Tolerance made into an absolute is as illiberal as intolerance made into an absolute; in many ways, it is the same thing. What the Old Westbury experience with diversity has shown me is that given certain purposes, a group is better off excluding certain points of view if such an action enhances the goals of the group. To give one more example, I taught this semester a seminar on "Power in America." In the first meeting, I explained the continuing debate between C. Wright Mills and his critics and indicated that this presented us with at least two choices. We could examine that debate in detail in an intensive pursuit of the "truth" of each side, or we could accept one point of view, preferably Mills's, and examine all of the implications of that view, ignoring the critics in order to see how far we could go with Mills. The students wanted to take that latter alternative, and we never returned to the Dahl-Bell *et el.* school of thought. Then one day we were visited by a political scientist from another institution who was extremely dismayed by our unconcern for the pluralist critics of Mills. He could not restrain himself, and he brought up all the standard arguments against the existence of an American power elite. What happened was simply that the members of the seminar explained to him the decision we had made at our first meeting, and on we went. My feeling is that he was flabbergasted by our "closed-mindedness" and "dogmatism." But that wasn't it at all. We had made an educational policy decision that too much diversity would inhibit our learning effectiveness. Given the context and our purposes, this decision is easily as justifiable as any other alternative. In other words, there just are not any totally satisfactory resolutions to the dilemmas which diversity presents to community.

Confrontation and Community

Closely related to diversity in the intellectual sense is pluralism in the institutional sense. Writers working from a sympathy toward institutional pluralism look with favor upon the existence of groups which compete against one another for the rewards which a political system can give. With the creation of a new political order such as Old Westbury College that institutional pluralism did not exist; no a priori groups were in conflict with any others. The creation of such a conflict brought plualism to the campus; the same creation destroyed community. The tensions between pluralism and community are worth exploring in the context of the college.

People come to a college nationally billed as "experimental" because of their dissatisfaction with institutions more familiar to them. At Old Westbury, there were those who felt the rigidity of academic life to be stultifying; those who were disenchanted with academic professionalism; those protesting the emphasis upon graduate study; those devoted to a return to a lost liberal arts; those upset by large lectures and impersonal contacts; those wishing to collapse departmental boundaries; those desiring to explore sensitivity training and other pedagogical devices; and those who, like myself, were so unhappy with existing higher education that they combined all these desires no matter how contradictory. This dissatisfaction and concomitant urge to create something new gave the initial group at Old Westbury something in common, and therefore we were closer to an educational community than most other American colleges, where the only thing held in common is a pension plan. The only way in which this mutual unhappiness could have been dealt with creatively would have been for the initial group to confront the differences in dissatisfaction and build something in common to counteract our distress. The worst thing would have been to permit each type of dissatisfaction to institutionalize itself, distinct from the others. The college began almost immediately to pursue this latter alternative.

The device used was a constituent-college form of organization. The idea of using constituent colleges as an alternative to departments had been an unexplored given from the beginning of planning operations. The only question was one of timing. During the search for new faculty, the name of someone particularly exciting but hard to get came up. The faculty selection committee recommended to the president that he be appointed to head a planning group which could possibly become a constituent college in the future.

The candidate came to the school and took a walk with President Wofford. Soon after, Wofford presented a "draft" of a proposal in which he announced the appointment of this candidate as provost of our first constituent college, one with a focus totally different from urban studies, which everyone on the campus, except apparently the president, had considered our eventual first college. During the ensuing protest, Wofford redrafted his announcement to say that a second provost would be appointed, one from inside the college, to head a constituent college emphasizing traditional liberal arts disciplines. A search would begin immediately for someone to head an urban studies college. Eventually someone was found, although he has turned down the offer at this writing.

Within six months of the opening of the college, we had three constituent colleges, two of them with provosts, to begin planning operations in 1969–1970. Wofford argued that his timing was "right," perhaps referring to the fact that most of the students, including some of the ones defined as "troublesome," had left campus to work in the field. His timing was questioned by a group which remained. This group, the one which by definition could not be pleased by his actions, was the one which argued that the move to constituent colleges was totally premature, that what we should be doing in our first year was working out our organizational problems, like the governance of the college, and finding value in our mutual alienation. These arguments were to no avail. The president had decided on three constituent colleges, and off we went. Our unity of experience is now a trinity, and communication between one end of the trinity and the other two is virtually nonexistent. In other words, the college did not wait until the inevitable pluralistic structure emerged. It went out and built it itself. Another thing that people had in common had been dissipated.

Confrontation is an essential for community. The creation of a pluralistic structure spells the end of confrontation. Instead of one series of ideas challenging another, they take their places side by side and each goes its own way. Because each side of ideas has the structure of a constituent college associated with it, it need never worry about becoming anachronistic. The structure will guarantee the need for the idea; as with the March of Dimes, a purpose will be found for the structure even after the polio vaccine has been discovered. As American society has adopted a pragmatic discourse which renders the confrontation of ideas irrelevant, the college has done the same. As American society has, because of that pragmatism, created institutions which will last until long after they serve a function, so has the college. The easiest way to deal with a possible confrontation is to reward both sides. In such fashion are community and pluralism at odds. In opting for the latter, Old Westbury again sacrificed a key element of the former.

THE POLITICAL THEORY OF COMMUNITY

Imagine what a conclusion I could write to this essay if my experiences with community at Old Westbury had been positive. Here is a model, I would say, that people involved in unresponsive, bureaucratic institutions could adopt in order to humanize both the institutions and themselves. Furthermore, I would sadistically add the clincher, it *is* possible to do it: look at my own experience. Unfortunately, that experience was negative, and I cannot write that stirring conclusion. There are, therefore, two other possibilities I see. I could say that the idea has not worked and that therefore community is a false goal which can never be realized in the type of society we have now. Or I could say that community is still worthwhile even though my experiences with it would seem to indicate otherwise. Even as I write this, I have not completely made up my mind, envisioning these two conclusions, one for each end of a continuum of moods that I often find myself in. But if I lean either way, it is toward the latter pole, both because I went into the Old Westbury experiment with a favorable attitude toward community and the confessional literature of the disillusioned repels me, and because there are good theoretical arguments to be made in behalf of community. Let me conclude with those arguments, though with the proviso that they are theoretical points which will obviously be difficult to implement.

Community is a political concept. That lesson, easy to forget, is what the Old Westbury experience taught me. Much of the attraction to community is antipolitical. People envision a retreat where the seamier aspects of politics—vituperation, mistrust, hypocrisy, pretension—can be ignored while a group of people live in peace and harmony. Such a concept is not mine. People who make decisions with respect to my life would probably enjoy my going off into a corner somewhere, loving all and trusting all; but because they make those decisions, I don't give them the pleasure. The type of community I think worth having is highly political—it seeks to serve as an alternative to the hierarchical, quasipluralistic, bureaucratic, complex society in which we live. Community should be viewed, not as the establishment of distinct (and, I would think, impotent) communes, but as a way of organizing people to understand, by contrast, the nature of the society in which they live, and as a way of showing that there are alternatives.

Community is first of all an alternative to mass society. Scott Greer has argued that what we must do in the face of mass society is not conjure up visions of simple nineteenth-century life but examine intermediate groups such as organizations and neighborhoods which act as surrogates for the massness of the contemporary city.[10] I would agree, but only insofar as those intermediate institutions can contravene Michels' Iron Law of Oligarchy and be made responsive and democratic. To do that, we can develop a concept of intraorganizational community relevant to colleges, factories, professional associations, neighborhoods. Intraorganizational community can serve to give people identity, but it can do more than that. It can be a way of making democratic theory applicable to nongovernmental institutions and it can be a reference point for others making the struggle in their own institutions. Clearly this is a difficult task. Perhaps another personal example can indicate the difficulty.

After about a month of teaching at Old Westbury, I returned to Rutgers University, where I had previously taught, to give a speech. In my talk I described my new job, contrasting it with my life at Rutgers, the whole point of which was, in my mind, to make them green with envy at what we were doing. After thirty minutes of rapturous description, the questions came from the floor, overwhelming me with their vehemence. It turns out that I had "copped out" by withdrawing into "my own thing" which, to them, was no solution at all. After recovering my composure, I gave some insignificant answer to their charge and returned home to think about what they said. Now, having thought it over, I have reached a conclusion: they were wrong. Old Westbury started out as an example of intraorganizational community. Had we there been more interested in this aspect of what we were doing, we could have created for ourselves, but also for anyone else who chose to examine what we were doing, an example of one way to deal with unresponsive institutions. True, for reasons described here, we never did that. No one is arguing that it is easy. But the lesson that people can learn is there, and it has been expressed by Tom Hayden much better than it could ever be expressed by me:

> The real alternative to bureaucratic welfarism is to be found budding in the experience of men who form communities—whether a freedom school, a community union, a teach-in, or

a wildcat strike—to struggle as equals for their own self-determination. Such communities come and go, existing at their best during intense periods of solidarity. But even where they fail to achieve institutional reality, these communities become a permanent part of this generation's consciousness of the possible. The new society still takes shape in the womb of the old.[11]

There is more to it than that. Community is more than an alternative to mass society; it can be conceived of as a method of political decision making. We almost naturally assume that the most efficient method of making decisions is a noncommunal one in which a few individuals arranged in some sort of hierarchical order make decisions for many more people who unfortunately do not possess the skills that the few are blessed with. Yet it is also true, as one student of public administration has pointed out, that "no competent research exists demonstrating the 'efficiency' of the bureaucratic model compared with some alternative." [12] Mainly, a cynic (realist) would add, because there have not been any significant alternatives. A communal approach to decision making, in which all affected parties participate in the process, is clearly a theoretical new way. We failed to work out that alternative at Old Westbury because people with power liked having it and did not particularly wish to share any of it. Perhaps I should have expected that, coming to a state university system. But that doesn't mean that the struggles I described were fruitless. We demonstrated that community is a powerful concept, which needs more than talk to render it operable but requires a surrender of certain prerogatives. If certain individuals had been more flexible, we might even have gained our goals. And we convinced ourselves that communal decision making would work when we obtained the means to try it.

If we move from activity within organizations to activity between organizations, community might be considered an alternative to institutional pluralism. Pluralism has much in common with hierarchical bureaucracy. Common goals are ignored in both. What exists becomes accepted as the only alternative, others being considered fallacious, naïve, impossible, utopian, contradictory, evil, simplistic, misguided, or pathetic. In both, a group of experts arises, constituting an elite which, by its own choice, decides on questions affecting everybody. Although pluralist writers would like us to believe that we have no alternatives, the converse of what I argued earlier appears true. Because community cannot exist with pluralism, the former could be substituted for the latter. Again, we at Old Westbury did not do that. And again, I think it could be done. Given the political problems described here, a group of people might choose to operate with common goals, without creating institutions which divide them. Somewhere in the theory of community, in other words, lies the alternative to pluralism.

I may not have convinced anyone that the concept of community has any potential. I may not have convinced myself. But I think I have. It remains to be seen whether any of these ideas could work in practice. One more controversy at Old Westbury could help me. That group, of which I am an active member, which lost nearly all the struggles discussed in this essay, developed in the course of their work a plan for a college which would be a community in the sense used here. With a curriculum on how man governs himself, ranging from the psychological to the international level, such a college would not divorce the study of governance from its practice. Students and faculty would govern the college in participatory-democracy form, the students for credit and the faculty for pay. A reasonably well developed plan for such a college, as a fourth constituent college for Old Westbury, was the basis of long discussions with President Wofford. He finally rejected the idea, something which surprised us because we thought he believed in the politics of co-option and we were (then) willing to be co-opted. But the plan exists and the people exist, and it might become a reality, perhaps at Old Westbury, more likely somewhere else. When it does, a more definite conclusion to this essay will be possible. At this point, the reader will have to live with the ambiguity that I have been living with.

ONE FURTHER NOTE

This essay was written during the second semester of the first year of Old Westbury College's existence. A majority—the articulate majority—of the college's students were working in the field that semester and thus had very little to do with the major decisions made by the President while they were away. In fact, these students (with good reason) were convinced that Wofford had waited until they left campus before announcing his total reorganization of Old Westbury into the three constituent colleges. Most of them were also convinced that the problem of decision-making power in the community had not been solved, and they planned to bring up the issue when they returned to the campus for the last two weeks of the second semester in what was supposed to be a review of the field program. When they did bring up the issue, the nature of the college changed significantly one more time in a way that needs description, for without it a visitor to Old Westbury who had read this essay to this point would hardly recognize the place.

The first scheduled event in the two-week field-evaluation period was the President's "State of the College Address." (Wofford constantly pretended that he was President of the United States and that we were the United States. He had read Richard Neustadt's advice to his former mentor, John Kennedy, and he actually tried to implement *Presidential Power*.) When Wofford totally ignored questions of power and governance, choosing instead to give his usual "Scott

Buchanan and I sat on a seesaw together" speech, the students walked out, presenting him later with a series of demands relating to the governance of the college. His refusal to talk about governance then led to a sit-in in his office by the white students, while blacks occupied the communications center. And so it came to pass that the smallest college in the United States, with a carefully selected student body of eighty-three, in its very first year of operation, had a sit-in, in which over fifty students occupied offices, twenty supported their demands without occupation, and the remainder went home or to Europe. On that note the first year of Old Westbury College came to an end.

Wofford's reaction was to deny to the press and to Albany that a sit-in had occurred. On the contrary, he maintained, students were sleeping in his office because he had invited them there, "to continue the dialogue." He had not, however, invited them to look through the official files of the college—he had taken his personal files out in his arms when the sit-in (invitation) began—and when they did so, the occupation officially became a sit-in, with periodic threats to call in the police. Meanwhile, back in the files, the students discovered that one of the named provosts had plans, with the President's consent, to build a personal empire on campus. His plans were described in a long letter to one of the students, combined with references to the low caliber of students and faculty but adoring praise for the President. The content of the letter, and the fact that a carbon had been sent to the President, were so embarrassing that when the students sent him a copy of the letter, the incipient provost announced that he would not be coming to Old Westbury after all. One down and two to go.

With the presence of the students in his office now producing results, and with the hawks in Albany after him, Wofford next tried the highly touted strategy of negotiating with the blacks, thereby attempting to isolate the whites.

This failed too, because the black students did not trust him, having just come back from the field. Their rejection of his peace offer meant that he had only two choices: to agree to the substance of the demands or to call the police. He finally did the smart thing; the students came out of the offices, and a constitution committee was created to implement the "midnight agreements" between Wofford and the students. People left for the summer, and the Constitution Committee sat down to its tasks.

More changes came about during the summer of 1969. In a move which surprised few people on campus, Wofford announced his resignation to become President of Bryn Mawr College in September 1970. While he remains, the two remaining constituent colleges have gone into operation, and one of them, the Urban Studies College, still without a provost, is functioning extremely well. Plans for the third college, emphasizing "learning by teaching," have been totally dropped, since nobody seemed to want it but the President and his ex-provost. A general program exists for students who do not wish to join one of the two constituent colleges. The Constitution Committee presented a document for ratification, but it failed to be ratified because too few people voted. Not many seemed to mind (except those who worked long and hard on the new constitution), for its purpose was to limit the powers of a president who was already a lame duck. A search has just begun for a new president. Two-hundred-odd students are now on campus, going to classes and doing all the things that students are expected to do. Those who engaged in the sit-in are now seeking from books an understanding of what last year was all about. The intellectual level of the campus is higher than it ever was. Within the limits set by constituent-college pluralism, a real learning environment has been created. It may seem ironic that it took political action to bring about this state of affairs, but that, after all, is in the nature of the new commu-

nity that inadvertently seems to have surrounded Old Westbury College in September 1969.

NOTES

1. For examples, see how the term is used in totally different ways
   in Robert Nisbet, *The Quest for Community* (New York, Oxford
   University Press, 1953); Maurice R. Stein, *The Eclipse of Community* (New York, Harper Torchbooks, 1964); and Scott Greer,
   The Emerging City (New York, The Free Press, 1962).
2. This is not exactly correct. There is a major difference between
   decentralization and community control. "After the Ocean Hill-
   Brownsville experiment had been formulated, the New York City
   Board of Education changed the wording of the philosophy from
   community control to community involvement." Richard Karp,
   "School Decentralization in New York: A Case Study," *Interplay,*
   August–September 1968, p. 11. Needless to say, the more militant
   local organizations adhered to the former concept, while the other
   partners to the alliance fell back upon the latter.
3. Robert Paul Wolff, *The Poverty of Liberalism* (Boston, Beacon
   Press, 1968), p. 163. His emphasis.
4. Old Westbury College, *Catalogue* (2nd printing), p. 2.
5. *Ibid.,* pp. 4, 6.
6. Ralph Keyes, "From Out of the Smoke," *Change in Higher Education,* I (March–April 1969), 13. A student planner was usually
   a student from another institution who received academic credit
   there for working on planning at Old Westbury.
7. Leo Schnore, "Community," in Neil J. Smelser, ed., *Sociology: An
   Introduction* (New York, John Wiley & Sons, 1967), pp. 82–150.
8. Peter Orleans, "On the Changing Conditions of Communal Life
   in the Contemporary City," unpublished paper. For a similar point
   of view, see Melvin M. Webber, "Order and Disorder: Community
   Without Propinquity," in Lowden Wingo, Jr., ed., *Cities and
   Space* (Baltimore, Johns Hopkins Press, 1963), pp. 23–56.
9. Herbert Marcuse, "Repressive Tolerance," in Robert Paul Wolff
   et al., A Critique of Pure Tolerance (Boston, Beacon Press, 1965).
10. Greer, *Emerging City,* and Greer and Orleans, "The Mass Society

and the Parapolitical Structure," *American Sociological Review,* XXVII (October 1962), 634–46.

11. Tom Hayden, "Welfare Liberalism and Social Change," *Dissent,* January-February 1966.

12. Robert Presthus, *The Organizational Society* (New York, Vintage Books, 1965), p. 56.

Civil Disobedience

and Corporate Authority

MICHAEL WALZER

I.

CIVIL DISOBEDIENCE is generally described as a nonrevolutionary encounter with the state. A man breaks the law, but does so in ways which do not challenge the legitimacy of the legal or political systems. He feels morally bound to disobey; he also recognizes the moral value of the state; civil disobedience is his way of maneuvering between these conflicting moralities. The precise requirements of civility have been specified by a number of writers, and while the specifications vary, they tend to impose a similar discipline on the disobedient persons. Above all, they impose the discipline of nonviolence. Civility, it is generally said, requires first the adoption of methods that do not directly coerce or oppress other members of society, and secondly, it requires nonresistance to state officials enforcing the law. I want to argue that there is a kind of disobedience that does not meet either of these requirements and yet sometimes falls within the range of civility.

Perhaps the actions I am going to describe should not be called civil disobedience at all; I do not want to quarrel about names. But it is arguable, I think, that narrow definitions of civil disobedience rule out certain sorts of unconventional yet nonrevolutionary politics which should not be regarded as attacks on civil order. These may well involve both coercion and violence, though always in severely limited ways. It is important to recognize the significance of such limits when making judgments about civility. The insistence on the absolute nonviolence of civil disobedience is, in any case, a little disingenuous, since it disregards, first, the coercive impact disobedience often has on innocent bystanders, and second, the actual violence it provokes and sometimes is intended to provoke, especially from the police. I do not doubt that it is preferable that no one be coerced and that police violence be met with passive resistance, but there may be occasions when neither of these is politically possible, and there may also be occasions, not necessarily the same ones, when they are not morally required. Such occasions, if they exist, would have to be described and delimited precisely. One of the dangers of a narrow definition of civil disobedience is that it simply rules out the effort to do this. By setting rigid limits to civil conduct, it virtually invites militants of various sorts to move beyond the bounds of civility altogether—and it invites the police to respond always as if they were confronting criminals. (Sometimes, of course, the police are confronting criminals, but it is important that we know, and that they know, when this is so and when it is not.)

The limits of civility are a matter of academic interest in more than the usual sense just now, and I do want to speak to the problems of university radicalism and to help mark out the moral space within which students (and faculties) can legitimately, if not legally, pursue their demands. But my more immediate focus will be on the past—for the sake, hopefully, of clarity and dispassion. There are historical cases in which the coercion of innocent bystanders and resistance to police authority have in fact proven compatible, or so it seems to me, with a kind of civility. The sit-down strikes against General Motors in 1936–1937 provide a classic example, to which I'll refer later in some detail. For now, it is enough to indicate the general principles under which such cases may be justified. They *may* be justified when the initial disobedience is directed against corporate bodies other than the state; when the encounter with these corporations, though not with the state that protects them; is revolutionary or quasi-revolutionary in character; and when the revolution is a democratic revolution, made in good faith. I will suggest later on just what these principles involve, and I will also argue very briefly that some (at least) of the recent student sit-ins, though they have been defended by reference to the 1936 strikes, cannot be justified in the same way.

II.

Americans today probably have a greater number of direct contacts with state officials than ever before. We continue, however, to have many contacts, perhaps more, that are mediated by corporate bodies. These corporations collect taxes on behalf of the state, maintain standards required by the state, spend state money, and above all, enforce a great variety of rules and regulations with the silent acquiescence and ultimate support of the state. Commercial, industrial, professional, and educational organizations, and to a lesser degree, religious organizations and trade unions all play these parts—and yet very few of these reproduce the democratic politics of the state. They have official or semi-official functions; they are enormously active and powerful in the day-to-day government of society, but the authority of their officers is rarely legitimized in any democratic fashion. These officers preside over what are essentially authoritarian regimes with no internal electoral system, no opposition parties, no free press or open communications network, no established judicial procedures, no channels for rank-and-file participation in decision making.[1] When the state acts to protect their authority, it does so through the property system, that is, it recognizes the corporation as the private

property of some determinate group of men and it protects
their right to do, within legal limits, what they please with
their property. When corporate officials defend themselves,
they often invoke functional arguments. They claim that
the parts they play in society can only be played by such men
as they, with their legally confirmed power, their control of
resources, their freedom from internal challenge, and their
ability to call on the police.[2]

Neither of these arguments justifies or requires absolute
power, and some of the subjects of corporate authority have
managed to win rights against it, rights which generally
come to them as citizens and are also protected by the state.
I am thinking of such things as the right to work no more
than a specified number of hours, the right to work in at
least minimally safe surroundings, and so on. The right to
strike is of the same sort, though it was for a longer time
unprotected. The claim of workers to shut down a factory
they did not own was once widely regarded as a denial of the
sanctity of private property and a threat to the efficient running of the economy. For years the strike (in the face of one
or another court injunction) was the most common form of
working-class civil disobedience, but it has long since been
allowed, and the strikers legally protected, by the state. I
should note that the right of students to strike is not similarly allowed, since students cannot, so far as I know, claim
state protection against expulsion after an unsuccessful
strike. In any case, such rights, even if securely held, would
still not be comparable to the rights a citizen has in a democratic state, and just how far they can or ought to be extended remains unclear, a matter of continuing public debate. By and large, the subjects of corporate authority are
. . . subjects, and state citizenship does not generate corporate citizenship, even when it guards against the worst
forms of corporate tyranny.

There is one argument in support of this subjection that
at least falls within the realm of democratic theory. This is

the argument from tacit consent, which holds that corporate subjects are, in some morally significant sense, voluntarily subject. By their willing entry into, and acceptance of the jurisdiction of, one or another corporate body, they commit themselves, on this view, to obey rules and regulations they have no part in making. They join the firm, go to work in the factory, enter the university, knowing in advance the nondemocratic character of all these organizations, knowing also who runs them and for what purposes. They are not deceived, at least no one is trying to deceive them, and so they are morally bound for the duration of their stay. And however subject they may be during that time to authoritarian pettiness and to oppressive rules and regulations, they are never the captives of the authorities. Their citizenship guarantees their ultimate recourse: if they don't like it where they are, they can leave.

This is a serious argument and deserves some attention. Residence in a democratic state does, I think, generate a prima facie obligation to obey the laws of that state—in part because of the benefits that are necessarily accepted along with residence, in part because of the expectations aroused among one's fellow residents, and finally because of the universality of obligation in a democracy, from which no resident can easily exclude himself. But the effects of residence in a nondemocratic state are surely very different. There the right of resistance and revolution may well be widely shared, and there is no reason why a new resident should not associate himself with the rebels rather than with the authorities. It is not obvious that the same distinction applies to the corporation, since the strict forms of political democracy are often said to be impractical in corporate bodies organized for industrial or educational purposes. But this is precisely what is at issue in most cases of corporate disobedience, and I see no reason to prejudge the issue by agreeing that tacit consent to nondemocratic corporations establishes any greater degree of obligation than tacit consent to nondemocratic states. In any case, arguments about the possible reaches of democracy are carried on almost continuously within both the corporation and the state; surely no one can bind himself not to join them; and it is one of the characteristics of political arguments in nondemocratic organizations that they will often take "illegal" forms. Such forms may even be necessary if the arguments are to be carried on at all. So there can be no binding commitment not to break corporate rules and regulations, or at least there can be no binding commitment until the best possible democratic procedure for establishing rules has been adopted.

There is another reason for rejecting the argument from tacit consent: corporate bodies do not offer anything like the same range of benefits that the state provides. Membership in them in no sense replaces citizenship in the state. A man may well provide himself with new benefits and even incur powerful, perhaps overriding, obligations by joining a corporate body, but he cannot be conceived as having yielded any of the legal rights he has as a citizen. Corporate officials may offer him a trade: we will pay you so much money, they may say, if you surrender the right to strike. That agreement, whatever its moral force, is not legally binding so long as the right to strike is recognized by the state. But the legal rights of a citizen are also matters of dispute, and so it is always possible for a corporate subject to break the rules and regulations, appealing to the laws of the state or to the established rights of citizenship as is authority for doing so.[3]

It is when such an appeal is not recognized by state officials that civil disobedience may begin. But for the moment, I want only to suggest that disobedience to corporate rules is probably justified whenever it is undertaken in good faith as part of a struggle for democratization or for socially recognized rights. By the phrase "in good faith," I mean to limit the occasions of justifiable disobedience to cases in which four conditions hold: when the oppressiveness of the corporate authorities can be specified in some rational way; when the social functions of the corporation have been taken into account in judging the rights its participants might enjoy; when concrete proposals for corporate reorganization have been brought forward; and when a serious effort has been made to win massive support for these proposals. I would assume also that whatever channels for "legal" reform are available within the corporation have been tried. But it is important to stress the fact that such channels do not always exist in the sorts of bodies I am considering here. Indeed, in many of them any serious demand for democratization may plausibly be called revolutionary, for it involves an attack upon the established authority system of the corporation. This has certainly been true, for example, of the demands of the labor movement, as one of its historians has noted: "If revolution is defined as a transfer of power from one social group to another, all forms of union activity which involve a challenge to the power of owners and managers are revolutionary." [4]

If this is so, then all the forms of revolutionary politics that we know from the history of authoritarian states may now be re-enacted on a smaller stage. In these kinds of situations, in fact, we ought to anticipate this kind of politics and not be shocked or surprised when it comes. Thus the presence of corporate police and spies (as in the auto plants before 1936) and the pervasive atmosphere of fearfulness generated by unlimited power will often impose secrecy and a severe discipline upon the revolutionary organization. At critical moments, initiatives may be seized by small minorities of militants who claim to represent their fellow subjects, but who also force them to make choices they did not anticipate and might well prefer not to make. Those who refuse to join the revolution may be threatened, mocked, perhaps beaten, their right to work systematically denied. Finally, the militants and their new supporters, now embattled and exposed, will often resist corporate countermoves and may do so even if these countermoves have state support. All this, secrecy, discipline, coercion, resistance, still falls or may fall, I want to argue, within the limits of civility—so long as the revolution is not aimed at the state itself and so long as the corporate authorities really are as oppressive as the rebels claim.

There is another condition, of course: that the corporate revolution not take the form of a violent coup, an attempt to blow up the central offices of the corporation or to murder or terrorize its personnel. It is crucial that violence on this scale, if it occurs, not occur at the initiative of the rebels. And in fact it rarely does occur at their initiative; in almost all the cases I can think of (there may be some recent exceptions), the rebels have followed a different course. Their strategy is almost always to shut down the corporation, to curtail its operations or to stop them altogether, until some new distribution of power is worked out. It is important to note that this first shutdown is different from all those that come later. Once the authority and cohesion of the corporate subjects have been recognized, strikes may become a permanent feature of the power system. The simple withdrawal of workers from their routine activities will then be sufficient to close the corporation, and even the threat to strike will be a valuable bargaining point in its ongoing politics. But this is not so earlier on, and the first strikes may have to take more direct and coercive forms. Generally, they involve the physical occupation of the corporate plant and the expulsion of nonstrikers. Occupation is preferable to withdrawal, because it can be achieved successfully without majority support, or immediate majority support, and majorities are not readily organized under authoritarian conditions. Occupation is also preferable because it precludes, at least for a time, the effective dismissal of the strikers and the resumption of corporate activity with new subjects. For these reasons, the sit-down or sit-in is a typical form of revolutionary activity in nondemocratic corporations.

The state then comes into the picture, not to enforce the laws against assault and murder, but to enforce the property laws. This is the paradox of corporate revolution: the revolutionaries encounter the state as trespassers. However serious their attack on corporate authority, they are guilty of only minor crimes in the eyes of the state, though one would not always guess this from the response of state officials. In fact, violence often, perhaps most often, begins with law enforcement.[5]

III.

In suggesting how disobedience to corporate rules and regulations might be justified, I have treated the corporation as a political community within the larger community of the state. I have discussed its government and the rights of its subject population. This is obviously not the way, or not the only way, the officials of the corporation and the state regard the matter. They see the corporation also as a piece of property, protected as property by the law. When corporate officials find "their" buildings occupied, their first response is to call on the police to clear them. The police sometimes come and sometimes do not. They are pledged to enforce the law, but they also take orders from the political leaders of the state, who may (and, I would suggest, ought to) see in the corporate revolution something more than a mere violation of the property laws. What is at issue here is not who owns the corporation, but what such ownership entails; above all, what, if any, governmental powers it entails. It is one of the characteristic features of feudal regimes that the ownership of property always entails governmental powers (and responsibilities): public functions such as war making, tax collecting, and adjudication are dispersed among a class of landlords, and the right to carry out such functions is literally owned along with the land. Clearly no modern state, even more clearly no democratic state, can permit or tolerate such a dispersal of powers. Corporate officials who carry out governmental or quasi-governmental functions (even the simple maintenance of social order within the corporation) must be responsible to the larger community, whose citizens they and their subjects are. But this means that the state has an interest in the internal politics of the corporation, an interest that may or may not be served by police intervention on behalf of private property. It is not farfetched, I think, to suggest that the interests of a democratic state are best served by corporate democratization—at least so long as this process does not seriously interfere with the social functions of the corporation, in which the larger community also has an interest.

It is important, in any case, for state officials to realize that when they enforce the trespass laws against strikers, they are also doing something else. They are acting to restore not merely the "law and order" of the state, but that of the corporation as well. They are enforcing another set of rules in addition to their own. And while they can argue that the strikers have every right and opportunity to work in public and try to change the first set of rules, they must recognize that the second set can, perhaps, only be changed by the very revolutionary action they are repressing. When police resist efforts to overthrow the state, they are behaving in a perfectly straightforward way. But the case is not straightforward when police resist efforts to overthrow corporate authority. Corporate authority is not the same as the authority of the property laws—it does not have their democratic legitimacy—and the differences between the two may require the police to use some discretion in moving against men who violate the laws of the state solely in order to challenge the authority of the corporation. The corporate rebels may, for example, be defending rights they actually have as citizens. Their violation of the law may be a means of bringing to the attention of their fellow citizens other, more important violations of the law.[6] And then the police must choose the laws they will enforce, and may reasonably choose to do as little as possible for the time being. Police inaction may even be justified if the rebels are wrong, or if the courts hold they are wrong, about their rights as citizens, for the size and scope of the strike may suggest changing communal values which the political leaders who command the police may choose to respect, if only in order to avoid violence.

The rebels may, of course, be wrong in other ways: the militant minority may not have even the silent and fearful sympathy of the others; its demands may be inconsistent with the continued fulfillment of important social functions. But corporate authorities always claim that these two conditions hold, and have done so in many cases where they clearly didn't. Since the truth is often difficult to discover, especially in the early hours or days of a rebellion, state officials must keep an open mind as long as they can. Police action may be necessary, but it is rarely necessary immediately. It is, however, almost always the demand of the corporate authorities that the police act quickly. If there is any hesitation, their subjects, they think, will rally around the militants—though it is obviously also possible that they will desert the militants, leaving them helpless and isolated. Time is the best test of the support the strikers actually have among the passive majority, but this has not, historically, been a test the authorities are willing to risk. Delay, moreover, pushes them toward negotiations with the strikers, and the beginning of talks is itself a victory for democratization, even if no other demands are allowed. Hence any refusal to enforce the law probably constitutes a kind of indirect intervention by the state against the corporation. It would be naïve to deny this; I can only suggest that the interests of a democratic state are sometimes served in this way.

If the police do enforce the law, then they must expect that the strikers will respond in the context of their own revolutionary situation. They are not at war with the state, but they are (or they may be) caught up in a political

struggle of the most serious sort, and direct police intervention, whatever its supposedly limited purposes, brings the
police into that struggle and into what may well appear the
closed circle of its strategic necessities. The more desperate
the struggle, the less likely they are to meet with either obedience or a merely passive resistance. Even active resistance
in such circumstances, however, does not necessarily constitute an attack upon the law and order that the state
represents. It may do so, of course, if state officials are totally
committed to the maintenance of corporate authority in its
established forms and if their interference on behalf of that
authority is not merely occasional but systematic. Clearly
there have been governments so committed, and to their
officials corporate revolution must look like (and may actually be) revolution *tout court*. But the history of liberal
government is a history of retreat from such commitments,
retreat from the total support, for example, of church prel-
ates (ecclesiastical authority, and above all the right to collect tithes, was once protected by the property laws), of industrial magnates, and so on. The occasion for such retreats
has generally been an act or a series of acts of corporate
rebellion which state officials decided they could not or discovered they need not repress.

Continuous repression, if it were possible, would virtually
force the rebels to expand their activity and challenge the
state directly. And there are always some militants among
the rebels who assume that such repression is inevitable.
Like the corporate authorities, they see civil order and corporate authority as inextricably intertwined. But this is
rarely, if ever, the case. Law and order is, indeed, always law
and order of a particular sort; it necessarily has a specific
social content. But law and order is also a universal myth;
the liberal state is at least potentially a universal organization; and in the name of its myths, its leaders can always or
almost always dissociate themselves from some particular
piece of social oppression. For this reason, corporate rebel-

lion is potentially a limited form of political action and potentially a kind of civil disobedience. The violation of property laws is not in itself an act of revolution against the state, and state officials acknowledge this and confirm it when they give up on such things as collecting tithes or clearing the factories.

If they intend to be civil and hope to be treated civilly, the rebellious subjects of corporate authority must in turn be careful not to make revolutionary claims against the state. Doubtless, the occasion calls for a certain rhetorical extravagance, but that can be ignored so long as the actions of the rebels bespeak a concern for the appropriate limits. In general, this is the case: the rebels argue by their actions that their goals and the commitments they have made to one another (their newfound solidarity) establish an obligation to disobey not all laws, but only *these* laws, for example, the trespass laws. They claim for their revolutionary organization not that it replaces the state or is a law unto itself, but only that it wins primacy in this or that limited area of social life. It requires its members to violate state laws *here,* not everywhere, and insofar as it justifies the use of violence against state officials, it does so only if they intervene against the revolution. The justification is local and temporary and does not challenge the general authority of the police to enforce the law. In fact, the rebels will often demand law enforcement—against the corporation—and explicitly pledge themselves to obedience, as they should do, whenever obedience is compatible with corporate democracy.

IV.

All the arguments I have thus far made are illustrated by the auto workers' sit-down strikes of 1936–1937, and I think the illustration is worth presenting in some detail since so little has been written about this form of civil disobedience. The right of workers to strike has come to be so widely accepted that its illegal and semilegal history and all the philosophical issues raised by that history have been forgotten. The sit-down, moreover, was not only called illegal by the local courts in 1937, it was eventually called illegal by the Supreme Court. And the strike that went so far to establish the right of corporate subjects to organize and defend themselves remains illegal today. Yet it is not the case that all corporate systems have been democratized, nor do all corporate subjects have the same rights. The questions raised in 1936–1937 still have to be answered.

I do not think that I need to describe at length the kind of oppression that existed in General Motors plants before the victory of the auto workers. Corporate officials possessed absolute authority over hiring and firing, the conditions of work, the pace of work, and the rates of pay. They used this power not only to maximize production and profit, but also to maintain the established authority system. In effect, they ran a miniature police state in the factories; and the organization of the workers, their incipient union, took on in response the features of an underground movement.[7] This movement claimed a kind of legality, not within the corporation, but within the state: its spokesmen insisted that they were acting in accordance with the National Labor Relations Act, which made the encouragement of union organization a matter of public policy, and in defense of those legal rights that workers were said to have in their jobs.[8] But though they might argue that their activity was democratically authorized outside the factories, inside it necessarily took revolutionary and sometimes nondemocratic forms.

There can be no doubt that the union enjoyed widespread sympathy among the workers. But union members did not make up anything like a majority at any of the struck plants, and in some this was true not only of members but also of supporters. Majority rule does not operate very well in the early stages of the struggle for democracy, when the majority is likely to be both passive and frightened, justifiably anxious for its jobs, and often resentful of militants who do not share that anxiety or who repress it in the name of possibly distant goals. Hence the way is always open for vanguard initiatives which are dangerous both practically and morally. Militants who seize the initiative always run the risk of finding themselves alone, deprived not only of effective support but of moral justification. In 1936, the risks paid off; the basis of a democratic movement did in fact exist, though this could not be known in advance with any certainty.

It is important to stress the risks the militants accepted and had to accept if they were to undertake any political action at all. But it is also important to stress all they did to minimize those risks. A long history of struggle and failure preceded the dramatic victory of 1937. The commitment of the union militants to corporate democracy is best evidenced by their months and years of work in the factories, building support, searching for activists, adjusting their own proposals to meet the interests of the men on the job. A strike might have been attempted without all that; angry men were never lacking in the auto plants. But there is a kind of legitimacy that can only be won by hard work. Without a disciplined base the civility of the strike would have been precarious at best, and it is not difficult to imagine isolated militants, faced with certain defeat, setting fire to a factory or shooting at the police.

But a successful strike requires not only that the militants find majority support, it also requires that they coerce minorities and often that they begin to do so before they have demonstrated the extent of their support. This is not a usual feature of civil disobedience against the state, but it has to be remembered that what is going on in the corporation is not civil disobedience at all but revolution. Exactly what this involves can be seen most clearly in the seizure of Chevrolet Plant No. 4, the turning point of the General Motors strike. The union was relatively weak in Plant No. 4,

and its seizure required careful planning. Company police
were lured away by a demonstration in another factory; several hundred union militants from Plant No. 6 were
brought in during a change of shifts; and these men, together with union supporters already inside, succeeded in
forcing the shutdown of No. 4. Before the strikers carried
the day, however, there was a time when uncommitted
workers were attacked from both sides. Here is the account
of a union official:

> A few of the staunchest unionists got into the aisles and be-
> gan marching around shouting . . . "Strike is on! Come on
> and help us!" Many of the workers stood waveringly at their
> posts. . . . And meanwhile the superintendents and foremen
> . . . tore about, starting the conveyors up again, yelling to
> the men to "get back to work or you're fired." . . . Some of
> the men began working again or at least made a desperate
> effort to do so under the tumultuous circumstances as they
> were still anxious to differentiate themselves from the strikers.
> But the ranks of the latter grew inexorably. . . . There was
> practically no physical violence. The men would merely act
> fierce and holler threats. There was huge Kenny Malone with
> wrench in hand tearing down the lines and yelling: "Get off
> your job, you dirty scab!" Yet he never touched a man. . . .[9]

This is a graphic description of a revolutionary moment, the
decisive overthrow of the absolutism of superintendents and
foremen. It is clear, I think, that one can justify the coercion
of the "wavering" workers only by reference to that end and
to the legitimate expectation that it was widely shared. For
the moment, however, the militants could only assume that
the end was widely shared; and such assumptions may have
to be sustained without proof for some time. In Plant No. 4
the political battle was won, but the moral outcome, so to
speak, remained inconclusive:

> The fight was over; the enormous plant was dead. . . . The
> unionists were in complete control. Everywhere they were
> speaking to groups of undecided workers. "We want you boys

to stay with us. It won't be long and everything will be settled. Then we'll have a union and things will be different." Many of the workers reached their decision (for the union) in this moment. Others went home, undeterred by the strikers. About two thousand remained and an equal number went off.[10]

I don't mean to suggest that *any* degree of coercion of undecided or neutral persons can be defended by reference to the end of corporate democracy. But it is likely that given the limits I have already sketched, virtually any degree of necessary coercion can be defended. Surely it would be dishonest for those of us who value democracy in corporations as well as in states to pretend that we would judge the GM strike differently if Kenny Malone had actually hit somebody with his wrench—though we are certainly glad (and should be glad) to be told that he didn't. But in discussing violence against state officials, somewhat different standards apply; at least, they apply if we believe the state to be so constituted that attempts on its authority are not easily justified. Within the corporation, revolutionary initiatives may well be appropriate; within the larger democratic community, they are inappropriate, and the corporate rebels demonstrate their civility only insofar as they make clear, as the auto workers did, that they intend no such initiatives. During the GM strike, for example, a number of workers were arrested, and the union leaders ordered mass demonstrations in front of the local police station. They thus used against the police legal forms of protest that they had declined to use against the corporation.

On the day after the seizure of Plant No. 4, a Michigan court issued an injunction against the strike, and the strikers began discussing among themselves what they would do if confronted by police or National Guardsmen. There were a few men in the factories and among the union's leaders who urged passive resistance. They thought the workers should allow themselves to be carried out of the factories. But a

much larger group favored active resistance, on the pragmatic grounds that there was no working-class tradition of
passivity and no religious or ideological foundation for a
politics of nonviolence. The spectacle of strikers being carried, limp and unresisting, in the hands of the hated police
would have, they argued, a profoundly disillusioning effect
on the families of the strikers and on all the men who had
so far refused to join the revolution. It would seem a terri-
ble defeat rather than a moral victory, an incongruous and
humiliating end to a period of heroic action. This argument
carried the day, and the strikers publicly committed themselves to fight back against any effort to use force to clear
the factories.[11]

At the same time, they did everything they could do, short
of leaving the factories, to avoid such an outcome. They established their own law and order, a strikers' discipline far
stricter than that of the foremen; they banned liquor from
the occupied plants, worked out informal agreements with
the police which permitted workers to come and go and food
to be brought in, and carried out all necessary repair and
maintenance work on factory machinery.[12] Above all, they
repeatedly stressed their willingness to negotiate a settlement. This last is a crucial token of civility. However radical
the demands, and even if those demands imply that the corporate authorities ought not to be authorities at all, the
rebels can never deny to their opponents the recognition
they themselves seek. The call for unconditional surrender
may sometimes be appropriate in time of war and civil war,
but it is never a political demand, nor is it compatible with
civil peace.

The argument in the factories indicates some of the problems of any absolute commitment to nonviolence. Men who
live in a democratic state can plausibly be said to be obli-
gated to preserve its peace, to accept the forms of its law and
order. But the strikers did not live only in the state. They
were members, as all of us are, of overlapping social circles,

and within the spheres specific to them—General Motors, the auto industry, the capitalist industrial system generally —they did not enjoy the benefits usually associated with the words *law and order*. These were worlds of oppression and struggle, in which the mutual forbearance necessary to civil disobedience did not exist. And in those worlds, state police had all too frequently played a role no different from that of company police, implicating themselves in the oppression and compromising their own authority. The point where the two circles overlapped had thus been dominated by the violence of the corporate world. It was only the refusal of Michigan's Governor Frank Murphy to enforce the court injunction—his own civil disobedience—that reestablished the state as a universal organization and a sphere of nonviolence, within which auto workers could conceivably incur serious obligations to the public peace.

Most of the criticisms of the strikers were simply refusals to recognize the pluralism of their social lives and the possible pluralism of their moral commitments. When A. Lawrence Lowell, president emeritus of Harvard University, said that the sit-downs constituted "an armed insurrection . . . defiance of law, order, and duly elected authorities," he was suggesting that the spheres of corporate and state authority coincided perfectly.[13] I have already argued that this is sometimes true, and when it is, civility on the part of the corporate rebels is almost impossible. But it was not true in Michigan in 1937. Governor Murphy, who had only a few months before become a "duly elected authority" with the support of the auto workers, symbolized this fact. His affirmation of the independence of the state recognized that the primary focus of the strike was on General Motors and not on Michigan or the United States; so ended the threat to civil order. By forcing negotiations between the corporate authorities and the union leadership, he began the long (and as yet incomplete) process of bringing some kind of legitimacy to General Motors. Until that process was well begun, there was no reason to deny to the workers the right to use (limited) force within the corporate world, against their oppressors, and against any allies their oppressors might call in. But I do not mean to state a general rule; the argument depends upon the specific character of the overlapping social circles.

Even if the police had gone in, the resistance of the workers would not have constituted an "armed insurrection," though it is not difficult to imagine an insurrection growing out of such an encounter. Particular, limited acts of resistance, coupled with appeals to community laws and values, do not necessarily break through the bounds of civil order. There was, in fact, an action of this sort early in the strike, a short, sharp battle between police and strikers (known, among the strikers at least, as the Battle of Bull's Run) which took place at the initiative of the police.[14] I do not believe that incidents of this sort detract in any serious way from the double description of the strike that I have attempted to sketch: revolution in the corporate world, civil disobedience in the state. Obviously that dualism breeds difficulty; neither label is precise. Together, I think, they capture something of the social and moral reality of the sit-down.

V.

Civil disobedience has often been divided into two types: direct disobedience, in which state laws thought to be unjust are openly defied; and indirect disobedience, in which state policies thought to be unjust are challenged by the violation of incidental laws, most often trespass laws. I have tried to describe a third type, more indirect than the second, in which the state is not challenged at all, but only those corporate authorities that the state (sometimes) protects. Here the disobedience takes place simultaneously in two different social arenas, the corporation and the state; and in judging that disobedience, different criteria must be applied to the

two, though I have tried to show that the two sets of criteria
are not entirely unrelated. When revolution is justified in
the corporation, then certain limited kinds of resistance,
even violent resistance, may be justified against state officials
protecting corporate property. I assume a strong presumption against such violence, however, and I would want to
justify it only when the oppression of the corporate subjects
is palpable and severe and the interference of the police of
such a kind that it leaves the rebels no alternative but resistance or defeat. At the same time, it seems to me that state
officials, recognizing the oppression, ought not to interfere:
ought to refrain, that is, from enforcing the property laws,
and so avoid even limited violence.

The character of private governments obviously varies a
great deal, and so the argument I have developed on the basis
of the General Motors strikes will not apply in any neat and
precise way to all other sit-downs. The student rebellions of
the sixties, for example, are very different from the labor
rebellions of the thirties. But I do believe that the same criteria can be used in framing our judgments in these two
cases, and in many others. This suggests the sorts of questions
we must ask student militants: What is the nature of the
oppression you experience? Have you worked seriously
among your fellow students (and among your teachers) to
build support for your new politics? Do you have, or potentially have, majority support? What are your specific proposals for university reform? and so on. By and large, I think,
these questions have not been adequately answered—chiefly
for two reasons that I can only mention here. First of all, contemporary universities are very different from the General
Motors plants of 1936 (or even of 1969). However authoritarian their administrations, their students enjoy personal
and civil liberties undreamt of in the factories, and these
liberties open the way for a great variety of political activities
short of the sit-in, or at least, short of the sit-in as I have
described it, with its attendant coercions. And yet, secondly,

contemporary student movements have rarely been able to win and hold majority support, in fact, they have rarely attempted in any politically serious way to do so. Their militants have too often rushed into adventures that cannot hope to win such support, in part because they have nothing to do with corporate democratization, in part because they call into question the very functions of the university the militants profess to value.

It is, nevertheless, not difficult to imagine universities so rigidly authoritarian and student movements so committed as to justify the sorts of politics I have been examining. There have certainly been justified sit-ins during the past several years, sit-ins that actually moved this or that university closer to whatever form of democracy is appropriate to the academic community. There have also been sit-ins justified in part, open at the same time to severe criticism, that resulted or might have resulted in similar movements. The theoretical model I have tried to elaborate permits us, I think, to defend such movements and their necessary methods—but always in a way that reveals to the participants themselves the nature and limits of their action.

The problems of university government indicate clearly the great importance of arguing about the possibilities of democracy in every institutional order, not only in the state. I don't mean to prejudge these arguments—at any rate, I don't mean to prejudge them absolutely. A government of equals may be possible in one setting; weighted voting, or some such recognition of inequality, may be necessary in another; collective bargaining between employees and managers may be appropriate in a third. The range of political decision making or of bargaining may have to be limited in this way or that, or it may not be limited at all.[15] There is no single desirable system of internal adjudication. But I think it can be said flatly that some kind of democratic legitimacy is always necessary to corporate authority. Insofar as corporations lack this legitimacy, their very existence breeds revolt, and the more private and autocratic their government is, the more angry, perhaps violent, the revolt will be. If democratic states choose to shelter corporate autocrats, then they must learn to shelter corporate rebels as well. And if the rebels are asked, as they should be, to maintain civility, then the authorities must see to it that civility is a genuine option for them and not merely a convenience for the autocrats.

NOTES

1. The list is adapted from Robert Pranger, *The Eclipse of Citizenship: Power and Participation in Contemporary Politics* (New York, Holt, Rinehart & Winston, 1968), esp. pp. 73–76. See also the excellent discussion in Grant McConnell, *Private Power and American Democracy* (New York, Alfred A. Knopf, 1966), Ch. 5. I should say at this point that I am not considering public corporations and civil services in this essay, though their employees may also be deprived of the benefits of internal democracy. Many of the arguments that I make later on may well apply to them, but their special position vis-à-vis a democratic government raises problems I cannot cope with here.

2. These are the implicit assumptions, for example, of Peter Drucker's *The Concept of the Corporation* (New York, New American Library, 1946). Drucker describes the suggestion box as a crucial channel for worker participation in corporate management and suggests no other channels (Ch. 3).

3. Perhaps there is a moral as well as a legal basis for such appeals: it can be argued, I think, that in discussing rights and obligations, one can always appeal from less to more democratic bodies. Obviously, this can work against the state as well as in its favor; for some examples, see my "Obligation to Disobey," in David Spitz, ed., *Political Theory and Social Change* (New York, Atherton Press, 1967).

4. Robert R. R. Brooks, *When Labor Organizes* (New Haven, Yale University Press, 1937), p. 112.

5. Charles Tilly suggests that this is also the case in Europe: "A large proportion of the European disturbances we have been surveying turned violent at exactly the moment when the authorities intervened to stop an illegal but nonviolent action . . . the great

bulk of the killing and wounding in those same disturbances was done by troops or police rather than by insurgents or demonstrators. "Collective Violence in European Perspective," in Hugh Davis Graham and Ted Robert Gurr, eds., *Violence in America, A Report to the National Commission on the Causes and Prevention of Violence* (New York, New American Library, 1969), p. 39.

6. This is the way the 1936–1937 strikes are justified in Joel Seidman, *Sit-Down,* League for Industrial Democracy Pamphlet (New York, 1937), p. 38.

7. See Henry Kraus, *The Many and the Few: A Chronicle of the Dynamic Auto Workers* (Los Angeles, Plantin Press, 1947), Ch. 1, for an account of what organizing was like before the sit-downs. Kraus was editor of the *Flint Auto Worker,* the local union newspaper, during 1936–1937.

8. Solomon Barkin, "Labor Unions and Workers' Rights in Jobs" in Arthur Kornhauser *et al.,* eds., *Industrial Conflict* (New York, McGraw-Hill Book Company, 1954), p. 127. These claims were eventually rejected by the courts. *Cf.* Leon Green "Sit-Down Strikes are Legal," *New Republic,* March 24, 1937.

9. Kraus, *The Many and the Few,* pp. 214–15.

10. *Ibid.,* p. 216.

11. In a letter to Governor Murphy; on the arguments within the union, see *ibid.,* pp. 220, 231–33.

12. Seidman, *Sit-Down,* pp. 32–36.

13. Quoted in J. Raymond Walsh, *C.I.O.: Industrial Unionism in Action* (New York, W. W. Norton & Company, 1937), p. 182.

14. Kraus, *The Many and the Few,* pp. 125ff. It should be noted that when compared to previous strikes in American history, "the sit-down strikes were exceptionally peaceful." Philip Taft and Philip Ross, "American Labor Violence: Its Causes, Character and Outcome," in Graham and Gurr, eds., *Violence in America,* p. 363. This was true largely because the workers were in the buildings, disengaged from company agents and the police. In labor disputes, violence most often erupts on the picket line.

15. Democratic decision making in the university does, I think, have to be limited: it is appropriate, for example, in the organization of day-to-day student life; in the classroom, not so.

Decentralization, Community Control,

and Revolution: Reflections on

Ocean Hill-Brownsville

PHILIP GREEN

I.

THE LAW in its majestic equality, wrote Anatole France, forbids rich and poor alike to sleep under bridges, to beg in the streets, and to steal bread. A contemporary connoisseur of equality might add that it also forbids black and white alike to establish segregated facilities, to sit in at public buildings . . . and to transfer teachers out of school districts in violation of union contracts.

II.

Important events, when we study them, yield important insights; but if we immerse ourselves in trivialities, our discoveries will share the inconsequence which distinquishes our subject matter. In recent years, unfortunately, American political science, especially on its home grounds, has taken as its preferred mode of analysis the attempt to build a science of politics from the materials of endlessly multiplied trivia: career patterns of twenty-seven district leaders; responses by twelve hundred citizens to abstract ambiguous questions about their hypothetical opinions; results of imitation conflicts simulated by bored graduate students. At the same time, political scientists seem often to avoid analysis of those signal developments or shifts in power that illuminate a new political landscape. The recent conflict in New York City between the governing board of the experimental school district in the largely black ghetto of Ocean Hill-Brownsville and the United Federation of Teachers (which struck the entire city three times over the dismissal of nineteen union teachers from that district's schools) was such an event; and so far, political science has turned toward it a blank face.

That conflict, to be sure, has already entered the realm of history, that is, become an event about which the facts will never quite be known. However, that this is so presents an opportunity for, as much as it constitutes an obstacle to, analysis. For "the facts," taking that phrase in its everyday sense, direct our attention to happenstance, to the accident of who said what to whom at the wrong time, who was a weak rather than a strong leader, and so on. The most circumstantial account of the New York crisis, for example— Martin Mayer's *The Teachers' Strike: New York, 1968*—is of exactly this nature, seeing virtually all the actors as foggy conspirators, or inexplicable charlatans, or intellectual and political incompetents. In the end such information, though fascinating as inside dope and gossip always are, is profoundly delusive. As Marx pointed out in *The Eighteenth Brumaire of Louis Bonaparte*, it draws our attention away from the real significance of the event: from what is revealed about the operational principles that underlie political institutions and processes.

These reflections, then, are intended to suggest a reconsideration of those principles in the United States.[1] They do not include, it must be admitted, a comprehensive report on the attitudes of residents toward their local school board or of teachers toward the union; or other such data which will surely be forthcoming. Rather, they are the tentative result

of my own intellectual confrontation with what suggests itself to me as the central meaning of the long and disastrous
battle, finally won by the union with the help of the city
administration and police force, between (largely) white
schoolteachers and the black community of Ocean Hill-
Brownsville.

III.

It is a truism, perhaps, to say that democratic theory has not
really solved the problem of legitimacy and consent. If so,
however, it is a truism that many writers prefer to ignore
entirely. Defenders of the majority-rule principle, especially, often seem to assert that with the discovery of that
principle in its modern form all the apparent dilemmas inherent in the existence of political authority have been re-
solved. At least, they suggest, this is so as long as one adds to
majoritarianism a dash of protection for minorities in the
form of due process, equal protection, free-speech requirements, and other formal constitutional provisions for "keeping open" the channels of opposition and dissent.

In fact, however, the notion of majority rule, whether or
not allied to that of constitutional protections, solves no
philosophical problems at all, although it does place some of
them in a new context. It is true, as Hobbes suggested in
broaching the notion of majority rule, that if all men are
roughly equal in their powers of physical destruction, and if
sovereign government is defined as that body which monop-
olizes those powers, then only a majority—at least 50 percent plus one—can securely form such a government and expect its dictates to be made good when opposed by physical
force. And if, furthermore (though Hobbes wished to avoid
this connection), the principle of that government's continuing legitimacy is *popular* rule, and force is exercised only in
the people's name, then generally speaking 50 percent plus
one of the people must give their consent to all the laws

which may call forth its exercise—else those laws would potentially be unenforceable.

These considerations no doubt explain why democracy appears to rank high among the most stable and secure forms of government in human history. In practice, if one must persuade, say, ninety-nine persons, roughly equal and in conflict, to undertake a course of action, the consent of fifty seems a minimal prerequisite for success, as they can then overcome the objections of the rest, but not vice versa. It is therefore always sensible in cases of conflict (except, of course, when limited by constitutional claims) to follow the wishes of the majority. It is the most practical thing to do, and assuming the issues for decision are of equal salience to everyone, also probably the fairest.

But in thus opting for stability, practicality, and even fairness, we have in no way established any principle that could resolve the really hard problems of political and ethical choice. If fifty out of ninety-nine persons want to do one thing and forty-nine another, we cannot possibly say for certain which group ought to have its way—until we know what exactly it is that each wants to do. Nor does the institution of a fundamental majoritarian social contract settle the argument except by assumption, for all sorts of situations can arise in which men may feel that the "contract" has not really been honored by those who implement it, or is for some other reason simply not binding.

What, then, does political theory have to say when basic institutions have lost their legitimacy in the eyes of a *minority* because for too long a time to be borne, the majority is thought to have done wrong or to have been oppressive? How to respond when the adequacy of constitutionalism is overtly denied, the implication of "tacit consent" expressly negated, Jefferson's rhetorical revolutionism taken seriously? As Michael Parenti's contribution to this volume illustrates, these questions are hardly hypothetical in the

United States today (or in France, or Italy, or Northern Ireland, or Canada, or West Germany, or Belgium).[2] But to this challenge, majoritarians and constitutionalists, except when they speak in the language of law and order, seem to have little to reply.

To be sure, it may be that once we depart from Hobbesian authoritarianism, such questions are finally unanswerable in the languge of rational theory, whether liberal democratic or any other. Certainly from any perspective which admits the necessity of political authority, it is ultimately indefensible as a matter of principle to leave the definition of the "legitimacy" of government up to every individual's or group's determination at will. In that sense, to speak of a "right" of revolution is meaningless, or self-contradictory.

But on the other hand, it ought to be recognized that resistance, rebellion, and revolution need no defense in principle: they occur not because someone has established their rightfulness in a logical argument, but because their spirit moves men too deeply to be withstood. Among recent evocations of that spirit, a book—Truman Nelson's *The Right of Revolution*—and a movie—Pontécorvo's *The Battle of Algiers*—are especially impressive at capturing its sheer intransigence and its irresistible claim on men. When it arises, furthermore, that spirit supersedes the claims of intellect and thus of theory; it exists as a brute fact, and we must simply choose up sides.

It is perfectly sensible, of course, to find the prospect conjured up by this line of reasoning frightening. But a political theorist ought to be aware of what he is doing before he succumbs finally to that fear, closes his mind against *all* potentially revolutionary claims, and registering his agreement with Hobbes's proposition that natural anarchy is the most dread of all possible states, takes an inalterable stand with the forces of "law and order." Such an unyielding permanent preference for the side of constituted authority as against

that of its opponents—*no matter what* the actual conditions
of the struggle, the demands of justice, or the moral nature
of the combatants—surely represents a more absolute commitment than most thoughtful men would want to make.
Nor will it do to limit Hobbes's absolutism to democratic
polities, thus hoping to qualify one's total opposition to revolutionary change; for whether a given polity actually is
"democratic" will always be a matter about which disagreement is possible, and which can in the end only be decided
by the citizens of that polity rather than by the definitions of
political theorists.

Therefore, at least for those who do admit even the faintest
possibility that the acts of a democratic, majoritarian government may at times be open to question,[3] there is something more to be said about the revolutionary spirit than the
mere uttering of expressions of sympathy or opposition, and
the New York school struggle offers an appropriate occasion
for saying it.

Let us look, for example, at the remarks of an observer
dedicated to both pluralism and liberalism (in its democratic socialist guise), writing in *Commentary,* a forum
whose general editorial policy is similarly inclined. In an article whose apparent purpose is to discredit the Ocean Hill-
Brownsville governing board and destroy sympathy for
black militants, Maurice Goldbloom claims that the board's
actions were consistently provocative and its demands consistently unreasonable. That is to say, they did not represent an understandable response to unbearable frustration
and oppression, but rather were deliberately couched so as
to frustrate the honest attempts of the New York City Board
of Education and the United Federation of Teachers to
give the "decentralized" experimental school district all
reasonable help. Defenders of the governing board have
claimed, says Goldbloom, that it could not function because
the Board of Education "refused to clarify its powers." On
the contrary:

. . . The problem was not that the Board of Education was unwilling to clarify the powers of the Governing Board; it was that the latter was unwilling to accept the clarification. It continued to demand that the Board of Education transfer powers to it which the latter had no legal right to transfer and in certain cases did not even possess. . . .

The guidelines finally issued gave the Local Boards all the powers the central Board felt it was legally entitled to delegate. These did not satisfy the Local Boards, and have been violently attacked by their apologists. Thus 'the NYCLU [New York Civil Liberties Union] pamphlet charges that the Board of Education "scuttled the experiment" with guidelines that "completely emasculated the experiment by stripping the Local Governing Board of virtually all of its substantive powers." The Niemeyer report is rather closer to the truth: "The suggested guidelines prepared by this Committee attempted to formulate the actual authority to be delegated to the Project Boards. In March 1968, however, the three Demonstration Projects agreed upon a consensus document *which demanded full authority, although the Board of Education could not go beyond the legal limits placed upon it by the State Education Law . . . in some local communities militant groups may be expected to continue to demand powers for which no one yet has proposed legislation. That is, in order for those who want to control all aspects of their local schools to accomplish their objectives, legislative changes would be required that would seriously affect many legal and contractual relationships affecting conditions of employment, such as tenure, that go far beyond the power presently held by the Board of Education."* 4

It is important to observe that Goldbloom (like all other commentators) is certain that the governing board's demands would not have been met by the state legislature and apparently agrees with the quoted Niemeyer report that these demands logically bear on the desire of certain groups of blacks "to control all aspects of their local schools." Thus his scorn for the board's approach is very revealing; it suggests as precisely as possible the limits of liberal pluralism. Diversity is encouraged, so long as consensus on the legitimacy of

PHILIP GREEN

the existing social framework is maintained. Tolerance of others' interests is the rule: so long as those interests can be met within the existing legal structure. But if the articulated demands of a disaffected group can *only* be met within a *changed* social framework or a *new* legal structure—too bad for pluralism then. Parenti's essay generally documents the nature of the American "consensus" with regard to ethnic diversity and interests; the New York school crisis shows us a graphic particular whose like we can expect to rediscover wherever majoritarianism is taken seriously. That, then, is Ocean Hill-Brownsville's distinctive revelation: the iron fist of undeviating authority in the velvet glove of liberal pluralism: Hobbes's ferocious eyes peering out from behind tolerant Madison's skull.

V.

But is not Hobbes correct, anarchy or authority our only alternatives, *any* openness to revolutionary claims an invitation to chaos? In another contribution to this volume, Michael Walzer challenges this assumption and suggests the possibility of a non-Hobbesian liberalism. His argument is that sovereign authority can and should respond with genuine tolerance to certain kinds of apparent disobedience (such as attempts to democratize undemocratic private institutions) without thereby subverting itself. To take his argument a considerable step further, it may also be possible to restrict (under certain conditions) both the scope and exercise of sovereignty to an extent that would make real rather than pseudo-pluralism a live option.

The argument, it will be seen, may seem to bear certain resemblances to the federalism of James Madison (or even the States' Rights of Calhoun), but the resemblances are only superficial. The federal system in which Madison saw such possibilities has without doubt offered avenues for the *advancement* of minorities to positions of limited political power, such as the Mormons in Utah, the Irish in a few big cities and states. But it has never—with perhaps one exception—offered *protection* for minorities (or communities) which were seriously unconventional or which put up serious resistance to the encroachment of "American" values and institutions on their own. The Mormons again are a perfect case in point, in that the price to them of attaining statehood for Utah was to surrender everything—most especially polygamy—that made their religion distinctively different from any other version of American Christianity. Only the southern states have successfully functioned in a protective manner, but then it is doubtful whether a popular national majority has ever been seriously inclined to challenge the White South's system of racial domination. Indeed, had that challenge ever been issued and intended to take real effect, the United States might be on its way to becoming a racially integrated society, and we would be discussing the problems of liberal centralism as revealed by events in, say, Quebec rather than New York City. And in any event, the case of the South—whose governments have clearly belonged in the category of "tyranny" rather than that of "democracy," for the most part—provides vivid evidence of the character that Madison's federalism has taken on. When sovereign powers are parceled out to *states* (and thence to localities) they are most often exercised with even less respect for opposition and resistance than exists at the national level.[5] When "decentralization" means the *dispersal* of powers to units of government that still rule without genuine consent, it is a sham. In the remainder of this essay I shall argue that if decentralization is to be taken seriously as a program, the exercise of certain powers based on legalized armed force cannot be merely *dispersed* to different constitutional arenas but must be altogether *forsworn* by organized public government at any level.

VI.

For the specific case of education, the argument in its simplest form may be stated as follows. A compulsory public
education system is inherently coercive and potentially intimidating of students and their parents. To a certain extent, the existence of a parallel *private* school system miti-
gates this condition if the private schools really offer alternative modes of education. Then parents who feel that the
public school abuses its powers may "vote with their feet"
and transfer their children to a private school . . . *if* they
possess the necessary financial resources.

Almost without exception, however, *black* parents resident in the big-city ghettos do *not* possess those resources
and are thus locked into the coercive public scoool system.
That is the way in which we must see the black parents and
children of Ocean Hill-Brownsville: the law compels them,
they are political subjects, not citizens. They must submit to
the various demands of authorities whom they may feel to be
either incompetent or illegitimate; they must engage in
types of behavior that they may feel to be inappropriate or
humiliating. And if through community leaders they attempt to capture that authority for themselves, they find, as
Goldbloom documents, that most of the important decisions
and resource allocations are being made elsewhere, outside
the small area in which their writ runs. Seized of de facto
control, they have nothing to control: they remain powerless. Power over their collective fate remains in the hands of
the state legislature and the central Board of Education—as
well as the latter's subcontractors in the United Federation
of Teachers and the Council of Supervisory Associations.
(And we must remember that such groups are not private
agencies but are rather quasi-public ones, by virtue both of
their contractual affiliations and of the fact that they do
work prescribed by public authority. Indeed, the UFT

could not win its struggle with the governing board except
by striking the whole public-school system, and thus bringing the city's police power into the lists on its behalf.)

This whole argument, of course, is stated by Goldbloom
himself in the passage quoted, although a different emotional affect is attached to it. But then critics of the governing
board do not deny that it was kept relatively powerless.
Rather, they wish to deny that the precise amount of power
possessed by that board is a consideration relevant to real
educational advancement. "Community control," that is, is
denigrated for being "cheap" and therefore educationally
ineffective; the union is claimed to be more truly dedicated
to educational betterment than the members of the governing board themselves.

From the viewpoint of the board and its supporters,
though, such complaints are beside the point. The effectiveness of educational reforms (and expenditures) per se is denied; community control (power) is asserted to be the sine
qua non of any useful program of change. In part, this is a
matter of ideology (that certain studies can be interpreted
to cast doubt on the utility of marginal expenditures for
ghetto education is an interesting but nonessential aspect of
the situation); in larger part, it is a matter of credibility.
White reformers are no longer believed in; their programs
are too little and too late; gradual improvements (e.g., the
rise in reading scores at Junior High School 271 before the
start of the decentralization experiment) are token and unsatisfactory. In the absence of immediate and (in some way)
real equality, only the feeling of self-determination, of control over the institutions to which one is subjected, can provide that morale without which no social group can long
sustain itself.

Regardless of whether these sentiments may seem reasonable to an outside observer, they are neither "right" nor
"wrong": they are revolutionary: they signal a breakdown of
legitimacy. They can, of course, be dealt with by resort to

repressive force. But that would clearly mean the end of the American dream of a plural society. Furthermore, given the nature of black consciousness today, the resort to force could only connote a final return to slavery after barely a century of "emancipation"; and whether a society so bent on large-scale injustice could escape decay or dissolution is a question that liberal upholders of law and order must ask themselves.

In the absence of a will to real social integration, then, decentralization (with its corollary, community control) presents itself as the only alternative to repression. It is such an alternative, first, because it and it alone is the program upon which the disaffected community has fixed its sights; and second, because it is a cure logically related to the disease that has turned out to be inherent in the liberal conception of public education. (Of course, we should not forget that analysis may show many other institutions to be, for similar or dissimilar reasons, in need of the same treatment: for example, the television oligopoly or centralized health services.) The combination of a compulsory education requirement and the lack of multiple channels within which to pursue it presents the problem; break that nexus and the problem begins to disappear. If compulsion is thought to be absolutely essential and unequivocally defensible on rational grounds—as military conscription, to take a similar example, is not defensible—then emphasis must be placed on the provision of supplementary local educational services.

The states and the cities, that is, must agree to forswear the exercise of their powers over all the institutions of public education, as they did not do in New York's so-called "decentralization." The simple powers of self-determination—controlling the allocation of one's own resources or the nature of one's personnel policies—that the lowliest private school possesses must be placed in the hands of those communities that demonstrate the seriousness of their demands. If that turns out to mean separatism, graft, nepotism, the spoils system, and general inefficiency—if "the majestic equality" of the law is violated on behalf of distressed minorities—we can only reflect that most civilized societies, including our own, have had no difficulty from time to time in enduring these shortcomings peacefully (especially as practised by the dominant social classes).

But if on the other hand, the servants of that law—in the guise of HEW, the Federal courts, the state legislatures, etc. —use its spurious formal equality as a justification for prohibiting community self-determination, then they will have themselves proclaimed the irrelevancy of that which they serve. Having thus effectively defined the issue as one of force against force, they will have no one but themselves to blame when the school windows are broken, and finally entire schools burned down or dynamited.

VII.

Of course, to prescribe decentralized community control as the indicated pluralist cure for a disease of liberal democracy raises the traditional question of whether the cure may not be worse than the disease. It is one thing to justify separatism or even corruption as necessary evils, quite another to countenance the prospect that traditional civil liberties may be destroyed. Specifically, that nineteen teachers were dismissed by the governing board in Ocean Hill-Brownsville without proper hearings and then prevented from reentering the schools by physical force is taken by critics to signify the disaster that community control portends for democracy. It is suggested that the very essence of liberalism itself—due process, rules of fairness, equal legal treatment for all citizens—is endangered. The law in its majestic equality is right after all: to have different rules for different groups is to have injustice; without duly enforced constitutional protections for all, the bullying of the weak by the strong is inevitable; nineteen union teachers today may be nineteen non-

union or radical or conservative or black teachers tomorrow.
The quest for pluralism will discover, not a multitude of self-
governing communities, but a surfeit of "McCarthyisms" (a
term Mayer uses to characterize the governing board's actions). And thus that pluralism—what I have called "genuine" pluralism—is not a complement to liberal society, but
one of its mortal enemies.

Superficially, all these criticisms are warranted. And yet to
stop there, to use the argument for due process as a means of
thwarting community control, is effectively to demonstrate
that the Hobbesian spirit underlying our liberal institutions
is hostile to the attainment not merely of pluralism, but of
social justice itself. Fearing for freedom, we invade it; in the
name of protecting the weak in principle, we harass those
who are truly weak in practice and leave them to the mercy
of the strong. The forms of fairness destroy its substance.

To see this more clearly, let us assume the very worst
about the events in Ocean Hill-Brownsville: that the governing board arbitrarily transferred out of the district nineteen qualified teachers without meeting the reasonable procedural requirements of a union contract; and that this was
done not because the teachers were guilty of any kind of untoward behavior, but purely in order to provoke a confrontation with the union—to test the limits of "community
control." [6]

Here is the heart of the contention that the governing
board engaged in an unacceptable version of "McCarthyism." The falsity of this argument, however, is betrayed by
the board's leading critic, Mayer himself, when to prove the
board's irrationalism he proclaims that it could not possibly
have hoped to win such a confrontation with a major, well-
organized union. Of course he is right, and thus he unwit-
tingly reveals a significant weakness in the liberal habit of
mind that treats all invasions of due process, all denials of
"equal protection," as meriting an indiscriminate denuncia-
tion.

For can anyone imagine it being said of McCarthy and his followers that *they* "could not possibly win" the confrontation with Theodore Kagan or Reed Harris or a schoolteacher, screenwriter, or folksinger whose path happened to be crossed by a congressional investigating committee? The very question is absurd. McCarthy consistently won (as his followers still win at times) until he took on bigger game than mere individuals. The decisive difference is that McCarthy and others who exercised his will (as distinct from the mass of his followers) were *leaders* of and *power wielders* in society: they were the powerful picking on the relatively powerless. By contrast, the blacks of Ocean Hill-Brownsville, even those described as "terrorists," are on the whole *victims* in and of American society, born losers, made losers, perpetual losers. To compare the spasms of self-defense in which they lash out at an oppressive society with the deadly and destructive operations of a marauding American senator is to be totally insensitive to the human dimensions of politics.

As for the members of the UFT, it may be possible to picture them too as "losers," but only in the terms of a complex Marxian theory of alienation which pictures the middle classes everywhere as victims of industrial society. In no way are they victims in same sense as that in which the blacks are victims: alienation is not oppression. Certainly, many occupational groups as well as ethnic minorities might more actively pursue self-determination—what used to be called "workers' control of industry." But the experimental school districts are hardly the major enemy of teachers' autonomy (which anyway means much more than mere formal due-process protections against being fired). For the teachers, who have long been notoriously backward in seeking job control, to persecute black separatists in pursuit of this end is equivalent to the United States' choosing Vietnam as the main battleground in its struggle to make the world "safe for democracy."

Nor can sentimentalism about the struggles of labor ob-

scure the fact that the teachers are *organized* labor: not a
buffeted, helpless mass, but a functioning solidary organization with social and financial resources and—despite the existence of an antistrike law for public servants—real collective bargaining power. The city board of education and the
state have certain legal powers over them, and they have certain real powers on their own behalf; to some extent they
countervail. The notion, then, that elements of a potential
coalition of the bottom classes have been set against each
other by Machiavellian elites cannot possibly stand; the two
forces are in no way partners in misery. Admittedly, organized workers, contrary to the assertions of complacent "pluralists" in the social science fraternity, are far from being full-
fledged partners with (for example) the real-estate and
financial interests in the governance of New York City.
Their "countervailing power" extends only to the necessities of self-defense and sheer organizational survival; except
perhaps for the building-trades unions, labor's power does
not extend so far as to constitute a real influence on the policies that shape the face—and the fate—of the city. Still, antistrike laws and all, organized teachers *have* made a place for
themselves in society and in the polity; the blacks have not,
and that is a difference more fundamental than their shared
exclusion from the realm where key decisions are made.

But even this comparison does not begin to tell the whole
story of the relationship between teachers and community:
of the face that "due process" wears in Ocean Hill-Brownsville. All of those commentaries on community control which
defend the union and protest the iniquity of the governing
board betray an insensitivity not merely to the human problems at stake but to the fundamental political issues as well.
They have, we might say, failed to receive the distinctive
revelation of Ocean Hill-Brownsville. They have made no
attempt to strike through the mask of liberal toleration and
see the coerciveness beneath: a coerciveness which when un-

checked weighs upon the victims of state power as heavily as though they did not live in a liberal democracy at all.

The truth, then, is that the teachers are, wittingly or not, agents of this coercive state power. Here is the testimony of one observer, an official of the New York Civil Liberties Union; it could be multiplied a thousandfold:

> I get calls every day here about cases we just can't handle. I just got one 10 mintues ago from a mother who said her son had been suspended for essentially petty kinds of things. He's a young kid, eight years old, third grade, and he's going to have a suspension hearing. And he's going to be shipped off to a 600 school, which has the same effect on a kid of that age as sending him off to prison.
>
> Talk about due process! There's absolutely no hearing. You have what's called a suspension hearing at which the child is not allowed to have a lawyer and which is a star chamber proceeding and a kangaroo court if there ever was one. . . . They consign a first-grade pupil very often to a 600 school when the pupil has said something aggressive to a teacher who is not used to having six-year-olds say something aggressive to her.[7]

In short, the school system is among other things a (potentially) *penal* system. Teachers and principals wield powers of suspension, expulsion, *involuntary transfer* (!); by misusing their pedagogical authority, or simply by using their disciplinary authority, they can set children irrevocably on the road to educational and thus social failure, or even to reform school and criminal careers. Unionized teachers, in sum, are not merely better adapted than are blacks to American society, they have power over blacks as well; and that power is not—was not, until the governing board took its decisive step—effectively countervailed.

That children—mere children, one is tempted to say— can be conceived of as having "rights" against public power may at first glance seem odd. But at least with regard to those old enough to think with some degree of rationality

about their grievances, it is not odd at all; especially in revolutionary situations, the breakdown in perceptions of legitimacy knows no age boundaries and is often, in fact, felt and
articulated more keenly by the relatively unsocialized
young.[8] And in any event we are talking about potential
conflicts not simply between teachers and schoolchildren,
but between teachers and a whole array of parents and community leaders, who compete with teachers to speak for and
in the name of the childrens' interests.

In this competition the teachers come armed by the law
with many weapons; the community, with virtually none. As
in a court of equity, then, the teachers can fairly plead for
relief only if their own hands are clean. Here, so to speak,
their hands are not clean, in that they ask for a form of relief
—due process—that they do not propose for and apparently
are not willing to give to others. In this particular case, in
sum, a general principle is once again revealed. Liberal society is constructed on the base of civil equality, yet formal
equality and real equality may sharply diverge, and to the extent that they do so the rules of liberalism become a mask for
privilege. The most grossly illiberal actions may then be
necessary to rectify that imbalance, or, as perhaps in the
Ocean Hill-Brownsville affair, to symbolically define the
condition of injustice and present a challenge to it. Lacking
the willingness to tolerate such appeals for equality, though,
liberalism becomes as much of a sham as does pluralism in
refusing to tolerate appeals for self-determination.

VIII.

There is still, we must note, another ground on which the
repression of such revolts has been justified. In addition to
invoking a prejudicial defense of due process, opponents of
community control also claim that black "militants," angry
schoolchildren, etc., are not truly "representative" of the
black community itself and therefore need not be treated

with seriousness. This supposed discrepancy between the demands of articulate community leaders and those of the apathetic masses, however, in no way bears on the legitimacy of the pluralist demand for self-determination. All it reveals, rather, is how perniciously the liberal majoritarian principle, like the principle of civil equality, can operate—how, that is, its tyranny can be all-encompassing, can dominate men's lives at the very lowest levels of social organization as well as at the highest.

The fact, unacknowledged by rigid devotees of majoritarianism, is that nothing important ever happens in any society because "the majority" *wills* it. Nor is the purpose of majority rule to "make things happen." (Did Hobbes imagine that a social contract came into existence because a majority spontaneously thought of it?) To repeat an earlier point, majority rule, both within representative assemblies and among competing political parties, is no more than a fair and practical device for legitimizing the actions of government in the absence of any of the more traditional grounds of legitimization. Actually to set the engine of government running, however, is always the work of a few, and often an unrepresentative few at that.

What is true of government is even more self-evidently true of social movements. Everywhere in democratic societies the political and economic life of both ascriptive communities and voluntary associations—including unions such as the UFT—is dominated by oligarchies or other kinds of elite leadership groups. These, in turn, are dependent for their self-maintenance on the usually apathetic behavior of a mass membership and are in many cases further helped to maintain their position by the cruder forms of domination.[9] The membership of most such groups, after all, consists of individuals who typically are not in any meaningful sense politicized or *willful* at all but live their organizational lives in a mental state compounded of tired resignation, the desire to be let alone, and daydreams of finding themselves suddenly in a better world without having had to lift a finger to bring it into existence. Thus we must expect that attempts at greater participation or self-government will be made in the first instance not through but *in spite of* the "majority will" and will often bear the combined onus of illegality and "elitism" because of this.

To take but one example relevant to this discussion: for a century the education of most American Catholics has been controlled by Catholic priests, who surely form the most unrepresentative leadership group to be found anywhere in the Western world. Yet American society, even including its liberal pluralists, has come to live peaceably with this situation; and indeed, were dissident parishioners to attempt the seizure of a church or a school building on the grounds that it belonged "to them" as much as to their priest, our peculiar notions of "property" would undoubtedly require that the force of law be thrown into the contest against them.

All this is commonplace. What it implies, clearly, is that dedication to majoritarianism as a principle to be imposed on those who try to institute social change, and the concomitant rejection of all kinds of vanguard activism as illegitimate, ultimately hide an acceptance of social stasis.[10] If decisive innovations, implacable demands, the use of force, had always to await the positive concurrence of a majority of the people in whose name action is taken, then nothing would ever happen, nothing would ever change. Walzer's description of the auto workers' revolt in 1937 (see pp. 235–42 below) could be duplicated in almost any similar instance: the activists make history; their fellows go along. And always the opponents of revolutionary action, be it in Algeria, Vietnam, Flint, or Ocean Hill-Brownsville, argue that "the people" do not really want change—as though thereby to absolve themselves from the charge of opposing it.

It is bitterly ironic, for example, that Goldbloom chastises black militants and their white supporters for lack of dedication to the California grape strike, a victory which, he writes, "would be of more direct benefit to American minority groups than any number of ads suggesting that we "Give a Damn' for the Ocean Hill Governing Board." As though the grape growers had not produced exactly the same arguments against the grape strike that Goldbloom has produced against community control!—the union is not representative, it intimidates the workers, they have spontaneously formed committees to oppose it, they are really well paid, the state has passed all sorts of reformist programs for their benefit, etc., etc. Everything, indeed, is noted except the one crucial fact: that the grape pickers are not free men, and that one of the hardest things in the human universe is for unfree men to act rebelliously and decisively: to act as though they were free. In fact, to return to our example, given the condition of the ghetto, the few statistics offered by the opponents of community control give an impression quite contrary to the one they are supposed to convey. It is astonishing, for example, that 22 percent of the school district's parents should have troubled themselves to participate in a school board election that they must have—correctly—anticipated would be allowed by the authorities to come to nothing. It is equally astonishing that after all the travail and torment inflicted on them, a majority of those willing to offer an opinion to Gallup Poll takers should support the actions of the governing board. For the work of mobilization, of arousing the quiescent, always requires much time and the use of many unpleasant or even brutal tactics.

Those who engage in such work certainly can and ought to be held accountable for what they do, as Rogin argues, but they can hardly be expected to meet the stringent requirements of democratic representation. (These, of course, are not met by "moderate" Negro leaders or by most labor leaders; nor even by many of our constitutional decision makers. Eldridge Cleaver and Bobby Seale are as "representative" as Congressman Jamie Whitten, and much less destructive.) For them, therefore, to be accountable in this setting generally means that they avoid gratuitous physical brutality; articulate real rather than imaginary grievances; are effective enough in mobilizing the community so that the inevitable innocent victims of the process at least do not suffer for nothing; and are engaged in a genuine attempt to bring about increased self-determination, not to turn their followers into puppets.

By any criterion of comparison with other insurgent groups, militant black community leaders have passed these tests. That the grievances and resentments they express speak to real community needs goes without saying (and cannot be obscured even by their occasional hyperbolic references to "cultural genocide"). In a short space of time, furthermore, their work of community mobilization has been amazingly effective: one has only to talk to any black high school or college student anywhere to know this. Nor, although the more militant among them may attempt to stifle dissent within the ghetto (building a *united* force is the object of the exercise, after all), is there any evidence that they wish to freeze their followers at a lower level of consciousness and self-realization than they themselves possess, as has been the case in so many Communist revolutions.

Finally, the physical and social costs (actual *and* potential) of their activities in black communities have been quite low—and especially in Ocean Hill-Brownsville. Even if we accept the stories about Robert "Sonny" Carson and his gang of toughs roaming the streets of Brooklyn on behalf of the governing board, we can still only be amused at the notion that this is "terrorism"—any scene from *The Battle of Algiers* would set us straight on that score. By all accounts, these are surely the most unimpressively armed assortment of "terrorists" in recent history; when a few burly men possessing a minimum of lethal weapons can intimidate a whole community, the only conclusion we can sensibly draw is that the apathetic citizenry feel no strong urge to oppose them.

The ghetto residents who react in this way are no more than recapitulating the relationship they have had with every other external political authority that ever set itself against them. But many of those same residents have also been inspired, activated, moved—mobilized. And *that* is an accomplishment that none of the "democratic" institutions of the white majority and pitifully few of its leaders (nor many black ones, either) can claim to have produced. To anyone who compares reports on firsthand experiences of life in the ghettos now with those from, say, five years ago, the accomplishment speaks for itself: it is strange to have to defend it. Of course, it is understandable that many observers will find the atmosphere surrounding most experiments in revolutionary social mobilization to be morally and aesthetically unpalatable; that is a matter of personal attitude that it is difficult to argue with. But to the extent that such social movements are also attacked from the standpoint of theoretical majoritarianism, as well as that of due-process liberalism, the standard by which they are judged is irrelevant—and to abide by it is unjust.

IX.

It cannot be denied, all the same, that vanguard activism in the public school system poses a serious problem for political analysis, though it is a problem obscured rather than clarified by adherence to liberal doctrines. The real point is that when community activists take over a *public* school, then public authority—sovereign power—is in *their* hands. Our earlier argument that if decentralization is not to be a sham, sovereign power must be forsworn rather than merely dispersed, potentially applies just as much to those who dominate others in the name of "community control" as to those who do so in the name of the legal state.

The governing board's critics, to be sure, have offered little or no evidence that in fact a significant number of the community's residents (or residents of the community served by the I.S. 201 experimental complex) perceive the new order in this way. But again, let us for the sake of discussion imagine the worst. Let us imagine that the board's actions are as intolerable to some parents as they are to Martin Mayer and Maurice Goldbloom. Since both class and generational conflicts are taking place within black communities, group unanimity is likely to remain, as Rogin describes it, a myth. (Alan Wolfe's essay in these pages vividly depicts some of the problems that can be expected to arise where "community" is the norm but the community is split.) What solution to this potential difficulty is indicated if a real dedication to plural democracy is to be maintained?

In such circumstances, I should think, the last course of action we would choose would be to return authority to the very same system that is the source of resentment and revolution in the first place. For whatever may be our judgment of the extent to which black militants truly incarnate the general will of the community, to suggest that the state legislature, the city board of education, and the UFT are somehow to be preferred in this respect is to insult our intelligence. If initial efforts at decentralization fail to eliminate all the problems of majority tyranny, then surely we desire not *less* decentralization, but *more*. If, that is, the rights of minorities within the minority community itself are at issue, if the realization of pluralism in the educational sector means, as I have argued, that dissident groups must be allowed control of their own schools, then the way to do justice to those who dissent from dissidence simply would be to provide an alternative system for them as well.

The state, that is, would provide a *dual* school system. One system would be governed by the conventional rules that govern all New York City schools: teachers working on a union contract; principals chosen under the "merit" system; resources allocated by the central board of education. We may assume, further, that militant leaders, demagogues, "outside agitators," etc., would not be welcomed within the classrooms of these schools.

The other school system—the "experiment"—would be run by an elected local board, as in Ocean Hill-Brownsville. It would initially be allocated resources comparable to those received by the first, but the decisions on how to spend those resources would all be made locally. (Which of these systems would be called "public" and which "private" would obviously be beside the point.) If the elected board were antiunion, it would seek out teachers willing to work without a union contract; it would select its own principals; community militants would presumably be welcomed into the classrooms of its schools. If those teachers could not teach, nor the principals administer, nor the militants be attractive to the pupils and parents, the system would inexorably break down. Since black parents desperately want educational improvement for their children, they will not easily forgive those who promise it but fail to provide it: if the conventional school system were functioning as well as its supporters say it can be made to function, the parents would flee the experimental system for the regular one.

The method of competition would be simple: a lump sum would be allocated to the entire school district each year and then divided among the school systems roughly according to how many pupils each enrolled. Success and failure, in conventional terms, would tell their own story. The smaller, less "successful" system might remain in operation to give its own version of education to those who continued to want it; but in general, the clients of the school system would have answered once and for all (as Gallup polls, themselves an agent of majority tyranny, do not) the speculations of outsiders as to who best "represents" them. In sum, that free choice which is the sine qua non of a functioning plural democracy would, for perhaps the first time in the history of our schools, have been available to "rich and poor alike." [11]

X.

In the second half of the twentieth century, there are few democratic polities in which the fundamental political problem remains how to ensure majority rule. On the contrary, in most of those societies, including that of the United States, it is the cultivation of diversity, and the protection from majority tyranny of racial, ethnic, economic, ideological, intellectual, religious, and cultural minorities, that pose the really vexing issues.

Each of these varieties of minority dissent, in turn, has its own needs and suggests unique solutions. For intellectual and ideological dissidents, the question *in extremis* becomes simply one of whether "liberal" society can be relaxed rather than rigid in the enforcement of formal public law: whether it can be truly tolerant of the demands of conscience and of conflicting obligations among the citizenry. For those who assert the right to a life style different from that of their fellows, the question is, rather, if the brutal force latent in the tyranny of majority opinion can be mitigated (and if in a given society it cannot be, all the constitutional protections in the world will not, as Judge Learned Hand suggested, make that society "liberal").

For ascriptive associations—racial, religious, or ethnic—the problems are essentially those of pluralism and decentralization. The incident we have been considering is a small but far from minor one that sharply illuminates one such problem. From any perspective which values democratic pluralism, an alternative school system should exist wherever a population, by the intensity with which they press their claims, express a real demand for it.[12] The creation of the experimental school district in Ocean Hill-Brownsville (and also at I.S. 201 in Manhattan) has been a step, however faltering, in that direction. Furthermore, as I have suggested, the problems of due process and representation this has brought to light are best dealt with by further carrying out the basic principles of decentralization.

Even, therefore, were we to accept the worst that has been said about that experiment and its managers, we could make no greater mistake than to counsel a return to the old system of public and private oligarchies, unchecked by those whom they are supposed to serve, bargaining at the table of sovereign power; or to counsel the creation of a trumped-up pseudodecentralization system in which those communities most adamantly demanding separatist control of "their own" institutions would be the very ones explicitly denied it.

As I have suggested earlier, that mistake would be a political catastrophe, in that the desire for community control, at least among blacks in the United States, can be turned back only by armed force; and a society that depends on overt force to maintain its order is a society in the throes of disintegration.

Worse, that mistake would also be a moral disaster. The real meaning of Ocean Hill-Brownsville is that in a community where almost all men and women had been only subjects of the state, a significant number became self-determining citizens; in a community where almost all had been victims, a significant number became actors. Of course, to make such a judgment, and to extend or withhold one's sympathies on that basis, is to assert, as I have done, that one is able to distinguish the victims from the actors. At times much careful thought may be required to keep us from making that distinction too hastily: but in the end, a political science which does not know who the victims are is no political science at all.

NOTES

1. I shall not offer here, except inferentially, a reply to Mayer's uncomprehending account of the New York School situation. For the best reply to Mayer and other critics of the governing board, the reader is referred to Jason Epstein's review of Mayer's book in *The New York Review of Books,* March 13, 1969.

2. See, for example, the essays in Robert Dahl, ed., *Political Oppositions in Western Democracies* (New Haven, Yale University Press, 1966), particularly those on the Netherlands and Belgium.

3. The following example may be taken as what ought to be a decisive test case. If a "democratic" society, through a parliament chosen by a majority from among freely competing political parties in free elections, decided to exterminate Jews or blacks or gypsies, would they be entitled to offer illegal resistance? Would they and their supporters be entitled to attempt to overthrow the freely elected government?

4. Maurice Goldbloom, "The New York School Crisis," *Commentary,* January 1969, pp. 49–50 (emphasis Goldbloom's).

5. Grant McConnell's *Private Power and American Democracy* (New York, Columbia University Press, 1968), Chs. 4 and 6, is perhaps the best current discussion of this development.

6. In imagining "the worst," I am considering only the worst that an experimental institution such as the Ocean Hill-Brownsville School District Governing Board could actually accomplish. It could not, for example, actually *fire* the teachers from the school system, thus leaving them jobless. That the charge that it did so is an untruth based on suppression of relevant information is revealed by Epstein in the review referred to above. The hypothetical statement which begins this passage should also not be taken as actually endorsing the claim that the dismissed teachers were totally guiltless in their behavior toward the decentralization experiment; the evidence so far offered on this point has been unpersuasive.

7. Quoted from the March 13, 1969, issue of the *Chelsea Clinton News*—a community paper which, through its consistently intelligent coverage of these issues, offers a living argument for decentralization of the news media.

8. A powerful argument that industrial societies ought for their own self-preservation to grant full citizenship to adolescents is presented

in Peter M. Marin's "The Open Truth and Fiery Vehemence of Youth," printed in *The Center Magazine* (January 1969) of the Center for the Study of Democratic Institutions at Santa Barbara.

9. Cf. Michael Rogin's contribution to this volume, pages 112–41. Overall, Rogin's picture of the AFL in the period of "nonpartisanship" perfectly describes a typical oligarchic group which could not be moved to new forms of action by ordinary internally democratic processes: thus the formation of the CIO.

10. Cf. Mancur L. Olson, Jr.'s *The Logic of Collective Action* (New York, Shocken Books, 1968), a theoretical economist's persuasive account, parallel in many respects to this one, of the characteristics that distinguish successful from unsuccessful attempts at group organization.

11. It should be noted that this scheme has little in common with proposals, such as Milton Friedman's, for making tuition grants to parents and letting them support the school of their choice. The apparent "choice," as usual in the case of laissez-faire policies, would not be real, in that the wealthy and well-to-do would be able to spend additional resources of their own on their children's education. Certain schools, equivalent to what are nowadays our private schools and well-financed suburban public schools, would choose, as now, to cater to those parents; the poor, the apathetic, and the unimaginative would have the leavings, which would, in the absence of a national commitment to greatly increased expenditures on education, look suspiciously like what are now our weakest public school systems.

12. Note that this proposal is in no way incompatible with, and may even be prerequisite to, the realization of the hope still clung to by a majority of blacks and whites that *in the long run* genuine integration among real political, social, and economic equals may be achieved. Whether such an outcome could be brought about without the destruction of all cultural differentiation, and whether that would or would not be a good thing, are questions that clearly require much more discussion than can be given them here. My argument is only that genuine pluralism will be a better state of affairs than the pseudopluralism of most modern states and that the "integration" of unequals means only the domination of one group by another. Cf. Michael Parenti's essay in this volume, pages 173–94.

Legitimacy in the Modern State

JOHN H. SCHAAR

I.

AUTHORITY is a word on everyone's lips today. The young attack it and the old demand respect for it. Parents have lost it and policemen enforce it. Experts claim it and artists spurn it, while scholars seek it and lawyers cite it. Philosophers reconcile it with liberty and theologians demonstrate its compatibility with conscience. Bureaucrats pretend they have it and politicians wish they did. Everybody agrees that there is less of it than there used to be. It seems that the matter stands now as a certain Mr. Wildman thought it stood in 1648: "Authority hath been broken into pieces." [1]

About the only people left who seem little affected by the situation are the political scientists. Authority used to be a central term in learned political discourse, perhaps the governing term in philosophical treatments of politics. Except for a few renegade Catholic philosophers, that is obviously no longer the case. You can read a dozen authoritative texts on the American political system, for example, and not find the concept seriously treated. Its use is restricted to discussions of such ritual matters as "the authority of the people" or to descriptions of the "authority" of this or that institution or office. Even the recent spate of writing on the theory of democracy contains no substantial treatment of the topic. [2]

Max Weber pretty thoroughly did our work for us here. His exposition of the three types of authority, or the three

grounds upon which claims to legitimate authority can be
based, has the same status in social science that an older trinity has in Christian theology. Since Weber, we have been
busy putting the phenomena into one or another of his
three boxes and charting the progress by which charismatic
authority becomes routinized into traditional authority,
which, under the impact of science and secularism, gives way
in turn to rational-legal authority. It all looks pretty good to
the political scientists, as more and more traditional societies
enter the transitional stage and gather their resources for the
hopeful journey toward the modern stage, where rational-
legal authority holds sway, along with prosperity, moderation, and a "participant" and empathetic citizenry. It is admitted, to be sure, that there are many obstacles on the path,
that some traditional folk still hold out, and that there are
even one or two troublesome cases of regression. But on the
whole, history is the story of the rational-legal state.[3]

But while the discipline cumulates, things outside jump.
We hear of riots and rebellions, demonstrations and assassinations. Heads of state in many modern countries cannot
safely go among the citizenry. Dignified ceremonies are rau-
cously interrupted by riotous crowds chanting obscenities at
the officials. Policemen have been transformed from protec-
tors into pigs. A lot of young people are trying drugs, and a
lot of older people are buying guns. A few months ago, a
man entered the employment security building in Olympia,
Washington, and tried to murder a computer. He failed, however, because 1401's brains were protected by a bulletproof
steel plate. Some developers recently announced plans for a
"maximum security subdivision" in Maryland at a minimum cost of $200,000 per house. The subdivision will be
ringed by a steel fence and patrolled by armed guards, the
shrubbery will hide electronic detectors, and visitors will be
checked through a blockhouse. In 1968, American governmental units hired 26,000 additional policemen, an increase

of 7 percent over 1967; 1968 was the second year in a row
during which police employment rose more steeply than any
other kind of public employment.[4]

We can feel the chill of some sentences Henry Adams
wrote over sixty years ago:

> The assumption of unity which was the mark of human
> thought in the middle-ages has yielded very slowly to the
> proofs of complexity. . . . Yet it is quite sure . . . that, at
> the accelerated rate of progression shown since 1600, it will
> not need another century or half century to tip thought up-
> side down. Law, in that case, would disappear as theory or *à
> priori* principle, and give place to force. Morality would be-
> come police. Explosives would reach cosmic violence. Disin-
> tegration would overcome integration.[5]

It is the thesis of this essay that legitimate authority is declining in the modern states; that, in a real sense, "law and
order" *is* the basic political question of our day. The seamless web of socialization described by such leading students
of the subject as Easton, Greenstein, Hess, and Hyman
shows rips and frays. Many of the sons are no longer sure
they want the legacy of the fathers. Among young people,
the peer group increasingly takes priority as the agency of
socialization, and the values it sponsors are new and hostile to
those of the adult world. Many people are seeking ways to
live in the system without belonging to it: their hearts are
elsewhere. Others, convinced that the organized system will
not in the long run permit the escape into private liberty, or
feeling that such an escape is ignoble, are acting politically
to transform the system. In the eyes of large and growing
numbers of men, the social and political landscape of America, the most advanced of the advanced states, is no green
and gentle place, where men may long abide. That landscape is, rather, a scene of wracked shapes and desert spaces.
What we mainly see are the eroded forms of once authoritative institutions and ideas. What we mainly hear are the
hollow winds of once compelling ideologies, and the un-

nerving gusts of new moods and slogans. What we mainly feel in our hearts is the granite consolidation of the technological and bureaucratic order, which may bring physical comfort and great collective power, or sterility, but not political liberty and moral autonomy. All the modern states, with the United States in the vanguard, are well advanced along a path toward a crisis of legitimacy.[6]

The essay has two subsidiary theses. First, that the crisis of legitimacy is a function of some of the basic, defining orientations of modernity itself; specifically, rationality, the cult of efficiency and power, ethical relativism, and equalitarianism. In effect, it will be argued that the modern mind, having now reached nearly full development, is turning back upon itself and undermining the very principles that once sustained order and obedience in the modern state. Secondly, it will be argued (mainly indirectly) that contemporary social science has failed to appreciate the precariousness of legitimate authority in the modern states because it is largely a product of the same phenomena it seeks to describe and therefore suffers the blindness of the eye examining itself.

What the thesis essentially asserts, then, is that the philosophical and experiential foundations of legitimacy in the modern states are gravely weakened, leaving obedience a matter of lingering habit, or expediency, or necessity, but not a matter of reason and principle, and of deepest sentiment and conviction. We are nearing the end of an era, and it is becoming clear that the decline of legitimate authority is the product of the ideal and material forces that have been the defining attributes of modern authority itself. This movement has been visible for a long time in most of the nonpolitical sectors of life—family, economy, education, religion—and it is now spreading rapidly into the political realm. The gigantic and seemingly impregnable control structures that surround and dominate men in the modern states are increasingly found to have at their centers, not a vital principle of authority, but something approaching a hollow space, a moral vacuum.

A preliminary word on the scope and perspective of the essay, and on its political and methodological orientations.

The major thesis and its subsidiaries can be expanded and elucidated in a number of ways. Its critical terms can be defined with precision, and its relevance to the contemporary political scene in the United States can be shown. Empirical evidence can be brought to bear on the propositions. But these propositions cannot be made operational, tested, and verified or falsified beyond reasonable doubt by the criteria of a rigorous behavioralism. This essay will report no opinion survey, present no input-output charts, attempt no stimulas-response or cognitive-dissonance analysis of legitimacy. It will, instead, utilize a variety of materials that help illuminate the problem, including some materials of dubious scientific quality. Perhaps it really is possible to say something about the truth without first polling a sample of one's contemporaries in order to get the facts.

The recent disturbances and novelties in the modern states have taken the political science profession largely by surprise. That is due in fair part, I think, to the very methods which now enjoy favor in the discipline and to the narrow standards set by those methods concerning the materials that qualify as worthy of professional attention. Those methods are poorly designed for dealing with change. The insistence upon rigor means that very often the methods are permitted to determine the subjects studied, rather than vice versa. The erection of the logical distinction between fact and value into a metaphysical dualism has simultaneously cut the profession off from the dominant concerns of modern philosophy and rendered it vulnerable to the grossest of all logical and practical errors, the idealization of the actual. The profession has devised a whole kit of tools for dealing with the routine and predictable but is largely at a loss in the face of genuine novelty. The virtual equation of operationalism and the verifiability theory of meaning with science has meant both a narrowing of many of the most basic concepts of political life and an inability even to perceive whole ranges of empirical phenomena. But this is not the place for a discourse on method: it must suffice to say that behavioral political science has some grave debilities on subjects such as those treated in this essay.

While the essay grew out of a concern with the recent appearance of novel, radical, and sometimes violent forms of speech and action in various sectors of modern life, it does not deal directly with those matters. It is clear to nearly everybody that a limited but quite significant "de-authorization" of the dominant institutions and ideas is taking place today. The causes and consequences of this movement have been treated in a thousand books, articles, and speeches, and no literate man can be unaware of the main analyses and proposed solutions. The essay has little to say on this level of the subject. It does not discuss the generation gap or the credibility gap. It has nothing to say specifically about permissiveness and firmness. It offers no analyses of the SDS or the University of California, no judgments on Anti-Communism or Imperialism. I would like to think that the essay does, however, deal with these matters in an important way by going beneath them to the underlying sources and dimensions of the present de-authorization.

No man can pretend to full moral and political neutrality on this subject. It is easy for one of my age and vocation to be simultaneously afraid, contemptuous, and envious of much of what today goes under the labels "youth culture" and "New Left." Their language and their manners are offensive. There are good reasons for worrying about their lack of discipline, their uncertain devotion to the practices of fair play, their instant communities of dope, music, and self-indulgent rhetoric, and their readiness for extreme actions. It is no true service to keep silent about these things, let alone to take the view that the young, the black, and the radical have a monopoly of the true, the beautiful, and the good.

On the other hand, he who veils fear and envy as patriotism, and hides contempt under the slogans of tolerance, or openly urges ferocity against the young and the radical, sins against life and the future. We are members one of another. The established, the respectable, and the frightened of this land appear on the edge of an utterly nihilistic war against the future—war against their own young, who *are* the future; and war against the black and the poor, who once were creators of wealth, but who now are seen only as expensive and dangerous nuisances. This war must be prevented, for we are members one of another. Furthermore, at their center and at their best, the youthful, black, and radical protest movements have served America well. Their criticisms of the repressiveness, unresponsiveness, bureaucratization, and hypocrisy of the dominant institutions have been incisive and courageous. Their rejection of the "technetronic society" now being built is an effort for the common redemption, without regard to differences of age, race, or station. So, too, is their call for a more democratic and humane society and their insistence that knowledge be integrated with identity, and both tied to commitment. In a basic way, this essay is an attempt to understand the ways in which certain modern definitions of knowledge and processes of control have contributed to the weakening of legitimate authority and the dehumanization of relations among men which the radicals of our day no longer ignore or endure.

II.

Start by comparing the traditional and common meanings of legitimacy with the usage of leading modern social scientists. The *Oxford English Dictionary* says the following:

Legitimacy: (a) of a government or the title of a sovereign: the condition of being in accordance with law or principle. . . .

(b) conformity to a rule or principle; lawfulness. In logic, conformity to sound reasoning.

Legitimate: (a) etymologically, the word expresses a status, which has been conferred or ratified by some authority. (b) conformable to law or rule. Sanctioned or authorized by law or right; lawful; proper. (c) normal, regular; conformable to a recognized standard type. (d) sanctioned by the laws of reasoning; logically admissible or inferable.

The most relevant entries from Webster's *Unabridged* are:

Legitimate: (1) lawfully begotten. . . . (2) real, genuine; not false, counterfeit, or spurious. (3) accordant with law or with established legal forms and requirements; lawful. (4) conforming to recognized principles, or accepted rules or standards.

Now, three current professional definitions:

1. Legitimacy involves the capacity of the system to engender and maintain the belief that the existing political institutions are the most appropriate ones for the society.[7]

2. In the tradition of Weber, legitimacy has been defined as "the degree to which institutions are valued for themselves and considered right and proper." [8]

3. We may define political legitimacy as the quality of "oughtness" that is perceived by the public to inhere in a political regime. That government is legitimate which is viewed as morally proper for a society.[9]

The contrast between the two sets of definitions, the traditional and lexical on the one side and the current scientific usage on the other, is basic and obvious. The older definitions all revolve around the element of law or right, and rest the force of a claim (whether it be a claim to political power or to the validity of a conclusion in an argument) upon foundations external to and independent of the mere assertion or opinion of the claimant (e.g., the laws of inheritance, the laws of logic). Thus, a claim to political power is legitimate only when the claimant can invoke some source of authority beyond or above himself. History shows a variety of such sources: immemorial custom, divine law, the law of nature, a constitution. As Arendt has pointed out, "In all these cases, legitimacy derives from something outside the range of human deeds; it is either not man-made at all . . . or has at least not been made by those who happen to be in power." [10]

The new definitions all dissolve legitimacy into belief or opinion. If a people holds the belief that existing institutions are "appropriate" or "morally proper," then those institutions are legitimate. That's all there is to it. By a surgical procedure, the older concept has been trimmed of its cumbersome "normative" and "philosophical" parts, leaving the term leaner, no doubt, but now fit for scientific duty. It might turn out that Occam's Razor has cut off a part or two that will be missed later on.

A few implications of these new formulations should be articulated.

First of all, when legitimacy is defined as consisting in belief alone, then the investigator can examine nothing outside popular opinion in order to decide whether a given regime or institution or command is legitimate or illegitimate. To borrow the language of the law, there can be no independent inquiry into the title. In effect, this analysis dissolves legitimacy into acceptance or acquiescence, thereby rendering opaque whole classes of basic and recurrent political phenomena, e.g., a group or individual refuses consent and obedience to the orders of a regime or institution on the ground that the regime or institution is illegitimate; a regime or institution is acknowledged to be legitimate as such, but consent is withheld from a particular order on the ground that the regime had no legitimate right to make that order; one consents or acquiesces out of interest or necessity, although he regards a regime or an order as illegitimate. In short, legitimacy and acquiescence, and legitimacy and consensus, are not the same, and the relations between them are heterogeneous. The older formulations made these empirical situations comprehesible, while the newer usages obfuscate them. The phenomenon of legitimacy, far from being identical with consensus, is rather, as Friedrich says, "a very particular form of consensus, which revolves around the question of the right or title to rule." [11] Legitimacy is that aspect of authority which refers to entitlement.

Another important feature of these new formulations, which emerges clearly when the definitions are examined within the context of the larger works in which they appear, is that they see legitimacy as a function of a system's ability to persuade members of its own appropriateness. The flow is from leaders to followers. Leaders lay down rules, promulgate policies, and disseminate symbols which tell followers how and what they should do and feel. Thus, Merelman explains legitimacy within the framework of stimulus-response psychology, which he rather narrowly equates with learning theory. The regime or the leaders provide the stimuli, first in the form of policies improving citizen welfare and later in the form of symbolic materials which function as secondary reinforcements, and the followers provide the responses, in the form of favorable attitudes toward the stimulators— which, to reiterate, is what Merelman means by legitimacy. The symbols become, in the minds of the followers, condensations of the practices and intentions of the rulers. Over time, if the rulers manipulate symbols skillfully, symbolic rewards alone may suffice to maintain supportive attitudes.[12] The symbols may actually conceal rather than reveal the real nature of the regime's policies and practices, as the symbols of democracy becloud the actual processes of rule in the modern states.

We should be clear about the understanding of the relationship between "community" and control that informs such a conception of legitimacy. Merelman and others in this tradition see a polity not as a people with a culture seeking together the forms of order and action that will preserve and enhance that culture, but as a mass or collective that is made into a unit of control by propaganda.[13] That is no doubt a fairly accurate conception of most modern systems of rule, but it is worth remembering that a politics of propaganda and ideology is not the only possible politics.[14]

Legitimacy, then, is almost entirely a matter of sentiment. Followers believe in a regime, or have faith in it, and that is what legitimacy is. The faith may be the product of conditioning, or it may be the fruit of symbolic bedazzlement, but in neither case is it in any significant degree the work of reason, judgment, or active participation in the processes of rule. In this analysis, people do not attribute legitimacy to authority because they recognize its claim to a foundation in some principle or source outside itself. This emerges clearly in Lipset's treatment of the specific institutional arrangements and procedures which are conducive to legitimacy: cross-pressures; widespread and multiple membership in voluntary associations; the two-party system; federalism, territorial rather than proportional representation.[15] In a most confusing way, an analysis of something called legitimacy first equates legitimacy with opinion, then goes to a restatement of the standard liberal-pluralist description of the structure of power in the United States, turns next to a discussion of stability, and finally resolves stability into passivity or acquiescence caused by cognitive confusion, conflict of interest, and inability to translate one's desires into political decisions due to certain institutional arrangements. Obviously, we are no longer talking about faith or belief at all, let alone legitimacy, but about confusion and indifference, stability and efficiency. There is where the contemporary social treatment of legitimate power rests. A fuller view is needed.

No matter where we go in space, nor how far back in time, we find power. Power is ancient and ubiquitous, a universal feature of social life. But if it is a fact, it is nonetheless a complex fact:

Power exists . . . only through the concurrence of all [its] properties . . . it draws its inner strength and the material succour which it receives, both from the continuously helping hand of habit and also from the imagination; it must possess both a reasonable authority and a magical influence; it must operate like nature herself, both by visible means and by hidden influence.[16]

Force can bring political power into being but cannot maintain it. For that, something else is required: "Will, not force," said T. H. Green, "is the basis of the state." Once power is established and set on course, as it were, then obedience is largely a matter of habit. But there are two critical points in the life of power when habit does not suffice. The first is at its birth, when habits of obedience have not formed. The other comes when the customary ways and limits of power are altered, when subjects are presented with new and disturbing uses of power and are asked to assume new burdens and accept new claims. At those two points—and most of the states of our day, old and new, are at one or the other of the two—theory must be called in to buttress and justify obedience. There is no denying a certain pragmatic or expediential element in all theories of legitimacy. Such theories are never offered idly, they never appear accidentially. Rather, they appear when the uses of power are matters of controversy, and they are weapons in the struggles of men to enjoy the benefits and escape the burdens of power. This is not to say that all theories of legitimacy are only or merely "rationalizations"; rather, it is to say that they have an element of rationalization in them.

Theory, then, by making power legitimate, turns it into authority. All theories of legitimacy take the form of establishing a principle which, while it resides outside power and is independent of it, locates or embeds power in a realm of things beyond the wills of the holders of power: the legitimacy of power stems from its *origin*. In addition, most theories of legitimacy simultaneously attempt to justify power by reference to its *ends*. As was suggested by the earlier quotation from Arendt, the originating principles have been many and diverse. So too have the ends. But in our time this great complexity has been reduced, in virtually all states, to a gratifying simplicity: for power or become authority, it must originate in "democratic consent" and aim at the "common good" or "public interest."

I shall not rehearse here in any detail the many assaults that have been made against both these concepts. They are familiar enough. Let it suffice to say that criticism and hard events have done their work: both concepts have been reduced to rubble. Democracy is the most prostituted word of our age, and any man who employs it in reference to any modern state should be suspect either of ignorance or of bad motives.[17] The public good has not fared much better. It is widely agreed among political scientists that it is more a term of political art than of political analysis, but if it has any cognitive content at all it can mean only the sum or aggregate of individual, subjective interests.[18]

That offered little trouble for a time, because it seemed perfectly compatible with popular sovereignty and majority rule, which everyone agreed were basic principles of democratic decision making. But then Arrow showed that there was no way to produce a unique social ordering of the preferences of individuals that would be compatible with the requirements of popular sovereignty and majority rule—thereby leaving both the theory of democracy and the concept of the public interest in a shambles.[19]

There the matter stands among the sophisticated. The most benighted savage of yesterday's anthropology, sacrificing to his totemic ancestor and groveling before his sacred king, is no worse off for a theory of legitimacy that will pass the tests of reason than is the most advanced "democratic" theorist among us today.

The case is not much better among ordinary men. Most of

them really know that "the people" do not run things: a plethora of surveys and voting studies confirms that. Hence, the test of legitimacy for them is not power's origins but its ends. And from this point of view, the "public interest" means just about what it has always meant: security and material abundance. The sacred king once had to make the crops grow and provide victory in battle. The government must now defend national security and enlarge the GNP. But it is increasingly clear that the nation-state can no longer guarantee the first at all and that in the modern states the second has been accomplished to the point where it threatens the irreversible degradation of the environment and the species.

We have finally made the engine that can smash all engines, the power that can destroy all power. Security today, bought at the price of billions, means that We shall have fifteen minutes warning that They intend to annihilate us, during which time we can also annihilate them. The most powerful state today cannot provide security but only revenge. There is not a person among us who has not himself imagined the destruction of all things by nuclear holocaust. Not since civilization began has man been so totally reduced to the status of temporary occupant of his home, the earth. The dream of total security through total power has ended in the reality of total vulnerability.[20]

The case with abundance comes out about the same way. Inexcusable injustices of distribution still prevail in the modern states, but the "battle of production" is nearing total victory. Societies have always been, in part, organizations for the production of the nutrients of life, but modern civilizations are dominated as no others have ever been by the law of production.[21] Modern production is dedicated almost entirely to consumption; and since consumption is limitless, so too is production. But to produce something means to destroy something else; hence, destruction keeps pace with production. There is the deepest law of modern production:

it must continue as long as there is anything left to destroy.
That is not metaphor but the precise dynamic of modern
economies.

Modern production has obscured the sun and stars toward
which men once aspired. It pollutes the air and chews up
great forests. It drinks whole lakes and rivers. It has already
consumed many species of creatures, and it is making ready
to consume the oceans. Its factories once ate children and
more recently have been fed slaves. This civilization of production periodically devours men by heaps and piles in war,
and it daily mangles the spirits of others in meaningless
labor. The only aim of this civilization is to live, that is, to
grow, and to grow it must consume. Ellul has shown, unan-
swerably I think, that the process must run until it consumes
those who think they run it—until man is absorbed into
technique and process. That will be the total victory in the
battle of production; and as always with total victories, no
atonement will avail.[22]

The modern state, then, insofar as it is provider and guar-
antor of increase, and insofar as its success in this task is a
source of legitimacy, has succeeded too well: its success has
become a threat to survival. The masses have not yet heard
this message, though some hints have begun to penetrate the
thicket of propaganda and inherited ideas. Most importantly, this understanding is growing among young people
and among the cultural elites: even Galbraith has anxiously
asked whether the impulse toward destruction might not be
an inherent dynamic of the new order.[23] Once again we
reach the same conclusion. The new state of production has
fulfilled its promise of abundance, but only at the price of
raising a new and formidable threat to freedom, and even to
survival.[24]

III.

I do not wish to poke about among these ruins. Rather, I shall take a backward look over the roads which have led to the modern condition, which, to say it again, is the condition of the shattering of authority. The modern condition is not "new" in the strict sense of the term. Rather, it is an intensification and a fulfillment of certain tendencies which are quite old. On the axiom that in the human sciences inquiry must begin where the subject begins, I wish to look at the basic elements, the principles or starting points, of the modern condition. The question is, What are the main routes by which modern states have reached the stage where power has lost most of the attributes of legitimate authority?

In order to be as clear as possible about the subject under discussion, it will be useful to say a few words about the nature of authority. Following Bertrand de Jouvenel, authority can be defined basically as "the faculty of gaining another man's assent." [25] The word's origins and rich associations suggest the place of authority in human life. An authority is one whose counsels we seek and trust and whose deeds we strive to imitate and enlarge. He is one who, while lacking most of the specific attributes of power as force, makes recommendations which cannot safely be ignored because they are usually right: "While power resides in the people, authority rests with the Senate [of Rome]." [26] An authority is one who starts lines of action which others complete. Hence he is, metaphorically, the father of their actions. A man or an institution becomes a father and augmenter of others' actions in one of two ways. First, by example: he shows others the way by going there first himself. Secondly, he has the ability to assure others that the actions he recommends are rightful and will succeed. Here, then, are the two basic functions of authority: it provides counsel and justification, and it increases the confidence and sense of

ability of those under it by assuring them that the actions it
recommends will succeed and will enlarge the actors. Seen in
this light, authority, far from confining and depleting men,
liberates and enriches them by bringing to birth that which
is potentially present. It is only under the impact of the liberal ideology that men came to formulate authority and
liberty as opposites and enemies. In an older understanding,
authority, while it defined and limited liberty, thereby also
fulfilled and directed it. As Nietzsche understood, absence of
horizons is not liberty but madness and impotence. Can anyone today still believe that liberty grows stronger as authority grows weaker?

If authority is to initiate actions and vouch for their rightness and success, it must have a rationale that backs its claim
to assent.[27] As Plato put it, each law must have a preamble, a
statement that walks before the law, justifying and explaining it. This rationale includes an account of reality, an explanation of why some acts are preferable to others, and a vision
of a worthwhile future toward which men can aspire. Put
differently, the rationale consists of a more or less coherent
body of shared memories, images, ideas, and ideals that gives
to those who share it an orientation in and toward time and
space. It links past, present, and future into a meaningful
whole, and ties means and ends into a continuum that tran-
scends a merely pragmatic or expediential calculation. Authorities at once personify or incarnate this rationale, this
conception of legitimacy, and are justified by it. Without
such rationales, or "stories," authority dissipates, leaving a
vacuum to be filled by power. As Adams put it, morality
becomes police.

This understanding of authority has concentrated so far
on what R. S. Peters has called its de facto aspects or dimensions. The concept also has what might be called de jure
meanings, as when Hobbes says "the right of doing any action, is called AUTHORITY. So that by authority is always
understood a right of doing any act; and *done by authority,*

done by commission, or license from him whose right it is." [28] Webster's clearly recognizes both usages, for while it gives "legal or rightful power; a right to command or to act," it also gives "power derived from opinion, respect, or esteem; influence of character, office, or station, or mental or moral superiority." The de jure usage welds authority with right and connects both with office or position in a system of rules and relations. This is the usage most commonly met in traditional political philosophy and in the philosophical analysis of such subjects as institution, obligation, command, and law. The reasons for this are obvious. Men live in societies, which means they regulate their relations with each other largely by systems of rules. This specifically human form of order can be maintained only if "there is general acceptance of procedural rules which lay down who is to originate rules, who is to decide about their concrete application . . . and who is entitled to introduce changes." [29] All these are functions of authority within human society.

The de facto and de jure uses of the term, while conceptually distinct at their outer margins, also have common dimensions. Both share the common root *auctor,* or originator. Furthermore, both share the idea of originator by right, though in the de facto sense the right or entitlement rests mainly upon the personal attributes of the individual who has authority, while de jure authority comes from position or office in a system of rules and practices. Finally, both stress ways of governing conduct by means other than force, manipulation, or propaganda. Authority commands, decides, recommends, and persuades, and resorts to force only when these fail. "To follow an authority is a voluntary act. Authority ends where voluntary assent ends. There is in every state a margin of obedience which is won only by the use of force or the threat of force: it is this margin which breaches liberty and demonstrates the failure of authority." [30]

In an older vocabulary, authority has both the cross and

the sword; but while the former is of its essence, the latter is
not.

IV.

A serious account of the contemporary problem of "law
and order" would be an account of the hollowing out of the
theoretical and empirical foundations upon which authority
(de jure and de facto) has rested in the states of the West.
Weber thought that the day of charismatic and traditional
structures of legitimacy was over and that both were being
displaced by rational-legal authority. But he did not see far
enough into the matter, for rational-legal authority has also
been undermined, leaving the great institutions it brought
into being gravely weakened from within. I cannot supply
anything like a full map of the routes leading to this end.
What follows is a sketch of the main routes on this journey
into emptiness.

1. *The Epistemological Route.* This route consists in
charting the connections between the status of the concept
of truth on the one side, and the growing feeling of disen-
gagement or alienation from authoritative structures of
order on the other. Until recently, the concept of truth
rested upon certain assumptions about the relations between
the knower and the known. Two of these assumptions are of
greatest importance: (1) the notion that man's cognitive
apparatus did not itself basically condition the quality and
nature of what was known; and (2) the notion that there
existed a kingdom of order outside man and independent of
him (e.g., the laws of nature, God, the laws of history).
Given the first assumption, truth always meant *discovery*.
Given the second, truth meant discovery of a *pre-established*
order. Discoveries made by the methods of science, philosophy, and theology were not fabrications of the human mind,
but faithful reflections or representations of an order independent of the discoverer. For man to increase his own har-

mony with the pre-established harmony outside himself, he had only to increase his knowledge of the world.[31] Given the right methods and concepts, increasing knowledge brought increasing harmony between man and the world. Anthropological and mythological researches have shown that in the ages before philosophy and science, myth served this same function of bringing men into contact with the sources of order outside themselves.

Given this concept of truth, social and political life too could be seen as a harmonious association of self and society with an objective order external to man and constituted by some force independent of him. Political societies were not works of human art and will, but were embedded in and even constituted by a larger order of being. Human authority rested on bases more "solid" than individual choice and will.

That older view of knowledge and truth has now just about disappeared, and with its disappearance men have lost most of their older principles of legitimation. In the older view, a structure of order could base its claim to legitimacy on some foundation other than the choices and opinions of the members. In the newer view, order becomes dependent upon will, with no source of rewards and punishments external to the system and its members. With that, the social and political world becomes "unfrozen" as it were, movable by skill and power, for it is seen that there is no necessity in any given arrangement of things. All things could be other than they are. It is the world of Sorel, rather than the world of Plato. It is not even a world in which change or becoming follows a necessary pattern. It is the world of Sartre, rather than the world of Hegel.[32]

Furthermore, the death of the older views also spelled death for the authoritative classes of priests and nobles who claimed a right to rule on the grounds that they possessed knowledge of the true order of things and of the methods needed for gaining further knowledge of that order. The oldest and most basic justification for hierarchy has dissolved. The only class that could conceivably make that claim today is the class of scientists. But in order to occupy this role, the scientific estate would have to transform itself into something very like a priesthood, along lines which Comte understood perfectly. The foundations for that are already present. For the masses, science is largely a matter of miracle, mystery, and authority. Translated into educational terms, the slogan that through science man has gained increasing knowledge of nature really means that a few men now know a great deal about how nature "works," while the rest of us are about as ignorant as we have always been. Translated into political terms, the slogan that through knowledge man has gained power really means that a few men have gained the means of unprecedented power over a great many other men. On the other hand, there are good reasons for thinking that the scientists and experts may not be able to perform the priestly role with enduring success. I shall indicate some of these reasons later.

When the secret that nature is no guide is finally known to all—the secret exposed by the Sophists and in our age by Nietzsche—the whole question of legitimacy will have to be reopened. Order will be seen as artificial, the result of will and choice alone, as vulnerable to change and challenge as will itself is. Structures of authority will not be able to invoke the ancient and once ubiquitous idea that each thing under the sun has its own right nature and place in the constitution of the whole. For centuries, this sense of the fitness and rightness of things set boundaries to men's pretensions to control and shaped their moral attitudes concerning the permissible limits within which they might legitimately impose their desires on the world around them. A basic piety toward the world and toward the processes that sustain it will disappear, and all things, including polities and men themselves, will come to appear artificial and malleable.[33] Whole new sets of arguments and images imposing limits on man's urge to satisfy his desires will have to be found. And until they are found, the idea and the very experience of legitimate authority cannot have anything like the bedrock importance they have heretofore had in political life.

2. *The Moral Route.* The knowledge that civilization begins when men understand that any shared custom at all is better than none is as old as Homer and as new as the researches of Lévi-Strauss. All morality is in the beginning group morality. Each tribe believes that there is no morality outside the tribe and that the tribe without its morality is no longer a tribe. Morality is, then, both a means and the basic means for preserving a community—holding it together, marking pathways through the landscape of social relations, defending it against threats from strangers and the gods. Men everywhere are taught to fear those who violate morality and to revere its authors and upholders.

Furthermore, as Nietzsche understood, and as scientific research increasingly confirms, nations and communities are "born." [34] And birth requires a father or author, the one who, whether mythologically or actually, brought the original laws and customs, thereby making a people a people.[35] The founder of a people is usually either a god or a messenger and mediator between gods and men: the creative moment in the birth of a nation is the birth of a religion.[36] Even the Enlightened American Founding Fathers saw the Constitution as a partial embodiment of that higher order called the Laws of Nature and of Nature's God. Prophets and messengers appear not only at the original birth, but also at times after the founding when the boundaries have been altered or obscured and need to be rectified. In addition, through actions based on myth and ritual, the people themselves also reenact and reaffirm the harmony between the ontological order and their own human realm. In sum, founders and prophets create and correct, and myth and ritual recreate and restore, a community identity set within a cosmology. Identity and legitimacy are thus inseparable.[37]

No one needs to be told that these ancient patterns of
thought no longer prevail. The old moralities of custom and
religion are husks and shells. With the growth of the special
modern form of individual self-consciousness as consciousness of separation, men lose sight of the dependence of the
group upon morality and of the dependence of morality
upon the group. These paths run parallel to the one, discussed earlier, by which men have journeyed toward epistemological emptiness. Individual withdrawal from the group
consciousness and individual rejection of received knowledge proceed concurrently. There is an intimate connection
between the decline of custom and "nature" as the setter of
boundaries in the social realm, and the Cartesian and
Hobbesian rejection of received opinion as the starting
point of the individual knower's search for knowledge. Each
man becomes his own author and oracle, his own boundary
setter and truth maker. The ego recognizes no source of
truth and morality external to itself.

Bacon, Descartes, and Hobbes first decisively stated this
modern perspective, and Rousseau formulated the basic political problem stemming from it. He was the first to understand fully, I think, that ours is the task of developing the
theory and institutions of a community in which men can be
both conscious and individual *and* share the moral bonds
and limits of the group. Rousseau thought, and much modern experience suggests he was right, that until such a polity
was built, modern men would often be, and would even
more often feel like, slaves, and that no modern state would
be truly legitimate.

Hobbes and just about all later writers in the liberal line
—T. H. Green nearly escaped—left this problem on shaky
foundations. Hobbes never conceived the possibility of a
selfhood which transcended the purely individual. Hence,
for him, there is no trouble so long as one self does not im-
pinge upon another. When that happens, Leviathan puts
curbs on all. In this perspective, order is a question of

power, and legitimacy is reduced to prudent calculations of self-interest. That line of thought remains dominant in Sartre, though the vocabulary has shifted to "seriality," and in much contemporary behavioral science, though the Hobbesian vocabulary of "prudence" has shifted to "satisficing" and "maximizing utility."

All this might be made a little more concrete by bringing it closer to home. The United States can be seen as a great experiment in the working out of these ideas. As Lipset has pointed out, the United States is in a very real sense the "first new nation." Our founding took place at an advanced stage of the progress toward epistemological and moral individualism which was sketched above. At the time of the founding, the doctrine and sentiment were already widespread that each individual comes into this world morally complete and self-sufficient, clothed with natural rights which are his by birth, and not in need of fellowship for moral growth and fulfillment. The human material of this new republic consisted of a gathering of men each of whom sought self-sufficiency and the satisfaction of his own desires. Wave after wave of immigrants replenished those urges, for to the immigrant, America largely meant freedom from inherited authorities and freedom to get rich. Community and society meant little more than the ground upon which each challenged or used others for his own gain. Others were accepted insofar as they were useful to one in his search for self-sufficiency. But once that goal was reached, the less one had to put up with the others the better. Millions upon millions of Americans strive for that goal, and what is more important, base their political views upon it. The state is a convenience in a private search; and when that search seems to succeed, it is no wonder that men tend to deny the desirability of political bonds, of acting together with others for the life that is just for all. We have no political or moral teaching that tells men they must remain bound to each other even one step beyond the point where those bonds are a drag and a burden on one's personal desires. Americans have always been dedicated to "getting ahead"; and getting ahead has always meant leaving others behind. Surely a large part of the zealous repression of radical protest in America yesterday and today has its roots in the fact that millions of men who are apparently "insiders" know how vulnerable the system is because they know how ambiguous their own attachments to it are. The slightest moral challenge exposes the fragile foundations of legitimacy in the modern state.

I am aware that my argument and conclusions here stand in opposition to the standard liberal-pluralist view of American politics. In that view, Americans are enthusiastic joiners. They seek goals through associational means more readily than do citizens in other lands.[38] In addition, Americans have been found to be less cynical about politics than the citizens of some other states. And Americans early learn attitudes of trust and respect for their regime and its authority figures.

But this literature is largely beside the point; and to the degree that it has been expressed doctrinally—as evidence for the democratic and participatory character of political decision making in the United States—it is misleading.[39] What matter here are questions of quality, not quantity. The professional literature glorifies the sheer, gross quantity of associational life—though it has never quite known what to say about the majority of adults who are members of no association except a religious one. Little is said about the quality and meaning of associational life, the narrowness of the constituencies, or the intentions that bring men together.[40] The associational life praised in the literature originates in and is pervaded by the kinds of liberal intentions and feelings described above. The individual takes little part in "group life," apart from lending his quantum of power to the whole. Membership is instrumental: the association is an efficient means for the achievement of individual goals, not an expression of a way of life valued in and for itself.

Affective life centers almost exclusively in the family, and other associations are more or less useful in the pursuit of private goals. Once the goal of self-sufficiency is reached, the individual retreats from group life. Or individuals are held in formal association by the subtle arts of managerial psychology, the not-so-subtle arts of bureaucratic control, the revision upwards of personal desires and demands, and the redefinition of material goals in symbolic terms. It is, then, a question not of how many associations there are, but of what being together means.[41]

This point, however, is a minor one, even though discussion of it occupies a large place in the professional literature. The main point remains: modern man has determined to live without collective ideals and disciplines, and thus without obedience to and reliance upon the authorities that embody, defend, and replenish those ideals. The work of dissolution is almost complete, and modern man now appears ready to attempt a life built upon no other ideal than happiness: comfort and self-expression. But if this is nihilism, it is nihilism with a change of accent that makes all the difference. Gone is the terror, and gone too the dedication to self-overcoming of the greatest nihilist. All ideals are suspect, all renunciations and disciplines seen as snares and stupidities, all corporate commitments nothing but self-imprisonments. Modern prophets rise to pronounce sublimation and self-mutilation the same. We, especially the young among us, presume that an individual can live fully and freely, with no counsel or authority other than his desires, engaged completely in the development of all his capacities save two—the capacity for memory and the capacity for faith.

No one can say where this will lead, for the attempt is without illuminating precedent. But it is clear that for our time, as Rieff has written, "the question is no longer as Do-

stoevski put it: 'Can civilized men believe?' Rather: Can un-
believing men be civilized?'' [42] Perhaps new prophets will
appear; perhaps tribalism will reappear; perhaps the old
faiths will be reborn; perhaps Weber's "specialists without
spirit, sensualists without heart" will stalk the land; or perhaps we really shall see the new technological Garden tilled
by children—simple, kind, sincere innocents, barbarians
with good hearts. But however it comes out, we must be
clear that already the development of the postmoral mentality places the question of authority and legitimacy on a
wholly new footing.[43]

3. *Rationality and Bureaucratic Coordination.* At least
one portion of the liberal impulse has reached near comple-
tion in the modern state: the urge to replace the visible with
the unseen hand.[44] Personal and visible power and leadership decline, supplanted by impersonal, anonymous, and automatic mechanisms of control and coordination. Overall, we
are confronted not with a situation of "power without authority," as Berle, Drucker, and others have described it,
though that is part of it, but with a situation of the "autonomy of process," as Ellul and Arendt have described it. The
results, as they bear on the meaning of authority and legitimacy, are mainly two: a reduction in the scope for human
freedom and responsibility; and the dehumanization—in
concrete ways—of leadership. We are beginning to gather
the bitter harvest of these triumphs of rationality in the
seemingly irrational, nihilistic, and self-indulgent violent
outbursts of our day.

It was mentioned before that modern civilizations seem
committed to no ideal beyond their own reproduction and
growth. A man from another era might say that collectively
we have sunk into mere life; the men of our era prefer to
call it a celebration of life. Setting that matter of judgment
aside, the point which must be understood is that this condition, combined with some of the basic characteristics of modern social systems and some of the basic components of the

modern climate of opinion, decisively alters most of our inherited conceptions of authority and leadership.

Our familiar ways of thinking prepare us to imagine that a society must have "someone" in charge, that there must be somewhere a center of power and authority. Things just would not work unless someone, somewhere, knew how they worked and was responsible for their working right. That image and experience of authority has almost no meaning today—as the people in power are the first to say. Modern societies have become increasingly like self-regulating machines, whose human tenders are needed only to make the minor adjustments demanded by the machine itself. As the whole system grows more and more complex, each individual is able to understand and control less and less of it. In area after area of both public and private life, no single identifiable office or individual commands either the knowledge or the authority to make decisions. A search for the responsible party leads through an endless maze of committees, bureaus, offices, and anonymous bodies.[45]

The functions of planning and control, and ultimately of decision making, are increasingly taken away from men and given over to machines and routine processes. Human participation in planning and control tends to be limited to supplying the machines with inputs of data and materials. And still the complexity grows. Modern man is haunted by the vision of a system grown so complex and so huge that it baffles human control. Perhaps the final solution to the problem of human governance will be to make a machine king. That is surely the immanent end toward which the efforts of all the linear programmers and systems analysts are headed.[46]

This is what I mean to suggest by the autonomy of process. The system works, not because recognizable human authority is in charge, but because its basic ends and its procedural assumptions are taken for granted and programmed into men and machines. Given the basic assumptions of growth as the main goal, and efficiency as the criterion of performance, human intervention is largely limited to making incremental adjustments, fundamentally of an equilibrating kind. The system is glacially resistant to genuine innovation, for it proceeds by its own momentum, imposes its own demands, and systematically screens out information of all kinds but one. The basic law of the whole is: Because we already have machines and processes and things of certain kinds, we shall get more machines and processes and things of closely related kinds, and this by the most efficient means. Ortega was profoundly right when a generation ago he described this situation as one of drift, though at that time men still thought they were in command. That delusion is no longer so widespread.[47]

The organization of the human resources needed to serve this process is done in the bureaucratic mode. It would be superfluous here to describe the essential characteristics of bureaucracy: that has been done capably by a number of writers. What I want to do instead is describe briefly what can best be called the bureaucratic epistemology, the operative definition of knowledge or information which is characteristic of all highly developed modern bureaucracies, for this is the screen through which information must pass before it becomes useful knowledge. This screen is one of the basic agencies by which the autonomy of process is assured.[48]

We are taught that the three great planning and control processes of modern society—bureaucracy, technology, and science—are all value-free means or instruments, just tools, which men must decide how to use by standards drawn from some other source than the realms of science, technology, and bureaucracy. This fairy tale is widely believed among the sophisticated and the naïve alike. Many things could be said about it, but here one thing is most important.[49] It is misleading to say that bureaucracy, for example—to focus on the force that matters most in a discussion of legitimacy—is a neutral means that can be used to achieve any end. Here, as in all human affairs, the means profoundly shape the ends. Bureaucracy may have no ultimate values, but it has a host of instrumental values, and among these is a conception of what counts as knowledge or useful information. This bureaucratic epistemology decisively shapes the outcomes—so decisively, in fact, that if you assign a certain task to a bureaucratic agency, you can largely say beforehand how the bureaucratic epistemology will constitute and alter the task itself. To put what follows in a phrase, if you were to assign the task of devising a religion to a bureaucracy, you could say beforehand that the product would be all law and no prophecy, all rule and no revelation.

More and more of men's energies are channeled through bureaucratic forms. Bureaucracy had advanced, as Weber pointed out, by virtue of its superiorities over other modes of directing human energy toward the ends of mastery over nature and other men. It is superior in speed, precision, economy, and clarity over alternative modes of controlling men and coordinating their energies. Hence, one can say, again with Weber, that modern bureaucracy is one of the supreme achievements of modern Western man. It is simultaneously an expression of the drive for rationality and predictability and one of the chief agencies in making the world ever more rational and predictable, for the bureaucratic mode of knowing becomes constitutive of the things known. In a way Hegel might barely recognize, the Rational does become the Real, and the Real the Rational.

Bureaucracy is rational in certain specific ways. First, it is in principle objective and impersonal, treating all cases without regard to their personal idiosyncrasies: all must stand in line. The objects of bureaucratic management are depersonalized. (Though, typically, each bureaucracy has a favored clientele group: all others must stand in line.) Secondly, bureaucracy is objective in the sense that the official is expected to detach his feelings from the conduct of his office. Subjectivity is for the private life. Thirdly, since bureauc-

racy proceeds by fixed rules and techniques, the incumbent
of an office is in principle replaceable by any other individual who knows the rules and procedures governing that
office and commands the skills appropriate to it.

This form of organizing human effort has a conception of
knowledge which is also rational in specifiable senses. In the
bureaucratic epistemology, the only legitimate instrument
of knowledge is objective, technically trained intellect, and
the only acceptable mode of discourse is the cognitive mode.
The quest for knowledge must follow specified rules and
procedures. Thus, many other paths to knowledge are
blocked. Specifically, everything thought of as "subjective"
and tainted by "feeling" must be suppressed. Any bureaucrat who based his decisions upon conscience, trained prudence, intuition, dreams, empathy, or even common sense
and personal experience would be ipso facto guilty of mal-
feasance. The bureaucrat must define whatever is to be done
as a problem, which implies that there is a solution and that
finding the right solution is a matter of finding the right
technique. In order to solve a problem, it must be broken
down into its component parts. Wholes can appear as nothing more than clusters of parts, as a whole car or watch is an
ensemble of parts. In order for wholes to be broken into
parts, things that are in appearance dissimilar must be made
similar. This is done by extracting one or a few aspects
which all the objects dealt with have in common and then
treating those aspects as though they were the whole. Thus,
there is in this conception of knowledge an urge toward abstraction and toward comparison and grouping by common
attributes. Abstraction and comparison in turn require
measuring tools that will yield comparable units: among the
favored ones are units of money, time, weight, distance, and
power. All such measurements and comparisons subordinate
qualitative dimensions, contextual meanings, and unique
and variable properties to the common, external, and quantifiable.[50]

This conception of knowledge also entails a whole conception of reality. Reality is that which is tangible, discrete, external, quantifiable, and capable of being precisely conveyed to others. Everything that is left over—and some might think that this is half of life—becomes curiously unreal or epiphenomenal. If it persists in its intrusions on the "real" world, then it must be treated as trouble; and those who act from motives embedded in the unreal world are treated as deviant cases, in need of repair or reproof. Bureaucrats still cannot quite believe that the human objects of "urban renewal" see themselves as victims.

All that remains to be added is the obvious point that he who would gain this kind of knowledge of this kind of reality must himself be a certain kind of man. The model is the knowledge seeker who is perfectly "objective" and dispassionate, detached from the objects of knowledge and manipulation, and blind to those aspects of the world that lie outside his immediate problem.

Now, when men treat themselves and their world this way, they and it increasingly become this way.[51] And somehow, this way includes consequences that an older vocabulary would have called horrible or evil. But if this is evil, it is evil of a special quality, the quality that Arendt calls banality. Bureaucracies staffed by "perfectly normal men" somehow perform horrors, but not out of ideology or love of evil. In 1576 the Duke of Alba marched into the Low Countries at the head of a uniform and thoroughly disciplined army of soldiers wholly devoted to the True Faith. When those soldiers, contrary to their disciplined and predictable appearance, began furiously burning and pillaging, the people called them "machines with devils inside." Today when we see bureaucracies perform their work of classifying, herding, expediting, and exterminating when necessary, we know they are machines without devils inside. What is inside is merely a certain conception of knowledge and the self, which has been long growing and which is widely distributed.

It is a conception which means by thought only a process of
rational and efficient calculation of the most efficient way to
handle materials, a conception which trains men how to behave efficiently, but not how to act responsibly. When
thought is so defined, the roles once filled by human leaders
wither and computers can perform them better than men.
Computer 1401 is worth much more to the State of Washington than the man who tried to kill it. In some remarkable
way, Eichmann was no more responsible than a computer.
Bureaucratic behavior is the most nearly perfect example
(along with certain areas of scientific and technical experimentation) of that mode of conduct which denies responsibility for the consequences of action on the grounds that it
lacks full knowledge of the reasons for action. All bureaucrats are innocent.

V.

Weber's account of charismatic authority leaves one with
a divided impression. On the one hand, he understood the
strong bonds and powerful currents of feeling that are possible between leaders and followers, and sensed that in some
way these relations were distinctively human. On the other,
Weber's tone suggests that charismatic authority is for the
childhood of the race and that the spread of rational-legal
authority, even though it too comes at a price, is somehow
progressive, more fitted to mature and independent adulthood. He frequently argues that we cannot return to that
earlier condition of ignorance and innocence, for "disen-
chantment" has gone too far, and he recommends the
Church with its music and incense for those who are too
"weak" to bear the burdens of the present. "Science as a Vocation" concludes on a note of warning to those "who today
tarry for new prophets and saviors" and urges all to "set to
work and meet the demands of the day." Modern life is disenchanted and hollowed of meaning, but we must manfully

live it anyway and not yearn for the gifts of faith and charisma. Each of us must, like Weber himself, see how much
he can bear.

But Weber's formulation puts this whole question on the
wrong footing. First of all, Weber "romanticized" charismatic authority, making it seem much more mysterious than
it really is. He also dealt mainly with very "strong" figures,
thereby skewing perception away from charismalike phenomena on a smaller scale and even in everyday life. He emphasized its dark aspects and saw it nearly always as the
ravishing of the weak and gullible by the strong and hyp-
notic, almost as Mann described it in "Mario and the Magi-
cian." But more importantly, the basic opposition is not between charismatic and rational authority, but between what
can only be called personal and human authority on the one
side and bureaucratic-rational manipulation and coordination on the other. It is obviously not charismatic leadership
that has been driven out by rational-legal authority, for our
age abounds in charismatic figures and putative prophets:
Rome of the second century of the Christian Era was no
richer. Such men have set the destinies of states, and they
may be met on every street corner and in every rock band.
The proliferation of these figures is plainly the dialectical
fruit of technological and bureaucratic coordination.

Rather, what is missing is humanly meaningful authority
and leadership. For this, the age shows a total incapacity.
Establishment officials and hippies alike share the conviction
that the only alternatives to the present system of coordination are repression or the riot of passion and anarchy. Both
groups, the high and the low, are unable to escape the crushing opposites that the world presents to us and that Weber
taught us to believe are the only possible choices. Both
groups conceive of authority almost exclusively in terms of
repression and denial and can hardly imagine obedience
based on mutual respect and affection. Confronted with the
structures of bureaucratic and technological coordination,

the young fear all authority and flee into the unreason of
drugs, music, astrology, and the *Book of Changes,* justifying
the flight by the doctrine of "do your own thing"—something that has never appeared on a large scale among any
populace outside Bedlam and the nursery, where it can be
indulged because there is a keeper who holds ultimate
power over the inmates. No doctrine was ever better designed to provide its holders with the illusion of autonomy
while delivering real power to the custodians. When those
in high positions are confronted with challenges, their first
response is to isolate themselves from the challengers by
tightening the old rules and imposing tougher new rules.
When the managers do attempt reforms in a "humanistic"
direction, the result is nearly always a deformity: to humanize leadership, institute coffee hours, fabricate human-
interest stories to show that the powerful one is human after
all, and bring in the makeup artists when he has to go
on television; to humanize bureaucracy, appoint T-groups
and ombudsmen; to humanize the law, introduce the in-
determinate sentence, special procedures and officials for
juvenile offenders, and psychiatrists who will put a technical
name on any state of mind for a fee. It is always an alliance
between "democratic" ideology and expert manipulation, in
a hopeless attempt to reconstruct something now almost forgotten—the idea and the experience of genuine authority.

To escape this trap, we must reject Weber's false opposites, and with it his test of manliness. It is not a question of
either retreating to charisma or advancing bravely to the rational-legal destiny, but of developing something different
from both. It is perfectly possible that the march toward the
rationally integrated world is not progressive at all, but a
wrong turning, a mistake, whose baneful consequences need
not be supinely accepted as inevitable or slavishly rationalized as developmental.[52]

It is certainly necessary to understand that natural human
authority has been overwhelmed by the combined impact of

the very forces, structures, and intellectual and moral orientations that we identify with modernity. A mere partial listing must suffice. Huge populations have made men strangers to each other and have made it necessary to develop efficient means of mass measurement and control. Centrally controlled communications systems can reach into all corners of the society, encroaching upon small human units of unique experience and outlook. Furthermore, the communications revolution makes possible the elaborate feedback circuitry necessary to the processes of automatic control. Intricate division of labor reduces common experience, producing both pluralistic ignorance and fragmentation of the process of work. The data explosion has produced microspecialization of the mind and the narrowing of perspectives on human problems. The relativization, materialization, and secularization of values makes it impossible for men to relate to one another on the basis of shared commitments to transcendent and demanding purposes and values. The sheer quantity and variety of artifacts and material needs and desires requires a vast system of administrative regulation and control, and thoroughly blurs the distinction between public and private, with the result that authorities cannot pretend to speak for public and objective goods but must accept the popular equation of private desire with public right.[53] The decline of tradition removes another rich source of shared meanings and limits, while rapid technological change proceeds by its own imperatives and enslaves its human attendants. All these add up to a scope and complexity so vast that humanly meaningful authority and leadership are baffled. Control must be accomplished either by bureaucratic coordination and self-regulating devices that govern the technical system by standards generated by the system itself, or by deliberately fabricated ideologies and images.

All these structures and processes will have to be confronted—and radically revised, in ways that no man can

clearly foresee—before humanly meaningful authority and
leadership can reappear.[54] But before that confrontation can
begin—or begin in ways that offer some prospect of a worthy
and merciful outcome—there must be an even more basic
shift in our understanding of the kind of knowledge that can
properly be accepted as constituting a claim to authority in
the human realm. I presented the administrative and scientific conception of knowledge as a specimen of what such
knowledge must not be. It remains to sketch what it must
be.

All leaders perform the same functions. They interpret
events, explore possible responses to problematic situations,
recommend courses of action, and vouch for the rightness
and success of actions taken. They advise, recommend, warn,
reprove, and command.[55] All this is so manifest in common
experience that the large social science literature which attempted to "explain" leadership by distinguishing between
"functional" and "trait" theories should have been seen
from the outset as superficial and unimportant, doomed to
trivial answers because it asked trivial questions. The fact
that it has been taken seriously supports the suggestion made
earlier that certain experiences of leadership and authority
really have become rare among men in the modern states.
The question is not whether leaders hold their positions by
performing certain functions or possessing certain traits.
The question is, rather, precisely how those functions are
construed and what kind of knowledge is understood to be
appropriate to their performance.

Each man is born, lives among others, and dies. Hence,
each man's life has three great underpinnings, which no
matter how far he travels must always be returned to and can
never be escaped for long. The three underpinnings present
themselves to each man as problems and as mysteries: the
problem and mystery of becoming a unique self: but still a
self living among and sharing much with others in family
and society: and finally a unique self among some significant

others, but still sharing with all humanity the condition of being human and mortal. Who am I as an individual? Who am I as a member of this society? Who am I as a man, a member of humanity? Each of the three questions contains within itself a host of questions, and the way a man formulates and responds to them composes the center and the structure of his life.

Given this, it can be said quite simply that humanly significant authorities are those who help men answer these questions in terms that men themselves implicitly understand. The leader offers interpretations and recommendations which set off resonances in the minds and spirits of other men. When leaders and followers interact on levels on mutual, subjective comprehension and sharing of meaning, then we can say that there exists humanly significant leadership. The relationship is one of mutuality, identification, and co-performance. The leader finds himself in the followers, and they find themselves in the leader. I am aware that to the rational and objective men of our day, this is mysticism. But it is those same rational men who cannot understand why the rational, objective, and expert administrators are losing authority, if not yet power, in all the modern states. The answer is mysteriously simple: to the degree that the rational, expert administrative leader achieves the objectivity and expertise which are the badges of his competence, he loses the ability to enter a relationship of mutual understanding with those who rely on him for counsel and encouragement.

Humanly significant leadership bases its claim to authority on a kind of knowledge which includes intuition, insight, and vision as indispensable elements. The leader strives to grasp and to communicate the essence of a situation in one organic and comprehensive conception. He conjoins elements which the analytic mind keeps tidily separate. He unites the normative with the empirical, and promiscuously mixes both with the moral and the aesthetic. The radical distinction between subjective and objective is unknown in this kind of knowledge, for everything is personal and comes from within the prepared consciousness of the knower, who is simultaneously believer and actor. When it is about men, this kind of knowledge is again personal. It strives to see within the self, and along with other selves. It is knowledge of character and destiny. Most of the facts which social scientists collect about men are in this epistemology superficial: information about a man's external attributes, rather than knowledge of who he is and what his possibilities are.

One who possesses and values this kind of knowledge bases his claims to its validity on grounds which are quicksand to the objective and rational man. One of the foundations is strength of conviction. A belief is true, or can be made true, when it is believed in strongly enough to base action on it, in precisely the way James described in his essay on "The Will To Believe." The other ground is the resonance set going between leader and followers when communications "make sense." When leader and followers begin to understand and respond to each other on a profound, personal level, each gains confidence that what is being communicated is true. All authority must believe that its knowledge is true. Rational, scientific authorities enjoy this confidence when they have followed the prescribed methods of inquiry and when their professional colleagues also share the belief. Personal authorities mean by verification the sympathetic vibrations set going by communications between leaders and followers who share a common background and outlook.

The language in which the knowledge appropriate to humanly significant leadership is expressed is also very different from the language of rational and objective discourse. It is a language profuse in illustration and anecdote, and rich in metaphor whose sources are the human body and the dramas of action and responsibility. This language is suggestive and alluring, pregnant, evocative. It is in all ways the opposite of the linear, constricted, jargonized discourse which is the ideal of objective communication. Decisions and recommendations are often expressed in parables and visions whose meanings are hidden to outsiders but translucent to those who have eyes to see. Teaching in this language is done mainly by story, example, and metaphor—modes of discourse which can probe depths of personal being inaccessible to objective and managerial discourse. Compare the Sermon on the Mount with the latest communiqué from the Office of Economic Opportunity in the War on Poverty; or Lincoln's Second Inaugural with Nixon's first.

The final distinctive characteristic of the knowledge appropriate to humanly meaningful authority is that it is dynamic and transactional. Currents of meaning and influence flow back and forth during the process of transmission, so that both the content of the message and the parties to the transaction are caught up and transformed in the flow. The contrast between this and objective discourse is decisive, for the goal of the latter is to send information economically from transmitter to receiver, altering neither the instruments nor the message in the process. Most of what modern information theory calls noise is of the essence of human communication between human authorities and their followers.

VI.

Very little of this—especially the material on leadership and authority—is new; and up until a short time ago it would have been unnecessary to say it. The tradition of political theory has always included leadership and authority among its central themes, and in that tradition the languages of discursive reason and of metaphor and myth were not permitted to fall apart and oppose each other either in the analysis of action or in the education of actors. As examples, consider Plato's theory of learning as remembrance, his emphasis on the right music and poetry in the education

of statemen, and his dialogues on justice and power. Aristotle said in the *Politics* that "the same education and the
same habits will be found to make a good man and a good
statesman and king." In the *Rhetoric* he tried to construct
the emphymeme as a tool specifically appropriate to practical discourse just as the syllogism was appropriate to theoretical discourse. Logic and rhetoric were important subjects in
the education of citizens because both taught ways of thinking and speaking which would make actors intelligible to
each other. Or consider the incomparable treatment of prudence, which is excellence in action, formulated by Aristotle
and perfected by Aquinas.[56] This treatment ascends from
custom and circumstance, through the psychology of motivation, to ethics and philosophy organized for the sake of action. Or take the literature of counsel, ranging from the profound and subtle works of More and Machiavelli through
the more limited works of Bacon and the "Mirror for
Princes" literature. All these branches of the tradition are
rich in precise observation of men and manners, historical
allusion, story, myth, and metaphor, and also in scientific
and philosophical argument and analysis. The tradition
starts with men where it finds them—located in a community, tied by custom and memory, full of prejudices, vices,
and fears, but also possessed of natural virtues—and strives
by a language appropriate to the subject to refine and enlarge character and knowledge so that men will be fit for
action and the exercise of authority.

In the modern world, and in the social science spawned by
that world, the "two sides" of this language have fallen
apart. We take it to be almost natural that the political
world, and the language and methods appropriate both to
understanding and to acting in that world, should be divided, as it were, between Sorel and McNamara. While I
have concentrated on the ideal and material conditions producing the crisis of legitimate authority, it should be clear
that that crisis also extends to our dominant ways of study-

ing these matters, which in turn conditions our ways of transmitting a political culture and preparing men to participate in it. Political Science has become a political problem.

In conclusion, there are senses, which I have tried to specify, in which de facto, humanly meaningful leadership *does* carry its own principle of legitimacy. But there are other senses in which it does not, or may not. There obviously can be illegitimate, albeit humanly meaningful authority. Without the setting and limits imposed by tradition, shared values and experience, institutions, and philosophical reason, humanly meaningful leadership can be as pathological and dangerous, and as illegitimate, as the processes of power-without-authority characteristic of modern states. Hence, one way to describe the crisis of legitimacy is to say that the basic features and tendencies of modernity have produced a situation in which the established processes and formal structures of control are at war with the conditions necessary for authority. In this battle, legitimacy is destroyed.

Events, institutions, and moral and epistemological ideas which, taken together, constitute modernity have virtually driven humanly meaningful authority and leadership from the field, replacing it with bureaucratic coordination and automatic control processes, supplemented when necessary by ideology and phony charisma. Furthermore, our methods of study have blocked us from seeing that such mechanisms of control are inherently vulnerable and in the long run unworkable, incapable of responding to men's needs for understanding and counsel on the basic, inescapable questions of human existence. So long as men remain what we have hitherto called human, they will require of power which strives to become authority that it respond to those questions in ways that have meaning for men. The current epidemic of revolts and uprisings, the current challenging of established institutions and processes, the thickening atmosphere of resentment and hostility, the dropout cultures of the young— these are something other than the romantic, reactionary, or nihilistic spasms which they are seen as in some quarters of the academy and the state. They are the cries of people who feel that the processes and powers which control their lives are inhuman and destructive. They are the desperate questionings of people who fear that their institutions and officials have no answers. They are overt signs of the underlying crisis of legistimacy in the modern state.

NOTES

1. From "The Whitehall Debates," in A.S.P. Wodehouse, ed., *Puritanism and Liberty* (London, J. M. Dent, 1938), p. 127.
2. The only important exception is Yves R. Simon, *Philosophy of Democratic Government* (Chicago, University of Chicago Press, 1951), pp. 1–72. Simon's book lies within the Aristotelian-Thomist tradition.
3. For a recent specimen, see the sections by Lerner in Daniel Lerner and Wilbur Schramm, eds., *Communication and Change in the Developing Countries* (Honolulu, East-West Center Press, 1967).
4. *San Francisco Chronicle*, June 5, 1969, p. 42.
5. Letter to Henry Osborne Taylor, January 17, 1905. In Harold Dean Cater, ed., *Henry Adams and His Friends*. Quoted here from William H. Jordy, *Henry Adams: Scientific Historian* (New Haven, Yale University Press, 1963), p. xi.
6. When I refer to a crisis of legitimacy, I mean more than an intensification of controversy about various public issues and policies— the kind of thing Dahl discusses in his analysis of the periodicity of opposition in the United States; or the kind of thing treated by the Michigan group under the category of critical or realigning elections. For a study of American voting patterns and electorial behavior that is important to an understanding of legitimacy in the United States, see Walter Dean Burnham, "The Changing Shape of the American Political Universe," *American Political Science Review*, LIX, No. 1 (March 1965), 7–28. What I mean by legitimacy will become clear as the essay proceeds.
7. Seymour Martin Lipset, *Political Man* (Garden City, N. Y., Doubleday, 1960), p. 77.

8. Robert Bierstedt, "Legitimacy," in *Dictionary of the Social Sciences* (New York, The Free Press, 1964), p. 386. Bierstedt is here paraphrasing Lipset, *Political Man.*

9. Richard M. Merelman, "Learning and Legitimacy," *American Political Science Review*, LX, No. 3 (September 1966), 548.

10. Hannah Arendt, "What Was Authority?" in Carl J. Friedrich, ed., *Authority* (Cambridge, Harvard University Press, 1958), p. 83.

11. Carl Joachim Friedrich, *Man and His Government: An Empirical Theory of Politics* (New York, McGraw-Hill Book Company, 1963), p. 233.

12. There is evidence that in the United States symbolic rewards alone do largely suffice. See Herbert McClosky, "Consensus and Ideology in American Politics," *American Political Science Review*, LVIII, No. 2 (June 1964), 361–82. A study of the tables on cynicism and futility shows that on item after item members of the general electorate express a strong sense of their own political powerlessness. Yet, 90 percent of the respondents say that they "usually have confidence that the government will do what is right."

13. David Easton's treatment, in *A Systems Analysis of Political Life* (New York, John Wiley & Sons, 1965), esp. Ch. 18, also remains within this perspective, although his reification of "the system" and his employment of the term as a noun of agency becloud what actually goes on. But consider: "Under the usual conception of legitimacy as a belief in the right of authorities to rule and members to obey . . . the major stimulus for the input of diffuse support would arise from efforts to reinforce such ideological convictions among the membership" (p. 288).

14. Lipset also sees legitimacy largely in terms of symbol manipulation. Thus, he says that "a major test of legitimacy is the extent to which given nations have developed a common 'secular political culture,' mainly national rituals and holidays." The United States has passed the test, for it possesses "a common homogeneous culture in the veneration accorded the Founding Fathers, Abraham Lincoln, Theodore Roosevelt, and their principles." (Lipset, *Political Man*, p. 80.) I refrain from comment on this pantheon.

15. *Ibid.*, pp. 88–92.

16. In Necker, *Du Pouvoir executif dans les Grands États*, 1792, p. 22. Quoted here from Bertrand de Jouvenel, *Power*, trans. by J. F. Huntington (London, Barchworth Press, 1948), p. 30.

17. Put less polemically: the looseness of the term is indicated by the fact that virtually every new or modern political ideology or sys-

tem has been identified somewhere in the literature as democratic. See, for example, C. B. Macpherson, *The Real World of Democracy* (Oxford, Oxford University Press, 1966).

18. I think this contemporary professional understanding of the public interest is a superficial one. It fails, for example, to consider Rousseau's effort to distinguish qualitatively between aggregated private interests and genuine common concerns. It fails also to come to terms with Burke's distinction between interest and opinion—an important distinction which appears in many everyday expressions, as when we say a man is "mistaken as to his interest." It excludes J. S. Mill's attempt to make qualitative distinctions between types of subjective interests and values. It is blind to Madison's distinctions between types of groups and publics: reasonable and long-range, versus passionate and temporary. Above all, the contemporary understanding restricts and debases the function of discussion in political life, reducing all speech to the lowest common denominator of "rationalization" or deception, or, at best, bargaining. American political parties and legislatures are not the whole of the political experience relevant to an understanding of the concept of public interest.

The whole question of the status and function of the notion of the public interest within the framework of democratic theory is complex and problematic. Historically, the notion has often played about the same role in domestic politics as "reason of state" or "national interest": it releases officials from restrictions imposed by the democratic principle of popular sovereignty. But if officials can claim authority, usually on grounds of superior knowledge, to determine the public good, then democracy, or democratic consent, is nothing more than a method for selecting rulers.

Richard E. Flathman, *The Public Interest* (New York, John Wiley & Sons, 1966) has tried to restore the concept to a status of philosophic dignity, with results that are, for me, murky. Brian Barry, *Political Argument* (London, Routledge and Kegan Paul, 1965), esp. Chs. 11–13, has laid solid foundations for further analytic work on the topic.

19. Kenneth Arrow, *Social Choice and Individual Values* (New York, John Wiley & Sons, 1963). Lindblom has argued that Arrow's conditions are not the preconditions of popular sovereignty. Lindblom's formulation, however, rests upon a very special understanding of democracy. He asks what process can produce the right ordering of preferences, answers that it is "partisan mutual adjustment," and concludes that this process is "democratic" *because* it produces the public good. See Charles E. Lindblom, *The Intelligence of Democracy* (New York, The Free Press, 1965).

20. I am aware that the typical, explicit popular response to this radical insecurity is: "Well, what can I do? Besides, we've all got to die sometime, anyway, and when you're dead, you're dead." That is now, as it has always been, the response of fools, though for ages wise men and saints had enough authority to persuade or impose upon men a belief in responsibility and immortality, so that fools were ashamed or afraid to speak their foolishness aloud. I am also aware that the typical, explicit professional response to this radical insecurity is something like, Total vulnerability is equal to security so long as the vulnerability is both mutual and really total. This is the strategy of deterrence. This theory redefines security to me, not freedom from fear, but the ability to believe that fears will not be realized. Such a notion of security requires endless and accelerating technological advance, increasing military power, and permanent inequalities of distribution. But all this is really beside the point. What matters here is that the "strongest" nation-states have failed the test of legitimacy through the provision of security. See Georges Bernanos, *Last Essays,* trans. Joan and Barry Ulanov (Chicago, Henry Regnery, 1955), esp. pp. 195–97.

21. Some perspective is provided by Walt Whitman's assessment, made over a century ago, that America had already overdeveloped the economic sector of life and should now turn to other efforts.

22. Jacques Ellul, *The Technological Society,* trans. John Wilkinson (New York, Vintage Books, 1967).

23. He, of course, did not put the point as bluntly as it is put here. Rather, he argued that high and ever-increasing military expenditures are an organic feature of the new industrial state, and concluded that "modern military and related procurement and policy are, in fact, extensively adapted to the needs of the industrial system." John Kenneth Galbraith, *The New Industrial State* (New York, New American Library, 1967), p. 241. See also Chs. 20 and 29.

24. Galbraith again: "If we continue to believe that the goals of the industrial system . . . are coordinate with life, then all of our lives will be in the service of these goals. . . . What will eventuate . . . will be the benign servitude of the household retainer who is taught to love her mistress and see her interests as her own, and not the compelled service of the field hand. But it will not be freedom." *Ibid.,* p. 405.

25. Bertrand de Jouvenel, *Sovereignty: An Inquiry into the Political Good,* trans. J. F. Huntington (Chicago, University of Chicago Press, 1957), pp. 203–4.

JOHN H. SCHAAR

26. Cicero, *De Legibus*, 3, 12, 38. Quoted here from Hannah Arendt, "What was Authority?" p. 100.

27. The rest of this paragraph is drawn from my "Violence in Juvenile Gangs: Some Notes and a Few Analogies," *American Journal of Orthopsychiatry*, XXXIII, No. 1 (January 1963), 33.

28. *Leviathan*, ed. Michael Oakeshott (Oxford, Blackwell, n.d.), p. 106. I have borrowed the de jure-de facto distinction for this discussion from R. S. Peters, "Authority," in Anthony Quinton, ed., *Political Philosophy* (Oxford, Oxford University Press, 1967), pp. 83–96, at p. 84.

29. Peters, *ibid.*, p. 94.

30. De Jouvenel, *Sovereignty*, p. 33.

31. Even Hume's thought reflects these patterns. Hume is, of course, famous for shattering the two-thousand-year-old concept of natural law—the idea that man could, by rational processes alone, discover universal norms of moral and political conduct. But while Hume, through his skeptical analysis of the character and functions of reason, undermined the ancient rationalist and transcendental conception of natural law, he replaced it by still another, more empirical, conception of natural law whose norms were as certain as those they replaced. He tried to show that the empirical existence of universal norms could be established by observation and that these norms were necessary products of social life. His logic was similar to that of the ancient theorists of the *jus gentium* and remarkably like that of modern linquistic philosophers, who argue that certain broad and necessary truths can be derived from the prerequisite conditions essential for the existence of a language. See Hume, *Treatise of Human Nature*, Book III, Part II, Sections I–VI; Part III, Section VI. See also his essay "That Politics May Be Reduced to a Science."

32. The scientific, objective, manipulative epistemology presupposes that the knower stands outside nature and studies it by assault. Thus: "A long time ago, we developed modern science as veritable outsiders of nature. In order to become scientific observers, we had to denature ourselves. We have succeeded. When we say, now, that we are reasonable we mean that we are engaged in calculations. When we hold something to be irrational we are merely indignant that our predictions have not been borne out, or perhaps, we are amused, for we make rash distinctions between the irrational and the stupid. When we say 'naturally,' we are hardly ever right." Hans Speier, "Shakespeare's 'The Tempest,'" reprinted in Speier, *Social Order and the Risks of War* (Cambridge, M.I.T. Press, 1969), p. 132.

33. For the impact of this upon the scope and nature of violence in the modern world, see Sheldon S. Wolin, "Violence and the Western Political Tradition," *American Journal of Orthopsychiatry*, XXXIII, No. 1 (January 1963), 15–29.

34. The words *nature* and *nation* come from the same root, the word for birth. Etymologically, a nation is a birth, hence a group of persons made kindred by common origin. Nations are also continually reborn, through the death of old customs and institutions and the generation of new ones. A nation has a unique birth and is also a continuous rebirth.

35. Law means limit or boundary. In Greek, the words for law, boundary line, and shepherd had the same root.

36. Vico expressed the point perfectly in his assertion that there were as many Joves, with as many names, as there are nations. *The New Science of Giambattista Vico,* trans. Thomas Goddard Bergin and Max Harold Fisch (Garden City, N. Y., Doubleday Anchor Books, 1961), pp. xxix, 31.

37. Machiavelli, obviously not under the spell of mythological thought, gave great attention to this problem of how to keep alive and intact the guiding spirit of a polity and in the end saw it as almost synonymous with popular remembrance of the founding premises: order and action perpetually re-created and renewed through remembrance of origins.

38. Tocqueville is frequently cited at this point in the standard exposition. But Tocqueville has been abused. He hoped and thought that, through voluntary associations, Americans could break out of the cell of individualism and learn the art of politics. But for this to happen, the associations themselves would have to be democratic and political in their internal character. That is rarely the case; but in its absence, Tocqueville's argument simply does not support the uses to which it has been put by contemporary pluralists.

39. Hopefully, Grant McConnell's work *Private Power and American Democracy* (New York, Alfred A. Knopf, 1966) will put an end to the idealization of the interest-group system as a process of partisan mutual adjustment which assures rationality and secures the public interest, thereby meeting the criteria of democracy. McConnell shows that "to a very considerable degree (the system of private power) makes a mockery of the vision by which one interest opposes another and ambition checks ambition. The large element of autonomy accorded to various fragments of government has gone far to isolate important matters of public policy from supposedly countervailing influences" (*ibid.,* p. 164).

40. I am, of course, speaking here of American writers, not of the European pluralist tradition of Von Gierke, Maitland, Duguit, Figgis, *et al.* Mary Parker Follett's *The New State: Group Organization the Solution of Popular Government* escapes these strictures.

41. At the least, it is a question of authorities here. Against the professional view of the seamless web of political socialization stand Malcolm X's *Autobiography* and, say, the two major studies by Kenneth Keniston. Against the voluminous professional accounts of the American as joiner stands the literature of the great American novels, which, from Melville to Faulkner, is an exploration of metaphysical and social isolation, a literature which sees the American as the wanderer, the one who does not belong.

42. Philip Rieff, *The Triumph of the Therapeutic: Uses of Faith After Freud* (New York, Harper & Row, Publishers, 1966), p. 4. Rieff's book is an important attempt to come to an understanding of the meanings of "postcommunal culture."

43. The spread of this new, postmoral mentality is bound to have corrosive consequences for the liberal doctrine of contract—the doctrine which bases government on consent of the governed and postulates an original contract by which the people who voluntarily set themselves under authority reserve the right to resist government when it abuses the agreement. The doctrine has always been a quicksand for logicians, a despair for sociologists and historians, and an invitation to resistance for men of conscience and just plain egotists. Historically, obedience has rarely been founded on contract; and as Hume said, "in the few cases where consent may seem to have taken place, it was commonly so irregular, so confined, or so much intermixed either with fraud or violence, that it cannot have any great authority." ("Of the Original Contract," in Frederick Watkins, ed., *Hume: Theory of Politics* [Edinburgh, Nelson, 1951], p. 201). Few men really consent to government, whether openly or tacitly. And as Jefferson understood, the logic of contract is incapable of binding men to the promises made by their predecessors. These logical shortcomings all become otiose in the face of the simple sociological fact that "obedience or subjugation becomes so familiar that most men never make any enquiry about its origin or cause, more than about the principle of gravity" (*ibid.*, p. 197). But all such habits are weakening in the modern states. As they weaken, the doctrine of consent becomes explosive. Every society rests upon a fiction, which usually encompasses both the society's origins and its ends, thereby helping make life and the world intelligible and endurable. Most of these fictions have failed. The fiction of contract and consent

was never one of the best (strongest). To take it seriously now would mean the dissolution of the modern state.

44. Ironic evidence is provided by the "Who Governs" literature. After prodigious professional labors we still have no authoritative answer. Apparently, everybody governs. Or nobody.

45. Admittedly, there are more sanguine vocabularies for describing the situation: "The fundamental axiom in the theory and practice of American pluralism is, I believe, this: Instead of a single center of sovereign power there must be multiple centers of power, none of which is or can be wholly sovereign. . . . Why this axiom? The theory and practice of American pluralism tends to assume, as I see it, that the existence of multiple centers of power, none of which is wholly sovereign, will help (may indeeed be necessary) to tame power, to secure the consent of all, and to settle conflicts peacefully." Robert Dahl, *Pluralist Democracy in the United States* (Chicago, Rand McNally & Co., 1967), p. 24.

This description, I believe, misses three central features of the situation: (1) it fails to point out that with all this dispersion there is still a powerful central tendency of policy, a pattern of movement; (2) it fails to point out that some persons and groups in the right positions and possessed of the right resources benefit much more from the system than do others—"noncumulative inequalities" is a dangerous euphemism; and (3) it fails to point out both the real nature of what is lost by the losers—identity, self-respect, and faith in others, as well as wealth and power—and the reparations those losers might someday demand. Thus: The chief of an Indian tribe, seeking redress for a grievance felt by his people, was advised to present his case to the government. He went from this office to that, was sent from one official to another and back again and again. He met no one who looked like himself, though everybody seemed to listen politely enough in the special way that bureaucrats listen. But much time passed, and nothing happened. The chief sadly concluded that the fault was his, because, despite his many interviews and diligent searchings, he had apparently failed to find the "government." Here indeed power was tamed, consent obtained, and conflict settled, but that Indian may not always conclude that the fault was his.

46. See Robert Boguslaw, *The New Utopians* (Englewood Cliffs, N.J., Prentice-Hall, 1965).

47. The description is not limited to control processes in the nongovernmental sector. In fact, any distinction between public and private, in both process and substance (except for the military power) would be very hard to draw in the United States. In 1908, Henry Adams wrote: "The assimilation of our forms of govern-

ment to the form of an industrial corporation . . . seems to me
steady though slow." (W. C. Ford, ed., *Letters of Henry Adams*
[Boston, Houghton Mifflin Company, 1930], Vol. II, p. 482.) Public, governmental bureaucracy grows apace: In 1947, there were
about 5.8 million people in government civilian employment, and
in 1963 there were 9.7 million; government expeditures, exclusive
of "defense," space, veteran, and debt outlays, grew eightfold between 1938 and 1963. The main impulse of large organizations, as
most students of the subject agree, is toward the maintenance and
growth of the organization itself, which requires increasing control over all aspects of the organizational environment.

48. The following draws heavily on Weber's classic analysis and on
the equally incisive work of Kenneth Keniston, *The Uncommitted: Alienated Youth in American Society* (New York, Dell Publishing Co., 1967), esp. pp. 253–72.

49. Though I cannot resist adding a brief appeal to those who still believe that science—especially social science—acquires "objective"
knowledge and that any such knowledge that can be acquired is
worthy of being acquired. Nietzsche exposed the fallacies here.
The number of things one might want to know is, in principle,
infinite. Therefore, every act of knowing requires a prior act of
choosing and desiring. The knowledge sought and gained necessarily reflects, in many ways, the impulses (values, intentions,
urges) which launched the search. Since it is a manifestation of
desire and choice, knowledge is subject to moral judgment; and
its "worth" is partly a function of the motives that led to its
acquisition. Our age, for example, has *chosen* to know how to
command *power* over nature and other men. Since Nietzsche, we
must recognize both the psychology and the morality of knowledge.

50. As a measure of the bureaucratization of American higher education, consider Clark Kerr's incisive definition of the multiversity
as "a mechanism held together by administrative rules and pow-
ered by money." *The Uses of the University* (Cambridge, Harvard
University Press, 1963), p. 20. He is talking about what used to be
called the community of scholars.

51. Reread W. H. Auden's "The Unknown Citizen," dedicated to
JS/07/M/378, in *Another Time* (New York, Random House, 1940).
Or C. Virgil Gheorghiu, *The Twenty-Fifth Hour* (New York, Al-
fred A. Knopf, 1950).

52. I wish to make it explicit here that while I have often treated
Weber critically, the "real" Weber was a far more powerful man
than the Weber canonized by social science. Social scientists have
borrowed Weber's discussion of the ideal-typical characteristics of
bureaucracy, but without his passionate concern to defend poli-

tics against bureaucracy. They have enthroned his fact-value distinction but have not even begun to come to terms with his profound criticism of the social science model of cumulative knowledge. They cite his dedication to science and rationality, but they
ignore his acceptance of Nietzsche's view of contemporary conceptions of science and rationality as potentially dehumanizing
forces. What was not "operational" in Weber has been largely ignored.

53. Perhaps this is excessive. Perhaps it is not yet a "popular equation." Most adult Americans do limit private desire by public
right. But among the young the equation is surely growing: either
private desire is equated with public right, or the existence of
anything like public right is simply denied, leaving only private
desire.

54. In the earlier ages of man, leaders were made by art to appear as
more than human: as divine or semidivine personages. Today the
ones who stand at the command posts and switching points are
made by art to appear as more than mechanical: as human beings.

55. This formulation cuts across Jouvenel's distinction between *dux*
and *rex*, though that distinction is very useful for locating the
performance of leadership roles within a social setting. Jouvenel,
Sovereignty, esp. pp. 40–70.

56. Aristotle, *Ethics* 6; Aquinas, *Summa Theologia*, i–ii 57.4–6; 58.4,
5; ii–ii 47–56.

"Hold On to Your Brains":

An Essay in Meta-theory

TRACY B. STRONG

What then is truth? . . . a sum of human relations, which have been enhanced, transposed and embellished rhetorically, and which after long use seem firm, canonical, and obligatory to a people: truths are illusions about which one has forgotten that this is what they are . . .

—Friedrich Nietzsche, *On Truth and Lie in the Extramoral Sense*

It is only through the habit of everyday life that we should think it perfectly plain and commonplace that a social relation of production should take on the form of a thing.

—Karl Marx, *Contribution to a Critique of Political Economy*

Extraordinary scientific achievements have a way these days of being used for the destruction of human beings (I mean their bodies, or their souls, *or their intelligence*). *So hold on to your brains.*

—Ludwig Wittgenstein to Norman Malcolm, December 1945

THIS IS AN ESSAY in meta-theory.* It is not itself political theory; rather it attempts to sketch out a typology of past historical conditions in which theory affected the beliefs and actions of men; it argues that such conditions are no longer characteristics of the present age; and finally it seeks to de-

* I am indebted to many people for their comments and suggestions, but most particularly to Nancy Lipton and Judith Shklar.

scribe the problems arising out of this fact and the sort of theory which would be appropriate to a new condition.

As such it is not *about* theorists: it does not attempt an exegesis of Rousseau or Hobbes to explain why they are "relevant" to our age. When this is done it seems often to occur in hasty bad faith: one allows that Plato "identified a problem"; one lauds "an insight"; one finally notes that "conditions" have "moved beyond" those under which the theorists wrote. Such work has its uses, not the least of them the comfort of a rationalized intellectual ancestry; in this essay, however, I will mention classical theorists only as examples of categories. I am not talking *about* them.

Nor does this essay attempt to find the "political message" in nonpolitical theorists. There is very little point in continuing an intellectual endeavor whose aim is merely to provide political glosses to texts of other disciplines. Those who have written about politics in a theoretical fashion, even when they are in the forefront of their fields, have in their politics tended to fall back on forms and doctrines developed mainly in the aftermath of the French Revolution. The plight of a Sartre trying to develop a Marxist political existentialism seems only equaled in its irrelevancy, if excelled in its honesty, by the silence of a Camus when confronted with the Algerian war. Closer to home, there is very little evidence that the brilliance of a Noam Chomsky in linguistics has anything to do with his laudable, though in the end very traditional, analysis of the war in Vietnam.

I. THE PROBLEM

In recent years, through the use of ever more sophisticated techniques of analysis, political scientists have accumulated an ever increasing body of information which has allowed substantially accurate forecasting of data correlations. In the face of this onslaught, so-called "traditional" political theorists have been reduced to fighting what amounts to a rearguard action. From time to time they have threatened to secede from departments, or they have formed departments of substantially like-minded people. For them the "relevance" of political theory has often come down to bemoaning the evils of this age, often in a moving and eloquent fashion.

This essay will have no part in this great debate between "behaviorists" and "traditionalists" which currently divides the profession of political science. Criticism of "numbers people" misses the point: the problem is with people, not with numbers. If an investigator insists, consciously or not, on maintaining an epistemology on the level of A. J. Ayer's *Language, Truth, and Logic,* we can only shake our heads in disbelief at his naïveté. The fact of the matter is that such an epistemology is untenable.[1]

Empirical behaviorists attempt to deal with the "facts." It is important to criticize their epistomology since it is precisely their relation to these facts that often constitutes a problem. Empiricism analyzes the whole as the sum of its parts,[2] in this as in much else partaking of a traditional liberal view of society. It sees "association by continuity."[3] It then proceeds to seek causal correlations (as we must call them) between parts. This simply fails to take into account what we know from the development of experimental science in the last thirty years.[4] To take the whole as the sum of its parts is a sort of social-science Pavlovism which has never learned that the whole is *different* from (not just greater than) the sum of its parts.[5]

To attempt to understand which facts occur together is not an illegitimate enterprise. Finding correlations is often interesting, sometimes useful, and frequently difficult. It also employs a large number of people. I do not find the oft-made accusation that such science is "value-laden" to be very telling. Since behaviorists are trying to depict the empirical manifestations of a society, they will inevitably reflect whatever values are implicit in the society. Indeed, they would not be performing their task adequately unless they did so.[6]

However, to take the conclusions of empirical behavioral science as ultimate or as real—that is, as describing how and why things work—is another matter. Since behaviorism seeks to understand correlations and not the nature of the unity of particular facts,[7] it misses the "essential." As Lévi-Strauss phrased it: "Marx followed Rousseau in saying—and once and for all as far as I can see—that social science is no more based than physics upon sense perceptions. Our object is to construct a model, examine its properties, and the way in which it reacts to laboratory tests, and then apply our own observations to the understandings of empirical happenings: these may turn out to be very different from what we had expected."[8] As the French phenomenologist Merleau-Ponty put it: "One must awaken the perspectival experience which has been buried by its own results."[9]

What we must do, then, to go below empirical science is to investigate Man in the World,[10] not through the addition of results achieved about each of them separately (science of man plus science of the world), but through an investigation of the structure of the field in which interactions occur.[11] However, if we stay "too close to empirical reality," as Raymond Aron noted, we will never reach a further stage of abstraction in which "we will discover the essential structures of a political order and the manner in which each political system manifests each of them and all together."[12]

A model for this endeavor has been described well by N. Troubetzkoy in his explanation of structural linguistics. "First, structural linguistics shifts from the study of *conscious* linguistic phenomena to study of their *unconscious* infrastructure; second, it does not treat *terms* as independent entities, taking instead as its basic of analysis the *relations* between terms; third, it introduces the concept of the *system*—'Modern phonemics does not merely proclaim that phonemes are always part of a system; it *shows* concrete phonemic systems and elucidates their structure; finally, structural linguistics aims at discovering *general laws,* either by induction 'or . . . by logical deduction, which would give them an absolute character.' " [13] This means that first we must move into a realm of abstract relations, of which the data are manifestations,[14] and second, that this realm underlies both ourselves and our data.[15] To use a vastly over-simplified analogy, we should not seek to understand what makes up a particular picture in the end of a kaleidoscope nor seek to compare successive pictures as the kaleidoscope is turned. We must seek to understand what a kaleidoscope *is.* Then particular manifestations of it will become clear and accurately understood.

We must, in other words, follow paths sketched out for us by Tocqueville, Weber, Nietzsche, and Lévi-Strauss. Following Montesquieu, Tocqueville sought to understand the *principe* of America; Nietzsche, as William Arrowsmith writes quite accurately, found the task of the classical scholar to be the construction of "something like a general field theory which would unify the crucial and complex features of Hellenic experience"; Weber sought the "spirit" of capitalism; Lévi-Strauss seeks "a single structural scheme existing and operating in different spatial and temporal context." [16] The problem is not that "what you see depends on where you sit," but rather that "nothing is more difficult than to know *exactly just what we do see.*" [17]

This points at the basic problem. If political theory is to result from a science conscious of and subject to all of the epistemological problems sketched out above, where will accurate analytical categories come from? They cannot exist independently of human understanding—that would require the acceptance of a version of natural law.[18] Most of us find such a position difficult to maintain.

Social scientists have attempted to resolve this problem in various ways. The most prevalent method is some form of functionalism—the notion that all societies must perform certain tasks or functions in order to remain in existence.

There have been many attacks on this specific theory: mostly on its theory of change. Most of these attacks have been rebutted,[19] and in its general outline functionalism has remained the dominant investigatory epistemology. Categories such as leadership, authority structures, and participation are held to be more or less useful ones.

Nevertheless, two problems immediately arise. First, social scientists have often gotten into trouble in applying them. E. R. Leach has delightfully chronicled the confusions of the British Colonial Office when it sought the leadership structures in Kachin Burma.[20] "Leadership" is simply meaningless in a Kachin context. Functionalist thinking sees good categories as abstract tools devoid of specific context which can be passed from scientist to scientist and society to society like a hammer. In practice, these tools are culture-bound.

Second, the notion that a society has certain functions which it must "perform" should give us pause. What and where is the "society" which "performs" these functions? Does it exist independently, or is it not rather more accurate to see it as coterminous with the performance of these functions.[21]

The functionalist appreciation has retroactively reified society. Society becomes a "thing" which "does" certain acts. Yet this is the same problem we found when we investigated the epistemological problems of empirical behavioralism: it is a separation of the investigator and the investigated, a denial of the coterminous nature of the two. Functional categories are to functionalists what the "facts" are to empirical behaviorists. Epistemologically speaking, they are only disguised versions of each other.

I have suggested (1) that concepts should emerge from under the data; (2) that they are nonempirical in nature *and* origin; and (3) that they correspond to the unity of the investigated, a unity which is different from the sum of the parts. To determine them thus requires a tremendous amount of work: complete immersion of the investigator in

the investigated until the epistemological distance is overcome. Since it took Lévi-Strauss a whole book—*Le Cru et la
Cuit*—to describe just one Bororo myth, any "complete"
analysis would be a huge undertaking. However, the power
of such concepts—even if incompletely and oversimply elaborated—can readily be seen from the persistent power of
Marx's analysis in *The Eighteenth Brumaire of Louis Bonaparte* and the lasting controversy over Weber's writings on
religion.

II. THE SOURCES OF THEORY

The preceding section is a preliminary conceptual sketch
of the epistemological problems of an adequate social science. Its basic point is that the development of concepts
must correspond to what our knowledge of the structure,
psychology, and phenomenology of perception (i.e., the formation of concepts) tells us. Good political theory will be an
activist presentation based on these concepts and knowledge.
This requires some explanation.

The conclusion to Lévi-Strauss' *Tristes Tropiques*—a
book which in many ways is a model for this sort of research
—is expressly a withdrawal from and a denial of activism
both in word and deed. In words which recall Max Weber
but with no sign of the torment which Weber felt, Lévi-
Strauss proclaims that the scientist must "accept the muti-
lated condition which is the price of his vocation. He has
chosen and must accept the consequences of his choice. His
place lies with the others and his role is to understand them.
Never can he act in their name, for their very otherness prevents him from thinking or willing in their place: to do so
would be tantamount to identifying himself with them. He
must also resign himself to taking no action in his own society, for fear of adopting a partisan position . . . his initial
choice will remain, and he will make no attempt to justify
that choice. It is a pure motiveless act. . . ." [22]

This lack of activism in the phenomenological sciences is due to an understanding of where concepts come from. If a concept can be formed on the basis of a reference point existing separately and independent from the observed, then social science acquires a sort of Archimedian fulcrum: it can explain things in terms of something else. This allows for causality, motion, a direction. Hence any theoretical understanding based on the epistemological principle that "there is something out there" contains an inherent dynamism or activism.* Old structures of truth and perception linger on, even though people no longer believe in them. Most people have an epistemology that would have been current in the early nineteenth century. They live on, in Nietzsche's angry accusation, in the "shadows of the dead God."

It is not surprising then that phenomenologists and structuralists, in their denial of independent reference points, have turned from explanation to description as the first task of the scientist.[23] Lacking an outside reference point, activism becomes impossible. We must take such a conclusion very seriously. If we are not able to move to an activist statement while retaining this basic epistemology, we must conclude that the theory is no longer possible.[24]

III. LANGUAGE AND THEORY

There can be no doubt that if theory has affected events, it must have been through the medium of language.[25] Most simply, people wrote, others listened and read and found in the words something that caused them to perceive and thus act differently than they otherwise would have. In the *European Revolution,* Tocqueville reports that during the French Revolution at first "one heard Montesquieu cited, but at the end no one was but Rousseau." The clear implica-

---

* I am not trying here to interject anything resembling the "fact-value problem." I am simply trying to investigate the consequences for theory of a certain type of epistemological view.

tion is that people found in Montesquieu and Rousseau a language by which to order and make sense of their actions. Norman Jacobson has suggested that American political science might have turned out much differently if "instead of the prudence of James Madison, the pieties of Thomas Paine had become the chief text for political education in America." [26] Again, the implication is clearly that the language a theorist uses—the grammar and concepts he leaves to posterity—places a broad parameter on the sorts of things that can be thought.[27]

This much is hard to deny. What we must ask ourselves at this point is if there is anything basic to the way people wrote *and were understood* that corresponds to the epistemological understanding which we set forth in section I. In other words, are there some basic underlying structures of language which in the past provided an epistemological activism for theory? I find such a conclusion in the works of Nietzsche and Wittgenstein, who investigated the effect of the structure of Western language on concepts. Both were driven in their investigations back to the roots of language, whose constraints they recognized without wishing to replace it with something else (emotive intuition, for instance, or, à la Buber, silence). "We cease to think if we do not do so under the constraint of language." [28]

We have spoken of the dangers and problems in the presupposition of causal relations among phenomena. Such considerations are well exemplified in language. One cannot separate society from its "functions" any more than a doer from a deed. As Nietzsche says: "The Doer is read back [*hingedichtet*] into the act—the act [*das Tun*] is all." [29] Thus, to say in general parlance that "the lightning flashes" or, in scientific circles, to speak of a force "moving something" is a "doing-doing" [*Tun-Tun*]; it is to state the same event as both cause and effect. "For all its detachments and freedom from emotion," Nietzsche says, "our science is still the dupe of linguistic habits." [30]

The same observation is made by such linguistical anthropologists as B. L. Whorf and Edward Sapir. "We are constantly reading into nature fictional acting entities, simply because our verbs must have substantives in front of them. We have to say 'It flashed' or 'A light flashed,' setting up an actor, 'it' or 'a light,' to perform an action, 'to flash.' Yet the flashing and the light are one and same!" [31]

What this is ultimately saying is that language brings on the tautology of causality. For instance, in the sentence "I am getting wet because it is raining," there is no logical way to distinguish "wet" (a quality) from "rain" (an occurrence and a datum). Thus the sentence might properly read "rainwetting and I together in time and space." In this formulation, though, the apparent causality has disappeared.[32] The logical extension of this notion is, as Whorf notes, that in certain circumstances language will inhibit understanding. "Western culture has made, through language, a provisional analysis of reality and, without correctives, holds resolutely to that analysis as final. The only correctives lie in all those tongues which . . . have arrived at different, but equally logical, provisional analyses." [33]

Language leads to errors; this is not an unmitigated disaster. Such errors, in fact, constitute the foundation of civilization. "Mathematics . . . for instance . . . would certainly have never evolved if one had known from the beginning that there are no real circles in nature, nor any absolute standards." Language, however, rapidly acquires a force of its own. It "drives humanity where it least wants to go." We are constantly led astray, says Nietzsche, "and are induced to think of things as simpler than they are, as separate, indivisible, and existing in the absolute. *Language contains a hidden philosophical mythology.*" [34]

Nietzsche and Wittgenstein thus set themselves a similar preliminary task: the unmasking of the mythologies and apparent absolutes of language. "The results of philosophy are the uncovering of one or another piece of plain nonsense and of bumps that the understanding has got by running its head up against the limits of language. These bumps make us see the value of discovery." [35] The process teaches us something about the consequence of language. For behind the falsifications of language lie the very basic "often extremely general facts of nature which are hardly ever mentioned because of their extreme generality." [36]

The effect of the above is to indicate how important the controlling effects of language are, especially in times of general social crisis. Both Thucydides and George Orwell exemplified this consciousness very well. In the former, we find an awareness of the power of language in controlling men's actions and of its basically ideological character: "When troubles had once begun in the cities, those who followed carried the revolutionary spirit further and further and determined to outdo the report of all who had preceded them by the ingenuity of their enterprises and the atrocity of their revenges. The meaning of words no longer had the same relation to things, but was changed by them as they thought proper." [37]

Orwell showed the same concern. "Political language . . . is designed to make lies sound truthful and murder respectable and to give an appearance of solidity to pure wind." [38] In *1984* he went so far as to construct a whole language—Newspeak—designed to make morally compatible concepts which are linguistically opposed in English. Generally speaking, a culture is neurotic and in trouble when circumstances compel it—as they did the American army major in Vietnam who had to speak of "destroying a village in order to save it"—to engage in acts which the morality and logic of its language do not permit.

In the past, then, theory was able to adopt an activist position vis-à-vis its audience due to the fact that a distinction of doer and deed was assumed in its "unconscious." That is, it was still possible to describe things that could be done and describe them in a way which made people feel that the not-yet-done was part of their potentiality. I am suggesting simply that at a given time in history, because, for instance, of the way that Rousseau wrote, many men were able to feel that what Rousseau described was something that they should and could try to be. Thucydides provided an emotional, projective example of this; Orwell, a manipulated, totalitarian one.

Central to an activist position was the notion of unrealized potentiality. There must exist for society and men something different to become. The minimum task of the theorist was to describe it, and to do this he had to have a fairly accurate perception of what was dynamic in the society and what was, in Marx's phrase, destined for the "ash-heap of history." What the theorist did, then, was in effect to "latch on" to history in one way or another through his understanding of it. The power of a theory was power leeched from the dynamism of history.

IV. TYPES OF THEORY:
THE USES AND ABUSES OF HISTORY

We must now turn to the various ways in which theorists did this. These appear in three main categories. I shall give specific examples in each category, but these are *only* examples. The theorists do not completely fit the categories, nor are the categories meant to appropriate the theorists.

1. First is *transcendental theory*. The name carries the burden of metaphysics for an age exclusively concerned with the facts. Yet all it means is "not subject to the vagaries of social or individual perception." This is political theory which escapes being ideology by *denying a past*. This is a point of view which accepts as its base only that which does not change. Hobbes's *Leviathan* and Plato's *Republic* could be examples. Those who see the *Republic* merely as an apology for the polis (as Karl Popper and to some degree Gilbert Murray do) or *Leviathan* as the apotheosis of the polit-

ical ambitions of the rising bourgeoisie (as C. B. Macpherson has so brilliantly argued) miss the point. Socrates and Plato were radicals in their day. Hobbes, bourgeois or no, wrote so well that neither Royalist nor Roundhead would offer him a post as ideologist. It is significant that Plato explicitly spells out the manner in which the Republic may be attained: either by accident (outside of history) or through the elimination of the past (by expelling everyone over ten years of age) and systematic reeducation. Hobbes, of course, felt obliged to start the Leviathan by engaging in systematic renaming.

Both Plato's and Hobbes's theories may have been inspirational in their time. They are dangerously inappropriate to the present. They assume that the model of the age can be dealt with by a model which denies time: the historical process is presumed to contain enough beneficial elements that one does not have to deal with it directly. By placing their cities outside the historical process, Plato and Hobbes assumed that in making a political statement (i.e., about common matters rather than about individual lives) they could allow the historical process to continue on for the time being without direct confrontation.[39] While profoundly radical in substance, the theories are conservative in statement.

2. Next, we have *historical theory*. This type formulates certain historical processes powerfully enough to make sense out of the past and to engender action for certain central values emerging out of the organizing principle. Machiavelli, Marx, and perhaps Weber fit in this category. In the *Discourses,* Machiavelli formulates those developments of an emergent politics in a theory of statesmanship which no one writing or governing after him could afford to ignore. Marx found a way to understand past history and a way (he thought) to predict future events. Max Weber understood the world in terms of demagification (*Entzauberung*) and progressive rationalization. His spell still hangs very heavily over those who would write about the Third World.

The danger with this approach is that history inevitably catches up. There arises a "conceptual lag" between the theory and "reality." The last man to be able to successfully apply the volitional theory of Machiavelli was probably Bismarck. As Henry Kissinger has made clear, after Bismarck and because of him the European system acquired a complexity which no one could hope to control.[40] Since capitalism proved less rigid than Marx had assumed, from historical experience modern Marxists have been obliged to pile up rationalizations. We are now told by structuralists that what Marx *said* was unimportant; it was *how* he went about it.[41] They have made him into a transcendentalist. Weber, when confronted with the reality of political change after the First World War, had no choice but to fall back on the state. While privately critical of Ludendorff and others, publicly he felt he had no choice but silent support.

Such theory was then radical by its statement; however, due to the subjugation of its content to the historical process, it became in the long run ideological and conserving. The list of demands in the *Manifesto* no longer appears to go against the dominant ideology of our times; it is hardly surprising that the young generation of new Marxists have turned to the young, almost transcendental Marx. Insofar as the problems to which the theory was designed to provide an answer persist—such as distributive justice—there are important points to be retained. If the nature of the problem changes, then so must the nature of the theory.[42]

3. The last type is cyclical *reconstructive theory*, which arises during periods of great social change after the breakdown of old value structures. It greatly changes the lives of men. Since it was "designed" to deal with specific problems, success would change it. Typically, the problems are anomie and lack of content. To the degree that the thought is successful, it provides meaning and thus is no longer necessary in its original form. Such theory has been well described by Michael Walzer in *The Revolution of the Saints*. In his last

chapter he describes how the dynamics of Calvin's Geneva, Jacobin France, and Leninist Russia were similar responses to a situation of social disintegration.

Cyclical-reconstructive theory acquires its power from its role in filling "value vacuums" at moments of "failure of nerve" and social upheaval. It is radical in both content and form. This, however, is its very problem: if it passes away it will become only a historical curiosity, as Engels was to point out about the Utopian Socialists. If, on the other hand, it succeeds, it is doomed thereby to become oppressive or conservative in history. Weber recognized this full well in the last pages of the *Protestant Ethic and the Spirit of Capitalism:* "The Puritan wanted to work in a calling; we are forced to do so. . . . The light cloak has become an iron cage."

In the end, cyclical-reconstructive political theory is temporary and not only succumbs to historical change but also requires historical change to arise. Without historical change, there is no vacuum; and without this vacuum, no chance to fill it with theory. In all three cases we have come down to the same fact: in one way or another, historical change is responsible for the demise and/or increasing social irrelevancy of theory. *History overcomes theory's activism,* either by disproving, subsuming, or perverting it.

V. THE PROBLEMS FOR PRESENT-DAY THEORY

In the past, political theory was concerned with the investigation of men in the communality. It was presupposed—correctly—that men could only survive in groups and, thus, that the nature of group relations was a key concept. In liberal theory, the nature of groups, or, to use psychological language, of the reality principle, was fundamentally economic and contractual in nature. It involved agreement to defer primary gratifications in order to conquer and appropriate the world in common. That this effort involved a fundamental change in the quality of relationships was better understood by Rousseau, Marx, and Durkheim than by Hobbes, Mill, and Locke.[43] Nevertheless, almost all political theory has presumed the existence of some form of public life; the question has been the theory and practice of the public.

Recently, however, doubt has been cast on the continued necessity of a public life for common survival. In individual cases[44] and in broad projections[45] a picture of "post-industrial society" has been evolved. What follows now is simply a short sketch of some of the problems which a theory will have to investigate. After that we will be able to proceed with an investigation of what the theory will look like, and from whence it will draw its power. One must repeat that there is nothing theoretical about the identification of problems through projections.

Central here is the proposition that upper-middle-class values (the breakdown of which leads to the "New Left") are not different in kind from those of the lower middle class. They only differ in that they occur in a condition of relative affluence. When monetary or economic achievement has reached a certain threshold it no longer provides an acceptable reality principle. At this point, man is left with no purposive incentives, having had only insignificant solidarity incentives due to the nature of the society (individualistic, achievement-oriented).[46] He moves then in the direction of normlessness. Since we can expect increasing affluence, there does not seem to be any *necessary* reason that our society cannot achieve a just distribution of goods—we can expect more and more people to arrive in the position of the upper middle class.

The middle-class values that seem to be disappearing can be listed:

    a. A concern about consequences (deferred gratification), to be replaced by what Kahn and Wiener call "sensate culture," based on impulse and spontaneity.

   b. Respect for authority, to be replaced by an actual decrease in authority.

   c. Adherence to group norms, to be replaced by increasing individualism.

   d. Decreasing intensity of perceived relation to the "system."

Most of these may be broadly summarized, not as Kahn does as caused by the lack of a goal, but rather as the lack of a group. Some of the consequences for individuals which emerge directly out of them and constitute a second set of problems for empirical work are:

   a. The nonexistence of roles.

   b. The inability to find a value referent valid both for oneself and for another.

   c. The prevalence of introspection.

   d. A valuation of experience purely for its own sake.

   e. An inability to criticize proffered solutions, especially when they are of the charismatic variety.

   f. A search for value confirmation in peer groups.[47]

   g. An inability to identify peer groups.

All these problems can and should be investigated separately. Taken together, they form the basis for a theoretical question: *What form of society corresponds to a situation where people no longer have to defer primary gratifications? How can one write about it accurately so that men understand it?*

Most people who have dealt with this problem have written about it in a manner which showed that they were not conscious of the difficulties involved. They have spoken as if the forces making for change were obvious. In other words, their expectations of change were premised upon the continuing existence of a dynamism which their theoretical analysis should have led them to question. Herman Kahn has admitted[48] that he thinks that people should "become tougher." Yet it is hard to see why the will of individuals should be able to resist the whole movement of a culture.

Men, especially large groups of them, are simply not rocks existing almost independently of the stream which flows around them. The same criticism applies to the proposals of Marcuse (in *Eros and Civilization*) and Norman O. Brown (*Love's Body*). The society which these men envisage seems to me to suffer from both romantic wish fulfillment of middle-class fantasies and from a surprising faith in the benevolence of technology. Both men wish to extend the erotic to all spheres of activity and permit, thereby, the substitution of play for work. Through vastly expanded technology, society will increase the amount of leisure time available to all men. Thus we could enter into a world with no "surplus repression." This is, in the end, very middle class. Men do not like their work, so we make it possible for them to play. Marcuse assumes that men will somehow know what they want to do, and more importantly, *what would constitute satisfaction.* Yet "identity" is one of the basic problems. It seems unlikely that under the identity which is falling away there is a better one which will emerge and allow the individual to recognize satisfaction. The dynamic which Marcuse proposes—a volitional restarting of the dialectic which modern society has brought to an end [49]—seems to me to suffer from the same problems that Kahn's does.

Norman O. Brown is more honest and more nihilistic: he foresees a world of polymorphous perversions. The depths are to be vigorously stirred and allowed full play. "The next generation needs to be told that the real fight is not the political fight, but to put an end to politics." His solution is love, which, "Cordelia-like," comes bearing "nothing." [50]

If the problems in these solutions lie in an inadequate analysis of the dynamics, it is then to this that we should turn. We suggested above three ways in which theory has acquired a dynamic in the past. The question we are now asking is, then, What is the relation of history to political theory in our time? This is a very difficult matter since, even if my conclusions *will be* correct, this relation has *not yet* achieved a paradigmatic form; thus counterexamples can always be adduced. My argument will have to be logical in form, then, although I shall try to adduce evidence from contemporary studies.

What I suggest is that the processes of history made transcendental and historical theory impossible and no longer produce the conditions required for cyclical-reconstructive theory. This is tantamount to saying that change does not occur in a "post-industrial" society by the same means that it did in the period which extends roughly from Socrates to Marx.

The argument rests on the notion that in the past ontogeny did in some broad outline recapitulate phylogeny and that this linkage provided the fulcrum from which conscious change could be meaningfully advocated. That is, the experiences people went through were structured in a manner similar enough to the outside world that people could feel they were part of an ongoing process.

When one says that ontogeny recapitulates phylogeny one is saying (a) that all men must pass through a series of stages in the development of their personality and (b) that these stages correspond in broad outline to ones which appear in history.[51] I believe the assertion of such a parallel can be justified in the following manner. If the development of the child shows any pattern which can be even remotely construed as evolutionary, this would be that of a gradual increase in domination. First, over the outside world: the child learns to deal with the world in a way so that (a) it does not destroy him and (b) he can make it do (or at least not defeat) his will. Secondly, over himself: during youth and adolescence one is able to dominate the environment with only a moderate amount of control over oneself—enough, shall we say, to allow calculations of pain and pleasure. After a period, though, it becomes necessary to create or influence the conditions under which one is going to control external events. Just reacting is no longer sufficient.

At this point ontogeny and phylogeny must part company. Historical development—Hegel to the contrary—is not the work of a creative Will which determines what all its stages are. One can make parallels between the two developments (man and history) as long as future development does not require what is in historical existence to create new conditions. The developments of the individual in "sensate culture" noted above seem to indicate that times of men have less and less relation to the history of mankind.

What this means for theory is that the individual's perception of history must be one of his decreasing relation to it. If historical developments have led the individual to a point where the developments mentioned above are occurring, then the individual has less and less relation to history. One could speak, in fact, of "an end to history," meaning by this an end to any parallel changes in the individual and in the broader society. As the individual has become more introspective, the society has become increasingly abstract and remote. As Kierkegaard put it: "The new development for our age cannot be political for politics is a dialectical relation between the individual and the community; but in our time the individual is in the process of becoming far too reflective to be able to be satisfied with being merely represented." [52] If the destiny of our times manifests itself in political terms, as Thomas Mann argued against Nietzsche, this destiny rarely involves men as political beings. As Lévi-Strauss says, "henceforth history will make itself by itself. And the society of men, placed outside . . . history would be able to exhibit once again that regular and as it were crystalline structure which the best preserved of primitive societies teach us is not antagonistic to the human condition." [53] Lévi-Strauss is here again true to his analysis; a similar though not so sanguine conclusion is attained by Michel Foucault in his most important book, *Les mots et les choses:* "Man finds himself as dispossessed of all that constituted the most manifest content of his History: nature no longer speaks to him of the creation or the end of the world, of his dependence or coming judgment. . . . The human being has no more history: or rather, since he speaks, works and lives, he finds himself bound up in histories which are neither subordinate nor homogenous. . . . He only constitutes himself as subject to History by the superimposition of the history of beings, the history of things, the history of words. He is subject to their pure happenings [*pures événements*]." [54]

The consequences of this on past types of theory can now be traced out. One may legitimately ask if the "end of history" is not simply the realization of transcendental theory. This is certainly in part what Hegel thought it was.[55] It would be if the individual were integrated into the pattern resulting out of such a realization. In Plato's *Republic*, there is the description of a state which requires from no one what he is unable to accomplish. This, however, is not what is described above. There we saw that society required nothing from the individual and he was reduced to, say, the role of the student in a multiversity, necessary perhaps in his presence but not in his being.

Transcendental theory depended, as we saw, on its opposition to history. In an age with no history there is nothing for it to distinguish itself from, and it inevitably must devolve into ideology. Thus it is not surprising that Daniel Bell, Raymond Aron, and others have proclaimed an "end to ideology." What has actually happened is the apotheosis of ideology, and Aron at least has had second thoughts.[56]

The effect on historical theory has been even more apparent. Like a horseman, historical theory depended on the existence of the horse. Thus the Marxist revolutionary is obliged to postpone the revolution indefinitely; the activist quality soon disappears—as the Chinese keep telling the Russians.[57] Liberal theory has, to a great degree, succeeded in some countries. It has thus destroyed through its success those conditions which previously made it a dynamic force.

Since there were a whole range of problems that it was simply not concerned with—problems which are now coming up—it too becomes, to the degree it is still adhered to, another conservative rationalization of the status quo.

Cyclical-reconstructive theory depended on periodic major social-political crises in values. To the degree that these are disappearing as necessary occurrences such theory will no longer appear.

VI. THE WRITING OF THEORY

It would appear from the above that there is little chance for any political theory written in any of the manners which have had some success in the past. Since the West, and the United States in particular, are probably going to be faced with a whole new set of problems in the relatively near future (say thirty-five to one hundred years), it would seem important to develop a political theory which could make a difference in the way people deal with those problems. This is highly problematic, since the consequence of what we have been saying above is that a certain paradigm of thought and action has pretty much played itself out. Other writers in this book have described the nature and operations of paradigms. There is no need to repeat their analysis here. I have a few suggestions which attempt to incorporate some of the analysis sketched out in the first part of this essay as to how one could begin to build the discovery of a new paradigm. One is a suggestion of format and the other of content; both of them are drawn from my understanding of the writings of Nietzsche.[58]

First as to format. How should one write in such a task? Few writers have engendered so many passionate personal interpretations as has Nietzsche. For this, he has been variously accused of inconsistency or confusion. I suggest, on the contrary, that Nietzsche's writing[59] provides a model of an appropriate style. Our problem is to find a form of writing which is intensely personal, yet which communicates a new general dynamic. We had found before that one of the problems emerging out of the end of history was the increasing disjuncture between these two areas. As I understand Nietzsche, he is writing in such a manner that everyone who reads him is forced or drawn to read *himself* into what Nietzsche wrote. Thus we have a pro-Semitic and anti-Semitic Nietzsche, a pro- and anti-Socrates Nietzsche, a Nietzsche concerned with releasing emotions and one concerned with controlling them, etc., etc. What I am saying is not that Nietzsche is all these things. He is Nietzsche. *We* (in our collectivity) are all these things. We project them onto Nietzsche's work. Since his writings contain an underlying structure which is both constructive and destructive, we are led to shape our projections in a certain way. These thoughts are, so to speak, reflected back to us in a somewhat distorted fashion. Since—if one keeps reading—one has to deal with them, they acquire a dynamic self-investigatory quality. If we deal with them long enough they should make us change in a definable direction.[60] Thus the activism of such theory will come not from its relation to history, but from its relation to new epistemology.

The question immediately arises, How will people understand it? If it is really a new epistemology (which it would have to be), how can it be apprehended consciously? The answer to this question is my second point. It will not be and it should not be. In his notes Nietzsche wrote, "one understands these things theoretically when they have been achieved in practice." By this he means that a whole new mode of life will have to be created. It is accurate to say that what is necessary is a restructuring of the unconscious. As we saw in our analysis of language, the shaping grammatical characteristics are hidden deep in our world. They provide part of the basic paradigm which theory would be seeking to replace. In terms of men, to speak of changing a paradigm amounts to saying, changing the unconscious. As Lévi-

Strauss put it: "It would be a matter . . . of stimulating an organic transformation which would consist essentially in a structural reorganization, by inducing the patient intensively to live out a myth—either received or created by him —whose structure would be, at the unconscious level, analogous to the structure whose genesis is sought on the organic level." [61] Wittgenstein also noted in *Remarks on the Foundations of Mathematics:* "The sickness of a time is cured by an alteration in the mode of life of human beings . . . not through a medicine invented by an individual." [62]

These are, in Marcuse's charming phrase, "very advanced thoughts." The implications are tremendous. As a start, they mean that political theorists will have to study a whole new set of disciplines (among them neurophysiology[63]). Much more investigatory science is necessary to understand what the limits and consequences of possible paradigms are.[64] We need a systematic methodology involving *all* sciences.[65]

We are, I think, going to be faced with a failure of nerve without proportion. To come out on another side will require both science and theory. Neither is in any condition for the task. As Nietzsche said: "All goals are annihilated. Men must give themselves one. They have given themselves all their past goals. But the pre-conditions for all earlier goals no longer exist. Science shows the river, but not the goal: it does give the pre-conditions to which the new goal must respond. . . ." and "among those who hold their being [*Dasein*] capable of eternal return, conditions such as no utopians have ever dreamed of become possible." [66]

NOTES

1. The work of Max Black, *Studies in Method and Language* (Ithaca, N.Y., Cornell University Press, 1959); Ernst Nagel, "A Formalization of Functionalism," in *Logic Without Metaphysics* (New York, The Free Press, 1956); and Ludwig Wittgenstein are just a few

352

TRACY B. STRONG

examples. The argument with other examples is well made in J. J. Katz, *The Philosophy of Language* (New York, Harper & Row, Publishers, 1966), pp. 240 ff.

2. Claude Lévi-Strauss, *La Pensée sauvage* (Paris, Plon, 1967), p. 35.
3. Maurice Merleau-Ponty, *The Structure of Behavior* (Boston, Beacon Press, 1967), p. 90.
4. Summaries of these experiments can be found in Merleau-Ponty, *Structure of Behavior;* in Merleau-Ponty, *The Primacy of Perception* (Evanston, Ill., Northwestern University Press, 1964), pp. 3–158; in Arthur Koestler's *The Act of Creation* and *The Ghost in the Machine.*
5. Maurice Merleau-Ponty, "The Child's Relation to Others," in *Primacy of Perception,* pp. 107–18, esp. pp. 107–8; *Structure of Behavior,* pp. 160–84.
6. Marc Bloch and Lucien Febvre, "De la logigue à l'ethique en histoire," cited in Paul Ricoeur, *History and Truth* (Evanston, Ill., Northwestern University Press, 1965), p. 30.
7. By "unity" I mean that "the properties of the object and the intention of the subject form a new whole." Cf. Merleau-Ponty, *Structure of Behavior,* pp. 12–19; 40 ff.
8. Claude Lévi-Strauss, *Tristes Tropiques* (New York, Atheneum Publishers, p. 61); cf. *La Pensée sauvage,* pp. 32–33.
9. Maurice Merleau-Ponty, *La Phénoménologie de la perception* (Paris, Gallimard, 1945), p. 77.
10. "We choose our world and the world chooses us." Maurice Merleau-Ponty, *The Phenomenology of Perception* (London, Routledge and Kegan Paul, 1962), p. 454.
11. Merleau-Ponty, *Structure of Behavior,* p. 127.
12. Raymond Aron, "Note sur la structure en sciences politiques," cited in Jean Viet, *Les Méthodes structuralistes dans les sciences sociales,* Paris, Éditions Mouton, 1967, p. 195.
13. N. Troubetzkoy, *La phonologie actuelle,* cited in Claude Lévi-Strauss, *Structural Anthropology* (Garden City, N.Y., Doubleday Anchor Books, 1967), p. 31. See B. L. Whorf's analysis of structures in the logic of English showing exactly what phonemic combinations could *not* occur: "Linguistics as an Exact Science," in *Language, Thought, and Reality* (Cambridge, Mass., The M.I.T. Press, 1956), p. 223.
14. Bruce Parain, *Recherches sur la nature et les fonctions du langage* (Paris, Nouvelle Revue Française, 1942), p. 36.
15. *Cf.* Merleau-Ponty, *Phenomenology of Perception,* p. 392; Ricoeur, *History and Truth,* p. 202.

16. For Tocqueville: *Democracy in America* (New York, Vintage Books, 1954), Vol. I, p. x; for Nietzsche: William Arrowsmith, "Nietzsche on the Classics and the Classicists," ARION II 4, p. 9; for Lévi-Strauss: *Structural Anthropology*, p. 22. That Weber fits into this group is borne out in his essay "Objectivity in Social Science and Social Policy," in *The Methodology of the Social Sciences* (Glencoe, Ill., The Free Press, 1949), esp. pp. 55, 96.

17. Merleau-Ponty, *La Phénoménologie de la perception*, p. 78. See also Paul Ricoeur, *Husserl: An Analysis of His Phenomenlogy* (Evanston, Ill., Northwestern University Press, 1967), p. 4; Merleau-Ponty, *Structure of Behavior*, p. 125; S. Strasser, *Phénoménologie et sciences de l'homme* (Louvain, Publications Universitaires de Louvain, 1967), pp. 129–46.

18. It is noteworthy that most of those who do retain such an acceptance do not accept the notion of the decline of political theory; e.g., Leo Strauss and Eric Voegelin. Cf. D. Germino, "The Revival of Political Theory," *Journal of Politics*, August 1963, pp. 437–60.

19. Best summarized in F. Cancian, "Functional Analysis of Change," *American Sociological Review*, December 1960.

20. E. R. Leach, *Political Systems of Highland Burma* (Boston, Beacon Press, 1965), pp. 182–95.

21. Even those who display some consciousness of the problems, such as Karl W. Deutsch in *Nationalism and Social Communication*, in the end do not offer any explanation for the boundaries of a specific set of overlapping clumps of communication. Kohn's simpler notion that nationalism is an "idea" is more accurate if not more immediately useful. Cf. Viet, *Les Méthodes structuralistes*, pp. 195–196; Anne M. Cohler, *Rousseau and Nationalism* (New York, Basic Books, forthcoming).

22. Lévi-Strauss, *Tristes Tropiques*, pp. 384–85.

23. E. Husserl, "Philosophy as a Rigorous Science," in *Phenomenology and the Crisis of Philosophy* (New York, Harper Torchbooks, 1965), pp. 106–7; cf. E. Husserl, *Ideas* (New York, Collier Books, 1962), pp. 191–93.

24. As does Judith Shklar in *After Utopia: The Decline of Political Faith* (Princeton, N.J., Princeton University Press, 1969) and *Facing up to Pluralism* (APSA mimeo, 1966).

25. Cf. Paul Ricoeur, "Work and the Word," in *History and Truth*, pp. 197–219 and esp. p. 216 ff.

26. Norman Jacobson, "Political Science and Political Education," *American Political Science Review*, September 1963, p. 563.

27. Parain, *Recherches,* pp. 21–36. The analysis of T. Kuhn in *The Structure of Scientific Revolutions,* which other authors in this book have dealt with, is highly relevant here.

28. Nietzsche in *Werke in drei Bänden,* ed. Karl Schlechta (Munich, Carl Hanser, Verlag, 1955), Vol. III, p. 862. There are similar considerations in Albert Einstein, "Reply to Criticism" in *Albert Einstein: Philosopher-Scientist,* ed. P. A. Schlipp (New York, Harper & Row, 1949) Vol. II, pp. 673–81, esp. p. 674.

29. Nietzsche, *On the Genealogy of Morals,* Essay I, #13.

30. Nietzsche, "The Four Great Errors," in *Twilight of the Idols,* #6.

31. Whorf, "Linguistics as an Exact Science," p. 243.

32. On this whole point see *ibid., passim;* E. Sapir, *Language: An Introduction to the Study of Speech* (New York, Harvest Books, 1955), pp. 99–100; for a sympathetic though telling criticism of Whorf's subsequent oversimplifications see Lévi-Strauss, *Structural Anthropology,* pp. 66–95; *cf.* also L. von Bertalanfy, *General System Theory* (New York, George Braziller, 1968), pp. 222–32.

33. Whorf, "Linguistics as an Exact Science," p. 244.

34. Friedrich Nietzsche, *Human, All-too-Human,* Vol. I, #11; *ibid.,* Vol. II, #11; *Richard Wagner in Bayreuth,* #5. Cf. Lévi-Strauss, *Structural Anthropology,* p. 56.

35. Ludwig Wittgenstein, *Philosophical Investigations,* 2nd ed. (New York, The Macmillan Company, 1953), #119.

36. *Ibid.,* p. 560.

37. Thucydides, *The Peloponnesian War,* iii, #81.

38. George Orwell, "Politics and the English Language," *A Collection of Essays* (Garden City, N.Y., Doubleday Anchor Books, 1954), p. 177.

39. This is well exemplified in the last pages of the *Protagoras.*

40. H. A. Kissinger, "Reflections on Bismarck: The White Revolutionary," *Daedalus,* Summer 1968. De Gaulle was a partial exception.

41. Lévi-Strauss, *Tristes Tropiques,* p. 61; L. Althusser, *Pour Marx* (Paris, François Maspero, 1966).

42. This is best argued in Max Weber, "Objectivity in Social Science . . . ," p. 84.

43. No one has made this point better recently than Mancur Olson, Jr., *The Logic of Collective Action* (Cambridge, Mass., Harvard University Press, 1965).

44. E.g. Kenneth Keniston, *The Uncommitted* (New York, Delta Books, 1967); Edgar Z. Friedenberg, *Coming of Age in America* (New York, Random House, 1965).

45. E.g. Herman Kahn and A. J. Wiener, *Towards the Year 2000* (New York, The Macmillan Company, 1967).

46. For a preliminary yet suggestive examination of incentives see Peter B. Clark and James Q. Wilson, "Incentive Systems: A Theory of Organization," *Administrative Science Quarterly*, Vol. VI (September 1961), pp. 129–66.

47. On this point see K. Benne, "The Uses of Fraternity," *Daedalus*, Summer 1964.

48. In conversation with the author during a session of the Defense Policy Seminar, Harvard, November 1968.

49. In *One Dimensional Man* Marcuse concludes that the negative destructive side of the historical dialectic has been subverted by modern society and thus no longer operates. In "Repressive Tolerance," his contribution to *A Critique of Pure Tolerance*, he argues for "withdrawing" tolerance from the right and center in order to get the dialectic moving again.

50. Norman O. Brown, "A Reply to Herbert Marcuse," in Marcuse, *Negations* (Boston, Beacon Press, 1968), pp. 246–47. Brown's notion frightens me, since I do not believe that things are as benevolent as he does. More investigation, though, is needed.

51. One could very easily establish a remarkably parallel set of categories between Erikson and Hegel in *The Phenomenology of Mind*.

52. Søren Kierkegaard, *Journals*, ed. Alexander Dru (New York, Harper Torchbooks, 1959), p. 97; cf. Nietzsche, *Human, All . . .*, Vol. I, #472.

53. Claude Lévi-Strauss, *The Scope of Anthropology*, Cape Editions, p. 49.

54. Michel Foucault, *Les Mots et les choses* (Paris, Nouvelle Revue Française, 1966), pp. 380–81.

55. G. W. F. Hegel, *The Phenomenology of Mind* (New York, Humanities Press, 1964), pp. 130, 267, 789–808.

56. Daniel Bell, *The End of Ideology;* Raymond Aron, *The Opium of the Intellectuals.* Aron's second thoughts are in "L'idéologie, support nécessaire de l'action," *Res Publica* 2 (3) 1960, pp. 276–86.

57. China and to a lesser degree Cuba are societies engaged in a conscious epistemological revolution. We should look below the surface nonsense of the "creative application of the thought of Mao Tse-tung" to understand the Great Proletarian Cultural Revolution as an epistemological revolution designed to induce in the Chinese people the attitude that nature can be mastered through

abstract thought, rather than (as in the Confucian mode) bent before like a reed. Franz Schurmann has well described the concurrent organizational revolution. We must investigate this structurally to understand the relation of the epistemological revolution and the organizational one. Preliminary reflection indicates they might work at cross-purposes. Can there be a "non-Weberian" bureaucracy in an advanced industrial state? What does "the administration of things" look like? No one knows. Few people appear to care.

58. I have gone into this whole matter more extensively in my "Friedrich Nietzsche: The Transfiguration of Politics," unpublished Ph.D. thesis, Harvard University, 1968.

59. *The Will to Power,* a book through which most people know Nietzsche, was not a book he ever wrote. It was put together by his executors. Much more typical is *The Genealogy of Morals* or *Beyond Good and Evil,* which are series of distinct though related paragraphs, not strings of aphorisms.

60. *Cf.* Merleau-Ponty, *Phenomenology of Perception,* p. 422; Foucault, *Les Mots et les choses,* pp. 396–97.

61. Lévi-Strauss, *Structural Anthropology,* p. 197.

62. Ludwig Wittgenstein, *Remarks on the Foundations of Mathematics* (Cambridge, Mass., The M.I.T. Press, 1967), p. 57.

63. Koestler has investigated this in his both overly simple and complex *The Ghost in the Machine* (New York, The Macmillan Company, 1967).

64. A few ideas of such limits are in Parain, *Recherches,* p. 178.

65. Piaget in *Le Structuralisme* (Paris, Presses Universitaires de France, 1968), p. 112, calls for this also; Foucault attempts it (*une archéologie des sciences humaines*) in *Les Mots et les choses.*

66. Friedrich Nietzsche, *Die Entschuld des Werdens,* ed. Baeumler (Stuttgart, Alfred Kroner Verlag, 1951), Vol. II, pp. 53–54, 476.

Political Arts and Political Sciences

WILSON CAREY McWILLIAMS

But if they are not sick, friend Polemarchus, the physician is useless
to them.

—*Republic*, I, 332e

MEN RARELY consult physicians except when they are ill,
and the case must be desperate indeed when the polity seeks
a remedy from political science. Politics is an art, and political science bears the same relation to it that the science of
nutrition does to cookery. We can imagine a nutritionist
who has mastered the art, and this, surely, would be a high
excellence. We are, however, forced to admit that there is no
necessary connection between the two and that the science
may even be an impediment to the art. From many a suspect
kitchen issue meals of more savor than emerge from the bur-
nished aluminum fortresses that are the citadels of the science. So it is with politics and political science.

Philip Green writes of journalistic reports of New York's
decentralization dispute that they "direct our attention to
happenstance, to the accident of who said what to whom at
the wrong time, who was a weak rather than a strong
leader." Personality, speech, chance: these, to anyone who
has read Thucydides—to say nothing of less intellectual experiences—are a fair description of what happens in politics
as perceived by the men who engage in it.

Those who involve themselves in the world of politics
must accept the fact that they are part of a world of com-

plexly related things, of imponderables and unpredictables in which information mixes darkly with gossip and old wives' tales. Political art demands a rash courage heated by the warm fires of compassion and desire to stand well among one's fellows. Science, political science especially, demands a colder bravery. It requires alienation, the belief that reality as most men perceive it is illusion only, in crucial respects; it demands the cruelly playful daring that dissolves verities and dissects phenomena, slicing off excrescent accidents to lay bare what is essential. Science is dangerous in politics at best, and so long as it is true to itself, men will ask it for counsel only when all other remedies have failed and even drastic risk seems indicated. Under other conditions, political scientists will seem whimsical fellows at best, dangerous madmen at worst, to those who live in the "real world."

Thought is the child of pain, not of euphoria. Political science was probably born when sons, standing with dripping hands above the slain father, realized that patriarchal authority creates dilemmas, not omniscience, or—more gently—when men found that the ways of custom differed between tribes, and some, seeing the many ways of life possible to man, wondered which was the best way to the best life. For societies at large, political thought becomes searching only when men suspect that the village wall will not hold back the terrors that all know wait outside it.

Not for nothing did Plato engage in empirical analysis when he spoke of political decay. When cookery produces ptomaine, even the antisepsis of nutritional science may seem preferable. When the political arts fail, and men find threatening powers—visible or invisible—inside the wall, it may seem less foolish to ask philosophers to be kings. We may demand, in fact, that they assume the throne.

The contemporary academy finds itself in much that position. Not long ago, colleges knew the blithe irresponsibility of educational impotence. Students came to us with characters already formed, with passions long since directed toward goals. What and how they were taught mattered little. Social science was "value-free" in the only possible sense: it was value-irrelevant.

All that is in the past. The great institutions which once shaped the identities of men—family, church, community, polity—are no longer havens. They have become *problems* for an increasing number of Americans, irrelevant at best, threatening at worst. Rousseau's anguish speaks for our time: ". . . there is neither country nor patriot. The very words should be struck from our language." [1] Students now come seeking, not bringing, selves.

Knowing our own inadequacies—to say nothing of those of our colleagues—our own confusions and puzzlements, we might prefer to avoid our new responsibility. But relevance is a fact, not a choice; abstinence is action when Macedonia cries. And despite maunderings of so many academics, the demand for "relevance," made with literal forcefulness, is hardly unique:

> Polemarchus said, Socrates, you appear . . . to be about to leave us.
> Not a bad guess, I said.
> Don't you see how many we are? he said.
> Surely.
> You must either prove yourselves the better men or stay here.
> Why, isn't there, I said, the alternative of persuading you that you ought to let us go?
> But could you persuade us, said he, if we refused to listen? [2]

Under such conditions, the only alternative is to prove oneself the better man *by* staying; as for Socrates, so for political science.

But, of course, political science is *not* Socrates; most of our professional compeers would be lucky to attain the eminence of Prodicus of Ceos. No one who has read the essays in this book could possibly come to any other conclusion. And the problem that poses is a simple one: the opportunity of science is a country's danger. When custom and the arts fail, men cast about for guides; but how are they to tell true guides from false, charlatan from scientist, sophist from statesman?

The shoe pinches and men feel pain; as Lewis Lipsitz makes clear, however, those who feel the pinch do not always —or even often—know its cause or its remedy. In political affairs, diagnoses are various: reactionaries insist that the problem is the foot and not the shoe; a school of "revolutionaries" traces the pain to the unnatural habit of wearing shoes at all. Should Americans, disquieted even when they know affluence, be wise enough to reject those diagnoses, they will still have to select a cobbler. And that task is far from easy.

Guidance is necessary, and for the best of reasons. Without it, students and citizens alike will opt for the diagnosis and the prescription which demand the least, which harmonize most easily with accepted belief. As William James wrote, when old ideas seem inadequate we look for new ones which we "can graft upon the ancient stock with a minimum disturbance." [3] That some men are moved to shatter old systems of belief and to create others does not disprove the rule: it only demonstrates that the meaning of the rule is personal, depending on what "can" means in the psyche of the individual. Great departures in thought are the result of greatness in *men,* not greatness in crisis. Indeed, the worse the trouble, the *easier* for most men; the blacker the fear, the more the inner eye is blinded by desperation, the more likely that crude sleight of hand can pass for miracle.

Tracy Strong speaks, rightly, of the power of new language and new world-views among men who know the inadequacy of the old, instancing the adoption of Rousseau by the revolutionaries in France. Yet Strong is also aware that the Jacobins invented their own Rousseau, giving their own meaning to his grammar, reducing subtleties and stern demands to simplicities and easy answers.

> *Success* has always been the greatest liar—and the "work" itself is a success; the great statesman, the conqueror, the discoverer are disguised in their creations until they are unrecognizable; the "work" of the artist, of the philosopher, only invents him who has created it, is *reputed* to have created it; the "great men," as they are reverenced, are poor little fictions composed afterwards, in the world of historical values, spurious coinage *prevails*.[4]

When a society can be described as radically diseased, when its citizens can be regarded as dehumanized or debased, it can hardly be expected to understand spontaneously—even to recognize—a physician of the soul.

The task of political science becomes more difficult as it becomes more vital. Even if it performed to perfection as a science, if it mastered the analysis of political things, it would be necessary for political science to learn the art of politics, the means by which men are taught and improved, by which political ideas can be translated into the lives of men.

Of course, as this book makes clear, political science fails on all these counts. In a certain sense, failure is inevitable. Science is, in an important sense, a polity, and the political order of political science is wildly diverse, disorganized, lacking "discipline"—a distinctive way of life. This has disturbed many political scientists; oddly enough, it has most offended those who in civic affairs were the strongest advocates of a political order identical with that of political science. For the profession of political science may be the *only* political order that corresponds in fact to "group theory." Here, if ever, men should be able to recognize their interest, at least in a narrow sense; groups and subgroups proliferate;

almost all of us have overlapping memberships that tie us to schools and professional friends other than our immediate colleagues. And all that holds the discipline together is an agreement—one which may be threatened in the future—about the rules of the game, the amenities and procedures of struggle.

What is defect for a polity may be virtue for a science. As several of the essays in this volume make clear, the messiness of political science is due to its adoption—however unwilling—of metaphysical diversity, its avoidance of "theoretic dogma." If this deprives political science of the monolithic security and drive of the natural sciences, it provides us with a structure more receptive to "discontinuous change," the breakthrough of mind that is a scientific revolution. And few of us would want to change it; even in a book devoted to an attack on established political science, there are few suggestions for changing the "liberal" structure of *our* polity, which admits men to citizenship on formal criteria alone.

This only emphasizes the need for an examination of the soul of political science, which means the spirit of political scientists themselves. There is no guarantee that our colleagues can diagnose and prescribe for the times, no assurance even that their remedies might not compound evils or create new ones. What else can be concluded from the fascination with process and unconcern with substance that give currency to a term like "charisma"? Since that miasmatic abstraction manages to enfold in one category both Jesus Christ and Adolf Hitler, its uses in analysis are suspect; since it manages to convey the notion that both represent the same "type" (kind, genre; read, *quality*) of authority, its moral impact is more dubious still. And if our colleagues are suspect, it is the least of our obligations to look closely at ourselves. If for no grander purpose, there is a need for some who will check and balance the worst tendencies of others; perhaps the former may help some others, and possibly many; at least, they will benefit themselves.

This is a universal law: a living thing can only be healthy, strong and productive within a limited horizon. . . .

"Arthur F. Bentley," John Schaar once told a class in American theory at Berkeley, "was simply a muddlehead." That might serve as a summary of our case against the dominant tendencies in political science: that they reflect muddleheadedness and little more.

It was understandable when political scientists reacted to the rediscovery of the unconscious and to the brutality of modern war and the threat of totalitarian politics by developing a deep suspicion of "the people." That pessimism, however, was immediately balanced by a wildly sanguine estimate of the ease of remedy. The same people who, in one sense, could be described as ill-informed, anomic, or irrational were presumed able to identify their problems, to choose organizations—if not to invent them—which could deal with those problems, and to select leaders who would adequately represent them. As Michael Rogin demonstrates with admirable clarity, this is nonsense; "functional" rationality depends always on a minimum of "substantive" rationality, and even within the suspect definitions of political science, that substantive reason is possessed only by a small minority of active citizens (distinguished by criteria—income, education, and the like—traditionally defined as the characteristics of an elite). One is reminded of Keynes's description of Lord Russell:

Bertie in particular sustained simultaneously a pair of opinions ludicrously incompatible. He held that in fact human affairs were carried on after a most irrational fashion, but that the remedy was quite simple and easy since all we had to do was to carry them on rationally. A discussion of practical affairs on these lines was really very boring.[5]

At best, the pluralist case was based on evidence that admitted of other interpretations. If sudden increases of participation during crises were associated with the totalitarian rise to power, might that not indicate the desirability of a more general participation *before* crisis forcibly thrust men into a political world of which they knew little, and to which they brought little save desperation? That view only gains prescriptive force from the fact that American pluralists, liberal democrats to the man, never suggested that the doors to participation should be *closed*. Most, in fact, sought to expand legal rights to participate, contenting themselves with the paradoxical argument that it would be better if these rights were not used. It was a muddled argument, even if we are happy with the illogic of those who made it.

Moreover, it is evident that Weimar was destroyed, *not* by participation, but by its inability to solve problems.[6] All the great political disasters serve to suggest that men who feel ignored, deprived, and environed by terrors arc likely to act badly. On its face, the pluralist argument seems to suggest that we should ignore such men, and greater neglect is not really likely to do more than increase the danger. Actually, the premise of the case is simply that the "group process" will progressively solve the problems of men, a gentle hope which is now in shards. Men have proved to feel themselves victimized on a basis far more complex and ubiquitous than pluralism allowed itself to believe. (For example, how many studies of "competence and affect" were designed to measure, not whether men felt *any* competence and affect toward the state, but how much they felt *relative* to other areas of life?)

If modern Americans—not to say modern man—have revealed unexpected problems, anguish, and resentment that political science almost alone seems not to have noticed, the reason for the blindness of our profession may be its curious epistemology. In the name of empiricism and the "data of experience," political science has created a structure of abstractions that block it from confronting experience. As Rogin points out, we do not "experience" a group *empiri-*

cally; nor, for that matter, do our senses show us a "process of socialization," being more likely to reveal parents trying to educate their children, and schools contributing to—or detracting from—the task. And the most towering illogic is required to transform a reprocessing of the data on punch cards into "empirical" research.

In this, as in so many things, political science is guilty of muddling categories, of dealing in vacuous "syntheses" that would daunt the vaguest of Hegelians. Perhaps the worst is David Truman's failure to preserve the distinction which he draws early in *The Governmental Process* between a "group" and an "association," a failure which has been typical of political science as a whole. Karl Mannheim warned us that groups large enough to be effective had become too large to be meaningful to the individual; Mannheim was aware that man's *senses*—and hence, in very large degree, his emotions—are limited and parochial.[7] Even when repression leads to projection or sublimation, one always reads the fatal signs of the limited physical self. ("The universe," D. H. Lawrence wrote of Whitman, "adds up to one. Which is Walt." [8])

The end of the nation-state has been repeatedly proclaimed by our fellows; others have felt it to be some sort of enduring monad of political life. Those who have proclaimed its demise have generally seen new, transnational forces uniting men over the bypassed boundaries of the old state. De Tocqueville, by contrast, guessed that the roots of loyalty would wear thin: "When the public sphere expands, the private sphere contracts." [9] *Function* may lead men to larger units; *substance* makes them cling to smaller ones, or to retreat into units smaller still. The smaller the sphere, the more important the man; the dyad, as Simmel knew, is the only relationship in which each member is *essential*.[10] And if we speak repeatedly of stability, we should understand that a part of its price is always individual feelings of importance. It is strange that political science has not noticed that the most latitudinarian of "significance tests" implies that it is the citizen who believes his behavior to be important who is irrational, not his anomic fellow who believes that he does not matter.

Alan Wolfe writes intelligently of his experience with community, and his argument that community cannot *be* the purpose *of* community and that community requires purpose is certainly correct, repeating the most sophisticated reflections of nineteenth-century American utopians.[11] Community demands purpose because in any case where men are vital to men they will get on one another's nerves and will need forgiveness from annoyance and conflict—and it is purpose which helps to provide the basis for forgiving.

As Wolfe argues, community does not exclude differences because it *cannot.* Sensually, empirically, physically, each man is a stranger to every other; feelings are always unique. What deludes us, sometimes, is that we can share an *idea* about feelings, a metaphoric judgment that your feelings are like, though quite distinct from, mine. It is the fact of physical uniqueness, however, that refutes Wolfe's generous desire to make the concept of community applicable to large institutions and free from the constraint of space. Rationally, it might be possible, but any community I might feel with a hundred million would be thin indeed; Hawthorne remarked that "a twenty-millionth of a sovereign" has only limited feelings of obligation and of unity with the whole.[12] Physicality draws around us the narrow circle of the senses; distant friends may be most important in my mind, but those I meet every day control the immediate rewards and deprivations of the body. And surely, to be aware of me *personally* requires more than an abstract knowledge of my existence. Wolfe knows that well enough, writing that "Confrontation is an essential of community."

We have all had the experience of meeting a friend after a lapse of years and have known the uneasiness that hangs over such a reunion. Men conquer the effects of space by holding

past communion in memory, but memory fails and each succeeding moment is a threat to it. When we meet again, we
must make a psychological leap from the past to the present,
with no guarantee of what we will find. The mind is not
bankrupt; old friends may pick up the threads when they
meet again, but only if they know the gentle forbearance
which separation in space makes necessary. Every summer,
the young learn the principle; vernal love which pledges a
fidelity stronger than time and space dies regularly with the
frost. Time and space are the conditions of fleshliness, the
first facts of life; those who do not or cannot understand this
can never comprehend political things.

Political science has scarcely been aware of the problem of
political space, of the limitations—or the possibilities—that
space imposes on political life. Madison and Hamilton, it
would appear, solved the problem for us in preferring the
great state which can offer men security, internal peace, and
material prosperity. The solution, however, *is* a choice of
values, a choice between values. The large state can give
men only a rough approximation of justice and a dignity
which is collective only. Justice in its highest forms requires
the small state (though the small state does not guarantee
it), in which the definition of what is due another can be
based on more than abstract knowledge of who the other *is,*
and in which men feel the smallest tension between the public's good and their own.

The decision to discard—or to attempt—that possibility
of high justice is not an easy one. If there is doubt, try
discussing "one-dimensionality" or estrangement with a
mother whose child has been saved from a once fatal disease
or with a farmer whose crops have flourished in what would
anciently have been a year of dearth. Yet the modern state is
fraudulent in important ways. As Schaar contends, the security and prosperity it so unevenly dispenses with one hand,
it threatens or destroys quite universally with the other.
Under those conditions it is no surprise if some Americans,

especially those who have known little of the favor and much of the exaction of the state, turn to the hope of justice and the smaller community even at the risk or the cost of disorder and violence. As Green implies, the surprise may be that they waited so long.

Political science, however, *has* been surprised. Despite our concern for predictive power, the professional journals of the past decade contain scarcely a hint of the storm which has become routine in the news of the day. The fact that the discipline has been taken unaware reflects its inability or unwillingness to recognize the ambiguity of the modern state, or of the large state as such. For even when the goods that the state provided seemed less offset by its perils, men lived uneasily, always marginally aware of something lost or missing in their lives.

The faults of political science in treating of political space are, as this implies, bound up with its defects in relation to political time. It has lacked a sense of the unity of modern history, and even those who speak of political dynamics— like the theorists of "political development"—have busily tried, gossiplike, to stigmatize as illegitimate the natural children of modernity. The premise of so much of their argument is that history *cannot* be producing things of which we disapprove, and hence, that things of which we disapprove must be at odds with the course of development. (Obviously, this also works in reverse: we cannot appropriately disapprove what is destined by history but must adjust or adapt to it.)

Few political scientists have honestly acknowledged that totalitarianism is a modern phenomenon, a "novel form of government," in Arendt's phrase, perhaps *the* distinctively "modern" form of regime, to which all others are as atavisms. In countless laboratories, thousands of cheerful innocents are perfecting the tools of control, removing their remaining defects. The old, almost ontological, restrictions which once put a limit to evil are being overcome. Leave aside the genetics labs; consider only the "decentralizing" tendency in modern industry that so delights many of our colleagues. In their joy, they overlook the fact that this tendency is made possible because new technologies of control make possible the imposition of *impersonal* controls from the center of decision making, eliminating in part one of the old weaknesses of gigantistic despotism: that the hand of the tyrant was limited by his span of personal control, which ran little further than his palace.

Kurt Vonnegut has recently done us—once again—the favor of speaking the truth.[13] Dresden is a sad memorial to the fact that the atomic bomb was not a qualitative change in the life of men; it was only part of a continuum. Just so, scientists who create life in test tubes and snuff it out when the experiment has been served are part of the same dimension as those who lit the furnaces of Dachau.

In the same sense, the "crisis of legitimacy" did not leap into being with Vietnam and ghetto riots. As Schaar indicates, it grew in partnership with the modern state and modern times. When most men—or those who mattered—rejected the authority of limits and made man's will and desire the sole standards of morality, they began that crisis, even though it may have become perceptible to political science only in our own times.

In 1838 Abraham Lincoln could already speak of a crisis of legitimacy in America. His language, more specific and certainly more eloquent, anticipated Weber's analysis and went more directly to the heart of things. The memory of old struggles and common combats against Britain, which had once given a sense of unity to America, was fading out, Lincoln argued. The human desire for glory, too, would not much longer suffer men to live in a state which was the creation of others and, however excellent, only reflected the glory of the creators. Hence, Lincoln concluded, America must accept the governance of iron, cold reason as the sole force that could sustain her.[14]

Examine the argument in detail. Tradition has already become the *memory of war;* men even then lived too distantly, too privately, to share a way of life. (America, Hawthorne wrote, is "too vast by far to be taken into one small human heart." [15]) Charisma is no longer a revelation of reality to men who have lived in darkness; it is merely the *glory of others.* Reason alone remains.

Yet reason sides only ambiguously with the modern state, as its rewards become less genuinely vital and beneficial to life. (*Apollo 11* is surely the most expensive circus in history, and *panem et circenses* was never, in any case, a good motto for republics.) And of course, the threats which multiply make reason hesitate; that thought has a "pale cast" is not the least of its virtues. "Force alone," de Jouvenel writes, "can establish Power, habit alone can maintain it in being, but to expand, it must have credit." [16] Reason, by itself, suspects the loan and considers foreclosure, constantly being tempted to reclaim the self from its contracts. (Why else did both Locke and Rousseau recognize that Hobbes's stern rationalism would make the state—for their different purposes—too weak?)

Reason falls short of providing legitimacy—at least, reason as modern men have understood it. Lincoln, its advocate, lived to fight the new war and to become the new hero that sustained the state beyond the point where reason faltered. And one can hardly ignore the fatal periodicity which has called up a war and a hero with virtually each new generation. For us, wars and heroes have become as threatening as they are beguiling, and even those who adore a Che Guevara have the moral prudence to select a warrior-hero who has been beaten. But to anyone who has read the record political time, present prudence is a moment's deliverance, not a guarantee for the future.

Limitless expansion of power, a pace of change that is ever accelerating: these have been the basic facts *and* values of modern history. Many—political scientists more than most

—advise us to keep pace with the times. To do so would be no more rational than keeping up with the Joneses, and very likely less so. History has only a slender claim to govern man at all, and the simplest maxim of our science is that government without limit, government which rejects limit on principle, is tyranny. When men have reached the point at which reason must fearfully counsel peace, whatever the price in justice—and so many, in different areas of life, are voicing that principle—they are in the environs of an ultimate tyranny. Then there is comfort when some men call for an "end to history," a limit to time.[17] Man, limited in time and space, is not suited to infinity in either.

> These, I conceive, you ought so far to surpass that they would not feel fit to be your opponents, but only to be your despised fellow-fighters against the enemy, if you mean really to make your mark with some noble act for that will be worthy both of yourself and of the city.
>
> —*Alcibiades* I, 119e

There is more than bad epistemology hidden in the doctrine of a radical separation between "fact" and "value." That precept presumes that the world (fact) is indifferent or hostile to value; it is based on the metaphysic which sets man at war with nature, which sets value in a contest with fact, with mastery as the prize.

Perhaps that is the reason political scientists have found it so difficult to speak of war as a human phenomenon: they see war as ubiquitous, pervasive in the condition of man and his relations with his fellows. War between man and man becomes only a subset of a more universal reality. The metaphors we use to describe politics—like "arena," with its image of political leaders as gladiators—reveal that we have reversed Clausewitz's dictum: for political science, politics is war conducted by other means.

That attitude is responsible for our failure as a science.
The essays in this book agree on one point if no other: political science lacks a critical standpoint, is bound up with the
parochialities of culture and history. If it fails to understand
political space and time, it is because it is trapped by them,
lacking the alienation which is associated with great science;
in fact, by defining alienation as a disease, social science
passes a verdict on itself.

Alienation is impossible when one looks at the world and
at men as enemies. We do not become alienated from our
foes; we become *like* them. The barbarians outside the gate,
as Cavafy knew, are really inside,[18] alienation is psychological distance, and the enemy is always close. In war, it is the
enemy who *rules:* "Nature," Bacon wrote, "to be com-
manded, must be obeyed."

There is no great service in the creed. Man is a part of
nature, and to make him an enemy to nature is to make him
a foe to himself. ("Humanity is in a condition of public war
of every man against every man and private war of each man
against himself." [19]) And given the logic of hostility, that is
to deliver him over to the part of himself he would master.

The desire for "objectivity" betrays a fear of what is
subjective, fleshly, and private in man; it is a defense against
what, in the attitude we are describing, is man's enemy in
himself—finitude, mortality, the things which—in an older
scheme—flesh is heir to. The adulation of those things, the
romanticism which makes a cult of spontaneity and desire, is
only an inversion of rationalism. The partisans of subjectivity engage in an ancient rite, eating the flesh and wearing
the skin of the feared thing in order to make themselves in
its image. War or propitiation share a trait: they are both
false. Man can escape what is private only in death, and can
limit himself to it only by the self-deception of madness.

For science, it is never a question of fact *versus* value, but
of fact allied with value, of fact *as* value. The problem of

science is that of winning men away from ignorance, opinion, and delusion: of enabling them to see truly. Despite the
mystique of "ought," our law does not say that a homicidal
maniac "ought" to respect human life or that a child
"ought" to be fully responsible. Someone might, indeed,
make those statements, but science need respect him no
more than another who argued that the world "ought" to be
flat.

Our grammar and our law realize that "ought" is an aux-
iliary of predication, a logical assertion that given x, y can be
expected ("ought to happen"). When Mill argued that the
visible was to the seen as the desirable was to the desired, he
was answered by the argument that the visible "is" what is
seen while the desirable "ought to be" desired. Nonsense, as
we *ought* to know; the visible *is not* seen by the blind or by
those who are not looking at it. It is what "ought to be" seen
by someone with eyes who does not avert his gaze. Im-
mensely more difficult, a science of value is—on principle—
no more impossible than a science of perception, and in
more than one sense they are the *same* science.

The problem of value is that man does avert his mental
eyes; and that, as Sanford Levinson suggests, is the reason
why so many of our "value" disputes are in fact disputes
about what the data really are. Born ignorant and weak,
man has one love in the beginning, himself, and one fear,
the rest of the world. His emotions, which draw around him
that circle whose center is always the self, *rule,* as they must;
the desires for physical comfort and security are the
guardians of survival, and life is needed before the good life
is possible. Those desires, however, are sometimes blind and
often blinding; the attacks on the theory of "instinct" in
psychology show, more than anything else, that whatever in-
stincts men have are hardly safe guides even to the simplest
objects.

That which exists independently of the self, especially

that which wills independently of the self, *threatens*—and threatens only more severely if it also benefits. Man's first "instinct" is a will to illusion, a desire that the danger should not be. The effort to master it derives from that will; so does the cunning effort to avert the danger by disguise, by becoming like it or as it would have us be. That last attempt is the desire for objectivity, the masking of subjectivity and the learning to fear it as a danger to the design of plotting man. Fear of others and the desire to overcome them lead, by the strange logic of the mind, to a fear of self; but the first premise remains.

The education which is *necessary* to human life is a product of force only, a response to the painful, unwilled lesson of weakness and incapacity. Anyone who has taught knows the *resistance* of students, a resistance which can be expressed in simple passivity—"I refuse to be involved with what *you* are doing"—or in the more active resistance which seeks to destroy one's mentors. (Aristotle, after all, can hardly speak of Plato without misconstruing him, and our insistence that a student do "original" research is merely an attempt to divert the threat to ourselves by *commanding* it.) Sophomores seize upon the doctrines of relativism and realism because they provide an intellectual defense ("that's only a value judgment"); and in the great anomic universities, applause at the end of a course—like applause in the theater—is meant to signal distance from the performer and to remind him that he is paid to act.

To be aware of these things is to set the problem of education; and *all* education is political education. It is to understand that rationalism is a false theory of man and of teaching, and to know that teaching is an *art* and—like all art—lives and designs within the boundaries set by its material. Political education, of which science is a "higher" form, is unnecessary education, education which will *not* happen of itself in human life and must result from design. And art—

especially the art of teaching—is relativistic in means because it is purposive in end. It proceeds deviously, by hints and suggestions, sometimes by white lies; it either masters rhetoric or it fails.

Political education is, in the most basic sense, a *seduction*. Men's emotions can be tempted as well as forced, drawn out of the fortress of the self. The emotions proceed by the rule of association, the dumb logic of empiricism. ("A cat who has sat on a hot stove lid will not sit on one again, and that is well," Mark Twain wrote, "but she will not sit on a cold one either." [20]) For millennia, men have been taught and have learned to associate the delights of eating with *sharing;* commensality is a powerful weapon of the community, transforming one of the most private of human feelings. So too, when men learn to associate security with "home," they may be taught that courage is the price of that security (just as, if they learn that the price is hypocrisy and cowardice, they may associate courage—by the old rule of negation—with what is "not home").

The world, left to itself, teaches man by what he perceives as a rape, by compulsion, and over protest (what else is a child's cry?). Education seeks to win willing assent, to induce another to give up—to desire to give up—emotional chastity, to delight in and identify with family, *patria,* and friends.

There is, after all, a part of man's psyche that would *know* the self—and must, consequently, know what *limits* it. Pick a favorite from the grab-bag of terms: "ego," "self-realization," "consciousness": the meaning is much the same. The critical political fact is that the ego cannot rule *alone*. It requires the assistance of emotion, and as Plato knew, if the passions can never be made complete allies, they can be trained to work in support of the mind.[21]

Education is, in this sense, the effort to give men a new birth, a more truly whole and knowing self. Mocking Socrates described his art as obstetric, thereby concealing that there is no delivery without conception and gestation, no new birth without impregnation. Not all impregnators are benign, of course, and our fear of "manipulation" tells of our knowledge of that fact. Yet manipulation simply means "touching," and he who cannot be touched emotionally is shut off in an isolation which ranks him lower than the beasts.

Words are the tools of higher education, and the early shaping of the emotions provides a fund of associations and symbols which are an essential part of language. Euben is perfectly right to say that it is false to argue that we can "operationally" define words at will. Words are common property, and the emotions hover around them. The attempt to free them of those associations is folly when it is not sophistry or propaganda.

Our colleagues have been right in their concern for precision in language. Precision, however, does not command that we invent a new language—or at least does not necessarily do so. The test of precision in language is *not* whether we have designed a form of speech which on its own terms excludes ambiguity or contradiction; that sort of formalism ought to have left political science years ago. Speech is not *intrinsic,* whatever else it may be. The test of precision in speech is that it accurately conveys meaning and understanding, or that it conveys them in the greatest possible degree, to those to whom it is addressed.

It is no objection against language that it is metaphoric: all communication *is* metaphor, the perception that the unique idea which is mine is akin to, like, that which is yours. Men *can* share ideas, but when an idea enters the mind of man it enters his fleshly self and becomes "his"; think only of the resentment we all feel at finding out that someone else has anticipated our discovery—even if he is a great man with whom we should feel proud to be allied.

Precision in communication is tested not by sounds or even by symbols but by the persons who see the symbols or hear the sounds. Who objects when a parent engages in the soft deceit of telling a child that the world is "round"?

In the same sense, it is no quarrel with language to say that it separates phenomena from qualities. Men can communicate only because they can make the separation. My love is not your love, and that is that, so far as phenomena are concerned; my hunger is not yours. We may, however, be able to speak about love and hunger and perhaps about selves.

There is a more vital reason for suspecting jargonistic efforts to remake our language. The older language was based on a presumption that the human fact was important; human virtue and vice, decision and conduct, had not vanished into "process" and "history"; man had been unable to conceal the fact that political process is made up of decisions. (That he can now conceal this suggests, as dramatists will know, that life has become comic and not tragic, and perhaps no more so than when men speak of a "tragic" quality in it.)

At the center of the older language of political science were terms which spoke personally, which spoke of relations which existed or might exist between men: *obligation, authority, justice, patriotism.* Not so much later, the terms changed into *liberty, equality, self-determination,* words which spoke of personal relations, to be sure, but which defined those relations on an entirely individualistic basis. The terms used to describe political units became correspondingly more abstract and formal: *authority* faded into *legitimacy, obligation* and *duty* into the more passive *loyalty, patria* into *state* or *nation.* So now, the language of political science has become so abstract as to be distinct in a radical way from the language men use, presuming that one cannot understand men on their own terms and—worse—that when they speak of communion it can only be understood by resolving it into a process, *communication,* that motives, similarly, must become *motivations,* and the like.

I am quite aware that this change reflects a change in the life of men. What is disturbing is that it also encourages that change, reinforces it by denying to those who learn that language that any other condition is possible. Consider the term "paradigm," so much used (principally in reference to Kuhn) in this book. It is not meant as a deprecation of Kuhn's work—which is superb—or of these essays, but the fact remains that the term misleads. The great scientific discoverers of the past did not believe that they were inventing paradigms, mere models of reality: they believed that they were discovering reality, or at least a part of it. To teach that they were in error on this crucial point is, first of all, to claim something that we do not really know. Second, it is to deprive our students—and ourselves—of any genuine communion with them. Will a student who sets out, with high ambition, to create a paradigm have the same passion that drove a man who sought to see truly? Is it not likely that he will settle for less, especially since the destruction of one's own ideas is a thing of pain? Men do not *tolerate* ambiguity if they are scientists; they *endure* it because they *must.* But the measure of the necessity is their passion for truth. "Paradigm," after all, is only a broader word for "hypothesis"; should science speak with the counsel of Bellarmine to Galileo?

The question of language is in part a question of our perception, in part one of teaching. And for the teaching which is the distinct role of political science in the political world of men, it is essential. Science rejects limit as politics cannot, and its ambition to know is boundless. What is madness among men is sanity among scientists; not for nothing did Plato call philosophy a divine madness.

Since the days when Socrates sat with Alcibiades, the great

role of political science has been the seduction of tyrants. The tyrant is shameless; he has no respect for custom and for propriety; he rejects the ordinary limits of political things. He is, in the modern phrase, a man without a superego; and since the superego is a product of the old institutions which are passing from power, he is—increasingly—ourselves and our students. And in political science, with its desire to attain mastery over men and things, there is more than a note of tyranny.

The difference between philosopher and scientist on the one hand, and tyrants on the other, does not lie in the basic structure of their personalities. It lies, first of all, in the fact that they have different *objects*, that they seek the love of different things. ("I am grieved for you, and for my love," said crafty Socrates to Alcibiades when he had persuaded that incautious young man to concede that he sought the admiration of Athenians.[22]) Tyrants are, in so many ways, alone that they seek the admiration of the very society whose beliefs they know to be folly in part, whose judgment they suspect is compounded of petty hopes and fears.

Tyrants desire intimacy without risk, and therefore it is necessary to teach them that they cannot risk being without intimacy: the scientist or the philosopher who would teach must be a powerful enemy, the sort of foe who may corrupt, in the sense of turning the student from his own path, but who cannot be corrupted, mastered, or swung from his own.[23] Not for nothing was Socrates savage with the Sophists; the young listener saw only too clearly the prospect of his own humiliation in what went before—and if the vicarious lesson did not suffice (as it does not with the extreme case of the tyrannical soul, because that soul denies likeness), that humiliation was something which the individual must be made to suffer himself. Teaching, in this sense, dare not be impersonal or objective: it must speak to the most intimate things in man, to the fear of ridicule that comes from our knowledge that in so many ways we are ridiculous. On that comment, there is surely no need of amplification for contemporary Americans.[24]

All this suggests that the scientist and philosopher is the supreme tyrant, and so, in a sense, he is. His passion is stronger, his madness of a higher order. The young men who ask Socrates to dispel the attraction of Gyges' ring are taught by a stimulation of their desire; from the desire to escape the limits of the law, they are encouraged to the brighter dream of giving law, of creating a city. (Just so, Alcibiades is encouraged to dream of worldwide, not merely Athenian, greatness.) There is more in this than seducer's cunning, though it is all of that. Those who have never imagined and thought through the best possible things, the ultimate human possibilities, the finest cities and glories, will hardly be able to know that politics is—even at best—inadequate among human things, and that human things are themselves not enough, not in part, but as a whole. The lesson of science and philosophy is the true extreme of the tyrant's passion, the highest form of the will to power: "man is something which must be surpassed." [25]

That is a dangerous lesson, but the same passion—though a lesser form of it—directed into the world of men, the inadequate world of men and politics, becomes the attempt to master that world, to defy the limits of political things. And from that, our own condition follows.

It is also a difficult lesson to teach, one which is impossible without the old words and rhetoric which appeal to the tyrannical passions: the best state, statecraft, obligation, authority, honor. Contemporary men need those perennial words more than their ancestors did. If modern lives tend to foster tyrant's hopes and sentiments, they create tools and weapons that make those hopes and feelings intolerable. And there is, perhaps, a possibility that many can be taught. The great powers of modern life reduce the tyrant's hopes to pettiness, to a small scale in which fear is never lost. So many men have the ring of Gyges, are become invisible, and suffer with the fact; for the kind of invisibility modern states offer is one achieved by shrinking man.

In any event, as Thoreau wrote, a man comes not to the world to do everything, but something. For political scientists, that something may be more morally compelling than for most, and not only because our subject matter enjoins it. Rather, it is because—as the reader of this book will learn more clearly than any other lesson—it is because our discipline attracts so many petty tyrants, little men of little dreams, who in their tawdriness discredit politics and science alike. Unworthy of being friends or enemies, they are hardly to be trusted with the task of training citizens, either for the polity or for the community of political science. But if we would take up the task, we must become worthy ourselves, the best possible friends and worst possible enemies to our students and to one another.

NOTES

1. Jean-Jacques Rousseau, *Émile*, trans. B. Foxley (New York, E. P. Dutton & Co., 1963), p. 8.
2. Plato, *Republic*, Book I, 327c.
3. William James, *Pragmatism* (New York and Cleveland, The World Publishing Company, 1968), p. 50.
4. Friedrich Nietzsche, *Beyond Good and Evil*, Sec. 269.
5. J. M. Keynes, *Essays and Sketches in Biography* (New York, Meridian Books, 1956), p. 255.
6. I am indebted to Kenneth Sherrill of Hunter College for reminding me of this among many greater debts.
7. Karl Mannheim, *Man and Society in an Age of Reconstruction* (New York, Harcourt, Brace & World, 1951), Pt. II; this is only one of many ideas I owe to this world.
8. D. H. Lawrence, *Studies in Classic American Literature* (New York, Doubleday, 1952), p. 178.
9. Alexis de Tocqueville, *Democracy in America*, Vol. II, Bk. iii, Ch. 13.

382 WILSON CAREY MCWILLIAMS

10. Kurt Wolff, trans., *The Sociology of Georg Simmel* (New York, The Free Press, 1950), pp. 118–44.
11. Compare Nathaniel Hawthorne's *Blithedale Romance* or J. H. Noyes, *A History of American Socialisms* (New York, Hillary House, 1961).
12. Hawthorne, *Works* (Boston, Houghton Mifflin Company, 1880): in *French and Italian Note Books,* Vol. II, p. 46.
13. Kurt Vonnegut, *Slaughterhouse-Five* (New York, Dell Publishing Co., 1969). Vonnegut may be the most consistently perceptive social commentator of the times.
14. R. P. Basler, ed., *Collected Works of Abraham Lincoln* (New Brunswick, N. J., Rutgers University Press, 1953), Vol. I, pp. 108–14. I apologize to Robert Eden of Harvard University for pre-empting a passage that is his by right. But he will understand, anyway.
15. "Chiefly About War Matters," *Atlantic,* Vol. XII (1863), p. 48.
16. Bertrand de Jouvenel, *On Power* (Boston, Beacon Press, 1962), p. 25.
17. Mario Savio, "An End to History," in Mitchell Cohen and Dennis Hale, eds., *The New Student Left* (Boston, Beacon Press, 1966), pp. 253–58.
18. I refer, of course, to his poem "Waiting for the Barbarians" in Auden's collection of his works.
19. Plato, *Laws,* Bk. I, 626d.
20. Mark Twain, *Following the Equator.*
21. See *Phaedrus, passim.*
22. *Alcibiades* I, 119c.
23. That is enough to suggest the importance of combating grantsmanship and government-sponsored research. At least, it is important to show that these do not influence us, but that will be difficult. And when under attack, the principle must always be that political science must have standards at least as high as Caesar expected of his wife.
24. The difficulty of striking home in the tyrannical soul is not so hard as it sounds, for the tyrant is never so unique as he believes. ("Yeah, into the evil!" cried the youth. "How is it possible that you have discovered my soul?" Zarathustra smiled and said, "Many a soul one will never discover unless one first invents it."—*Thus Spake Zarathustra,* Ch. 8; see also Plato, *Republic,* Bk. IX).
25. *Thus Spake Zarathustra,* Ch. 14.

Notes on Contributors

KENNETH M. DOLBEARE, Professor of Political Science and Chairman of the Department at the University of Washington, is the author of two text-readers, *Directions in American Political Thought* and *Power and Change in the United States* (both 1969), and of *Little Groups of Neighbors: The Selective Service System* (1968), with James W. Davis Jr., and is about to publish *American Politics: Public Policy, Conflict, and Change* (with Murray Edelman). Born in Mineola, New York, in 1930, he is a graduate of Haverford College in Pennsylvania (B.A. 1951) and Columbia University (Ph.D. 1965), and has taught at Hofstra University and the University of Wisconsin. In 1969, he received a Guggenheim Fellowship to study the redistribution of political power through citizen participation.

J. PETER EUBEN, Assistant Professor of Politics and a Fellow at Crown College, University of California, Santa Cruz, was born in Calicoon, New York, in 1939. He did his undergraduate work at Swarthmore in philosophy and political science, spent a term at Exeter College, Oxford, England, and a year as a Research Fellow at the London School of Economics (1966–1967), and received his Ph.D. from the University of California, Berkeley, in 1968.

PHILIP GREEN, Associate Professor of Political Science at Smith College, is the author of *Deadly Logic: The Theory of Nuclear Deterrence* (1966) and coeditor of *The Political Imagination in Literature* (1969), and has contributed articles to numerous magazines including *The New Republic, Commentary, Dissent,* and *World Politics*. Born in New York City in 1932, he attended Swarthmore (B.A. 1954), and Princeton University (Ph.D. 1965), where he was a Fellow of the Center for International Studies Fellow. He taught at Princeton and Haverford before coming to Smith.

SANFORD LEVINSON was born in Hendersonville, North Carolina, in 1941, attended Duke University (B.A. 1962) and Harvard University

(Ph.D. 1969), and was the recipient of a Woodrow Wilson Fellowship. He has contributed articles to *Dissent, Yale Law Journal, Harvard Review,* and *The New Republic.* Formerly Assistant Professor of Political Science at Ohio State University, he is now attending Stanford University Law School on a Russell Sage Fellowship.

LEWIS LIPSITZ, Associate Professor of Political Science at the University of North Carolina, was born in Brooklyn, New York, in 1938, and attended the University of Wisconsin (B.A. 1957) and Yale (Ph.D. 1964.) He has worked as a newspaper reporter, written a book of poetry, *Cold Water,* and edited *American Government: Policy Making: Behavior and Controversy* (1967), as well as contributing to numerous magazines, and received a National Endowment for the Arts Writer's Grant.

WILSON CAREY MCWILLIAMS is the author of *The Idea of Fraternity in American Politics* and a contributor to numerous publications, including the *New York Times, Commonweal,* and *The American Political Science Review.* He received his B.A. and Ph.D. from the University of California at Berkeley and is now Professor of Political Science at Livingston College, Rutgers University.

MICHAEL PARENTI, Assistant Professor of Political Science at the Institute of Government and Political Affairs, the University of Illinois, has written *The Anti-Communist Impulse* (1969) and *Power and the Powerless,* and has contributed articles to various magazines. Born in New York City in 1933, he received his B.A. at the City College of New York and his Ph.D. at Yale.

MICHAEL ROGIN, Assistant Professor of Political Science at the University of California, Berkeley, was born in Mt. Kisco, New York, in 1937, and graduated from Harvard College (B.A. 1958), receiving his Ph.D. from the University of Chicago. In 1962–1963 he was a Visiting Lecturer at Makerere College, Uganda, and in 1967–1968 he was a Visiting Fulbright Lecturer at the University of Sussex, England. A contributor to numerous magazines, he is the author of *The Intellectuals and McCarthy: The Radical Specter* (1967) and, with John L.

Shover, *Political Change in California: Elections and Social Movements, 1890–1966* (1970).

JOHN H. SCHAAR, Professor of Political Science at the University of California, Berkeley, was born in Pennsylvania in 1928 and received his B.A. and Ph.D. degrees at the University of California, Los Angeles. The recipient of a Guggenheim Fellowship, he formerly taught at UCLA and Mount Holyoke College and is the author of two books, *Loyalty in America* (1957) and *Escape from Authority* (1961).

TRACY B. STRONG, Professor of Political Science at the University of Pittsburgh, was born in China in 1943, and raised in the Far East and Europe. He attended Oberlin College (B.A. 1963) and Harvard (Ph.D. 1968), and is currently working on a book on Nietzsche.

MICHAEL WALZER, Professor of Political Science at Harvard, has written *Revolution of the Saints: A Study in the Origins of Radical Politics* (1965), and coedited (with Philip Green) *The Political Imagination in Literature* (1969). His essay will be incorporated in a book of his own, *The Obligation to Disobey,* to be published this year. Born in New York City in 1935, he graduated from Brandeis University (B.A. 1956), spent a year at Cambridge, England, on a Fulbright Scholarship (1956–1957), and received his Ph.D. from Harvard (1961), and has previously taught at Princeton. He has been on the editorial board of *Dissent* since 1960 and contributes to other professional journals.

ALAN WOLFE was born in Philadelphia in 1942, received his B.A. from Temple University and his Ph.D. from the University of Pennsylvania, and has been teaching at Old Westbury College of the State University of New York. He has contributed to several magazines including *Center Magazine, Urban Affairs Quarterly,* and *Antioch Review,* and has a forthcoming book entitled *Foundations of Political Science.*

Index

Abundance, 289–90
Acculturation, 174–5, 178, 179, 184
Activism, 334–5
Adams, Henry, 278, 325 n.
Afro-American, refusal of leaders and professional men to be identified as, 184–5
Agitprop, 24
Alcibiades, 378, 379, 380
Alienation, 12, 372
Almond, Gabriel, 8, 12; on emergence of new paradigm, 42, 49 n.
Ambiguity, 35
American Federation of Labor (AFL), 120–36; shifts in attitude toward politics, 121–6; opposition of leaders to unemployment insurance, wage and hour laws, and other social legislation, 124; alliance with Democratic Party, 124; resolution, favoring government ownership of railroads, 125; endorsement of Robert La Follette, 125–6; craft unions and urban machines, 126–35; alliance of craft unions with Tammany Hall, 127–9; opposition to La Follette by local craft unions, 128–9; leadership independence in, 131–135; interests of leadership met by nonpartisanship, 132–6; support of Vietnam war by labor leaders, 141 n.; see also Gompers, Samuel; Nonpartisanship of labor unions

American Political Science Association, 12, 112
Americanization, 179
Amish, the, 177
Apathy, 15–16, 143; see also Political participation
Apollo 11, 370
Arendt, Hannah, 11, 45, 288, 302, 368
Aristotle, 316
Aron, Raymond, 331, 348
Arrow, Kenneth, 288
Arrowsmith, William, 332
Assimilation, 173–7; melting pot and, 174; ideological paradigm of, 174; absence of, 174–5; and acculturation, 174–5, 178, 179, 184; cultural and social systems, 174–6; nativist, 178–9; and Americanization, 179; black identity and counterassimilation, 180–7; black militants on, 183–185; Alvin Poussaint on, 184; see also Ethnics
Associational life, 300–1
Austin, J. L., 18
Authority, 276–7, 333; and legitimate power, 287; nature of, 291–4; de facto aspects of, 292, 293, 294; de jure aspects of, 293, 294; and development of postmoral mentality, 302, 324 n.; and leadership, 309, 312–17; see also Legitimate authority
Authority, charismatic: Max Weber on, 308–9

"Autonomy of process," 302
Ayer, A. J., 330

Ball, Terrence, 52 *n.*
Battle of Algiers, The (film), 251, 268
Beard, Charles A., 74
Behavioral approach in political science, 8, 12–13, 17, 21–3, 38–9, 330–1; and "postbehavioral revolution," 85, 88–92
Behaviorists, empirical: *see* Empiricism
Bell, Daniel, 348; on alienation, 12
Bentley, Arthur F., 113, 137 *n.*, 363; on public-interest "spooks," 114
Berelson, Bernard, 5, 6, 16–17, 20
Bismarck, Otto von, 341
Black community: mobilization of, 264–9; representativeness of leaders, 264–9
Black community control, 187, 190, 195–6, 221 *n.*
Black culture, 189–90; dismissal of reassertion of, by Black Panthers, 189
Black identity and counterassimilation, 180–7
Black militants: on assimilation, 183–5; and community control, 264, 270
Black Muslims, 185
Black nationalism, 182–3, 186; Michael Parenti on, 184
Black Panthers: emphasis on class consciousness, 188–9; dismissal of reassertion of black culture, 189
Black power, negative reaction to, 182
"Black racism," 185
Black radicalism, 187–92
Black "revolution" in cultural and personal identification, 185–7
Black separatism, 182; advocacy of community control of local schools, and black studies programs, 187
Boggs, James, 182
Brown, H. Rap, 189

Brown, Norman O., 345
Bryan, William Jennings, 122
Brzezinski, Zbigniew, 71
Bunche, Ralph, 187, 190
Bureaucracy, 304–8, 309, 310, 311; Max Weber on, 305, 326–7 *n.*
Burke, Edmund: on mass belief systems, 144–9
Burtt, E. A.: on metaphysics, 25–6; on paradigms, 41–2

Calhoun, John C.: States' Rights of, 254
Camus, Albert, 329
Carmichael, Stokely: on integration, 183–4
Caucus for a New Political Science, The, vii
Centers for Change, 196
China, epistemological revolution in, 355–6 *n.*
Chomsky, Noam, 329
Citizenship: Lewis Lipsitz on "democracy" and political silence, 143–4; Lewis Lipsitz on political grievances of the poor, 152–69; ethnic groups and, 177–9; Michael Walzer on rights of, 226–8; Philip Green on conflicting obligations of, 272
Civil disobedience, 223–4; and corporate authority, 223–46; nonviolence of, 224; justifiable cases of, 225; types of, 242–3; *see also* Corporate disobedience
Civility, 223–4
Class consciousness, emphasis of Black Panthers on, 188–9
Clausewitz, Karl von, 371
Cleaver, Eldridge, 188, 267
Cloward, Richard A., 182; on integration, 183
Coffin, William Sloane, Jr., 192
Communal living, 197
Communism, 10, 12; *see also* Nazism
Community: conditions of, 195–222, 366; concept of, 197–8, 204, 206–207, 214–18; Old Westbury Col-

Community: conditions of
(*continued*)
lege experiment, 198–221; power
and, 200–4; space and, 204–7;
diversity and, 207–10; confrontation and, 210–13; pluralism and,
210–13; political theory of, 213–
218; as alternative to mass society, 214–15
Community action program (CAP),
Daniel Moynihan's critique of,
105–9
Community control of schools, 187,
190, 195–6, 221 *n.*, 257–73; black
militants and, 264, 270; *see also*
Decentralization
Community experiments, 196–7
"Consensus and Ideology in American Politics" (McClosky), 165–6
Conservatism, 48 *n.*
Converse, Philip: on ideology, 150,
154, 166, 167; on mass beliefs,
150–1
Corporation, the: disobedience
against, 228–42; justifiable cases
of disobedience against, 228–31;
revolution against, 229–35; sit-
down or sit-in during revolution
against, 230; police action during
revolution against, 231–5; sit-
down strike against General
Motors, 235–42; *see also* Civil
disobedience
Craft unions: and local politics,
126–35; alliance of, with Tammany Hall, 127–9
Cru et la Cuit, Le (Lévi-Strauss),
334
Cuba, epistemological revolution in,
355–6 *n.*
Cultural systems *vs.* social systems,
174–5
Cyclical reconstructive theory, 341–
342, 349

Dahl, Robert, 7, 8, 10, 11, 33, 44,
47 *n.*, 318 *n.;* on democratic stability, 11; on political participation, 11, 15; on behavioral
approach in political science,

12–13, 17; on the "real world,"
18, 19; on objectivity, 29, 30
David, Henry: on nonpartisanship
of interest groups, 121
Decentralization of schools, 255,
256–73; and community control,
195, 221 *n.;* Philip Green on
dual school system, 270–1; *see
also* Community control of
schools; Ocean Hill-Brownsville
district
"Democracy," 249–50; and political
silence, 143; use of term, 288
Democratic stability, 11–12, 14
Demonology, 37–8
Deputy, The (Hochhuth), 3–4
Descartes, René, 298
Desegregation, Nathan Wright, Jr.,
on, 183
Discourses (Machiavelli), 340
Disobedience: *see* Civil disobedience; Corporation, the: disobedience against
Dolbeare, Kenneth M., viii, 69; on
policy analysis, 85–111; on Moynihan's critique of community
action program, 105–9
Donovan, John, 73
Drop City (community), 197
Due process, prejudicial defense of
in Ocean Hill-Brownsville, 259–
264
Durkheim, Émile, 343

Easton, David: on policy analysis,
91; on legitimacy, 319 *n.*
Edelman, Murray, 94
*Eighteenth Brumaire of Louis Bo-
naparte, The* (Marx), 145, 248,
334
Ellul, Jacques, 302; on battle of
production, 290
"Empirical world," 20–3, 78
Empiricism, 21, 364–5, 375; criti-
cism of, by Tracy Strong, 330–1
Engels, Friedrich, 144, 342
Eros and Civilization (Marcuse), 345
Esalen Institute, 197
Ethnics, 173–7; and absence of
wide-scale assimilation, 175–6;

Ethnics (*continued*)
  quasi-autonomous cultural enclaves of, 177; *see also* Assimilation
Euben, J. Peter, viii, 60, 77, 376;
  on political science and political
  silence, 3–58
Eulau, Heinz, 8, 25; on empirical
  discipline in political science,
  21; on objectivity, 24, 28, 29
European Revolution (Tocqueville),
  335

Fact-value linkage, 21, 24, 60, 61,
  70, 74, 371, 372–3
Federalism, 254–5
Feigl, Herbert, 30; on precision,
  32–3
Feyerabend, Paul, 24
Force, 287, 370
Ford Foundation, 195
Form, William, 166
Foucault, Michel, 347–8
France, Anatole, 247
Frazier, E. Franklin, 184–5
Freud, Sigmund, 10
Friedman, Milton, 275 *n*.
Functionalism, 332–3; problems of,
  333

Galbraith, John K.: on battle of
  production, 290
General Motors, sit-down strike
  against, 224, 235–42; background
  of, 236–8; nonviolence of, 240
Genovese, Eugene, 65, 73; on Lynd's
  writings on American history,
  72
Goldbloom, Maurice, 266–7, 270;
  on Ocean Hill-Brownsville governing board, 242–3, 256, 257
Goldman, Irving, 173
Gompers, Samuel, 120, 122, 124,
  125, 128; nonpartisan policies,
  120, 122, 123, 125, 128–9; opposition to unemployment insurance,
  wage and hour laws, and other
  social legislation, 124; *see also*
  American Federation of Labor

Governmental Process, The (Truman), 112–18, 135, 365
Green, Philip, viii; on decentralization, community control, and
  revolution, 247–75; on Martin
  Mayer's report of New York City
  teachers' strike, 248–9, 274 *n*.,
  357; on majority-rule principle,
  249–51, 265–6; on Ocean Hill-
  Brownsville district, 259–73,
  274 *n*.; on New York City school
  system, 263–4; on dual school
  system, 270–1; on pluralism, 272,
  275 *n*.
Green, T. H., 287, 298
Greer, Scott, 214
Grievances, 145, 147, 149, 150, 151;
  political, of the poor, 152–69;
  distinguished from issues, 167;
  see also Political grievances of
  the poor
Group interest, Robert Michels on,
  112–13; *see also* Interest groups
Group theory, of David Truman,
  112, 113–20; *see also* Organized
  groups
Guevara, Che, 370

Hamilton, Alexander, 367
Hamilton, Richard, 165
Hand, Learned, 5, 272
Hare, Nathan, 185
Hartz, Louis, 6
Hasidic Jews, 177
Hayden, Tom, 215–16
Hegel, Georg W., 295, 305, 347, 348
Historical theory, 339–40, 348
History of Western Philosophy
  (Russell), 23–4
Hobbes, Thomas, 10–11, 14, 252,
  254, 298, 329, 339, 340, 343, 370;
  and state of nature, 10, 13; on
  precision, 32, 34–6; on majority
  rule, 249; on natural anarchy,
  251
Hochhuth, Rolf, 3–4
Hofstadter, Richard, 74
Hog Farm (community), 197
Hume, David, 23, 322 *n*., 324 *n*.
Humphrey, Hubert, 83 *n*.

Hutterites, 177
Hylan, John F., 127

Idealism *vs.* realism, 4–6
Ideology: Daniel Lerner on, 24; Edmund Burke on, 146; Karl Marx on, 146–7, 148; Robert Lane on, 149–50; Lewis Lipsitz on, 166–9; of limitless assimilation, 182–3
Ideology, end of, 49 *n.*, 70–1, 348
Incrementalism, 48 *n.*
Industrial Workers of the World (IWW), 123
Integration, black militants on, 183–4; *see also* Assimilation
Interest groups, as "spooks," 113–114; *see also* Group interest; "Public interest"
Isaacs, Harold, 184

Jacobson, Norman, 4, 336
James, William, 360
Jefferson, Thomas, 6, 7, 251
Johnson, Lyndon B., 83 *n.*
Jones, LeRoi, 188
Jouvenal, Bernard de: on authority, 291, 370
Justice, 367

Kahn, Herman, 343, 344, 345
Kallen, Horace, 174
Kariel, Henry, 44
Keniston, Kenneth, 3
Keynes, J. M., 363
Kierkegaard, Søren, 347
King, Martin Luther, 182
Kissinger, Henry, 76, 341
Knights of Labor, 131
Koinona (community), 197
Kuhn, Thomas, 8, 22, 31, 39, 42, 73; on normal science, 21, 62; on paradigms, 21, 24–5, 39–42, 62, 63–4, 378; on textbooks, 62–3

La Follette, Robert M.: endorsement of, by AFL, 125–6; opposition to, by local craft unions, 128–9
Laing, R. D., 82–3 *n.*

Lane, Robert: on ideology of the common man, 149–50, 166, 167
Language, 33, 360; and theory, 335–339; effect of, on concepts, 336–338; political, 338; precision in, 376–8
Language, Truth, and Logic (Ayer), 330
Lasswell, Harold: on policy analysis, 91
"Law and order," 278; contemporary problem of, 294
Lawrence, D. H., 365
Leach, E. R., 333
Leadership, 309, 312–17, 333
Legitimacy: definitions of, contrasted, 282–5, 319 *n.;* John Schaar, on new professional definitions of, 284–6, 319 *n.*
Legitimacy in the modern state, 276–327, 369; crisis of, 279
Legitimate authority: Max Weber, on three grounds for claims to, 277; weakening of, 278, 279–82; *see also* Authority
Legitimate power, 286–9; and authority, 287
Lenin, Vladimir, 17
Lerner, Daniel, 30; on research, 24
Leviathan (Hobbes), 34–5, 339, 340
Levinson, Sanford, viii, 373; on teaching political science, 59–84
Lévi-Strauss, Claude, ix, 297, 331, 332, 334, 347, 351
Liberal-conservative dimension, absence of meaning for the poor, 152–4
Lincoln, Abraham: on crisis of legitimacy, 369, 370
Lindblom, Charles, 73, 320 *n.*
Linguistics, structural: Troubetzkoy on, 331–2
Lipset, Seymour, 6, 229; on legitimacy, 283, 286, 319 *n.*
Lipsitz, Lewis, viii, 360; on mass beliefs, 142–51; on political grievances of the poor, 152–69
Living Theatre, 197
Locke, John, 6, 343
Love's Body (Brown), 345

Lowell, A. Lawrence: on sit-downs, 241
Lowi, Theodore: on pluralism, 69
Lynd, Staughton, 65, 72
Lysenko case, 31

Machiavelli, Niccolò, 316, 340 ·
Macpherson, C. B., 340
Madison, James, 336, 367; federalism of, 254–5
Majority-rule principle, 249–51, 265–6; and "public good," 288
Mann, Thomas, 347
Mannheim, Karl, 365
Marcuse, Herbert, 209, 345
Marin, Peter M.: on full citizenship for adolescents, 274–5 n.
Markel, Julian, 65
Marshall, Thurgood, 190
Marx, Karl, 69, 248, 328, 334, 340, 341, 343; on mass belief systems, 144–9; on political silence, 148
Mass belief systems: Karl Marx vs. Edmund Burke on, 144–9; contemporary political-science ideas about, 149–51; see also Grievances; Prejudices
Mass politics, 143–4
Mass society, community as an alternative to, 214–15
Maximum Feasible Misunderstanding (Moynihan), 105
Mayer, Martin, 270; on teachers' strike in New York City, 248, 260, 274 n.
"McCarthyism," as used to characterize Ocean Hill-Brownsville governing board, 260–1
McClosky, Herbert, 165–6
McConnell, Grant, 323 n.
McWilliams, Wilson Carey, ix; on political arts and political sciences, 357–82
"Melting pot" and assimilation, 174
Merelman, Richard M.: on legitimacy, 283, 285
Merleau-Ponty, Maurice, ix, 331
Metaphor, 35–6
Metaphysics, 25–6

Michels, Robert: on organized groups and oligarchy, 112–13, 214; on conflicts of interest among leaders and members, 113; on public-interest "spook," 114
Middle-class values, 343–4; breakdown of, 343–4
Mills, C. Wright, 145, 210
Mobilization, of black community, 264–9
Modern Political Analysis (Dahl), 17, 29, 30
Montesquieu, Charles, 332, 335–6
Moore, Barrington, 72
Morality, 297–302
Mormons, 255
Morningstar (community), 197
Mots et les choses, Les (Foucault), 347–8
Moynihan, Daniel P.: critique of community action program (CAP), 105–9
Muhammad, Elijah, 185
Murphy, Frank, 241
Murray, Gilbert, 339
Muste, A. J., 181

Nativist assimilation, 178–9
Nature, state of, 10–11, 13, 35, 36
Nature of man: see Nature, state of
Nazism, 36, 37, 40, 41, 42, 45; and political science, 8–14, 22
Negroes, refusal to be identified as Afro-American, 184–5; see also Black
Nelson, Truman, 251
New Buffalo Commune, 197
New York City: decentralization of schools, 195–6, 255, 256–73; teachers' strike in, 248; Neimeyer report on guidelines for local school boards, 253; suspension, expulsion, and transfer of students in, 263–4; teachers vs. schoolchildren, parents, and community leaders, 263–4; see also Decentralization of schools; Ocean Hill-Brownsville district

New York Civil Liberties Union,
253; on suspension, expulsion,
and transfer of students, 263
"New York School Crisis, The"
(Goldbloom), 252–3
Newark Community Union Project,
196
Newton, Huey P., 188
Nietzsche, Friedrich, ix, 292, 296,
297, 328, 332, 336, 337, 347, 351;
on effect of language on concepts, 336, 337; Tracy Strong, on
writing style, 349–50
1984 (Orwell), 338
Nonpartisanship of labor unions,
120–36; as a cover-up for union
alliances with political machines, 129–30; interests of leadership met by, 132–6; *see also*
American Federation of Labor;
Gompers, Samuel
Nonviolence, 223–4, 240
"Normal science," 21, 62

Oakeshott, Michael, 19, 75, 78
Obedience, 279, 293, 324 *n.*
Objective standards of public policy consequences, 98–9
Objectivity: and political science,
24–31, 37, 38, 372; in the classroom, 59–60, 65, 66–7, 70
Ocean Hill-Brownsville district,
187, 196, 248–9, 259–73; Maurice
Goldbloom's criticism of governing board, 242–3, 256, 257;
Philip Green on, 259–64; and
prejudicial defense of due process, 259–64; actions of governing
board described as "McCarthyism," 260–1; *see also* Decentralization of schools
Old Westbury College experiment,
198–221; problems faced by,
200–13; power and community,
200–4; space and community,
204–7; diversity and community,
207–10; confrontation and community, 210–13; constituent colleges, 211–13

Oligarchy and organized groups,
265, 275 *n.;* Robert Michels on,
112–13
Ontogeny and phylogeny, 346–7
Organized groups, and oligarchy,
112–13; *see also* Group interest;
Group theory
Ortega, José, 304
Orwell, George, 339; on political
language, 338

Paine, Thomas, 336
Paradigms, 21, 22, 24–5, 39–45, 62,
71, 73, 378; assimilationist, 174
Parenti, Michael, viii, 134, 250–1,
254; on assimilation and coun-
terassimilation, 173–94; on analytic distinction between cultural
system and social system, 174–5
Participation, political, 11, 14–17,
363–4
Peters, R. S.: on authority, 292
Phonemics, 331–2
Phylogeny and ontogeny, 346–7
Piven, Frances Fox, 182; on integration, 183
Plato, 292, 295, 315, 339, 340, 348,
358, 378
Pluralism, 64, 69, 210–13, 253–4,
258, 259–60, 262, 270, 275 *n.,*
325 *n.,* 363–4
Police action during corporate disobedience, 231–5
Policy, public: *see* Public policy
Policy research, 85–6, 89; application of a more comprehensive
approach, 105–10; *see also* Public policy analysis
Political arts and political sciences,
357–82
Political change: public policy consequences and, 100–5; identification of, 100–1; examination of
processes of, 101; need to seek
reasons for, 101–2; need to seek
reasons for lack of, 101–2; tracing of policy consequences to
understand change, or lack of it,
102–3; changing patterns of,
103–4

Political education, 374–5
Political grievances of the poor, 152–69; absence of meaning in liberal-conservative dimension, 152–3; racial differences in, 153, 169 *n.*, 170 *n.*, 171 *n.;* about spending money on space programs and foreign aid, 154; on government spending, 155–6; on what is most important for good government, 156–8; in connection with personal problems, 158–61; on whether or not America is a "free country," 161–3; on whether the government supplies help to ordinary man, 163–165; on American involvement in Vietnam war, 165; conclusions about, 166–9
Political participation, 11, 14–17, 363–4
Political science, 8–46; and Nazism, 8–14, 22; behavioral approach in, 8, 12–13, 17, 21–3, 38–9; state of nature and, 10–11; objectivity and, 24–31, 37, 38; precision and, 31–8; as taught in the classroom, 59–85; means-end relations, 69, 71, 72; "postbehavioral revolution" in, 85, 88–92; language of, 376–8
Political science courses: objectivity in the classroom, 59–60, 65, 66–67, 70; task of teacher, 59, 61, 66, 67, 69, 71, 73–80; teacher's selection of problems, 67; teacher's choice of empirical theories, 71; fact-value linkage, 74; responsibilities of teacher, 76, 79; fundamental task of, 79
Political science profession, unpreparedness for riots, demonstrations, and assassinations, 280–1, 368
Political Science and Public Policy (Social Science Research Council), 85
Political silence, 143–4; Karl Marx on, 148

Political theory: *see* Theory
Politics of Poverty, The (Donovan), 73
Popper, Karl, 339
Popular sovereignty, 288, 320 *n.*
Populist democracy, 17–18
"Postbehavioral revolution," 85, 88–92; and concern for substance of policies, 90–2
Postmoral mentality, 302, 324 *n.*
Poussaint, Alvin: on assimilation, 184
Power, legitimate, 286–9, 370–1
"Power without authority," 302
Precision, political science and, 31–38
Preface to Democratic Theory, A (Dahl), 7, 17
Prejudices, 145, 148, 150, 151
Production, battle of, 289–90
Progressive Historians, The (Hofstadter), 74
Protestant Ethic and the Spirit of Capitalism, The (Weber), 342
"Public interest": David Truman on, 114–19 *passim;* Michael Rogin on, 114, 115; and majority rule, 288; John Schaar on status and function of, 288–9, 320 *n.*
"Public-interest spooks," David Truman on, 114
Public policy analysis, 85–111; Sanford Levinson on choice of topics for, 76–80; approaches used in, 89–90; concern for substance of policies, 90–2; *see also* Policy research
Public policy consequences, 92–105; and evaluation of performance, 94–100; and political change, 100–5; identification of, 100–1; illustrations of tracing of, to understand political change or lack of it, 102–3
Public policy evaluation, 94–100; political science teacher's choice of problems for, 67–72; objects of, 94–5; standards for, 95, 98–9; dangers encountered in, 95–8

Racial differences in political grievances of the poor, 153, 169 *n.*, 170 *n.*, 171*n.*

Rationality, and bureaucratic coordination, 302–8

"Real world," 38, 39; theories of, 18–27; *see also* Realism

Realism, 4–6, 19, 77, 374; *vs.* idealism, 4–6; *see also* Real world

Reconstructive theory, 341–2, 349

Remarks on the Foundations of Mathematics (Wittgenstein), 351

Representativeness, of black community leaders, 264–9

"Repressive Tolerance" (Marcuse), 209

Republic (Plato), 339, 340, 348

Revolution, 251–2; "right" of, 251; epistemological, in China and Cuba, 355–6 *n.; see also* Corporation, the: revolution against

Revolution of the Saints, The (Walzer), 341–2

Rieff, Philip, 301–2

Right of Revolution, The (Nelson), 251

Riots, demonstrations, and assassinations, unpreparedness of political science profession for, 280–1, 368

Rogin, Michael, viii, 267, 363, 364; on nonpartisanship and the group interest, 112–41; on David Truman's "group theory," 112–120

Rousseau, Jean Jacques, 6, 7, 298, 329, 335–6, 339, 343, 359, 360–1, 370

Russell, Bertrand: on disinterested inquiry, 23–4; on objectivity, 27

Rytina, Joan, 166

Sapir, Edward, 337

Sartre, Jean Paul, 295, 299, 329

Schaar, John, ix, 61, 363, 367; on apathy, 16; on legitimate authority in the modern state, 276–327, 369; on status and function of "public interest," 288, 320 *n.;* on total vulnerability,

289, 321 *n.;* on Max Weber, 308–310, 326–7 *n.*

Schlick, Moritz: on objectivity, 28

Schmitt, Carl, 17

Schnore, Leo, 206

School system, dual; Philip Green on, 270–1

Schurmann, Franz, 356 *n.*

"Science of Muddling Through, The" (Lindblom), 73

Science of politics: *see* Political science

Scientific revolution, 63–4

Seale, Bobby, 188–9, 267

Security, and total vulnerability, 289, 321 *n.*

Selective Service System, operations and impact of, 103

Shriver, Sargent, 200

Silence, political, 143–4, 148

Simmel, Georg, 365

Sit-down or sit-in, corporate, 230

Smith, Alfred E., 128

Social Origins of Dictatorship and Democracy (Moore), 72

Social Science Research Council, 85

Social systems *vs.* cultural systems, 174–5

Socrates, 66, 378, 379, 380

Sovereign authority, 254–5, 269; *see also* Authority

Space programs and foreign aid, attitude of poor toward, 154

Stability, democratic, 11–12, 14

Stalin, Joseph, 10

Strong, Tracy B., ix, 360–1; essay in meta-theory, 328–56; criticism of empiricism by, 330–1; *see also* Theory

Structure of Scientific Revolutions, The (Kuhn), 8, 39, 62

Student rebellions, 243–4

Supreme Court decisions on school prayers, 102

Synanon, 197

Tammany Hall, alliance of craft unions with, 127–9

Taylor, Charles, 26

*Teachers' Strike: New York, 1968,
    The* (Mayer), 248
Theory: sources of, 334–5; language
    and, 335–9; types of, 339–42;
    transcendental, 339–40, 348; his-
    torical, 340–1, 348; cyclical recon-
    structive, 341–2, 349; problems
    for present-day theory, 342–9;
    writing of, 349–51
Thoreau, Henry David, 381
Thucydides, 338, 357
Tilly, Charles, 245 *n.*
Tocqueville, Alexis de, 323 *n.*, 332,
    335, 365
Tolerance, 209–10
Totalitarianism, 7, 37, 45, 368; and
    political science, 9, 11
Transcendental theory, 339–40, 348
Tristes Tropiques (Lévi-Strauss),
    334
Troubetzkoy, N.: on structural lin-
    guistics, 331–2
Truman David, 12, 135, 365; on
    emergence of new paradigm, 42;
    "group theory" of, 112, 113–20;
    on nonpartisanship, 130–1; on
    leadership desires and member-
    ship benefits, 132
Truth, concept of, 294–5
Tyrants, 379–80

United Federation of Teachers in
    New York, 187, 248, 252, 256–7,
    261
Universities, student rebellions in,
    243–4
Unskilled jobs, massive obliteration
    of, 175–6, 181
USCO (commune), 197

"Value-free" research, 95
Vietnam war: support of by labor
    leaders, 141 *n.;* attitude of poor
    people on American involve-
    ment in, 165

Violence, 224
Vonnegut, Kurt, 369
Vulnerability, total: John Schaar
    on, 289, 321 *n.*

Waismann, F., 33–4
Walker, Jack: on mass beliefs, 149
Walzer, Michael, viii, 34, 266, 341–
    342; on civil disobedience and
    corporate authority, 223–46; on
    sovereign authority, 254
Washington Free Community, 196
Watkins, J. W. N., 36
Weber, Max, 59, 64, 68, 70, 72, 332,
    334, 340, 341, 342, 369; on task
    of teacher of social science, 59,
    61, 66, 69; on means and ends
    linkage, 69; on three types of
    authority, 276–7; on rational-
    legal authority, 294; on bu-
    reaucracy, 305, 326–7 *n.;* on
    charismatic authority, 308–9;
    John Schaar on, 308–10, 326–7 *n.*
White, Henry: on organized labor
    and politics, 121
Whitman, Walt, 321 *n.*, 365
Whitten, Jamie, 267
Who Governs (Dahl), 7, 17
Whorf, B. L., 337
Whyte, William F., 28
Wilson, Woodrow, 177, 178
Wittgenstein, Ludwig, 328, 351; on
    effect of language on concepts,
    336, 337–8
Wofford, Harris, 200, 201–3, 208,
    212, 218–20
Wolfe, Alan, viii, 270; on conditions
    of community, 195–222, 366; on
    Old Westbury College experi-
    ment, 198–221; on political the-
    ory of community, 213–18
Wright, Nathan, Jr.: desegregation,
    183

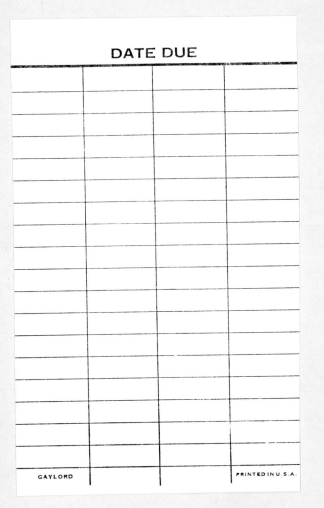

DATE DUE

GAYLORD   PRINTED IN U.S.A.